AF225312

Unveiling Your Sacred Truth

*The innermost essence of all of the Buddha's teachings,
together with a supplementary explanation of the methods for entering
into the profound path of the Kalachakra Six Vajra Yogas.*

བདེ་གཤེགས་སྙིང་པོའི་འཇིག་རྟེན་རྟོགས་ལྡན་གསར་པའི་ཁྱད་ཆོས

ༀ།།ཟབ་ལམ་རྡོ་རྗེའི་རྣལ་འབྱོར་དྲུག་ལ་འཇུག་ཆལ་འཕྲོས་དོན་དང་བཅས་པ་ཀུན་འདུས་རྣལ་བསྡུན་ཡང་སྙིང༌།།

— BOOK TWO —

The Internal Reality

by Shar Khentrul Jamphel Lodrö

ཤར་མཁན་སྤྲུལ་རིན་པོ་ཆེ་འཇམ་དཔལ་བློ་གྲོས

Dzokden

Author: Shar Khentrul Jamphel Lodrö

First Edition

ISBN (Paperback): 978-1-958229-59-0
ISBN (ePub): 978-1-958229-60-6

Published by:
Dzokden

This work was produced by Dzokden, a non-profit institution operated entirely by volunteers. This organization is dedicated to propagating a non-sectarian view of all the world's spiritual traditions and to teaching Buddhism in a way that is both completely authentic and at the same time practical and accessible to Western culture. It is especially dedicated to spreading the Jonang tradition, a rare gem from a remote part of Tibet that preserves the precious teachings of the Kalachakra.

For more information about scheduled activities or available materials, or if you would like to make a donation, please contact:

Dzokden
3436 Divisadero Street
San Francisco, CA 94123
USA
www.dzokden.org
office@dzokden.org

Contents

至尊藏哇赤列南杰觉囊派第四十七任法王壤塘藏哇大藏寺金刚寺主

HIS HOLINESS TSANGWA TRINLÉ NAMGYAL

The 47th Vajra Throne Holder of the Great Eastern Monastery of Dzamthang Tsangwa and Lord of the Jonang Dharma.

༄༅། །ཤར་མཁན་སྤྲུལ་འཇམ་དཔལ་བློ་གྲོས་མཆོག་གིས་དུས་ཡུན་རིང་པོར་ས་དགེ་བཀའ་རྙིང་ཇོ་ནང་དང་བཅས་པའི་ལྟ་གྲུབ་ལ་ཐོས་བསམ་སྒོམ་པ་ཡང་དག་བྱས་ནས་བོད་བརྒྱུད་ནང་བསྟན་ཀུན་ལ་ཤེས་ནས་དད་པ་ཐོབ། ཁོང་གིས་ཆོས་བརྒྱུད་རིས་མེད་ཀྱི་ཆོས་འབྱུང་ལྟ་གྲུབ་བཅས་ཀྱི་དཔེ་དེབ་གལ་ཆེན་མང་དུ་བྲིས་པ་སོགས་བསྟན་པ་ལ་ཕན་པའི་ཕྱག་ལས་གལ་ཆེན་གནང་བཞིན་ཡོད།

ཁོང་གིས་ཆོས་བརྒྱུད་རིས་མེད་ཀྱི་དགེ་བའི་བཤེས་གཉེན་མང་དུ་བསྟེན་ཞིང་། རྩ་བའི་བླ་མ་དངོས་ནི། ངེས་པ་དོན་གྱི་མཁས་གྲུབ་གཉིས་ལྡན། རྗེ་བཙུན་བླ་མ་བློ་བཟང་ཕྲིན་ལས་སམ་ཡོངས་གྲགས་སུ་བླ་མ་བློས་འཕྲིན་ཚང་ཡིན། བླ་མ་དམ་པ་ཁོང་གི་མདུན་ནས་མདོ་སྔགས་གཉིས་ལ་ཐོས་བསམ་སྒོམ་པ་ཡུན་རིང་བྱས། ལྷག་པར་དུ་དཔལ་དུས་ཀྱི་འཁོར་ལོའི་རྫོགས་རིམ་སྦྱོར་བ་ཡན་ལག་དྲུག་གི་ཉམས་ལེན་ལ་འབད་པ་ཡང་དག་བྱས་མཐར། བླ་མ་དམ་པ་གང་གིས་ཁོང་ལ་ཆོས་ལུགས་རིས་མེད་ཀྱི་མཁན་པོའི་མཚན་གནས་གནང་། དེའི་མ་ཚད་བླ་མ་དམ་པ་གང་གི་སྐུ་ཚེ་ཧྲིལ་པོར་བཞེས་པའི་མཁན་ཞུ་བྱིན་རླབས་ཅན་གཅིག་པུ་དེ་དང་། ཁོང་གི་སྐུ་ཚེ་ཧྲིལ་པོར་འཆིང་བའི་ཕྱག་དཔེ་བྱིན་ཅན་དེ་གཉིས་ཀ་གནང་ཏེ་མ་འོངས་པར་འགྲོ་དོན་རྒྱ་ཆེན་ཡོད་པར་ལུང་དུ་བསྟན།

ཁོང་ཆུང་དུས་དགེ་རྒྱེ་མཁན་སྤྲུལ་གྱི་ཡང་སྲིད་དུ་ངོས་བཟུང་ཡང་། སྐུ་ཚེ་ལ་བར་ཆད་ཟློག་ཆེད་དུ་གསང་རྒྱ་དམ་པོ་བྱས་ཡོད་འདུག བླ་མ་འདི་བ་ཚང་གིས་བར་ཆད་ཐམས་ཅད་བསལ་ཏེ་གསང་རྒྱ་བཀྲོལ་ཆོག་པའི་བཀའ་གནང་ཐོབ་ནས་ཕྱིས་སུ་བཀྲ་ཤིས་ཆོས་ཐང་དགོན་པས་ཁོང་ཨ་ཤུལ་ལྷ་བཟོས་བླ་མའི་ཡང་སྲིད་དུ་ངོས་འཛིན་མཛད་སྐྱོའི་དགའ་སྟོན་ཞིག་ཀྱང་གནང་སྐྱོང་འདུག

ད་ལྟ་ནི་ངེས་དོན་མདོ་བཅུ་དང་། སྙིང་པོའི་མདོ་བཅུ་ཡི་དགོངས་པ་མཐར་ཐུག་བླ་ན་མེད་པ་དབུ་མ་གཞན་སྟོང་གི་ལྟ་གྲུབ་ཀྱི་ཟབ་གནད་དང་། བྱང་ཤམྦྷ་ལའི་རིས་གསང་ཟབ་མོའི་ཆོས། དཔལ་དུས་ཀྱི་འཁོར་ལོའི་སྔོན་འགྲོ་དངོས་གཞི་དང་བཅས་པའི་ཆོས་སྐོར་ལ་ཉམས་ལེན་དང་། དེ་དག་བོད་སྐད་ནས་དབྱིན་སྐད་དུ་བྲིས་ཤིང་། དབྱིན་སྐད་ནས་སྐད་ཡིག་གཞན་པ་དུ་ཡང་འགྱུར་བཞིན་ཡོད་འདུག་ལ། མ་འོངས་པར་སྐད་རིགས་ཆེ་ཤེས་མང་དག་ཅིག་གི་ཐོག་ཏུ་བསྒྱུར་རྩིས་གནང་གི་འདུག ད་ལྟ་འཛམ་གླིང་ཤར་ནུབ་གཉིས་ཀྱི་ཡུལ་གྲུ་ཁག་ཏུ་དབུ་མ་གཞན་སྟོང་གི་ལྟ་བ་དར་སྤེལ་དང་། དེས་ཕན་ཐོགས་རྒྱ་ཆེར་གནང་བཞིན་པ་ལེགས་ན། ཐུན་ཀྱིས་དཔལ་རྒྱལ་བ་ཇོ་ནང་བ་ཀུན་གྱི་ཚབ་ཞུས་ཏེ་ཁོང་ལ་བསྔགས་བརྗོད་དང་རྗེས་སུ་ཡི་རངས་ཡོད་པ་མ་ཟད། རྒྱབ་སྐྱོར་ཡང་མཐའ་གཅིག་ཏུ་ཞུ་གི་ཡོད།

དེས་མི་ཚད། མཁན་སྤྲུལ་ཁོང་གི་ལྷག་བསམ་དང་སྙིང་སྟོབས་ལ་ཆེ་མཐོང་ཡོད་ལ། ཆེས་དཀོན་པའི་དཔལ་དུས་ཀྱི་འཁོར་ལོའི་བསྟན་པའི་ཁུར་ཆེན་བཞེས་ནས་ཆོས་ལུགས་རིས་མེད་ལ་ཤུགས་སྐྱོན་གནང་ཏེ། སྐྱེ་ཚོགས་ཀུན་མཐུན་ལ་ལག་རྗེས་བཞག་ན་འཛམ་གླིང་ཞི་བདེ་ལ་ཕན་པ་མ་ཟད། མཐར་རང་ཅག་དུས་བཞི་ཕྱི་མའི་རྫོགས་ལྡན་གྱི་སྐལ་བཟང་དེ་ལ་རིག་ཐུབ་པའི་མཐུན་རྐྱེན་ཆེས་གལ་ཆེན་ཞིག་ཡིན་པས། ཐུན་གྱིས་ཁོང་གི་མཛད་པ་དེ་དག་ལ་སྙིང་ནས་རྗེས་སུ་ཡི་རངས་ཡོད།

མ་ཟད་མཁན་སྤྲུལ་མཆོག་ལ་མཐུན་འགྱུར་དང་རྒྱབ་སྐྱོར་གནང་མཁན་འཛམ་གླིང་གི་མི་སྣ་སུ་འདྲ་ཞིག་བྱུང་བ་ཀུན་ལ། བདག་གིས་ངོས་ནས་ཡི་རངས་དང་བཀའ་དྲིན་ཆེ་ཞུ་རྒྱུ་ཡིན། འདི་ནི་སྐྱེ་ཚོགས་ཀུན་མཐུན་དང་ཞི་བདེ་ཡང་དག་འོང་བར་ཕན་པའི་དགོན་ཞིང་མཆོག་གི་ཟབ་ཆོས་ཞིག་ཡིན་པས་མ་འོངས་པར་བྱང་ཤམྦྷ་ལ་རུ་ལྡན་འཛོམས་ཀྱི་སྐྱབས་འཇུག་སྨོན་ལམ་དང་བཅས།

༄། གཙང་བའི་ཁྲི་རབས་ཞེ་བདུན་པ་ཤཱཀྱ་མཆོག་སྤྲུལ་འཇིགས་མེད་རྡོ་རྗེ་ཞལ་སྔ་ནས་ཀྱིས།
ཤར་འཛམ་ཐང་གཙང་ཆེན་གཟིམ་ཁང་ཆོས་ཀྱི་སོ་བྲང་ནས།
བོད་རབ་བྱུང་བཅུ་བདུན་པའི་རབ་གནས་མི་ཕྱུལ་ཤོད་ཟླ་དྲུག་པའི་༡༨ ལ།། །།

གཙང་བ་སྐུ་འཕྲེང་བརྒྱད་པ་ཤཱཀྱ་མཆོག་སྤྲུལ་འཇིགས་མེད་རྡོ་རྗེ་ཕྱོགས་ལས་རྣམ་པར་རྒྱལ་བའི་སྡེ།

无上怙主殊胜化身吉美多杰尊胜第八任藏哇活佛

The 8th Tsangwa Geitrul, Supreme Incarnation of All the Victorious Ones, Jigmé Dorjé

Preface by His Holiness Jigmé Dorje

Shar Khentrul Jamphel Lodrö has attained great faith in the teachings of Tibetan Buddhism through his intensive study of the five traditions of Nyingma, Sakya, Kagyu, Jonang and Geluk. On the basis of these teachings, he has written many great books on subjects such as the history of the Dharma and non-sectarian philosophical views. Through this work he has brought great benefit to the doctrine.

While having studied under many great masters from each of the traditions, his root master was the truly learned and accomplished master Jetsun Lama Lobsang Trinlé, also known as Lama Trinlé Tsang. From him, he spent a long time learning the complete teachings of Sutra and Tantra, specifically, the six branch practices of the Kalachakra Completion Stage. In recognition of his great effort to achieve mastery of all traditions, Jamphel Lodrö was awarded the title of Rimé Master by his root teacher. In particular, he was given the highly blessed Khenpo-hat which had been worn by Lama Lobsang Trinlé throughout that master's life. This hat carries with it profound blessings and is a sign that Jamphel Lodrö will bring great welfare to beings in the future.

As a child, Jamphel Lodrö was recognised as the immediate reincarnation of the Golok lama Getse Khentrul; however, this truth was kept secret in order to expel obstacles to his life. Many years later, with permission from his root master and after all obstacles had been dispelled, the seal was lifted and he was publicly recognised as the second incarnation of the Washul Lhazu Lama—Ngawang Chözin Gyatso.

Presently, he has been giving extensive teachings on the sutras of definitive meaning and the profound philosophical views of Zhentong Madhyamaka, as well as the preliminary practices which form the foundation for the practice of Kalachakra. He has made great effort to make these teachings available in

The Great Monastery of Dzamthang Tsangwa

the Tibetan and English languages, with the aim to eventually translate them into many other languages in the future. Due to his determination to make the Zhentong philosophy accessible, many people all over this world have received great benefit and for that I am very grateful. I rejoice and thank him on behalf of all Jonang practitioners, and fully support him in his many activities.

I would particularly like to express my highest regard for his courage to take responsibility for the most rare and profound teachings of the Kalachakra as an authentic holder of the lineage, as well as for his emphasis for all traditions to come together in the name of global peace and harmony. From the bottom of my heart, I rejoice in these great deeds for they are truly the causes for a golden age to arise.

To all those who are currently supporting Khentrul Rinpoché to achieve these activities, I would like to express my heartfelt thanks to you and rejoice in the vast merit that you are creating. It is most rare to have the opportunity to encounter these teachings which can bring so much peace and harmony to this world. I make prayers and aspirations that in the future, we will all gather together in the sublime northern realm of Shambhala.

Written at the Dharma palace of the Great Eastern Monastery of Dzamthang Tsangwa by the 47th Vajra Throne Holder Tsangwa Geitrul, Supreme Incarnation Jigme Dorje on the sixth month of the fire monkey year during the 17th rabjung (August, 2016).

Shar Khentrul Jamphel Lodrö Rinpoché

Acknowledgments

On behalf of the Tibetan Buddhist Rimé Institute, I would like to thank everyone who has been involved in making this book a reality. First and foremost is of course our kind teacher Khentrul Rinpoché, whose profound teachings and patient guidance has made the Kalachakra System accessible to us all. We are eternally grateful for the opportunity to meet with this incredible path and for being involved in preparing this book series.

On a personal note, I would like to express my enormous gratitude towards Rinpoché for giving me the opportunity to help him manifest this great vision. While I realise the words I have offered will never truly capture the depth of his wisdom, it brings me great joy to think that in some small way this work may bring people closer to Kalachakra and closer to Rinpoché, who for me is the embodiment of these teachings. I recognise that my capacity is limited by my own obscurations and therefore I take full responsibility for any mistakes that may have found their way into this text. I welcome any feedback that could help improve this book in order to make it as beneficial as possible.

Furthermore, I would specifically like to thank the members of the editorial team who have worked diligently over the last six months to prepare this latest installment in the *Sacred Truth Series*. We sincerely appreciate the effort and determination of Vanessa Mason, Holly Reilly and Dorothy Welton. I am particularly grateful to Julie O'Donnell and Jackie Bao who have been instrumental in creating the conditions for the work to be completed.

It is our sincere aspiration that this book provides you with an authentic doorway to enter into the Kalachakra Path. May it bring benefit to your life and may it become the cause for you and all sentient beings to achieve lasting genuine happiness and freedom from suffering. May the teachings of the Jonang Dharma flourish throughout this world and may the Golden Age of Shambhala be realised.

Joe Flumerfelt
Belgrave, Australia
August 2016

Shakyamuni Buddha

Introduction

Unveiling Your Sacred Truth was written to expound the spiritual path as taught by Buddha Shakyamuni. Throughout this text, I have attempted to present the core tenets of Buddhism in an approachable way without losing the essence of the Buddha's ancient wisdom. It is my hope that *Unveiling Your Sacred Truth* will enable you to live purposefully and compassionately.

When you pick-up a Dharma book such as this one, you are not simply reading the words of the author. Through *Unveiling Your Sacred Truth* you connect with the unparalleled wisdom of the Buddha and come to know the great practitioners of the past and present who realised Buddha Dharma for themselves. This Buddhist ancestry—known as a lineage—is critical for spiritual development as it is their stories, commentaries and realisations that we rely upon for guidance and inspiration.

The Buddha's teachings were taught for an extensive variety of people, each experiencing dissatisfaction and suffering in different ways. As a result, there are different levels of benefit from studying these teachings that we can all aspire to achieve. On the most basic level, we can each find practical tools to help us lessen our day-to-day stresses and to live a more meaningful life. On a deeper level, we can realise our incredible potential and cultivate the causes for long-lasting, genuine happiness for both ourselves and others.

Of all the Buddha's teachings, the system that I personally feel most connected with is that of the Kalachakra Tantra. In my opinion, it is the most skilful system for realising this extraordinary potential and for actualising enlightenment within a single lifetime. While most people relate these teachings to advanced esoteric practices, the Kalachakra Path is in fact a complete system which is suitable for practitioners at all stages of their spiritual development.

OVERVIEW OF THE KALACHAKRA PATH

Kalachakra literally means *wheel* (chakra) of *time* (kala). It is the name given to a system of practices that originated with the Buddha Shakyamuni and has been passed down through the ages in an unbroken lineage to this day. The Kalachakra system is focused on helping people make sense of their experiences in such a way that allows them to cultivate greater peace and harmony in their personal lives and their relationships with others.

The Kalachakra is unique in that it provides teachings on a comprehensive scope of topics that support a wide variety of practitioners at different stages in their spiritual development. Within one unified framework, we find a wealth of profound wisdom that is both immediately relevant and direct in its approach.

The main subject matter of *Unveiling Your Sacred Truth* is the presentation of the complete Kalachakra Path. This path is progressive in nature, providing clear step-by-step instructions for guiding you through the many layers of your lived experience. I have broken this path into three separate books, with each emphasising a specific layer of reality, moving in a linear fashion from gross to subtle. As such, it is recommended that the material be studied in sequence so the necessary foundations can be developed for each subsequent practice.

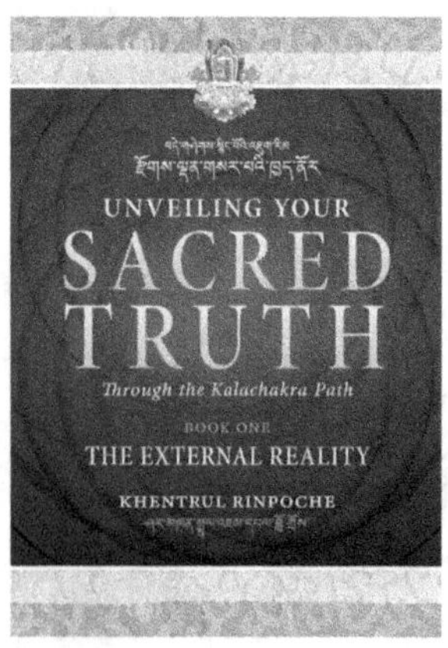

Book One: The External Reality

We begin our journey by first studying the characteristics of our immediate experience. Specifically we examine the ordinary world that we encounter each and every day, with the aim of developing the wisdom to live a more meaningful and balanced life. At this stage, the emphasis is on pragmatic strategies which are firmly rooted in an experiential approach to understanding reality.

Introducing many potentially new ideas, this book challenges us to expand our perspective regarding the nature of our shared universe. These ideas form the basis for understanding a Buddhist worldview and for developing a profound system of contemplative practice.

Book Two:
The Internal Reality

With our focus turned outward, we can develop strategies for coping with the disarray and upheavals that occur in our lives, finding ways to apply wisdom to act constructively in the face of adversity. But no matter how effective our methods, they cannot generate the long lasting transformation needed to break the cycle of our suffering and open the door to genuine happiness. For this we must turn inward and look directly at our mind, giving ourselves the opportunity to experience its natural potential.

In this second book, we explore the experiential world of appearances and how they actually exist. While we continue to work with concepts on a theoretical level, the emphasis begins to shift toward a more practical orientation. It is not enough to merely understand these concepts intellectually, we need to develop a first-hand experience of them. Through practice, we convert understanding into realisation, allowing ourselves to truly integrate these ideas into our way of being.

Divided into three parts, each section emphasises the development of the foundational qualities needed before engaging with the practices of Buddhist Tantra. Just as we cultivate the soil before planting a crop, these teachings lay the groundwork to help us gather the necessary conditions for reaping a bountiful harvest.

Relying on a Valid Source of Refuge

According to the teachings of the Buddha, we have been aimlessly wandering through cyclic existence since beginningless time, taking rebirth after rebirth after rebirth. Because we fail to recognise the true nature of our reality, we perpetuate our suffering in an endless loop. Unless we change this situation, we will continue this existence for all of eternity. Reflecting on this reality generates the strong desire to break free from samsara and raises the question of how we can actually achieve this freedom.

Although every single sentient being shares the desire to experience genuine happiness and to be free from suffering, it is not a state of being that arises naturally or easily. Substantial training and effort is required to transform and liberate the mind from its present condition of turmoil and conflict, to one of sustainable peace and harmony. The *Kalachakra Path* offers us a direct route to achieving this result, providing an extraordinary range of methods that can quickly penetrate to the most profound layer of our experience. Not only can we accomplish personal liberation, but also the enlightened state of Buddhahood. Understanding the structure of this path, bestows us with a detailed map to guide us to our ultimate and sacred truth.

Walking a path such as this is not unlike an expedition into unknown territory. It is a journey of pitfalls, wrong turns and unforeseen obstacles. To develop the willingness and effort to overcome these difficulties requires inspiration and a confidence in what is promised at the end of the journey. To do this, we can look to those who have walked this path before us. Through studying the history and life stories of the great masters of the *Jonang-Shambhala Lineage*, we are introduced to more than two thousand years of combined experience that has given shape to the very path presented in this book, and offers us the encouragement we need to take our first steps.

With the inspiration to practice, we need the guidance of *an authentic Dharma teacher* to steer us through the process. Although there are many teachers in the world, only the jewel-like holders of the Vajra Yoga Lineage are qualified to teach the Kalachakra Path. As they are exceedingly rare and precious, we must make great effort to develop our connection with them. For this reason, it is necessary to clearly understand what to look for in a teacher and how to make the most of this dynamic relationship.

As we set forth on our journey under the guidance of an authentic teacher, we learn that the foundation of the Kalachakra Path is faith in the *Three Jewels*. This profound teaching provides us with clarity regarding the sources of refuge capable of freeing us from cyclic existence. Through our unwavering reliance on these supports, we can be certain our life remains oriented in a positive direction, leading us to the genuine happiness we seek.

Entering the Path of a Bodhisattva

With a firm conviction in the power of the Three Jewels, it is possible to end our personal suffering by cutting through the cycle of existence. This alone however is not enough to bring us to full and complete enlightenment. We must open our awareness and expand our motivation to incorporate the limitless sentient beings who, just like us, have been trapped in the suffering of samsara since beginningless time.

Reflecting on our relationships with others, we come to recognise that without their enormous kindness we could not have existed in this world, nor experienced even a moment of happiness, and yet these beings who have so lovingly cared for us, endlessly perpetuate their suffering. Like a mother seeing her only child trapped in a fire, we develop the unshakeable determination to do whatever we can to help them. From this basis of *love and compassion* we generate the supreme altruistic intention of *Bodhicitta*—the mind which seeks to achieve enlightenment for the benefit of all sentient beings.

Only this extraordinary mind is a valid motivation for engaging in the Kalachakra Path. As we nurture and strengthen this aspiration, it becomes the driving force behind all of our actions and we enter into the *Mahayana Path of the Bodhisattvas.* This path of the compassionate warrior is dedicated to benefitting others and lays the foundation for all the unique practices of the Kalachakra system.

As we study the teachings of the Bodhisattva Path, we discover the two trainings vital for the attainment of a fully enlightened Buddha—the *Six Perfections* and the *Four Ways to Gather a Following*. While these two trainings offer the methods for realising our own aim of liberation and the aims of others to be free from suffering, the profound wisdom of *Zhentong Philosophy* provides the view for engagement with these practices and those specific to the Kalachakra Path. Drawing from the vast scriptures of the Three Turnings of the Wheel of Dharma, we establish a conceptual view which highlights the definitive nature of reality and clearly indicates how we can experience that nature.

Preparing the Mind for Tantra

Relying exclusively on the practices of the Mahayana will undoubtedly dissolve the layers of ignorance we have built over countless lives and lead us to the achievement of full enlightenment. Unfortunately this purification takes billions of lifetimes to complete, and during this lengthy timeframe, the sentient beings we care for so dearly continue to suffer unbearably. The path of Buddhist Tantra gives us the opportunity to speed up the process. With its vast array of skilful means, we can quickly cut through our delusions to reveal and rest in our ultimate nature. As these methods enable us to completely purify our mind in a single lifetime, it is known as the lightning vehicle.

To make use of these profound methods however, we need to create the conditions to realise our sacred truth, which is currently hidden from us like a jewel buried deeply underground. Developing the discipline and commitment to a *daily recitation practice* helps us to dig down through the many layers of our confusion and clear the obscurations that prevent the radiance of this jewel from fully manifesting. In this tradition, the main text used to do this is the *Divine Ladder: Preliminary and Main Practices of the Profound Kalachakra Vajrayoga* by the great Jonang master, Jetsun Taranatha. This text provides a structured method for familiarising ourselves with all the intermediate realisations required to directly experience the nature of reality.

The *Kalachakra Preliminary Practices* are divided into three sets: outer, inner and unique. The remaining part of this book focuses on the instructions for meditating on the outer and inner preliminaries. Specifically we examine the preliminary practices of *Taking Refuge, Generating Bodhicitta, Vajrasattva Purification and Mandala Offerings*. The final three preliminaries of Guru Yoga, Deity Yoga and The Three Isolations are detailed in Book Three of this series.

Book Three:
The Enlightened Reality

By working with our internal reality we slowly refine our ability to distinguish between the impure appearances of the external reality and the pure appearances of the enlightened reality. Like cleaning the lens of a telescope, clearing the gross obscurations from our mind enables us to catch a glimmer of our true nature. While this nature is not yet completely manifest, establishing a first glimpse provides us with a foundation on which to expand until we can fully experience the luminosity of our most sacred truth.

Whereas the preceding two books of this series work with teachings common to all Tibetan Buddhist traditions, this final book presents the unique practices of the Kalachakra Tantra. For the practitioner who is ready to dedicate themselves to yogic practice, these profound methods offer everything needed to achieve enlightenment within a single lifetime.

GETTING THE MOST OUT OF THIS BOOK

As you read through the material, it can be helpful to keep a few key points in mind. The following is some general advice that applies to any form of Dharma study, whether reading a book or listening to a teaching.

The Right Attitude for Studying Dharma

When we encounter the Buddhist teachings, it is important to generate an attitude of great enthusiasm. If we can recognise that these teachings introduce ideas that can ultimately lead us to greater peace and harmony, this should be a relatively easy task. That being said, cultivating a bright and alert mind is a skill that takes time to develop and prolonged effort is required to overcome the different obstacles that may arise. One teaching that highlights these difficulties is known as the *Three Defects of a Pot*:

- We should not be like an **upside-down pot** on which liquid is being poured, being distracted or so closed minded that the teachings cannot penetrate. Listen with an open mind, a ready mind.

- Nor should we be like a **pot with a hole in it**. No matter how much liquid is poured in, it drips away and we retain nothing of what is learnt.

- Finally, do not be a **pot containing poison**. Avoid falling prey to preconceptions and fixed ideas. This will cause you to misconstrue what you hear and manipulate Dharma into something it is not, like nectar poured into poison.

As you read through each chapter, try to maintain an open, receptive attitude that is fully engaged in the material and free from any preconceptions or judgemental attitudes. Every now and again check to see the quality of attention you bring to your reading. Remind yourself of this simple teaching whenever you need the inspiration to improve your method of study.

Stopping to Reflect

Throughout this text different exercises have been inserted to give you the opportunity to reflect upon the material being studied. As it is important not to become overwhelmed by the theory and potentially challenging ideas, breaking up your reading with short periods of personal reflection can provide valuable insights into how the material relates to your personal experience.

If a section does not follow with a particular exercise, it is still a good habit to select passages of the text to reread a few times and make sure you really comprehend the essence of what is being said. Every now and again, put the book down and consider how these teachings relate to your life. By thinking of examples from your own experience, you will be able to illustrate the various principles and enhance your understanding.

Another good habit to develop is writing down questions that arise while reading. Keep a notepad nearby and when a question comes up, simply jot it down. When you are finished reading a section, look back at your questions and see whether they have been answered. If your questions persist, consider discussing the topic with a teacher or a Dharma friend when the opportunity arises.

Taking Joy in the Journey

Finally, no matter what your motivation is, I am confident that if you maintain an open heart and an open mind, the timeless wisdom of the Buddha-Dharma has the capacity to bring you great benefit.

Remember that this is a journey of discovery; a process of transformation. As it takes time for the concepts and practices to develop in your mind, it is important to be patient with yourself. Work through the ideas at your own pace and take as much time as you need. After you finish reading some chapters, revisit them and see if your understanding has shifted. Often you will find that later teachings shed new light on earlier ones, peeling back layers and uncovering a deeper meaning.

Above all, cultivate a sense of joy in having this precious opportunity. It shouldn't be dry, or tedious, but think of it like an adventure and revel in the challenges it presents. In Buddhism we often speak about planting the seeds for future realisation; this simply means that no matter how much confusion we face here and now, it is the basis for understanding to arise in the future.

"In the beginner's mind there are many possibilities,
but in the expert's mind there are few"
— Shunryu Suzuki —

PART ONE

Relying on a Valid Source of Refuge

CHAPTER ONE

The Kalachakra Path to Peace and Harmony

Right now, something very special is happening. Through the power of interdependence, a number of extremely rare and precious conditions have come together to create a brief but powerful window of opportunity. We have been given a valuable chance to bring immense meaning and purpose into our lives and be guided toward our heart's most profound desire.

To understand and appreciate these exceptional circumstances, we should first consider who we are and where we find ourselves at this particular moment in time. Of the vast range of possible forms a sentient being can take, the fact that we have been born here and now into this human life is certainly grounds for generating a sense of sheer wonder. We could just as easily have been born as one of the billions of animals that populate this planet, or worse, as one of the countless hungry ghosts or hell beings. Our lives could be completely consumed by endless suffering and torment. But they are not; we are human.

Likewise, it is possible that we could have been born into the extravagant and decadent world of the desire realm gods, or lost in the oblivious absorption of the form or formless realms. On the surface such an existence may appear desirable, but eventually it will come to an end and the harsh reality of time wasted must be faced. So while our lives could be filled with blissful distractions, they are not; we are human.

Within our human birth we experience intense sorrow and pain but we also have relief from this suffering which makes it more bearable. During these intervals we have the chance to experience joy and pleasure and it is this potential for both the good and the bad that gives meaning to our lives, for it is in our struggles we learn to appreciate our triumphs, and by reflecting on our experiences, we have the possibility to develop insight. We can use our extraordinary intelligence to identify the causes for our suffering and the causes for our happiness.

Although we may be lucky enough to feel we have everything we need to bring happiness to ourselves and those around us, we must be conscientious as the leisure of our life could just as easily lead us to complacency and laziness. Our minds can become dull and confused, carried away by an endless stream of self-made distractions. In the blink of an eye, we could find ourselves on our deathbed, looking back and wondering, "Where did the time go?"

The reality of our present existence is that life is impermanent. Conditions gather together, but then just as easily disperse and although we may presently find ourselves in a good situation, tomorrow we could find ourselves in turmoil. There is no certainty in what our future holds, only in the inevitably that it will be different from what we are experiencing now.

And so we cannot give in to degeneration. We must be vigilant in how we use the little time we have and recognise that our conditions will not remain forever. By developing the wisdom that realises their impermanent nature, we can seize these conditions of a human form and make our lives truly meaningful. Unlike any other form of life, we have a choice. We can choose to simply endure, or we can choose to do something more.

While such a realisation has great significance, it is only part of the tremendous opportunity that has arisen. If we reflect on the countless world systems that exist, pervaded by countless sentient beings, we have the incredibly good fortune to be born in a world during a time when a Buddha has manifested and bestowed teachings. But not just any teachings, Buddha Shakyamuni turned the wheel of Dharma four times. In the first, he taught the truth of dependent origination; in the second, he taught the truth of emptiness; in the third he taught the truth of our ultimate Buddha-nature; and in the fourth, he turned the wheel of Tantra, revealing the deepest of truths and methods. And of these, the most profound and most expansive was that of the Kalachakra Tantra.

This unparalleled teaching was not only received, it was diligently practiced in the subtle realm of Shambhala, where for millennia it has remained a shining beacon of hope for all who encounter it. Fortunately for us, some of those teachings reached this gross realm of experience and have been passed from the hearts and minds of highly realised masters to those of their dedicated students. For generations this unbroken lineage has protected these teachings, ensuring the heart essence was never lost. These highly realised men and women understood that failing to put these precious and rare teachings into practice would cause them to eventually fade away. Without practice, they would first deteriorate into a fragmented approach, losing sight of the complete picture. The number of masters with authentic realisations would then diminish until there was no one left to guide the next generations. Finally, the focus would then shift to study alone and the teachings would become just another intellectual exercise. Eventually, these valuable texts would become mere artefacts of a forgotten past. However, due to the extraordinary effort of these lineage masters, not only have the Kalachakra teachings survived to this day, we also have the incredible opportunity to practice them in an authentic way.

We can exemplify our sincere appreciation by never forgetting why these teachings have come to exist. Their sole purpose is to relieve our suffering and to provide us with the wisdom we need to break free from the endless cycles of ignorance and confusion. For far too long we have been beaten by the currents of the raging river we call life, trapped in a cage of our own making.

We have been granted genuine hope in the form of this dazzling ray of light. How foolish would we be not to take advantage of it? Now is the time to put this wisdom into practice by integrating it into every aspect of our experience; to become the very embodiment of that light. Through striving to be the very best we can be, we can achieve a profound peace of mind as well as becoming a shining example for those around us.

THE BENEFITS OF PRACTICING KALACHAKRA

In part three of the previous book of the *Unveiling Your Sacred Truth* series, we learnt that authentic spiritual paths are a collection of wisdom and methods that can be used to guide us towards genuine happiness. While there are many forms of spirituality in this world, we specifically explored the various approaches presented within the context of the Buddha's teachings. These teachings are filled with a wide range of techniques, designed for the individual needs of different practitioners during different stages of their spiritual development. Such diversity provides an incredible degree of flexibility and depth which allows a single practitioner to make the most of their unique conditions as they unveil increasingly more subtle layers of truth about their experience.

Where previously our aim was to gain a broad understanding of the context of spiritual paths, our focus now becomes more selective. While breadth is indeed important, there comes a time in everyone's spiritual journey when the need to go deeper arises. To bring this depth into our practice, it is necessary to narrow our focus to a specific path that has the potential to guide us through the many layers of our confusion.

The path that is presented in both this book and the next is based on the teachings of the Kalachakra Tantra. This system of practice has a number of advantages which makes it unique among the many systems you may encounter. These characteristics have earned Kalachakra the honour of being called the *King of Tantra*.

Expansive Scope

The Kalachakra is essentially a unified theory of reality. Through its profound understanding of reality's ultimate nature, it encompasses the totality of all the countless manifestations which that reality takes. It is for this reason that all systems of practice, whether Buddhist or non-Buddhist, can be considered to fall within the pervasive aspect of Kalachakra.

Although this may be the ultimate nature of the Kalachakra teachings, conventionally the Kalachakra we know is considered to be Buddhist doctrine. Within this context, it is unique in its remarkable detail regarding all aspects of human experience, as well as presenting in-depth discussions of cosmology, medicine and technology as a support for its main subject—how to achieve enlightenment within a single lifetime.

When compared to other traditions, all of the Buddha's teachings—whether sutra or tantra—can be understood through the study of Kalachakra. The same cannot be said for those traditions that tend to have a more narrow focus of interest. In fact, it is quite common for them to refer to the Kalachakra as it contains information not found anywhere else.

Clarity of Presentation

In general, the language used in Buddhist teachings becomes increasingly difficult to understand in direct correlation to the profundity of the truth being communicated. Initially the teachings are quite pragmatic and straight-forward, helping us develop a firm foundation of understanding. We are then challenged to see things differently as we begin to work with apparent contradictions that shake up our view. This is followed by a range of teachings that focus on a symbolic level of understanding to prevent us from becoming locked into our fixed concepts. Kalachakra breaks this pattern by turning it on its head. Where others use language that is often vague or suggestive, Kalachakra applies incredible detail and precision to its descriptions. The more profound the truth, the more direct and comprehensive the teachings become.

This unique feature makes Kalachakra particularly suited for times of great degeneration. When the minds of sentient beings are pure, symbolic teachings can be very effective. However, as the minds of sentient beings are clouded over by increasingly more intense obscurations, the lack of clarity in the teachings can lead to greater degrees of misinterpretation. As people cease to understand the intent of the teachings, distorted views begin to arise and they lose their capacity to bring benefit. For this reason, because the Kalachakra emphasises clarity in all aspects of the teachings, it is able to maintain its strength even in times of conflict and turmoil.

Profound Methods

The expansive scope and great clarity of the Kalachakra view spans the totality of all experience, but this view alone would be pointless without practical strategies for using our understanding to drive personal transformation. Fortunately, the Kalachakra has an abundance of profound methods that incorporate every aspect of our reality in order to accelerate the process of realisation and help us achieve our spiritual goals as quickly as possible.

Many people hold the view that Kalachakra is a very complex system and are therefore filled with doubt at the prospect of taking it as their practice. This is a sign of being too heavily focused on the theory and not enough on the practice. When practiced correctly, the essence of Kalachakra is extremely direct and does not require mastery of endless volumes of text. The information is certainly accessible if needed, but is not always necessary. Many great practitioners who have attained the highest of realisations may never have studied a single book in their entire life. By relying on the pith instructions of their teachers, they learnt how to practice, and through applying these instructions, realisations naturally arose.

In Kalachakra, nothing is simply black or white, nor is there only one single way to do things. If you understand the nature of your situation, you can select the methods that will be most beneficial to you. Sometimes this may mean developing a conceptual model and other times it may mean meditating on a mind free from concepts. Like a skilled tradesman, it is better to have a toolbox full of tools, than to need a tool and not have it.

ACHIEVING PERSONAL TRANSFORMATION THROUGH THE KALACHAKRA PATH

In this book and the following book in this series, we will study the specific theories and practices that form what can be referred to as the *Kalachakra Path*. This system of practice is specially designed to guide you through a process of transformation which can result in the manifestation of your greatest potential.

To provide a clear picture of what will be examined, we will rely on the same framework of analysis used when discussing the different vehicles in Buddhism (see Book One)—ground, path and result. In this context, the *ground* is a set of conditions which act as the basis for engaging in a path; the *path* is a strategy for how to use those conditions to achieve specific changes in our experience; and the *result* is the experience itself that is produced by practicing that path.

Ground—The Inseparability of Ground and Result

No matter who we are, whether we are young or old, male or female, human or otherwise, we all carry with us the same profound nature that is our most sacred truth. Each of us belongs to the family of Buddhas, sharing the nature of Buddhas as our innate and natural lineage.

If we allow ourselves to recognise this inner capacity, we can begin to see our potential for achieving the perfection of all good qualities and the eradication of all faults. This is the sublime state of a fully enlightened Buddha. Without the perception that comprehends such potential, our minds are overwhelmed with doubt, making enlightenment seem completely beyond our grasp.

For this reason the Kalachakra places an enormous emphasis on achieving the realisation of Buddha-nature. From beginning to end, the Kalachakra identifies this nature within a seemingly infinite array of manifestations. By recognising that every moment of our experience is a result of our Buddha-nature, then every single instance of our experience becomes an opportunity for realisation. In this way there is nothing which, under the right conditions, cannot be used as a support for the path.

While our nature has been primordially pure since beginningless time, our experience of it has become clouded by layers and layers of obscuring concepts. Like a jewel buried deep in the ground, we have lost sight of our innate purity and as a consequence, we perpetuate for ourselves an endless cycle of suffering. The Kalachakra Path does not need to create purity as the purity already exists. It merely needs to remove the conditions which prevent that purity from fully manifesting.

Unfortunately, our minds are currently limited by two primary obscurations: ignorance and bias. *Ignorance* in this context refers specifically to the ignorance which grasps onto reality as existing in the way that it appears. It is this misconception that leads to the division of reality into the dualistic perspective of subject and object. When we grasp onto appearances as being a self, from that moment on we relate all our experiences back to this concept.

On the basis of this ignorance we develop another form of misconception known as *bias*. This type of ignorance grasps onto some appearances as desirable and others as undesirable, projecting our own value judgement onto what we perceive. As a result, we hold tightly to some aspects while rejecting everything else, separating our experiences and fracturing our minds into a web of tangled thoughts and emotions.

The stronger our ignorance and bias, the more limited our mind's capacity becomes, as if we were to bind our nature within chains. To free ourselves from these constraints, we must cut through all forms of ignorance and bias for only then will the innate purity of our nature be able to fully manifest.

Simply removing the obstacles however is not enough, we must also develop the conditions to ensure they do not return. This is done by completely habituating our minds to the *wisdom* that realises the sublime emptiness of reality and the non-referential *compassion* that encompasses all things. These two aspects of wisdom and compassion function like the two wings of a bird.

Together, they allow us to soar high above our limitations and establish the conditions for Buddhahood.

As the great Kadam master Atisha Dipamkara often said, "Wisdom without method is bondage. Method without wisdom is bondage." Neither of these qualities is sufficient in isolation. Without the method of love and compassion, there is no room in our lives for change, as our focus is simply too narrow for wisdom to be effective. Conversely, without wisdom, our love and compassion remains superficial and limited. We need both of these qualities if we are to be successful.

Path—Taking Reality as the Path

To gain insight into the actual methods used by Kalachakra to purify our mind of obscurations, we can discuss the meaning of the name itself. Kalachakra is a Sanskrit word made up of two terms; *kala* meaning "time" and *chakra* meaning "wheel", literally translated into English as "Wheel of Time". Beyond its mere function as a name, Kalachakra embodies the very essence of the ground, path and result. By understanding the different ways these two terms are used, we can develop familiarity with the system's methodology.

The first thing to note is that Kalachakra refers to the totality of all our experience. It is a label that is used to refer to both reality itself and every possible manifestation of that reality. By realising the nature of Kalachakra, we are in fact realising the nature of everything. This means that no matter what level of experience we are discussing, it is all contained within the concept of Kalachakra.

From the perspective of practice, we can say that Kalachakra takes *reality as the path*. This refers to the way we work directly with our perceptions of reality at different stages in our spiritual development. The aim is to use our direct experience as an opportunity to recognise how Kalachakra is manifesting and to reveal its underlying nature. As we progress along the path, we start with a gross level of experience and slowly refine our realisation until eventually arriving at a direct experience of our Buddha-nature.

To simplify this process, we can speak of three main levels of reality: (1) the External Reality, (2) the Internal Reality and (3) the Enlightened Reality. Each level represents a different aspect of how reality is experienced. Therefore, the meaning of Kalachakra changes based on the context in which it is being used.

The External Reality

The External Reality refers to the objective nature of the universe in which sentient beings live, comprising the entire vastness of space and encompassing all the stars and planets. It also includes the countless unseen realms that as humans we don't experience directly but which still influence the appearances in our minds. For example, there are the lower realms of animals, hungry ghosts and hell-beings, and the celestial realms of various types of gods. In essence, the external reality is the environment in which we live.

When we consider the nature of this environment, there are two observations we can make. The first is that everything is impermanent, constantly changing in both gross and subtle ways. Even when something seems solid or fixed, if we investigate closely we can see that it is made of very subtle particles which are in a constant state of flux. There is nothing in the physical universe that is not like this. We refer to this impermanent nature as *time*.

Normally, when we think of time, we think of a beginning, middle and an end (or past, present and future), but these are merely conceptual ways of referring to how things change, not how they actually exist. When we observe how matter appears to us, we find that mass and energy do not appear out of thin air, as something can never arise from nothing. What we classify as the beginning of something is really just the moment in which enough energy has come together, enabling us to perceive it. It then appears to remain stable for a time as the energy holds a similar configuration, until finally it seems to dissolve when that energy is redistributed. The energy was previously in one configuration and then transformed into another. This process is symbolised by a circle, with no beginning, middle or end. This is what the word *wheel* refers to.

In this context, Kalachakra refers to the never ending process of transformation that governs the way the external universe manifests in our experience. This process is without a beginning and without an end, a cycle of change that repeats over and over again, in every single moment.

By understanding this nature, we achieve two main benefits. Firstly, when we realise the impermanent nature of the external universe, it becomes very hard to believe that it is substantially real. Comprehension of this constant shifting from one form to another reduces our clinging to it being only one way forever. It's like the notion that we are all made of stardust. Over millennia, the atoms that constitute our bodies right now have also comprised many other previous forms. When our bodies eventually decompose, those atoms will then become the building blocks of innumerable forms in the future.

Secondly, when we realise the cyclical nature of reality, we gain insight into the nature of imputation, by identifying the ways our experience is influenced by our interpretation of what appears to us. We see a beginning where no beginning exists. We see an end where no end exists. These are both conceptual imputations that we use to make sense of our world. When we investigate more closely, we discover that the things we believe to exist are not independently separate from our minds. They are instead dependent upon the act of imputation.

Exercise 1.1 — Patterns of Change

- *In a relaxed posture, establish a neutral mind through the practice of mindfulness of breathing.*

- *Identify an object that you have encountered in your life. It can be anything other than yourself.*

- *Now consider where this object came from. Try to trace it back to the moment where you would say it began. What observations can you make about this moment?*

- *Then consider the manner in which this object abides. Does it remain static, or is it changing? If so, how does it change?*

- *Finally, consider how this object will one day disappear. If it hasn't already, simply imagine how you think this will happen. What conditions do you think can trigger this change? Where does the matter go?*

- *As you consider these points, rest your awareness in any insights that arise. When you are ready, you can repeat the process by choosing another object or you can end your session.*

The Internal Reality

Within the environment of the External Reality, we can distinguish two groups of phenomena: animate and inanimate objects. The defining difference between these two is the presence of dualistic mind. While both are comprised equally of subtle particles, the particles of an animate object have been appropriated by a stream of consciousness. We call this combination of body and mind a *sentient being*.

The glue which binds body and mind together is a form of grasping that sees the body as part of the mind's conception of self. The strength of this grasping determines the influence these two aspects have over each other. Once the bond is formed at the moment of conception, the body develops in accordance with the karmic conditioning of the mind, whereas the mind experiences reality through the physical conditioning of the body.

Just as the physical universe is dominated by a constant process of transformation, so too is the mind. In this sense, there is no difference between the internal and external. In fact, the patterns of subtle energy within the body are closely correlated to the patterns of energy in the environment. For instance, the cycles of breathing that occur during a single day correspond to the movements of various planets and stars over the course of a year. Virtually every pattern of change we experience internally as a sentient being is connected with some aspect of the external cosmos.

The implication of this connection is that by changing the patterns of energy within ourselves, we influence the patterns of energy around us. If only a few people make these changes the impact may be negligible, but it can quickly multiply based on the numbers of people adopting the new pattern. This is the principle which drives the notion of how the practice of Kalachakra is able to effect change on a larger scale. By establishing peace and harmony within our bodies and minds, we are actively contributing to the peace and harmony of the world in which we live.

With this in mind, the meaning of Kalachakra has now shifted inwards to identify the nature of the subjective aspect of our experience. Previously, the term *wheel* referred to an endless cycle with no beginning and no end. This is another way of saying that every moment is connected to every other moment through the continuity of transformation. If you could track the movements of every single particle, you would be able to connect the dots between the presently arising state and a previous state of existence. Likewise, the state of our mind now is the result of a series of changes that connect us to the experience of our past. It is this interconnected nature that we associate with *wheel*. Subjectively, this feeling of connection manifests as love and kindness.

Our ordinary perception of love is actually a mixture of love and attachment. While attachment focuses on getting what we want, authentic love is focused on the needs of others. In the most universal sense, love is the desire for others to experience genuine, lasting happiness. Because love centres on others, it has the effect of dissolving our bias of self-cherishing, opening up our hearts and allowing us to develop meaningful connections with those around us.

As you strengthen your connections through authentic love and kindness, you slowly expand your sphere of interest to include more and more people. In time, your love becomes less conditioned, allowing it to grow immeasurably until it encompasses all sentient beings regardless of their relationship with you.

The closer you feel towards others, the more you care about their welfare and it is this caring that manifests in the form of compassion. Because of its interdependent nature with love and kindness, the more love we feel, the stronger our compassion grows. Although it may start at a superficial level of merely empathising with the suffering of others, in time, it too will expand outwards until you feel personally responsible for helping every single sentient being, without exception. The more you dedicate yourself to their welfare, the less focused you are on feeding your self-cherishing. This clears away more bias and creates the conditions for you to realise your ultimate nature.

We can relate this sort of compassion to the concept of *time*. No matter the situation or who is experiencing it, time keeps moving forward, it never stops. In the same way genuine compassion cares equally about all sentient beings across time and therefore never gives up. Whether or not they are experiencing suffering or happiness at this present moment is irrelevant. Genuine compassion is able to see the big picture. It cares about both sentient beings' present welfare and their future welfare.

We can then say that Kalachakra has the essence of love and compassion. When cultivated correctly, this essence connects us with anyone we encounter in the same way a mother does with her child. This realisation alone is truly extraordinary. Just imagine the impact it would have if everyone cultivated these qualities.

In addition to the enormous benefit this perspective brings to sentient beings, we are also guided toward two very important insights into the nature of reality. The first is the interconnected aspect of all phenomena. The more our awareness of this interconnection develops, the less we grasp onto the notion that we are separate entities operating independently from the world. This realisation of the dependent nature of all things leads to the realisation of the emptiness of an inherently existent self. When this wisdom is combined with the genuine compassion that feels a sense of personal responsibility for all sentient beings, we achieve a non-referential form of compassion that is known as "being endowed with the essence of emptiness and compassion".

Exercise 1.2 — Cultivating Connections

- *In a relaxed posture, establish a neutral mind through the practice of mindfulness of breathing.*

- *Bring to mind a person you feel a strong connection to. Try to feel as though they are present with you.*

- *Think of this person's hopes and dreams for their life. Try to go beyond the surface level and look at the essence of what motivates them.*

- *Now compare this with your own hopes and dreams. What similarities can you identify?*

- *Just as you hope to fulfill your heart's desire, cultivate the wish that this person receives everything they need to make their dreams come true.*

- *Allow this person to fade back into the mind and rest in an open awareness until someone else arises. No matter who it is, try to connect with their underlying motivation and develop the wish that they experience happiness.*

- *Repeat this process for as long as you like.*

The Enlightened Reality

Through working with the External and Internal forms of Kalachakra, it is possible to reveal the ultimate nature of conventional reality as the emptiness of inherent existence. This realisation clears away the tangled web of concepts that have prevented us from experiencing our most profound nature. Now, with the driving force of our bodhicitta motivation, we turn our focus to the definitive meaning that transcends the dualistic mind completely. Since it refers to reality from the perspective of an enlightened being, this is known as the Enlightened Reality.

When we consider the nature of the awareness that experiences love and compassion, we also discover its blissful nature. The more we open our hearts, the more bliss arises in the mind. This is a strong indication that bliss is a fundamental aspect of the nature of our minds. As love and compassion rely on connection as their basis, we can relate the feeling of bliss as the concept of a *wheel*.

For ordinary beings, the bliss we experience is intermittent, changing in dependence on causes and conditions. When we realise emptiness on the basis of dependent origination, we give rise to a non-referential compassion that is not affected by change. No matter what the circumstances, it remains stable and manifest. This in turn leads to an experience of bliss that also does not fluctuate. Where *time* previously referred to impermanence and change, now it is connected with the ideas of permanence and the absence of change.

When these two aspects are combined, we experience what is known as *immutable bliss*. It is a state of mind that abides unwaveringly in the bliss that is generated from not grasping onto dualistic appearances. This type of bliss is symbolised by the male deity of Kalachakra.

If we then consider the nature of the appearances that are the basis for generating this form of non-referential love and compassion, we find that they are also empty in nature. But this emptiness is not a mere vacuity, it is a field of infinite potential that is beyond atoms or particles and completely transcends the physical realm of experience. While simultaneously being everything, it is not fixed in any way, therefore it transcends both existence and non-existence. Such reality is known as *empty-form* because it is empty of all conceptual fabrications which limit its potential. This very suchness is the diverse nature of reality and is symbolised by the female deity of Vishvamata.

For the enlightened mind, immutable bliss and empty-form are experienced as the inseparable union of Kalachakra and Vishvamata, the single taste that is the definitive meaning of ultimate reality. Even though we may use different words to describe their different aspects, we must always remember that they are referring to the same nature. These are merely skilful means to focus our awareness and bring us closer to realisation.

Exercise 1.3 — Resting in Equanimity

- *In a relaxed posture, set your mind at ease through the practice of mindfulness of breathing.*

- *Open your eyes and rest your gaze gently in the space in front of you.*

- *With each out breath, release whatever thoughts you may have. Allow your mind to become spacious and open.*

- *Rest the mind in stillness for as long as you can, free from any sort of grasping.*

- *If the mind begins to move again, simply use the out breath to release the grasping and return to equanimity.*

- *With an unbroken stream of awareness, continue in this way until the end of your session.*

Result—The Perfection of Peace and Harmony

The essential method of Kalachakra is to cultivate love and compassion to such a degree that all forms of bias are removed and the mind is able to abide in a pervasive and unchanging experience of peace and harmony. This profound realisation is known as *Shambhala*. To achieve Shambhala is synonymous with full and complete enlightenment or the perfect manifestation of our primordially pure Buddha-nature. Because this nature is equally present at the time of the ground and the time of the result, Shambhala is considered to be both the source of the Kalachakra teachings and the fruition of its practice.

While ultimately Shambhala is the perfection of peace and harmony, conventionally, it can manifest in a variety of ways depending on the purity of one's mind. As such, we can identify many intermediate steps along the path that are also given the name Shambhala. All of these manifestations represent provisional opportunities for us to achieve realisation of the definitive meaning of Ultimate Shambhala and are produced through the practice of Kalachakra. This means that even if you are unable to complete the path at this time, you can be sure to create the opportunity to do so in a future life.

Realms of Opportunity in the Aspect of Shambhala

The first level of Shambhala that can manifest in our experience as a result of practicing Kalachakra is what is known as *Realms of Opportunity in the Aspect of Shambhala*. These experiences are not a fully qualified manifestation of Shambhala but represent a partial aspect of its nature. They are referred to as realms of opportunity, because they offer us a chance to become more familiar with our definitive nature. The following aspects can all be experienced during an ordinary human rebirth:

1. **Essential Aspect:** The essence of Shambhala is *love and compassion.* It manifests in our lives whenever we experience a genuine connection with other sentient beings. For instance the love felt by a parent for their child.

2. **Vast Aspect:** When the qualities of love and compassion are cultivated through a spiritual path, the scope of our connection expands outwards. When taken to its fullest expression, it encompasses all sentient beings. It is this *expansive quality* that is the manifestation of Shambhala's vastness.

3. **Unbiased Aspect:** Bias has the nature of creating divisions, whereas love and compassion have the nature of making connections. The more expansive our love and compassion becomes, the more our bias is dissolved. The unbiased aspect of Shambhala manifests as an experience of *equanimity* that cares equally for others regardless of their specific characteristics.

4. **Unified Aspect:** The unity of Shambhala manifests in the *wisdom* that realises our fundamental nature, for instance, the wisdom that comprehends the unanimous desire to be happy and to be free from suffering. Through connecting with our similarities, the differences which divide us cease to have any power.

The Golden Age of Shambhala

Practicing the Kalachakra Path increases our cultivation of the qualities of love and compassion, generating powerful karmic connections to the beings in this world. At the same time, we are also habituating our minds to the aspects of Shambhala and this creates the karmic causes for us to be born during the *Golden Age of Shambhala.*

In general, a "golden age" is a term given to a period of time when the dominant values of a society have shifted to spiritual values such as love, compassion and wisdom. They normally arise after periods of great degeneration and suffering. At such times, people tend to recognise the need to change their ways and are therefore more receptive to new views.

The Golden Age of Shambhala specifically refers to a period in which the Kalachakra teachings will flourish in this world, giving rise to a form of enlightened society that is conducive to spiritual practice. It is during this time that anyone who has not yet achieved enlightenment but has previously cultivated a connection with Kalachakra, will be born on this planet in a human body.

When this golden age will actually occur is unclear. There are prophecies that exist which state it will happen in a few hundred years, however these numbers should not be understood as being fixed. Whether or not a golden age arises depends entirely on the minds of the sentient beings of this planet. If we continue to hold to wrong views that promote ignorance and bias, it will be impossible to experience a golden age. If on the other hand we each make peace and harmony our priority, a golden age could arise much sooner than we imagine.

Shambhala—the perfection of peace and harmony

The Sublime Nirmanakaya Realm of Shambhala

The next level of experience is known as the *Sublime Nirmanakaya Realm of Shambhala* and is the first manifestation that can be described as a fully qualified form of Shambhala. This means it is a complete manifestation produced by all of Shambhala's aspects. While the previous forms of Shambhala manifest at a gross level of experience, this realm manifests at a much more subtle level of experience. To be born there requires three main conditions:

1. **Karmic Connection:** First, we must become familiar with the aspects of Shambhala through the practice of Kalachakra. This realm is the result of more than two thousand years of Kalachakra practice, and as the teachings of Kalachakra originated in Shambhala, to engage in Kalachakra practice during this life creates a very strong karmic connection with that realm.

2. **Strong Aspiration:** Secondly, we must develop a strong aspiration to be born there, particularly at the time of death. This aspiration will strengthen our karmic propensities, causing them to ripen and propel us into our next rebirth.

3. **Stability of Mind:** Finally, we must develop a sufficient degree of stability in our minds in order to maintain the necessary degree of subtlety during the *Bardo of Becoming*. This stability is naturally developed through the meditative practices used in the Kalachakra Path.

The following is a short description of how the Sublime Realm of Shambhala is experienced by those who are born there:

The entire realm is surrounded by an impenetrable barrier of snow mountains which are so high they are impossible to cross. As one descends from the crystal-like peaks, down into the valleys below, one passes through rocky outcrops, woodland forests and lush jungles. Eventually the mountainside transforms into rolling hills of green grass and fragrant flowers. The whole landscape emits a warm glow that self-illuminates the entire world, dispelling all darkness from every corner.

Looking down upon the kingdom there are eight great regions forming an outer ring around a central one—like the petals of an eight-petalled lotus. Each of these regions is divided by natural boundaries of winding rivers and towering mountains. Unlike those on the outer border, these mountains are filled with vibrant green valleys offering ample opportunity to travel from one region to the next. While the landscape of each region varies considerably, they are all a mixture of luscious grasslands and magnificent forests. The countless rivers that wind their way through the land connect a huge network of lakes that contain pristine, nectar-like water which sparkles and reflects the natural splendour of the environment.

From the perspective of the humans who live there, the land is filled with all kinds of beautiful animals and birds who sing melodious songs and ornament the landscape. These are all emanations of the Bodhisattva Kings and serve to provide comfort and inspiration to the citizens of Shambhala. The green valleys are filled with rich pastures, orchards and gardens. The land organically gives rise to an endless array of foods ensuring ample nourishment for everyone.

Within each outer region there are twelve kingdoms, divided naturally by the lay of the land. Each kingdom has ten million cities that sit in perfect balance with the surrounding countryside. In the central region of the land is an immense mountain rising high above all the surrounding valleys. It is known as Mount Kailasha. At its summit is the capital city of Shambhala—the magnificent Kalapa. The city is surrounded by two lotus filled lakes and a vast oasis of pleasure gardens.

All humans born here start their lives endowed with a wealth of virtuous qualities; in particular, they all have phenomenal propensities for love and compassion. Each child is born to a human mother, but unlike ordinary birth, there is no pain. Both parents feel an enormous amount of love for their child, however they do not view them as their own. They instead love all children equally, regardless of who physically gave birth to them. As long as a child needs them, there are adults who are capable of nurturing them and offering support.

From very early on, children are introduced to the spiritual views emphasised in their particular region. Due to their extremely well developed spiritual qualities, they progress very quickly along their respective paths. Like riding a bicycle, they re-learn much of what they were taught in previous lives and so are able to develop deep levels of meditative absorption at a very young age.

Since food, clothing and shelter are available in abundance, it is not necessary for anyone to work for money or for people to trade in goods. Within this culture the leaders of the various kingdoms do not need to impose laws on their people and do not need to rule through might and power. In each of the 96 kingdoms there is a governor who acts as a spiritual role model and mentor for the people within their kingdom.

While individuals may grow up in one kingdom of Shambhala, they are not attached to the geography nor its culture. When the time is right, they often travel to other kingdoms where they continue their studies and advance on their spiritual path. The relationships formed between people are not based on belonging to this or that group, but are closely tied to their level of spiritual development.

Another common relationship is between students and teachers. Everyone in Shambhala recognises the responsibility of those with higher realisations to guide and support those with less. As there is no sense of competition, everyone works together to help each other actualise their potential.

As individuals progress through each stage of their path, they slowly migrate from the outer kingdoms towards the centre. Like all rivers flowing into the ocean, everyone eventually arrives at the base of Mount Kailasha. Ascending the mountain, they reach the pleasure groves where they are initiated into the enlightened mandala of Kalachakra. Through the uncommon practices of the *Kalachakra Six Vajra Yogas*, they enter into the city of Kalapa where they are eventually granted an audience with the King. Here they experience the face of Kalachakra and realise the ultimate manifestation of Shambhala.

This extraordinary realm of opportunity is produced through the combined aspirations of bodhisattvas and the karmic connections of the sentient beings of this world. Because it is a realm that arises from karma, it is possible to cultivate the causes to be born there, and due to the aspirations of the Bodhisattvas, it is the perfect environment to complete our spiritual journey. Anyone born into this realm is guaranteed to achieve enlightenment within the span of a single human lifetime. For this reason, it is no longer considered to be part of Samsara.

The Sambhogakaya Realm of Shambhala

For those who have perfected the practices of the Kalachakra Generation Stage and have developed familiarity with the experience of empty-forms, it is possible to use the dream-like appearances that arise during the transitionary period after death as an opportunity to realise the definitive meaning of Shambhala. This is known as the *Sambhogakaya Realm of Shambhala.*

Although this is not the same as complete enlightenment, by abiding in this experience, a practitioner achieves an extraordinary degree of realisation similar to a tenth level bodhisattva. In such a state, you would experience all sights as enlightened deities, all sounds as mantras, and all thoughts as primordial wisdom. From here, an infinite number of ways to complete the accumulations of merit and wisdom can be manifested.

The Dharmakaya Realm of Shambhala

The final manifestation of Shambhala is the culmination of the path, the ultimate experience of the perfection of peace and harmony. This realisation is known as the *Dharmakaya Realm of Shambhala* and occurs as the result of mastering the *Six Vajra Yogas* of the Kalachakra Completion Stage. It can be achieved in two ways:

1. **During the Clear-Light of Death:** At the moment of death, when our minds separate completely from our bodies, it dissolves back into its own primordial nature of Shambhala. If we have enough awareness during this process, we can abide in that nature.

2. **During this Life:** Through dedicating our lives to the practice of the *Six Vajra Yogas*, it is possible to generate the conditions for the mind to experience the unity of immutable bliss and empty-form which is inseparable from the definitive meaning of Shambhala.

In both instances, by abiding in the ultimate nature of Shambhala, our karmic propensities are naturally consumed and are no longer able to condition our experience. Once the last traces are removed, we will have attained complete enlightenment.

Very few people have the necessary conditions to dedicate their lives completely to spiritual practice, but this does not mean that we cannot benefit from practicing Kalachakra. As we can see from the various manifestations of Shambhala, there are many intermediate results that greatly improve our capacity to experience peace and harmony.

This should give us great confidence to always practice to the best of our abilities, regardless of the conditions that are present. Remember, the Kalachakra Path is achieved one step at a time. Even if we only cultivate a little more love and compassion in our lives, it is still an amazing achievement that brings us one step closer to enlightenment.

Similarly, do not worry if you have difficulty understanding some of the concepts discussed above. This is merely a sign that you are encountering new and unfamiliar ideas. In this chapter our goal was to establish a very broad overview of the unique characteristics of the Kalachakra Path and why it is such a powerful system for achieving realisations. Now as we continue, we will expand upon these ideas to develop a much more robust understanding.

REVIEW OF KEY POINTS

- Right now we have a rare opportunity based on three key conditions: (1) we have attained a precious human rebirth, (2) we are gifted with the intelligence that is able to distinguish the causes of our suffering, and (3) we have encountered the Kalachakra teachings which are the cause for genuine happiness.

- These conditions are impermanent and so will not be here forever. Therefore, we need to take advantage of them as much as possible.

- Since beginningless time we have been cycling through Samsara, experiencing every type of suffering. Now is the time to break that cycle.

- Our aim is to develop greater peace and harmony in our lives. To do this, we need a spiritual path to show us how to overcome our negative habits and cultivate our positive qualities.

- The Kalachakra Path is considered the King of Tantra for three reasons: (1) expansive scope; (2) clarity of presentation; and (3) profound methods.

- The ground of the Kalachakra Path is the innate purity of our Buddha-nature which pervades every moment of our experience. This purity is limited by the presence of ignorance and bias in the mind. We can overcome these limitations through the cultivation of wisdom and compassion.

- The Kalachakra Path works with reality on many levels in order to connect us with our ultimate nature of peace and harmony. The three types of reality are: (1) External Reality, (2) Internal Reality and (3) Enlightened Reality.

- The External Reality works with understanding processes of transformation found in the objective experience of our environment in order to develop realisations of impermanence and the emptiness of imputed natures.

- The Internal Reality works with the subjective experience of sentient beings in order to cultivate the qualities of love and compassion. These qualities form the basis for realising the emptiness of dependent natures.

- The Enlightened Reality works with non-dual awareness in order to realise the union of immutable bliss and empty-form. This is the basis for realising the sublime emptiness of our fully established nature.

- The result of the Kalachakra Path is the manifestation of Shambhala—the perfection of peace and harmony.

- Shambhala manifests in different ways depending on your spiritual maturity. From gross to subtle, there are five forms it can take: (1) Realms of Opportunity with the Aspect of Shambhala, (2) The Golden Age of Shambhala, (3) The Sublime Nirmanakaya Realm of Shambhala, (4) The Sambhogakaya Realm of Shambhala and (5) The Dharmakaya Realm of Shambhala. All of these experiences of Shambhala are produced by practicing the Kalachakra Path.

CHAPTER TWO

Connecting with the Jonang-Shambhala Lineage

Shakyamuni Buddha is known to have manifested in our world more than two and half millennia ago. He taught in the Noble Land of India for approximately fifty years before he passed into parinirvana. His entire life was a Dharma teaching that demonstrated the very principles of the discourses he taught and as such, he made a profound impact on all who had the great fortune to meet him.

During his time in this world, the Buddha taught on many different levels of experience. As a result of his enlightened realisation, he was able to enter into profound states of absorption which allowed him to operate within different dimensions of incredible subtlety. Consequently he was not limited to teaching only those who were in his physical presence. Many times, while he may have appeared to be simply meditating, he was in fact manifesting his mind in countless ways for the benefit of sentient beings.

The Kalachakra Path that we discussed in the previous chapter is one example of a teaching the Buddha gave from a more subtle dimension of experience. As he expounded the *Perfection of Wisdom Sutras* on the summit of Vulture's Peak Mountain near Rajagriha in the north-east of India, his mind was simultaneously manifesting as the *Primordial Buddha of Kalachakra* in the south of India, inside the famed Dhanyakataka Stupa near modern day Amaravati.

At that time, through the power of his vajra-like absorption, the Buddha rested in the Dharmakaya state of the Primordial Buddha. To the tenth level bodhisattvas who had gathered there he appeared in the Sambhogakaya form of Kalachakra with four faces and twenty-four arms, embracing his consort Vishvamata in union. It was to this form that the Bodhisattva King of Shambhala Suchandra first requested the teachings of Kalachakra.

The Buddha granted his request and proceeded to turn the wheel of Tantra by expounding the vast and profound teaching known as the *Primordial Buddha in Twelve-Thousand Lines*. While he gave this teaching from his principal face, he also gave teachings from each of his other three faces. In this way he transmitted four distinct classes of tantra suited for beings of varying capacities.

Similar to the Buddha, King Suchandra and his ninety-six bodhisattva governors were also meditating in deep absorption. When they had received all of the teachings that the Buddha had to offer them, they returned their awareness back to their bodies in the Sublime Realm of Shambhala. It was there that King Suchandra wrote down the teachings and began to propagate the wisdom of Kalachakra.

The Dharma King Suchandra—an emanation of Vajrapani himself—is considered the first Kalachakra lineage holder. This is a simple way of saying that the teachings were passed from the Buddha to Suchandra and it was then Suchandra who was responsible for propagating them to his students. But more importantly than this, to become a lineage holder refers to the fact that Suchandra was the first to actualise the Kalachakra teachings in his mindstream, effectively becoming the living embodiment of the definitive meaning of those teachings. We can therefore identify two types of lineage:

1. **Lineage of Transmission:** This first type of lineage is focused on the communication of teachings from master to disciple. A skilled master can use any aspect of his body, speech or mind to transmit teachings. For instance it may be an oral transmission through words, or a direct transfer of understanding from mind to mind. It can also take the symbolic form of a physical action such as when Tilopa struck Naropa on the head with his sandal. Whatever form the transmission takes, the essence is that through the act of giving the transmission, the master creates the conditions for realisation to arise in the mindstream of the student.

   In the Tibetan tradition, oral transmissions are known as *lung*, which literally means wind or air. The aim of such a transmission is to ensure that a specific teaching is passed on without distortion, thereby maintaining its pure connection back to the moment when it was first uttered by the

The Supreme Dharma King of Shambhala, Suchandra

Buddha. It is generally considered good practice to seek transmission of a teaching from an authentic lineage holder before actually engaging in its practice. This ensures that you are establishing the best karmic propensities to actualise the teachings. First request the teachings, then receive the transmission and finally practice what you have received.

2. **Lineage of Realisation:** The second type of lineage is a direct result of having received the first. To become a lineage holder, it is not enough to merely have heard a teaching, for even a fly can be fortunate enough to hear the sounds made by a teacher. It doesn't mean that they are able to understand and integrate the meaning of those teachings into their lives.

   To truly *hold* a lineage means to have achieved realisation on the basis of those teachings. When this occurs, the student's mind effectively manifests the qualities of the master's mind, achieving the intended result for the transmission to be given.

   In order for a lineage to be considered *alive*, it must be held by lineage holders who can transmit not only the words but more importantly their meaning. It requires enormous dedication to the teachings to become a lineage holder and it is only through the infinite kindness of these masters that we are able to encounter authentic teachings in this age of degeneration.

THE IMPORTANCE OF RELYING ON A LINEAGE

Buddhism in general places a great deal of emphasis on the notion of lineage. This is partly because in the years after the Buddha's passing, the Sangha community preserved the teachings through oral recitation of the entire canon. It wasn't until later that these teachings were written down as texts and the only way to access them was by relying on a lineage.

In the present day, technology has allowed us to document and store information more than any other time in history. At the push of a button, from anywhere in the world, we can find scriptures and commentaries available in a wide number of languages. Does this mean lineages are no longer relevant? I would say the exact opposite is true. Now, more than ever, connecting with an authentic lineage is not only relevant, it is essential.

To begin with, unlike the ease with which we now can access information, students once had to travel vast distances at great peril in order to receive the teachings. They would also be willing to give all of their worldly possessions in order to receive a single verse of the precious Dharma, whereas now we expect everything to be free. These contrasting examples point to a major shift in the value attributed to the teachings. The more common the teachings become in our minds, the less appreciation we have for their incredible capacity. Without appreciation, there is no strength to our practice and the benefit they were originally designed to produce is no longer received. By actively seeking out authentic lineage holders who can bestow the teachings from an authentic lineage, we can be sure to avoid this scenario.

We should always remember our purpose for practicing a spiritual path in the first place. While we all long for genuine peace and harmony in our lives, who can we look to as an example for actually achieving these results? The answer is the Buddha and all the highly realised beings who dedicate their lives to putting his teachings into practice. These are the lineage holders who embody our greatest potential and demonstrate the path we can all walk. Without these venerable role models to inspire our minds and connect us to our ultimate nature, how can we ever hope to achieve realisations? For this reason, they should be cherished from the depths of our hearts.

From another perspective, consider the importance we place on our regular ancestry and the pride many people have for belonging to a particular family. Think of the great efforts people go through to simply find out where their families originated. We may obtain some interesting facts regarding the origins of our genetic material and if we are lucky we may find one or two people in our family tree to inspire us, but there's no guarantee of this.

A spiritual lineage on the other hand is much more profound. Each member of this lineage has effectively transformed their minds into the minds of their masters, manifesting their amazing qualities. By connecting with an authentic lineage holder, instead of the teachings being something far off in a distant past, they become immediately accessible and relevant. In this way, the mind of the Buddha continues to live on, bringing his teachings into the present moment and giving us the extraordinary opportunity to receive the teachings from the Buddha himself.

HOW TO DEVELOP FAITH IN A LINEAGE

The primary method for connecting with a spiritual lineage is by working closely with a lineage holder as your spiritual guide. Such a guide is a living embodiment of the path we are following and therefore provides the most immediate and effective method for attaining realisations. The next chapter will discuss this aspect in detail, and so for the moment we will look at strengthening our awareness of the context in which we are practicing.

We do this through studying the life stories of past Kalachakra lineage masters. Developing familiarity with their spiritual journeys arouses feelings of respect and appreciation. Such an attitude makes us more worthy recipients for receiving the teachings and strengthens our resolve to follow in the footsteps of these great masters. It also prevents us from falling into the trap of viewing our spiritual practice as something ordinary or common and heightens the importance the teachings play in our lives, bringing extraordinary meaning to our actions.

Practically speaking, the first step is to become familiar with who the lineage masters are. It can be helpful to start with identifying the general evolution of the lineage and then slowly over time, adding more detail to each period. If you can, I highly recommend memorising the names of the lineage masters to heighten your awareness of them in your practice. You can find a list of the full lineage as an appendix to this book.

Once you have an overall sense of the relationships over time, you can focus more attention on extracting the essential points for each master. If a detailed history is available, you can spend time reflecting on the way the master developed their qualities over the course of their life. A great deal can be learned from paying attention to the teachings they relied on, their attitudes towards them and the types of activities they engaged in.

Finally, when you have developed a strong awareness of the lineage masters, use their lives as examples of how to study, reflect and meditate, and strive to develop their qualities in your own experience. When faced with challenges, consider how they would handle the situation and do your best to emulate them in everything you do. By keeping them close to your heart, you allow their enlightened presence to inspire your mind and guide you in all your actions.

THE JONANG-SHAMBHALA LINEAGE

While the Kalachakra teachings have existed in the Sublime Realm of Shambhala for more than two thousand years, they were only transmitted to our world a little more than one thousand years ago during the ninth and tenth centuries. If we look at the present holders of the Kalachakra lineage, we can see it has survived primarily within the different traditions of Tibetan Buddhism. Of the six main traditions, there are four which actively promote the Kalachakra teachings: the Sakya, Kagyu, Jonang and Geluk. Of these four, only the Jonang has maintained an unbroken lineage of the Kalachakra completion stage practices known as the *Six Vajra Yogas*. It is for this reason the Jonang Tradition is considered to be the most complete Kalachakra lineage in this world.

From the perspective of practicing Kalachakra, each of the teachings within all the different traditions is considered authentic and so has the capacity to guide you towards enlightenment. The main difference between the Jonang and the other traditions is that while the others mostly use Kalachakra as a supplement to their main practice of other systems, only the Jonang focuses one hundred percent on the practice of Kalachakra. As a result, the Jonang have developed a uniquely profound insight into the nature of this system and how to most effectively use it for achieving enlightenment.

The following history details the evolution of the Jonang-Shambhala lineage over the course of the last few millennia. What we currently refer to as the Jonang Tradition is actually a combination of two streams of teachings which emerged from two perspectives: the causal perspective of the Buddha's sutra teachings and the resultant perspective of the Buddha's tantra teachings. Both of these streams were combined in the fourteenth century by the Omniscient Dharma Lord of the Three Times, Dolpopa Sherab Gyaltsen. Since then, his unified system of sutra and tantra has formed the basis for all Jonang curriculums.

As will be illustrated, the Jonang originated in the Tsang province of Central Tibet where it thrived for several hundred years. By the seventeenth century, the political landscape shifted and the tradition found itself in the middle of various power struggles that saw its monasteries gradually converted and its teachings banned. Fortunately, the Jonang followers had previously established major monastic institutions in the remote regions of Eastern Tibet and it was there the tradition continued to flourish.

To help develop a broad overview for understanding the context of the teachings presented in this book, the following section provides you with a summary of the main people and events which have shaped the Jonang Tradition. If you would like a more detailed presentation of this history you can find one in my book *Demystifying Shambhala*. There are also condensed histories of each lineage holder in my book *Hidden Treasure of the Profound Path*.

The Tantric Lineage of the Kalachakra Six Vajra Yogas

The **Dharma King Suchandra** is largely credited with establishing the Kalachakra teachings in the kingdom of Shambhala. He did this by firstly compiling all the teachings he had received from the Buddha to produce the *Kalachakra Root Text—The Supreme Primordial Buddha*. He then went on to construct a mammoth three dimensional mandala in the pleasure grove of Malaya, to the east of the capital city Kalapa. On the basis of this enlightened mandala he bestowed empowerments and gave many teachings to the people living in the central region of Shambhala.

Recognising that the Root Text was too difficult for most people to understand, Suchandra composed a detailed commentary of sixty thousand verses. As a result of this text, the Kalachakra teachings flourished within the royal courts of Kalapa, giving rise to a succession of highly realised Dharma Kings who carried on the work that Suchandra had started.

Only a few hundred years before the start of the common era, the Kingdom of Shambhala had already transformed significantly. Although Kalachakra was widely recognised as being an extraordinary method for realising the definitive meaning of reality, it was mostly practiced in the central region of Kalapa. The vast majority of people in the surrounding regions of the country were still divided along traditional religious lines.

At this time, the **Dharma King Yashas**, who was said to be an emanation of Manjushri, realised through the power of his clairvoyance that the society of Shambhala was at a crossroads. Due to certain practices within the culture, divisions of bias were being strengthened and if left to develop, these forms of bias would prevent his people from experiencing the ultimate freedom of their sublime nature. For this reason, he made great efforts to remedy the situation.

Manjushri Yashas met with all the different communities in his kingdom and, using his profound wisdom, showed them how to interpret their own teachings in a way that would guide them to the most profound truth. There were those, however, who would not accept his unshakeable logic, and with the need to use more forceful methods, the King issued a decree that everyone in Shambhala should participate in a Kalachakra empowerment as recognition of their shared nature.

One group of Brahmins, believing this was an attempt to convert them to another religion, chose to reject the King's decree and instead left Shambhala to travel southward towards India. Determined to prove that his intentions were motivated purely out of great compassion for their welfare, the King demonstrated his incredible powers. Finally being convinced of his wisdom, the Brahmins returned to Shambhala where King Yashas proceeded to unite his people into a single vajra family. From this moment on, the Dharma Kings of Shambhala were given the name *Kalki*, meaning "Holder of the Caste."

In the Kalachakra Tantra, twenty-five Kalkis are prophesied to each reign for approximately one hundred years and this present era falls during the time of the twenty-first Kalki, Aniruddha. Through the guidance of these Kalkis, the teachings of Kalachakra flourished throughout the kingdom of Shambhala. This was largely made possible due to the kindness of the **Second Kalki King Pundarika**—an emanation of Avalokiteshvara—who wrote the *Stainless Light* commentary on the *Abridged Kalachakra Tantra* that had been composed by his father Manjushri Yashas. Through these two texts, the Kalachakra became increasingly more accessible and allowed a much wider audience to draw benefit from its wisdom.

Over the centuries as a direct result of their continuous practice of the Kalachakra, the minds of the citizens of Shambhala became increasingly refined. Eventually the entire kingdom became so subtle it was no longer accessible to the coarse minds of ordinary beings. From the perspective of the outside world, Shambhala had disappeared into the archives of history, kept alive only by legends and folklore, but for those with a pure enough intention and a mind made subtle through meditation, Shambhala could still be experienced.

And so it was that during the reign of the Eleventh Kalki King Aja, a gifted yogi by the name of **Manjuvajra** would be responsible for retrieving the profound pith instructions of the Kalachakra teachings from Shambhala and bringing them into this realm of existence for the benefit of all sentient beings. Born in the eastern region of Bengal and growing up during a time when Buddhism was thriving, Manjuvajra studied in the great monastic universities of Odantapuri and Nalanda, becoming a great scholar and expert of the five sciences.

During his studies, Manjuvajra received many teachings from Pindo Acharya who held a textual transmission of Pundarika's commentary known as *Stainless Light*. While his mind was greatly inspired by this text, he longed to put its teachings into practice, for at this time there was no lineage describing how the Kalachakra could be applied to one's own experience. With great determination, Manjuvajra set out in search of Shambhala's ancient pith instructions.

After travelling northward, he met an emanation of Kalki Aja who agreed to bestow upon him the higher and highest empowerments as well as the instructions that he sought. Over the course of many months, Manjuvajra put these instructions into practice and attained incredible degrees of realisation. As his mind became sufficiently subtle, Manjuvajra was able to travel directly to Shambhala where he received from the Kalki himself, a complete system of practice in accordance with the Kalachakra Tantra.

When Manjuvajra returned his awareness to this gross realm of experience, he proceeded to pass the teachings on to all who would listen. Recognised as an accomplished Mahasiddha, he became known far and wide as the *Great Kalachakrapada*.

Of his many disciples, one of his closest was **Shri Badrabhodhi**. Like his master, he was a renowned yogi and was often referred to as the *Second Kalachakrapada*. After attaining complete enlightenment through the perfection of the Six Vajra Yogas, Shri Badra founded a Kalachakra temple at the famed Nalanda University in Magadha. There he taught the Kalachakra to many students, twelve of whom are said to have achieved the supreme attainment of rainbow body.

Although it was Shri Badra who established the practice of Kalachakra in Nalanda, it would be his student who would assert its dominance as the *King of Tantra*. The great scholar-practitioner known as **Nalendrapa** once posted the *Kalachakra Tenfold Symbol of Power* above the main gate of the university. Below the symbol he wrote a short verse that stated:

Those who do not understand the Primordial Buddha, do not understand Kalachakra; Those who do not understand Kalachakra do not understand the Names of Manjushri; Those who do not understand the Names of Manjushri do not understand the awareness body of Vajradhara; Those who do not understand the awareness body of Vajradhara do not understand the mantrayana; Those who do not understand the mantrayana are all those in cyclic existence, and are not on the path of the victorious Vajradhara. This being so, all pure teachers should rely on the Primordial Buddha, and take with them all pure students intent on liberation.

In response to his challenge, more than five hundred Nalanda scholars debated with Nalendrapa and each was defeated by his flawless logic. In this way, the most acclaimed masters came to recognise the Kalachakra to be the definitive meaning of the Buddha's teachings. Invited to become Abbot of Nalanda, Nalendrapa became master to an ocean of disciples and it is believed that during this time, the number of people attaining high realisations through Kalachakra was more than all the other systems combined.

From Nalanda, the teachings of Kalachakra extended outwards. Meanwhile, a Buddhist revival was developing in the Tibetan provinces of Ü and Tsang; as a result many translators were travelling south to request teachings from the great Indian panditas and mahasiddhas. By the beginning of the eleventh century, a number of Kalachakra practice lineages had found their way into the snowy mountains of Tibet. One such lineage was known as the *Dro Tradition of the Six Vajra Yogas.*

This tradition flowed through the great **Kashmiri Pandita Somanatha**. Originally born into a Brahmin family in the west, Somanatha had travelled to Nalanda in search of commentary on a Kalachakra text he had encountered during his earlier studies. Under the guidance of Nalendrapa, Somanatha grew to become a highly realised master of the Six Vajra Yogas. He eventually returned to his homeland of Kashmir where he was invited to Tibet to help translate the Stainless Light.

In Tibet, Somanatha worked closely with the Tibetan translator **Drotön Sherab Drakpa** from whom the tradition gets its name. Whereas Dro Lotsawa concentrated on making the Kalachakra teachings available in the Tibetan language, another of Somantha's students by the name of **Lhaje Gompa** focused on putting those teachings into practice. As word of the incredible strength of their realisations spread, students began to gather and among them, the most accomplished was the great scholar and practitioner **Drotön Namla Tsek**. Under the direct guidance of Somanatha and Lhaje Gompa, Namla Tsek would go on to propagate the Kalachakra teachings widely in the region of Western Tibet.

At this time, the pith instructions for practicing the Six Vajra Yogas were kept secret, passed between master and student in a whispered lineage. Somanatha himself is known to have only taught the complete path to his three main students. The lineage was then given to **Yumo Mikyo Dorjé** who became an accomplished mahasiddha in his own right. In addition to his many supernatural abilities, Yumowa is most widely known as being one of the first Tibetans to write on his direct experience of the profound definitive meaning based on his practice of the Kalachakra Tantra. These writings are now considered to be a forerunner to the later work of great Jonang masters such as Dolpopa Sherab Gyaltsen.

After Yumo, the lineage would be preserved by his immediate family for two generations. The teachings first passed to Yumo's spiritual and biological son, **Seachok Dharmeshvara**. Gifted with an extraordinary intellect, Dharmeshvara was considered a child prodigy. From a very early age he wrote extensive commentaries on very difficult treatises and by the time he was twenty he had mastered everything his father had taught him. Dharmeshvara's legacy was then passed on to his three children: **Namkha'i Özer, Machik Tulku Jobum** and **Sechen Namkha'i Gyaltsen.**

While Namkha'i Özer became a renowned scholar and author of various texts, his sister Machik Tulku Jobum became a highly realised yogini. It is said that when she first practiced the Six Vajra Yogas, she attained realisation of the first yoga after only a single day and by the end of the week, she had achieved complete mastery over all her subtle winds. The stories of her incredible siddhis were heard far and wide. The younger brother of Namkha'i Özer and Machik Jobum was originally born with severe hearing and speech impairments. Only through the kindness of his siblings was Namkha'i Gyaltsen able to overcome these limitations and achieve the highest of attainments.

He established *Semoché Monastery* in the Ölung region of Central Tibet, and it was at this time that restrictions on the lineage were slightly loosened as the Six Vajra Yogas began to be taught more openly. Semochen passed the teachings to his heart disciple **Jamyang Sarma Sherab Özer.** Originally a student of the Nyingma Tradition, Jamsar Sherab was guided by a vision of Manjushri telling him to seek out Semoché and request teachings from him. After receiving all of the ripening empowerments, Jamsar Sherab entered into retreat on the Six Vajra Yogas and achieved a direct realisation of the definitive meaning of reality. During the remainder of his life, he dedicated himself to teaching the practices of Kalachakra, establishing a number of remote meditation hermitages.

Another disciple of Semochen, the omniscient **Chöku Özer** would take up the mantle from Jamsar Sherab. Recognised as the reincarnation of the great Indian Kalachakra master Shakyashri, Chöku Özer was known for his incredibly stable realisation of immutable bliss. It is held that his mind never wavered from this pristine wisdom for even a moment.

By the middle of the thirteenth century, the Kalachakra teachings were truly flourishing in the provinces of Ü and Tsang. More than seventeen different practice lineages of the Six Vajra Yogas were being propagated, as well as a variety of Kalachakra textual traditions. All of these lineages would eventually be unified into a single vajra stream through the enormous efforts of **Kunpang Thukje Tsondru.**

Kunpangje grew up studying within the Sakya Tradition where he received the Kalachakra teachings in accordance with the Ra Lineage. Quickly mastering his studies of the Stainless Light commentary, he travelled to Kyangdur Monastery to receive teachings from the great Chöku Özer. It was there he was instructed in the profound path of the Six Vajra Yogas as presented in the Dro Lineage. On the basis of these instructions, Kunpangje became a highly accomplished yogi.

Driven by a great desire to master every aspect of the Kalachakra, Kunpangje travelled throughout the region requesting the transmissions of each Kalachakra lineage. Once he had successfully gathered them all together, he went into strict retreat to put their instructions into practice. Travelling from hermitage to hermitage, he remained in isolation meditating on the profound meaning of the teachings, and as a result of his incredible diligence, Thukje Tsondru was visited by many enlightened beings, including the Kalki Kings of Shambhala. They each bestowed immeasurable blessings upon him and empowered him to uphold the complete Kalachakra teachings.

When a local spirit invited him to take up residence in the Jomonang Valley, Thukje Tsondru agreed and so the Jonang Mountain Retreat was founded. As he meditated in the valley, his composition of a root text for the Six Vajra Yogas was to be the first time the pith instructions had been committed to writing. Word of his realisations spread throughout the land and students from all over Tibet flocked to the mountain retreat to receive guidance from this unparalleled master. Soon his followers became known as the *Glorious Tradition of Jonang*.

Just before his passing in 1313, Thukje Tsondru appointed his heart disciple **Jangsem Gyalwa Yeshe** to be the new regent of Jonang Monastery. Originally a follower of the Karma Kagyu Tradition, Gyalwa Yeshe had travelled to Jonang when told of his strong karmic connection with the great Kalachakra master by the Karmapa. Filled with unbridled faith and devotion in Thukje Tsondru, Gyalwa Yeshe dedicated his life to meditating on all he had received. He remained on the Vajra Throne of Jonang for seven years before passing the responsibility of the lineage to his dharma brother **Khetsun Yonten Gyatso**.

After studying intensively within the Sakya Tradition, Yonten Gyatso was directed by the Sakya Throne Holder to seek out Thukje Tsondru as his teacher.

For the next thirty-eight years, Yonten Gyatso received an ocean of teachings on Kalachakra and achieved a wealth of realisations in reliance on his extensive practice of the Six Vajra Yogas. When his friend and teacher Gyalwa Yeshé passed into parinirvana, Yonten Gyatso became the next throne holder of Jonang Monastery.

The Sutric Lineage of Zhentong Madhyamaka

When the Jonang Mountain Retreat was founded, it was essentially a community of yogis dedicated to the advanced practices of the Kalachakra Tantra. At any given time it was possible to find over six hundred meditators in the various hermitages and caves that filled the valley. The great majority of these practitioners received their spiritual education in other traditions such as the Nyingma, Kadam, Sakya or Kagyu. It wasn't until the arrival of the omniscient Dolpopa Sherab Gyaltsen that the Jonang would develop a systematic monastic curriculum that clearly distinguished its practitioners from the other traditions.

While Dolpopa is most well known for his innovative philosophical ideas regarding the ultimate nature of reality, everything he presented was firmly rooted in an unbroken lineage that can be traced back to the sutra teachings of Shakyamuni Buddha and the Bodhisattva Maitreya. We call these teachings *The Sutric Lineage of Zhentong Madhyamaka*, which means the "Middle Way View of Other-Emptiness."

At the core of this view we find the doctrine of Buddha-nature that was expounded by the **Buddha** during the *Third Turning of the Wheel of Dharma*. In this tradition, the three turnings represent a progressive sequence of development for realising the definitive meaning as revealed by the Buddha in relation to the spiritual maturity of his disciples. In the first turning the Buddha focuses on the provisional truth of dependent origination. In the second turning he presents the ultimate nature of conventional truths as an emptiness of inherent self-existence (Self-Emptiness). Finally, in the third turning, he reveals the ultimate nature of reality itself to be a sublime emptiness that is empty of all forms of conceptual fabrications (Other-Emptiness).

This approach was also taken by the great pioneer of the Mahayana, **Arya Nagarjuna**. Like the Buddha, Nagarjuna presented his teachings in three progressive collections: the *Collection of Advice*, the *Collection of Middle Way Reasoning* and the *Collection of Praises*. It was in this third collection that Nagarjuna detailed the nature of ultimate reality in accordance with his experience of Buddha-nature. Even though later scholars would connect Nagarjuna mostly to his treatises on Middle Way Philosophy, an examination of the totality of his writings clearly indicates his profound realisation of Other-Emptiness.

By the fourth century, a second great pioneer would emerge to build upon the foundations laid down by both the Buddha and Nagarjuna. The expansive teachings of **Arya Asanga** not only shaped how the Mahayana was practiced in India, they also revolutionised how people conceived of the ultimate nature of reality. In Asanga's *Tradition of Yogacara Madhyamaka*, emphasis was placed on how to transcend one's conceptual mind through the practices of meditation. This was an experiential approach, based on the teachings as revealed to Asanga by the Bodhisattva Maitreya.

Recognising that some of Maitreya's teachings were too profound to propagate immediately, Asanga concealed them in a stupa to be discovered when the time was appropriate to receive them. For the remainder of his life he focused on the more accessible texts of Maitreya, but unfortunately this sequence of events has led many to misinterpret his teachings as exclusively propounding a Mind-Only Philosophy. It would not be until much later that the true intent of his teachings would be revealed.

The Yogacara Tradition was propagated by a string of exceptional scholar-practitioners such as **Vasubandhu**, **Dignaga**, **Sthiramati** and **Chandragomin**. Due to the profound realisations and prolific writings of these masters, Asanga's teachings became the foundation for the monastic curriculums of great universities like Nalanda and Vikramashila. From these famous centres of Buddhist thought, the teachings of Asanga were transmitted to an ocean of students who gave rise to countless branches of the lineage.

In the eleventh century, an accomplished yogi by the name of **Maitripa** discovered the teachings Asanga had hidden away so many hundreds of years earlier. With the blessings of the Bodhisattva Maitreya, he began teaching these texts in Vikramashila and quickly gained a dedicated following. In reliance on all *Five Treatises of Maitreya*, it then became possible to develop a clear understanding of the intent behind Asanga's teachings and therefore use them to reveal the definitive meaning of ultimate reality.

From Maitripa, the teachings passed through his disciples **Ratnakarashanti** and **Anandakirti**. It was Anandakirti who travelled to the western region of Kashmir and gave the teachings to the **Kashmiri Scholar Sañjana**. To prevent the loss of these treasure teachings and pith instructions, Sañjana proceeded to record them in writing.

When the Tibetan translator Ngok Loden Sherab learned of the teachings Sañjana had received, he requested the textual transmission of Maitreya's treatise *The Sublime Continuum*. Accompanying him was an aging Tibetan by the name of Tsen Kawoché Drimé Özer, who wished to receive from Sañjana the profound pith instructions for meditating on the teachings of the Bodhisattva Maitreya. As Ngok Lotsawa left before he could receive these teachings, Drimé Özer sought help from another translator, **Zu Gawa'i Dorje**, who generously agreed to translate all of Sañjana's teachings into Tibetan. From Gawa'i Dorje, the pith instructions then passed to **Tsen Kawoché** who began propagating them in Tibet. It was at this time the lineage became known as *The Contemplative Tradition of Maitreya*.

The lineage entered Tibet during the twelfth century at a time when the New Translation schools were just beginning to take shape. From Tsen Kawoché it was given to **Dharma Tsondru**, a master of the Zhijé lineage of Padampa Sangye. It was then passed on as a whispered lineage to **Dolpa Nyen Yeshe Jungné**, **Jangchup Kyap** and **Zhonu Jangchup** of the Kadam School that had been founded by the great Indian master Atisha Dipamkara.

Eventually the lineage was established in the great Kadam Monastery of Narlang by the master **Kyotön Monlam Tsultrim**. His student **Chomden Rikpé Raldri** became famous for establishing one of the first printing presses in Tibet and subsequently compiling and publishing the complete Tibetan Canon of the Buddha's teachings and commentaries.

At the start of the fourteenth century, the lineage was brought to Sakya Monastery after Rikpé Raldri's student **Kyitön Jamyang Drakpa** chose to leave

Nartang due to a number of political issues that arose. At Sakya, he dedicated his time to teaching the Kalachakra Tantra and the Treatises of Maitreya. It was Kyitönpa who would go on to become one of Dolpopa's most influential teachers.

The Unified System of Sutra and Tantra

From the tenth century, as a result of the oceans of Dharma flooding into the country and the hard work of dedicated translators, Tibet was experiencing a spiritual renaissance. By the fourteenth century, the views of the Tibetan masters had grown significantly in sophistication and they were now producing a variety of treatises that presented their unique approaches in the form of comprehensive systems of philosophy. On the basis of these systems, the distinctions between the different schools became increasingly pronounced.

For the Jonang, it was the writings of **Dolpopa Sherab Gyaltsen** that would define their unique heritage. Born in the Dolpo region of Western Tibet, Sherab Gyaltsen grew up practicing in the Nyingma Tradition. As a young man he ran away from home when his parents forbade him to study with the Sakya Lama Kyitönpa who had visited his region on his way to Mustang. Under Kyitönpa's direct tutelage, Dolpopa quickly excelled in his studies of philosophy, epistemology, psychology and cosmology. When Kyitönpa returned to Sakya Monastery, Dolpopa was soon to follow.

During his time at Sakya, Dolpopa studied the Kalachakra Tantra and the works of Maitreya and Asanga. Under the guidance of some of the most learned masters of his time, he was recognised as a great scholar of both sutra and tantra and before long, Dolpopa was asked to become a teacher to the other students in Sakya.

With an insatiable desire to learn, Dolpopa travelled extensively to the many monasteries of his region, studying under the masters of the main traditions and participating in many debates. Due to his incredibly sharpened intellect and his comprehensive understanding of the full breadth of the Dharma, he was often referred to as *kunkyen*, meaning "omniscient."

At the age of only twenty-eight, Dolpopa was offered the throne of Sakya Monastery as its abbot. His tenure was short lived, however, as during the

The Omniscient One, Dolpopa Sherab Gyaltsen

coming year he visited the Jomonang Valley and met with the enigmatic Khetsun Yonten Gyatso. Dolpopa was so impressed by the degree of realisations achieved by the Jonang practitioners that he decided to give up his position and dedicate his life to meditation.

After receiving the complete transmission of the teachings from Yonten Gyatso, Dolpopa entered into strict retreat and was able to attain realisation of the first four of the Six Vajra Yogas. It was during this time that the *Zhentong View* arose in his mind. Because he was not yet ready to share his discovery, he dedicated the years to follow to refining his ideas and to perfecting his experience of the first three yogas. When he did finally emerge, Yonten Gyatso asked him to assume the vajra throne of Jonang and after careful deliberation, he agreed and became Yonten Gyatso's successor.

From this point on, Dolpopa divided his time between periods of teaching and retreat. Like his master Kyitönpa, he always emphasised Kalachakra and the teachings of Maitreya. No matter what subject he taught, he would always relate it back to Pundarika's great commentary.

When his beloved master Yonten Gyatso passed away in 1327, Dolpopa chose to honour him by constructing a massive stupa. Although many people thought he was crazy for attempting such a mammoth task, Dolpopa and his many students persevered and completed what would become one of the largest stupas in all of Tibet. During its construction, Dolpopa began to teach his view of other-emptiness publicly for the first time. His revolutionary ideas generated a great deal of debate, which Dolpopa would then use to refine his presentation and strengthen his position.

As a result of this process, Dolpopa composed his masterpiece entitled *Mountain Doctrine: An Ocean of Definitive Meaning*. This comprehensive text drew from a large number of sources to present and defend Dolpopa's controversial assertions. Within this one source, he clearly demonstrated the shared intent of all the Buddha's teachings and thereby unified the view found in both the sutras and tantras.

Over the years, Dolpopa would continue to write a treasure trove of philosophical and practical texts that became the core curriculum for all Jonang practitioners. With the assistance of his fourteen heart disciples, the Zhentong View extended throughout the provinces of Ü and Tsang and there were very few who did not consider Dolpopa as their teacher.

During this period, the Jonang Tradition itself was growing outside of the Jomonang Valley. Many of Dolpopa's closest students were either given existing monasteries or built them with the offerings they received. One particular student by the name of Ratnashri, travelled into the eastern provinces of Amdo and Kham and founded Chöje Monastery in the region of Dzamthang. Under the guidance of their great leaders, hundreds of branch monasteries were constructed in the neighbouring regions and in this way, the Jonang established a very strong presence in the East.

After Dolpopa's passing in 1361, the vajra throne of Jonang passed to one of his closest disciples **Chokgyalwa Choklé Namgyal**. For more than fifteen years, Choklé Namgyal carried on the tradition Dolpopa had started, championing the Zhentong View and guiding an ever increasing community of dedicated practitioners. Eventually, he chose to retire and took up retreat in the hermitage of Se Karchung.

Succeeding Choklé Namgyal was the great Zhentong master **Tsungmed Nyabön Kunga**. After studying closely with Dolpopa for most of his life, Nyabön Kunga spent time teaching in Sakya Monastery before founding his own monastery of Tsechen. From his seat at Tsechen, Nyabön Kunga amassed a large following of students who subsequently went on to propagate the Jonang teachings.

The Rimé Philosophy that Transcends All Bias

As opposing philosophical views began to gain traction in Central Tibet, many Jonang practitioners chose to foster an unbiased approach that recognised the value of the diversity found within the major traditions of the time. Following in the footsteps of the great Jonang masters before him, Nyabön Kunga's heart disciple **Drupchen Kunga Lodrö** spent more than fifty years in solitary retreat, studying and mastering not only the Kalachakra, but all of the *Eight Great Practice Lineages*. Rather than fuelling sectarian divisions, he promoted a deep respect for each school and the need to go beyond intellectual debate by grounding one's view in experience. This approach was then advocated by his successors **Jamyang Konchok Zangpo, Namkha Chökyong, and Panchen Namkha Palzang.**

By the sixteenth century, under the leadership of Namkha Palzang's student **Lochen Ratnabadra,** the emphasis within the tradition had shifted away from philosophical study and focused predominantly on meditative practice. Due to the richness of lineages now present within the community, Jonang Monastery had become a hub for all those wishing to dedicate their lives to the yogic paths of Buddhist Tantra, regardless of the tradition they belonged to.

This period of unbiased wisdom was personified by the great rimé master **Palden Kunga Drolchok.** For much of his life, he travelled the provinces of Ü and Tsang gathering teachings from each of the major traditions and diligently putting them into practice. He held a particularly strong connection to both the Shangpa Kagyu teachings of the Dakini Niguma and the Kalachakra teachings of the Six Vajra Yogas. After the passing of his root teacher Lochen Ratnabadra, Kunga Drolchok became the new head of the Jonang Tradition, and dedicated the next twenty years of his life to giving extensive teachings, practicing in retreat and writing texts. One of his most significant accomplishments was his creation of the first non-sectarian compilation known as *Drolchok's Quintessential Instructions.* This collection of practices presented the pith instructions of the eight practice lineages side-by-side in a single unified text. Before he passed away, Kunga Drolchok transmitted everything he had received to his three heart disciples: **Khenchen Lungrig Gyatso,** Khidrup Sangye Yeshe and Khiwang Jampa Lhundrup.

Some years after Kunga Drolchok entered parinirvana, his reincarnation was recognised as a young boy named Kunga Nyingpo. It is said that just one year after this child's birth, he was heard to proclaim, "I am Kunga Drolchok!" News of this exceptional being spread to his students and a few years later he was officially recognised by Lungrig Gyatso. When he was enthroned at Kunga Drolchok's monastery, Chölung Jangtse, he was given the name Drolwai Gönpo.

As a reincarnated lama, Drolwai Gönpo received the best possible education from Kunga Drolchok's main disciples. Together, they bestowed upon him the same vast range of teachings they had received from their kind master, ripening his mindstream to give rise to countless realisations. He found particular inspiration in the writings of Dolpopa that he received from Lungrig Gyatso. When he was only fourteen, he encountered a highly realised Indian Mahasiddha by the name of Buddhaguptanatha. Filled with enormous faith and devotion, Drolwai Gönpo spent considerable time listening to many of this master's rare teachings and would go on to work alongside other Indian scholars and adepts, translating a number of Sanskrit texts into Tibetan.

Due to the enormous influence of these Indian masters, Drolwai Gönpo soon became known by the Sanskrit version of his name, **Jetsun Taranatha**. His ties to India were further strengthened when he was able to remember his life as the Indian Mahasiddha Nakpopa. On the basis of his memories and the stories told to him by Buddhaguptanatha, Taranatha composed an extensive history of India that to this day is still used as an authentic source.

In 1588, Taranatha was enthroned as the head of the Jonang Tradition and while he gave teachings there once a year, for the most part he wandered the countryside visiting countless monasteries and hermitages. During his discussions with many Jonang practitioners, it became apparent to him that a number of mistaken conceptions had developed in relation to Dolpopa's original presentation of the Zhentong View. Determined to clear away all confusion and reinvigorate the purity of the Jonang philosophy, Taranatha composed a number of important texts on the subject of Other-Emptiness. Thanks to his tireless efforts, the teachings of Dolpopa were restored to their former glory.

The performance of Taranatha's immeasurable activities to ensure the flourishing of the Jonang Dharma exemplified him as a true rimé master, just like his predecessor, and picking up where Kunga Drolchok left off, he expanded upon *Drolchok's Quintessential Instructions* to produce the *One Hundred and Eight Quintessential Instructions of the Jonang*. This comprehensive text would become the primary inspiration for many of the writings of the great Jamgön Kongtrul Lodrö Thaye, who would pioneer the Rimé Movement later in the 19th century.

The Great Rimé Master, Jetsun Taranatha

Survival in the Face of Persecution

The seventeenth century was a period of great unrest in Central Tibet. Extended wars between the clans of Ü and Tsang had resulted in stark political divisions that promoted sectarian rivalries and different forms of persecution. Unlike their brothers of the Sakya, Kagyu and Geluk traditions, the Jonang had never held power and so were largely able to avoid involvement in political turmoil. Unfortunately however, when Taranatha accepted patronage from the ruling Tsangpa King, the Jonang became a target for his Mongolian rivals.

After Taranatha's death in 1635, the Jonang Monasteries of Central Tibet were systematically converted into Geluk institutions by order of the Government in Lhasa. This transformation was part of a much greater campaign to establish the new ruler's base of power and to remove all potential threats. To help legitimise this process, the Jonang doctrine was labelled as "heretical" and subsequently banned.

The main centre of the Jonang Tradition at this time was in Takten Damchö Ling. This monastic university had been constructed by Jetsun Taranatha and symbolised everything the tradition stood for. Despite Taranatha's successor **Kunga Rinchen Gyatso's** valiant attempts to preserve the integrity of the institution's curriculum, external pressures proved too strong. Eventually he chose to leave the monastery, entering into strict retreat in remote places. By the year 1658, the monastery was officially renamed to Ganden Phuntsok Ling.

Following the loss of its most prominent institution, many Jonang practitioners began to migrate eastward to Dzamthang where the Jonang Dharma continued to flourish. Due to the efforts of lineage masters like **Khidrup Lodrö Namgyal** and **Drupchen Ngawang Trinlé**, the monastery of Dzamthang Tsangwa was established alongside the great monasteries of Chöje and Tsechu. These three universities became the new heart of the Jonang community.

Dzamthang Tsangwa quickly rose in distinction under the skilful leadership of **Ngawang Tenzin Namgyal, Kunzang Trinlé Namgyal** and **Konchok Jigmé Namgyal**—the subsequent reincarnations of the monastery's founder Lodrö Namgyal. Each concentrated heavily on the core practices of the tradition, emphasising above all else the practice of the Kalachakra Six Vajra Yogas. With their guidance, the Jonang established many new monasteries in the Golok and Amdo Ngawa regions, effectively expanding their presence and ensuring their survival.

By the nineteenth century, a number of great masters such as Jamyang Khyentse Wangpo and Jamgön Kongtrul Lodrö Thaye recognised that due to sectarian rivalries, many important lineages were in danger of being lost. With the wish to preserve the rich cultural heritage that Tibet had inherited from India, these masters worked tirelessly to promote the values of an unbiased approach. Since the Jonang had a long history of promoting this philosophy, they provided a fundamental source for many of the rare lineages that were in danger of becoming extinct.

One of the teachers that Jamgön Kongtrul relied upon was **Ngawang Chöpel Gyatso**. After spending many years meditating on the Kalachakra Completion Stage, as well as the Nyingma teachings of Dzogchen and the Shangpa teachings of Niguma, Chöpel Gyatso was chosen by Jigmé Namgyal to take his place as the Vajra Master of Dzamthang Tsangwa. Giving countless teachings from all of the major traditions, Chöpel Gyatso was mostly known as the "Tsangwa Gelong". He was succeeded by his three heart disciples: **Ngawang Chökyi Pakpa**, **Ngawang Chöjor Gyatso** and **Ngawang Chözin Gyatso**.

While all three were renowned as highly accomplished yogis, Chözin Gyatso was particularly recognised for his extraordinary accomplishments. Believed to be an emanation of the Bodhisattva Akashagarbha, Chözin Gyatso took ordination from Chöpel Gyatso when he was very young. Soon after, he went into strict retreat practicing the Six Vajra Yogas and very quickly progressed through all six branches, achieving unprecedented realisations at each stage. He would go on to refine those realisations through the practice of Object Severance (Chöd).

After working on behalf of Tsangwa Monastery for many years, Chözin Gyatso elected to stay in retreat at the hermitage of Tashi Lhari Tse, where he guided a select group of very gifted students in the practices of the Six Vajra Yogas. Among his closest disciples were **Ngawang Tenpa Rabgye**, Bamda Thubten Gelek Gyatso and Lama Tsoknyi Gyatso.

Having practiced with Chözin Gyatso since he was only twelve years old, Tenpa Rabgye was a highly accomplished practitioner of the Kalachakra Completion Stage. After his master passed away, Tenpa Rabgye moved to Tsangwa Monastery where he studied under some of the greatest Jonang masters of his time. Having completed his studies, he returned to his hometown and took up residence in Chayul Monastery where he would eventually become its Abbot.

It was in Chayul that **Lama Lobsang Trinlé** was given the complete lineage from Tenpa Rabgye. After practicing all of the common and uncommon preliminaries, Lobsang Trinlé received all of the ripening empowerments and was then guided in the practice of the Six Vajra Yogas. After only two weeks, he attained the ten signs of the first yoga. Following his retreat he continued diligently in his practice while maintaining the external conduct of an extremely pure monk.

At the age of thirty-two, Lobsang Trinlé contracted leprosy and became very ill. To overcome this disease he entered into strict retreat, and for five years he devoted himself to the intensive practice of Vajrapani. During this retreat he experienced his sickness emerging from his body in the form of thousands of worms which then absorbed into the offering cakes laid out on his altar. In time he was completely cured of his leprosy and the offering cakes took on extraordinary medicinal properties.

When he finally emerged from his retreat in 1954, he found Tibet undergoing immense changes as a result of the Chinese Communist influence. By this point, he had become a highly realised scholar-practitioner and so was invited to become the teacher of Ngawang Chözin Gyatso's hermitage, Tashi Chöthang Monastery, but as the Communist government began to impose restrictions on the Tibetan people, spiritual practice became increasingly difficult. Over a span of roughly twenty-five years, many Jonang monasteries were destroyed, with their monks forced to practice in secret. Lobsang Trinlé spent much of this time working within various communities as a healer, secretly stockpiling sacred relics such as statues and texts, and preserving the Dharma in whatever ways he could.

After the death of Mao Zedong, many restrictions were loosened and monks were allowed to begin rebuilding their spiritual institutions. Lobsang Trinlé returned to Tashi Chöthang and focused his energy on training the next generation of teachers, ensuring the lineage was not lost. Through the dedicated efforts of lamas like him, the flame of the Jonang Dharma has remained strong and continues to flourish in the eastern provinces of Tibet. At the time of writing this book, the Vajra Throne of Dzamthang Tsangwa is held by the most recent incarnation of Lodrö Namgyal, **His Holiness Jigmé Dorje.**

REVIEW OF KEY POINTS

- There are two types of lineage: (1) a lineage of transmission represents the communication of teachings between master and student, and (2) a lineage of realisation which represents the manifest qualities in the minds of the people who put those teachings into practice.

- Working with a spiritual lineage establishes a connection to those who have developed the realisations we seek to develop in ourselves. They act as role models that inspire the mind and demonstrate our potential.

- We can develop faith in a spiritual lineage through familiarising ourselves with the stories of past masters, reflecting on their qualities and then striving to produce those qualities in our own minds.

- The Jonang-Shambhala Lineage represents the unbroken transmission of the Kalachakra teachings from the time of the Buddha. It is the only lineage to contain all of the pith instructions for the advanced completion stage practices.

- The Jonang Tradition is a unified system that is the result of combining the Sutric Lineage of Zhentong Madhyamaka and the Tantric Lineage of the Kalachakra Tantra.

- The two main lineage masters for the Jonang are the Omniscient Dolpopa Sherab Gyaltsen and Jetsun Taranatha.

- The Jonang has a long history of cultivating an unbiased philosophy towards the views and practices of all Tibetan traditions.

- Since the seventeenth century the heart of the Jonang Tradition has thrived in the remote regions of Eastern Tibet. The main monastic institutions of Chöje, Tsechu and Tsangwa are all located in Dzamthang, with many branch monasteries established in Gyalrong, Golok and Amdo Ngawa.

CHAPTER THREE

How to Follow an Authentic Dharma Teacher

Exploring the histories of the great lineage masters provides a sense of perspective for the amazing benefit that can come from practicing the Kalachakra teachings. Each story arouses a sense of awe and wonder, gaining insight into how these masters overcame their obstacles and obscurations to achieve extraordinary realisations. Their stories inspire us to one day follow in their footsteps, giving rise to the question, "Who can show me how to walk this path?"

To find an answer, we can turn to the Buddha's own teachings in the *Sutra of Ksitigarbha*:

> *Notice that all of the Buddha's immeasurable good qualities and activities to transform the minds of sentient beings arise from proper reliance on the Dharma teacher. Therefore, rely on, become close to, serve and venerate the teacher, just as you would all the Buddhas.*

As the Buddha was preparing to enter parinirvana, he told his students not to be sad, assuring them that he would continue to manifest in the form of spiritual teachers. By properly relying on them, it would be possible to achieve all of his enlightened qualities. In this way, he urged us to turn to spiritual teachers for guidance.

However, with an abundance of books by authentic teachers and realised lamas presenting teachings online, we may wonder if having a teacher is still necessary? We may think that it is enough to merely read and listen to the Dharma. While there are indeed many wonderful ways to acquire information about the Dharma, there is a considerable difference between understanding the words intellectually and realising their meaning within your own experience.

Since beginningless time our minds have been deeply conditioned by karmic propensities, trapping us in cyclic existence. To break this endless cycle, we require the support and guidance of a teacher who has the ability to tailor the teachings to our specific needs—adjusting them to the dynamic state of our minds. Like a skilled doctor, they know the course of treatment and the medicine to prescribe that will bring us the greatest benefit. For this reason, developing a meaningful relationship with a teacher is a vital component to achieving genuine peace and harmony.

The sheer complexity of practicing a spiritual path is another reason why having a teacher is so important. Filled with pitfalls and false endings, following a path such as Kalachakra is not a straightforward process. As it leads to increasingly more subtle layers of experience, the deeper you go, the easier it becomes to get lost or confused. With the blessings and guidance of authentic spiritual teachers who have actualised the path in their own mindstreams, you will be better prepared to overcome the many obstacles you will face on your journey, maintaining focus and moving forward toward your ultimate goal.

For the Kalachakra Path a spiritual guide is particularly important, since all of the advanced practices are only accessible through a qualified lineage master who holds the profound pith instructions of the tradition. Such instructions have been passed down from generation to generation and represent the essential methods used to achieve authentic realisations. A teacher will only bestow this level of instruction to students they are confident will benefit from them. For this to occur a student must first invest the time and energy into developing a meaningful and heartfelt relationship with a teacher.

Such a relationship is established in three phases: (1) first, we investigate potential teachers and evaluate our capacity to learn from them; (2) then, we practice devotion towards them by putting their teachings into practice; and (3) by emulating their qualities, we actualise the lineage in our minds. We will now look at each of these phases in turn.

CHOOSING A QUALIFIED TEACHER

Throughout our regular lives we are faced with important milestones that require us to assess our preferences and evaluate our options. There is a great deal to consider when selecting a career, buying a house, or starting a family. If this is true for making worldly decisions, then consider the importance of a decision that will impact not only this life, but all of our future lives as well, as in the case of choosing a spiritual teacher.

To receive the most benefit from working with a spiritual teacher, a foundation of trust needs to be developed. This form of trust doesn't come from mere blind faith, but rather from a clear understanding of the nature of the relationship between ourselves and our teacher. The main obstacle to achieving this aspect of trust is our afflicted doubt which can cause us to second guess our steps along the path, preventing us from being open to change. The first step on our journey must therefore be to remove any doubts regarding our teacher.

This is a process that does not usually happen overnight. Time is often needed to get to know a teacher as their qualities are not always immediately apparent to us. Sometimes we may think a teacher has great qualities, only to discover their motivation is not particularly pure. Just as we would not get married after a first date, we should not rush into committing ourselves to a spiritual teacher until we have developed the confidence we need.

That being said, we must also be careful not to be overly judgemental. While scepticism can be beneficial in the beginning, if it overwhelms us, it will be impossible for a teacher to fulfil our expectations. Failing to develop a healthy view of our teacher will prevent us from committing to anyone. Our relationships will remain superficial as we bounce from teacher to teacher, never giving ourselves the opportunity to actualise our deeper potential.

To overcome these issues, it is essential to remember that a spiritual teacher is one condition for working with our own afflictions. As such work is internal and not external, who the teacher appears to be and what they appear to do is much less important than the effect they have on our mind. If, after spending time with a particular teacher, you experience some degree of benefit, this alone can be enough to build a foundation of respect and devotion.

TYPES OF TEACHERS

Actively seeking a spiritual teacher can often lead to a misconception that one single person should be able to fulfil all our needs. This "all or nothing" kind of attitude can lead to disappointment and be a major obstacle for developing a constructive relationship. A healthier approach is to recognise that throughout our life we will have many different types of teachers. Some will come into our lives only briefly, while others will be a recurring presence over many lifetimes. Regardless of the time we share with them, what makes a person a teacher is their ability to transmit a level of wisdom that brings benefit to our mind. From the perspective of the degree of benefit we can hope to receive, we can identify four main types of teachers:

1. **Worldly Teacher:** This type of teacher is responsible for transmitting knowledge that helps us function in the external world and tends to focus on aspects such as language, social skills and training for specific jobs. The benefit we receive from a worldly teacher is generally limited to this life.

2. **Dharma Friend:** Sacred Dharma can be understood as any phenomenon which demonstrates the nature of reality and acts as a direct antidote to ignorance. By learning about Dharma we gain insight into our experience and develop wisdom, creating the causes for liberation. Anyone who makes us aware of sacred Dharma can be considered a "Dharma friend".

   A Dharma friend does not necessarily need to be a fully qualified master. What defines them as a teacher is a knowledge of Dharma that we do not possess and through their kindness we have the opportunity to learn something new. For instance, they may show us how to meditate, or perhaps shed light on a difficult subject. Whether they share volumes of wisdom or a single insight, if their influence helps reinforce the Dharma in our minds, they are actively contributing to our long term happiness in both this and future lives.

3. **Spiritual Guide:** While all spiritual guides are Dharma friends, not all Dharma friends are spiritual guides. The main distinction is that a spiritual guide is an authentic lineage holder that teaches us how to progress along the path and how to actualise the Dharma. To do this, they must develop a strong working relationship with their students, as the better they know us, the more able they are to offer advice that meets our specific needs.

   Working closely with a spiritual guide greatly strengthens our karmic connection, ensuring that we will meet our teachers again in the future. In this way, authentic spiritual guides stay with us from lifetime to lifetime until we have achieved the ultimate benefit of perfect enlightenment.

4. **Vajra Master:** The final type of teacher is a very particular type of spiritual guide. While performing all the same functions as a spiritual guide, a vajra master specifically clears away the obscurations preventing us from realising our ultimate nature. They do this by using various techniques that challenge our habitual patterns and cut through the ignorance of our mind.

   Entering into a spiritual relationship with a vajra master carries with it much more weight than that of other kinds of teachers. Because it is based on the student giving the teacher permission to completely eradicate all traces of their self-grasping, students must have sufficient strength of mind to endure such a process. For this reason, it is generally recommended to first establish a firm foundation in the Dharma before entering into a relationship with a vajra master.

   The main benefit of working with a vajra master is that progress along the path is very rapid. Realisations which would normally take billions of lives to achieve become possible within the span of a single lifetime. This is due to the fact that the Guru creates a wealth of opportunities to purify our negative karma. As long as our compassion for the suffering of sentient beings is strong enough, we should have no problem tolerating short-term difficulties for the guarantee of infinite benefits in the long-term.

The early stages of our lives are generally focused on gaining a worldly education from *worldly teachers.* As we mature, a desire for deeper meaning often develops and this can lead to seeking *Dharma friends* who can share the wisdom they have acquired.

It is not uncommon for people to have many Dharma friends before eventually meeting a teacher they feel a strong connection to. It is at this point they may relate to such a teacher as their *spiritual guide* and over time, teacher and student build a foundation of trust and wisdom through their shared experiences.

If the teacher is qualified and the student has developed a strong altruistic motivation, a *vajra relationship* may be entered into. Once a student makes a commitment to a *vajra master*, there is no turning back and all scepticism and doubt must have been eliminated.

As we are only just setting out on the path, our main concern should be on developing a meaningful relationship with an authentic spiritual guide. Deciding whether or not to enter into a vajra relationship is not something that should be rushed into. It is far more important at this stage to develop the correct foundations so that if the opportunity to work with a vajra master arises, we have the strength of mind to do so.

Exercise 3.1 — Identifying the Teachers in Your Life

- *In a relaxed posture, establish a neutral mind through the practice of mindfulness of breathing.*

- *Think back to your early childhood and begin walking through the major phases that have occurred.*

- *Consider the different people who have been influential in your life, sharing their wisdom with you or guiding you in some way.*

- *Bring to mind the types of lessons you learned from each. What category of teacher would each person belong to?*

- *Visualise each teacher in the space before you. If you like, group them in a way that is meaningful to you.*

- *Rest your mind in the awareness of all your teachers, together in one place.*

Examining Your Own Qualities

Many people enter into a spiritual relationship with very fixed ideas and expectations of how a teacher should behave, how they should act in relation to them and what they should receive from them. Such preconceptions can lead to a conditional relationship that limits potential benefit.

By first reflecting on our own capacity, we can derive a better understanding of where we are on our spiritual journey and therefore what kind of teachers we are able to connect with. This means recognising the level of teachings we understand and to what degree we are willing and able to commit to Dharma practice. For instance, working with a vajra master requires a genuine inspiration to achieve enlightenment, eagerness to practice Dharma and unwavering devotion toward the teacher. A great deal of courage, strong faith and willingness to change are also important. If you do not yet possess these qualities, then you should recognise that and do what you can to cultivate them. It is essential to always be honest with yourself to avoid creating false expectations.

In order to see the good qualities in other people, we need to cultivate certain qualities within ourselves. This will help us recognise what a particular teacher has to offer and develop our confidence in them. These qualities are:

1. **Impartiality:** When listening to teachings or interacting with a teacher, it is important to always maintain an open mind. The moment bias develops, barriers are constructed that prevent you from hearing what a teacher has to offer. In the beginning it is better to simply absorb as much as you can and avoid making too many judgements.

2. **Intelligence:** Although being open minded will help you gather information, you should not accept everything you hear. The strongest type of faith arises on the basis of sound reasoning and experience. For this reason, you should reflect deeply on the teachings you receive and evaluate whether or not they are beneficial to your mind. If you identify wisdom in the teachings, then put them into practice and try to integrate them into your experience. Being discerning about what to adopt and what to abandon prevents you from being influenced by false teachers.

3. **Diligence:** You cannot put a time limit on when you will find a spiritual guide. It may take months or it could take your entire life; this is simply the nature of your karmic connections. As a teacher's qualities may not appear to you straight away, you may need to cultivate the relationship for quite some time. Understanding this, being diligent will prevent you from giving up in the face of challenges. Even though you may not have a strong connection with any spiritual guide, you should still cherish the Dharma friends currently present in your life. Have faith that through their teachings, your mind will continue to develop and eventually, when the conditions come together, your spiritual guide will appear.

Exercise 3.2 — Looking in the Mirror

- *In a relaxed posture, establish a neutral mind through the practice of mindfulness of breathing.*

- *Spend some time reflecting on the following questions. Think about each line from many angles before moving to the next.*

- *Why do you want to find a spiritual guide?*

- *What do you hope to achieve by establishing this relationship?*

- *What qualities do you think are important in a teacher?*

- *Now consider each of the following qualities and evaluate your own capacity:*

    - *Are you judgemental and opinionated or do you think you are open minded? Think of examples by looking at your relationships with family and friends.*

    - *Are you naturally sceptical or do you find it easy to accept new ideas? Think of examples where you were faced with new information that required you to think differently. How did you react?*

    - *Do you finish what you start or do you give up easily? Think of different activities you have participated in and how you reacted to challenges or hardships.*

- *Rest for a moment in any insights that arise.*

Examining the Qualities of a Teacher

After preparing yourself for working with a teacher, you can now begin the process of examining the teachers you encounter. In today's world a vast number of people claim to be spiritual teachers and while some are authentic, many are not. As this need to distinguish between the two has become increasingly important, the following are some basic guidelines to help you use your time wisely.

Signs of a False Teacher

An appearance of the following characteristics may indicate the need to distance yourself from a particular teacher. Although it is impossible to know exactly what is going on in a teacher's mind, if we see these signs, we can be fairly certain that their teachings will not bring any significant benefit.

1. **Impure Intentions:** Even though a teacher may have studied, reflected and meditated, if they have done so to gain a position of importance within their spiritual community we can say they have an impure intention. These teachers are often very attached to their reputation and do whatever they can to avoid losing their status. Because their main concerns are worldly in nature, they often care very little about training their students, or if they do, they teach in a way that emphasises their own popularity rather than having the best interests of their students at heart. Instead of helping individuals overcome their afflictions, these teachers tend to focus on telling them what they want to hear to promote generosity of offerings. This sort of false teacher is unfortunately very common and as their teachings are easily accessible, they often attract large numbers of people who lack discerning wisdom and whose blind faith is easily manipulated.

2. **Lacking True Realisation:** When a teacher does not follow an authentic lineage or has not trained with an authentic lineage master, they are not qualified to teach within that tradition. Their defining characteristic is their failure to take the teachings to heart and integrate them into their experience. Such teachers might have academic qualifications

but because they have not developed realisations, their minds remain afflicted, reducing their ability to maintain sufficient discipline. While they may present an external display of love and compassion, internally they can harbour hatred and jealousy and so are unsuitable as guides to enlightenment. Relying on this type of teacher will only reinforce your own delusions and greatly hinder your progress along the path.

3. **Close-Minded:** These teachers are not especially well qualified, yet when they begin to attract a following, they develop great pride and even arrogance, exaggerating their own good qualities while being unaware of the attributes of a truly authentic teacher. They are likened to a frog that has lived its whole life in a well and is totally unaware of the existence of the great ocean beyond. These teachers tend to compete for students and wealth, focusing all their energy on building expensive monuments, temples and stupas. They are not interested in actually teaching anything, but only in creating magnificent displays of their illusory greatness.

These types of teachers are the main cause for the decline of the Dharma in this world. As the Omniscient Dolpopa once proclaimed, "Buddhism will decline in five stages, the last being like a peacock, where everything looks beautiful on the outside but is decaying on the inside." Likewise, the great Lama Tsongkhapa also said, "My tradition of Buddhism will decline in wealth when my monks and temples become rich."

As Dharma practitioners, it is our responsibility to prevent the Dharma from degenerating in this manner. We cannot afford to place our trust in fraudulent lamas, monks or communities. We must therefore develop our intelligence and awareness so we can identify these signs of corruption and avoid them as much as possible.

Signs of an Authentic Teacher

In these degenerate times, it is very rare to find a single perfect spiritual guide that fulfils all of our requirements. This is mainly due to our impure perception which obscures our seeing the actual qualities possessed by an authentic teacher. For this reason, it is worth familiarising ourselves with the recognised attributes of an authentic teacher before beginning our examination. As Arya Maitreya said in the *Ornament of Mahayana Sutras*:

Rely on a Mahayana teacher who is disciplined, serene and thoroughly pacified, has good qualities surpassing those of the students, is energetic, has a wealth of scriptural knowledge, possesses loving concern, has a thorough knowledge of reality and skill in instructing disciples, and never loses inspiration.

In total we can identify ten qualities that are strong signs of an authentic spiritual guide. As it is exceptional to find a teacher with all of these qualities, if you have the good fortune to do so, you should cherish them with all your heart and devote yourself to them as much as you possibly can.

1. **Maintains ethical discipline:** Within the Buddhist traditions of Tibet, ethical discipline is divided into three types, (1) the external vows of Self-Liberation, (2) the internal vows of a Bodhisattva, and (3) the secret vows of the Vajrayana. Ideally we should look for a spiritual guide who holds all three levels of vow. Such a teacher is qualified to guide us in both the preliminary and advanced practices, providing us with the opportunity to achieve enlightenment within a single lifetime.

2. **Mind is tamed by meditation:** A spiritual guide should have spent time working with meditation in order to calm the mind and establish a basis of serenity. Ideally they will have achieved the state of Shamatha, but this is not always necessary. The essence is that the teacher's mind is calm, stable and vividly clear, with strong mindfulness and a sharp mentality.

3. **Afflictions are thoroughly pacified:** As long as a spiritual guide is dominated by afflicted states of mind, it will be difficult for them to help others. We should therefore look for a teacher who has trained to reduce the strength of their own afflictions and, at the very least, be free from strong afflictions such as hatred or jealousy. Ideally the teacher will have realised emptiness which acts as an antidote to all afflicted states of mind.

4. **Has more qualities than the student:** For a student to learn from a spiritual guide, the teacher's qualities must surpass those of the student. It is not necessary for all the teacher's qualities to be greater than your own, as superiority of only one quality is enough to receive benefit. Knowing the strengths of a teacher can help focus attention to specific aspects. Sometimes it may be necessary to work with multiple teachers, each with differing capacities. This can maximise your ability to overcome your limitations, the fruitfulness of your relationship and your progress along the path.

5. **Has enthusiasm for Dharma:** Authentic spiritual guides focus all their energy on studying, practicing and teaching the Dharma. They are enthusiastic and passionate about the teachings and love to share them whenever they can. Because of their enthusiasm, they engage in many Dharma activities and are dedicated to bringing benefit to their students. Such a teacher is able to inspire their students to make the Dharma a priority in their lives and help them to avoid getting lost in worldly pursuits.

6. **Has a strong spiritual education:** The Buddha's teachings are vast and profound, providing a wide range of advice for a great diversity of practitioners. For a spiritual guide to be effective as a teacher, they need to be able to draw on that body of knowledge to adapt to the needs of their students. Ideally this means spending substantial time studying and reflecting on the scriptures. The most essential point however is not the number of quotes they can memorise but rather their ability to capture the meaning and essence of the teaching. A teacher who is not a great scholar but has a strong grasp of the Dharma can definitely bring benefit to their students.

7. **Honestly cares about others:** The only authentic reason to teach the Dharma is for the benefit of others. For this reason it is important to look for a teacher who is genuinely invested in seeing their students grow and when the need arises, they are willing to reach out and help their students in whatever ways they can. Like a loving parent who raises their child to face the world when they are ready to leave home, a caring teacher will not be attached to their students but with love and compassion, will only act in their best interest.

8. **Has some degree of realisation:** Ultimately, a spiritual guide's purpose is to lead you to your definitive nature, but if they have never experienced it for themselves, this is an impossibility. While it is extremely difficult to gauge a teacher's level of realisation, by spending enough time with them, it is possible to develop a feeling for when they are simply quoting from a text or when their insight comes from within. The main point is to not be satisfied with a teacher who merely has intellectual knowledge of profound topics. Remember that to become an authentic lineage holder, a teacher must have attained realisations.

9. **Is skilled in communication:** To effectively transmit the Dharma, a spiritual guide should communicate the teachings in a way that is appropriate to the audience they are addressing. By using different approaches they are able to find the best method to cut through a student's confusion. This does not mean all teachers have be highly articulate and educated as when it comes to communication, it's not about quantity, but quality. Some of the best teachers are able to communicate incredible wisdom through only a few simple words.

10. **Unwavering perseverance:** Sentient beings have been wandering in samsara since beginningless time and as such have accumulated very strong habits. Great effort, time and an enormous amount of repetition is required to shift our way of thinking. An authentic spiritual guide has an incredible degree of perseverance that never gives up in the face of challenge. No matter how long it takes and no matter what they have to do, such a teacher is willing to work with sentient beings to help them break free from their suffering. Although they may temporarily withdraw to regroup or increase their capacity, they never lose their motivation to bring benefit to others.

As choosing a spiritual guide is perhaps one of the most important decisions of your life, the connections you make now will play a crucial role in propelling you forward along the path, not only in this life but also in future lives until your ultimate achievement of enlightenment. Therefore, take the time to examine your teachers to the best of your ability until you feel confident they have the capacity to guide you on the path.

With this in mind, finding someone who manifests all these ten qualities is very rare, so we need to be prepared to work with someone who is not perfect. As long as the teacher has superior qualities to the student, genuinely cares about their welfare and is motivated purely by love and compassion, there is a solid foundation for growth to occur. This coupled with your spiritual guide being trained within an authentic lineage means that although their realisations may not be perfect, having access to the wisdom of the lineage makes it possible to guide students towards enlightenment. No matter what faults you may perceive in the teacher, as long as the lineage is pure, you can be sure the teachings hold the blessings of the Buddha.

Finally, always remember that the most effective teacher is one we can relate to on a personal level. For as long as we manifest as a human being with all our imperfections and faults, then so too will our teachers. The very fact of our similarity is what allows them to form a connection with us and this is the ultimate expression of their kindness. In short, don't expect a teacher to be super-human as it is their ordinary aspect which is most precious and is what will guide us to genuine peace and harmony.

Exercise 3.3 — Remembering the Kindness of Your Teachers

- *In a relaxed posture, establish a neutral mind through the practice of mindfulness of breathing.*

- *In the space before you, bring to mind all the teachers who have been influential in your life so far.*

- *Choose one teacher and think about the different qualities they possess that you admire and the ways they have influenced your life.*

- *Contemplate the benefits you have received from this teacher.*

- *If a sense of gratitude arises, rest your mind in this feeling for as long as it lasts. When it begins to fade away, focus on another teacher and repeat the process.*

Developing a Relationship with a Teacher

Thoroughly examining both yourself and your teacher creates the possibility of entering into a healthy spiritual relationship, the nature of which is quite different from the ordinary relationships we usually cultivate. Normally we are driven by some degree of self-cherishing where we feel some aspect is missing in our lives and so seek relationships that may help fill a void. This could be a romantic relationship to curb feelings of loneliness, a business relationship to assist us to achieve our goals, or a friendship which fulfils our need for support.

When a relationship is based on self-cherishing, a person can often have difficulty withstanding hardship and problems. For instance, the sharp rise in the number of divorced people in industrialised countries is a strong indicator that the foundations of our relationships have become weak and uncertain. The moment a person stops fulfilling our needs, we can be quick to abandon them in favour of someone who we think will give us more.

For a spiritual relationship to be meaningful, we must break this pattern. We cannot expect a spiritual guide to simply wave a wand and make our problems magically disappear, although if this was possible they would not hesitate. Unfortunately this is not how it works. The teacher's purpose in the relationship is to create conditions for us to grow as individuals and it is then up to us to actually create the causes for change to occur.

Types of Relationships between Teachers and Students

To cultivate a strong and healthy relationship with your spiritual guide, it can be helpful to consider the ways in which relationships evolve over time. As interactions occur and experiences are shared, a bond is developed between teacher and student. The stronger that bond becomes, the more effective the relationship will be.

Babysitter and Baby

At this level of the relationship, the student is concerned with temporarily improving the conditions of their current life. A crisis can often motivate a person to seek spiritual guidance, but if the concepts and practices challenge them too strongly, this sort of student will often stop attending classes and go in search of something easier.

In such instances, a skilful teacher must work very gently, like a babysitter caring for an infant. Until the mind of the student grows strong enough to challenge its habitual tendencies, the teacher must be content with simply planting seeds for the future.

From the student's side there is very little devotion toward the teacher. They are easily swayed by appearances and it takes very little to scare them away. For the relationship to grow beyond this superficial level, the student needs to establish a strong desire to actually make changes in their life.

Salesman and Customer

Once a student develops the desire to improve their life and consider the actuality of change, they become much more receptive to what a teacher has to offer. A certain open-mindedness develops and they are at least willing to reflect on the ideas presented in the teachings.

At this stage, the student actively tries to acquire knowledge and they see the teacher as a source of wisdom. This can be likened to a customer engaging with a salesman to gather information before proceeding with a transaction. There needs to be a mutual respect between both parties where the teacher respects the student's wish to grow and the student respects the teacher's experience.

The main limitation of this sort of relationship is that the student can grasp too strongly onto the notion that they know what is best for their own wellbeing; the customer is always right. Pride tends to blind a student to certain shortcomings, preventing their spiritual growth. This can be overcome by developing greater trust in the teacher's capacity to see things from a different perspective.

Siblings in a Family

Trust grows slowly on the basis of experience. The more a teacher demonstrates their trustworthiness, the more willing a student will be to turn to them for advice. Once trust is established, the teacher takes on the role of advisor to the student and although the student may still be very independent, they value the input from their teacher and seriously consider what they counsel.

At this level of relationship, the teacher is like an older sibling. The connection has now become much stronger allowing the two to work through increasingly more difficult layers of obscuration. Spirituality now plays a major role in the student's life and they hold a deep respect and admiration for the teacher who guides them along the path.

When a student reaches this point, the teacher can start challenging their habitual tendencies, using a wider range of methods to help the student develop their qualities at a much faster rate. There is a considerably stronger level of commitment on both sides as the teacher sees that the student is willing to make the effort required for transformation to occur.

The only limitation of this type of relationship is based on the degree of dedication expressed by the student. It basically comes down to the time they are willing to devote in order to achieving realisations. The more time they invest, the more benefit they will receive, both in the short term and in the long term.

Mother and Child

Through building a solid foundation of trust, the student will eventually arrive at a point in their spiritual development when they see that their spiritual guide has nothing but unconditional love for their well being; just like a mother for her child. At this stage, the student has developed an extraordinary degree of pure perception and feels a great swell of devotion towards their master.

This relationship is characterised by an unwavering trust between student and teacher that allows the teacher to work very skilfully with the student's subtle obscurations. For this to occur successfully, there must be a total surrender on the part of the student and a willingness to do whatever is needed to achieve enlightenment. Subsequently there can be absolutely no doubt whatsoever in the qualities of the teacher. The time for scepticism has long since passed.

If a student can strip away all forms of resistance, the teacher can introduce them to their ultimate nature. This direct experience is what the student has been working toward and on the basis of that experience, they can very quickly complete the path.

In the beginning of our relationship with a teacher, there can be a desire to be very close to them in order to learn as much as possible. While this intention is good, there is a need to be careful. In Tibet, we often say, "A guru is like a fire. If you get too close, you get burned; if you stay too far away, you don't get enough heat." This indicates the necessity of developing a balanced and healthy approach. We don't want to become obsessive and attached to our teachers, nor do we want to be indifferent to them. Try to meet regularly with your teacher to maintain the connection but also give yourself the opportunity to integrate the advice they give.

How to Enter Into a Dharma Relationship

Many unfortunate misunderstandings can arise when there is a lack of clarity regarding the type of relationship a teacher and student are working within. Participation of a student in formal rituals like vow ceremonies or empowerments can be an indicator to the teacher that the student wants to enter into a specific type of relationship. Problems can occur however if the student is not yet ready to move to the next stage, and so to avoid this, it is important to develop mindfulness of your actions to ensure both you and your teacher are on the same page.

Whether you relate to a teacher as a Dharma friend, a spiritual guide or a vajra master, ultimately depends on your own perception. Whereas seeing a teacher as a Dharma friend carries with it no particular level of commitment, viewing them as either a spiritual guide or a vajra master does. You should therefore be aware of the corresponding commitments before entering into these relationships.

Traditionally, to begin a relationship with a spiritual guide, a formal request for them to become your teacher is made or you participate in a ceremony where they bestow vows. The moment you receive vows from a teacher, they should be considered your *Vow Preceptor* and with this comes an expected degree of respect and devotion that forms the basis for developing a spiritual relationship.

To enter into a relationship with a vajra master, one needs to attend an empowerment ceremony which includes receiving the *Tantric Vows*. Even if you feel you are not ready to maintain this level of commitment, you should still participate. It is so rare in this world to have this opportunity that we cannot waste it. Therefore, do not worry whether you will be able to maintain the vows tomorrow, instead focus on developing a sincere aspiration to uphold them on that day. In this way, you will receive the blessings of the ceremony and will be laying the karmic seeds to keep the vows in the future.

Remember the choice of whether to enter into a spiritual relationship or not is always up to you. No one can force you to be a student to a teacher. At the same time however, we must take care to not mislead our teachers with our actions. Be honest about where you are on your spiritual journey and if you have doubts, keep the lines of communication open by discussing them with your teacher.

PRACTICING DEVOTION TOWARDS YOUR TEACHER

Once you have chosen a spiritual guide, the next phase of practice is how to actually follow that teacher. At this point, you should feel a level of confidence in having found someone who is both suitable for your particular stage of development and who is committed to helping you achieve your spiritual aims.

A qualified teacher can benefit you in two ways: (1) they are a source for the transmission of teachings which connect you to the lineage; and (2) they are an object worthy of devotion who inspires you to engage in virtuous actions. The first focuses on the wisdom you need to attain realisations and the second is the method through which those realisations are achieved.

The term *devotion* has been mentioned several times already in this chapter, so what does it specifically mean? To "devote oneself" refers to using our body, speech and mind to perform actions which honour or please a particular object of devotion. For instance, you could devote yourself to your parents by honouring their wishes and performing their requested actions. Similarly, you devote yourself to your teacher by practicing the Dharma.

To understand why devotion is so important is to understand the nature of our relationship with our spiritual guide. The relationship is formed on the basis of a desire to achieve lasting peace and harmony by freeing oneself and others from suffering. This motivation defines both our connection with our teacher and the purpose of our activities. Through the practice of devotion we use that connection as a support for developing the wisdom which acts as an antidote to the ignorance that currently dominates our mind. In this way, the entire path is contained within the context of devoting oneself to a spiritual guide.

Three Ways to Please the Teacher

If we consider the quality of our relationships with other people, the vast majority are based on worldly concerns such as providing money or fulfilling an emotional need. Conversely, your relationship with your spiritual guide is unique as they will be the only person who explicitly connects you with your inner wisdom. Karmically speaking, this makes them the most powerful person in your life. Because of the weight of this relationship, any actions done in connection to a spiritual guide have an incredible impact on the karmic propensities produced. Therefore, if you want to progress quickly along the path, you should devote yourself to pleasing your teacher.

For a sceptical mind, it is easy to develop misconceptions regarding the practice of devotion, viewing it as a form of enslavement where a teacher takes advantage of their students for their own personal gain. This outlook completely misses the point of the practice as devotion is not about bringing benefit to the teacher, but bringing benefit to the student. Through the act of making offerings to the teacher, a student develops strong virtuous habits which will ripen in the form of genuine happiness. The teacher creates the conditions for you to make those offerings and form those habits.

If you have taken the time to ensure the teacher is authentic, there is no danger whatsoever of them becoming attached to the offerings you make. In fact, for such teachers, worldly gain does not please them. As their only desire is for sentient beings to be free from suffering, their minds are greatly pleased by anything that helps sentient beings achieve this goal. When they see their students making the effort to develop virtuous qualities, they rejoice as they know the students are stepping closer to enlightenment.

To reach the end of the path, we must amass enormous quantities of merit and wisdom. Only the perfection of these two karmic propensities will lead us to Buddhahood. The practice of devotion therefore focuses on three forms of offering that are specifically designed to complete these accumulations: (1) making offerings of practice, (2) making offerings of service, and (3) making offerings of material support. While the first is used to accumulate wisdom, the last two concern the accumulation of merit.

Offering Practice

The most important offering we can make to a spiritual guide is the effort to achieve realisations by practicing the Dharma. Through studying the teachings, reflecting on their meaning and meditating to integrate that meaning into our lives, we give rise to realisations. We then become authentic holders of the lineage with the capacity to transmit wisdom to the next generation of practitioners. As long as there are lineage holders in this world, the Dharma will survive and continue to bring benefit to sentient beings. Knowing the Dharma is thriving in the world fills the mind of your spiritual guide with immense joy and is the greatest gift you could ever give them.

Offering practice occurs every time you dedicate your activities toward enlightenment. It does not require the teacher to acknowledge your realisations in any way. In fact, seeking recognition from your spiritual guide can act as a powerful obstacle to your practice as it feeds a sense of pride and self-cherishing. We should not be searching for approval from outside of ourselves. We should instead be like the Buddha who, when asked who could vouch for his realisations, simply extended his finger to the ground and proclaimed the earth as his witness.

Exercise 3.4 — Integrating Practice into Life

- *In a relaxed posture, establish a neutral mind through the practice of mindfulness of breathing.*

- *Bring to mind the spiritual teachers you have met in your life.*

- *For each teacher:*

    - *Consider the teachings you received.*

    - *What are the practices related to those teachings?*

    - *What are the benefits of engaging in those practices?*

- *Now review the conditions present in your life right now. Which practices do you think are most relevant for you at this time?*

- *What opportunities can you identify to use for practice?*

- *Develop a strong resolve to take advantage of those opportunities.*

- *Rest your awareness in this resolve.*

Offering Service

A spiritual guide is not an inherently powerful object. The power comes from how we as students relate to them. When we recognise the connection between the teacher and our own sacred truth, every interaction with them becomes an opportunity to connect with our deeper nature. The more we strengthen that connection, the more powerful the teacher becomes.

It is this premise that drives the practice of offering service. Here we use whatever skills of body, speech and mind we have to facilitate the activities of the teacher. This could be as simple as offering a cup of tea to quench their thirst, or it can be more involved such as managing a Dharma Centre in your city or town.

The key to effectively offering service is to recognise what your teacher aspires to achieve and what they need to actualise those aspirations. Most authentic teachers spend as much time as possible engaged in Dharma activities which either directly or indirectly promote the teachings or bring long lasting benefit to sentient beings. Recognising that worldly concerns only serve as a distraction to the pursuits of a spiritual guide, a student could offer to cook meals for the teacher or clean their home and wash their clothes. By doing this, they ensure their teacher maintains their health while also freeing up time so they can focus on the Dharma.

Another way to serve a teacher is to identify your specific skills and how you could use them to help your teacher realise their goals. By communicating with your teacher to establish what they want to achieve, you can gain a clear under-standing of their vision and what opportunities exist for you to act. Students often take a passive approach and wait for their teacher to request something of them. This requires a great deal of energy on behalf of the teacher who has far better things to do than push his students into action. What could have been an offering of service from a sincere wish to bring benefit, can turn into a sort of duty or chore, which is not the correct attitude to have. To get the most out of this practice, we need to take control of our actions and cultivate the desire to help from within and in this way, service becomes joyful and meaningful to the student volunteering their time and effort.

In addition to offering service directly to our teacher, we should also consider ways we can serve our spiritual community. As the community is an extension of the teacher, by helping our Dharma brothers and sisters we are also actively assisting the teacher to fulfil their purpose. This could take the form of volunteering at a local Dharma Centre, organising spiritual events where people can connect with the Dharma or simply offering words of advice when needed. Just as we should be attentive to the needs of our teacher, we should also be considerate of the needs of his students.

Exercise 3.5 — Identifying Opportunities to Serve

- *In a relaxed posture, establish a neutral mind through the practice of mindfulness of breathing.*

- *Bring to mind the teacher you feel the strongest connection with.*

- *Reflect on the activities of this teacher. Consider projects they are presently working on and those they may aspire to work on in the future.*

- *What is needed to complete these activities? Think not only about the main activities but also the many conditions required to dedicate oneself to this work.*

- *Can you think of any skills you have that might allow you to help your teacher achieve their goals?*

- *What steps could you take to put those skills to use.*

- *Develop the desire to volunteer your services.*

Offering Material Support

There are times when the conditions are not present for us to participate in the way we desire. Even though we may possess skills that could be constructive, we may lack the time or conviction to put them to use. Fortunately, if helping directly is not possible, indirect support is another option.

In this case, the focus is not on what actions you can perform, but more the resources you have available to you. These resources can be used as conditions to support the work of others. For instance, by offering food to your teacher, you create the condition for them to eat and sustain their body. As long as they are healthy, they can continue to work for the benefit of others.

In regards to making donations to a teacher, we must make effort to remove any misconceptions that limit the benefit we can draw from such acts of generosity. As long as we have investigated our teacher previously, we should be confident that donations will be directed toward authentic Dharma activities.

This means that everything we give becomes a condition for sentient beings to achieve enlightenment. As such, an authentic teacher is not pleased by simply having money, they are pleased by what they can do with it.

If you do not feel you can trust your teacher, this is something you need to examine. Before directing attention to the faults of others, start by looking inward to your own attitudes. How does your perception of a particular situation prevent you from practicing generosity? Do these attitudes bring you or others benefit? Look closely at your motivation and try to consider the long term implications of your actions.

For those who would like to practice offering material support, the following are some suggested ways of maximising the benefit you can achieve:

1. **Commissioning holy objects:** These objects are symbols of enlightened qualities and inspire the minds of all who see them. They can include things like paintings, statues or stupas. Through your generosity, you could sponsor the purchase of materials or contribute to the cost of hiring an artisan to produce the object.

2. **Publishing books and translations:** Through the writing of books and the translation of existing texts, the Dharma becomes more accessible to a much wider audience. You can help expand the reach of the teachings by providing for the basic needs of writers and translators, or by sponsoring the printing of the books themselves.

3. **Sponsoring dedicated practitioners:** Devoting oneself to achieving realisations often means reducing one's involvement in worldly activities like managing a household and generating income. This means that dedicated practitioners need to rely heavily on the generosity of others in order to survive. You can help them by sponsoring their living costs so they can concentrate on formal practice.

4. **Sponsoring events:** Teachers can only bring benefit to sentient beings they have previously formed connections with. By sponsoring a teaching or retreat, you reduce the cost of the event and allow more people the

opportunity to attend. This creates the conditions for the teacher to form more Dharma connections that will ultimately be the cause for them to achieve enlightenment.

5. **Building temples and retreat centres:** Creating spaces that are dedicated to Dharma practice is a powerful way to gather people together and focus their minds on virtuous activities. Supporting the purchase of land or the construction of buildings to be used by a spiritual community is a wonderful way to establish the Dharma in a particular place.

If you have a genuine desire to practice generosity, it is worth sitting down with your teacher to discuss ideas for making the most of the resources you have. As a spiritual guide will generally have a much broader view of what needs to be achieved, they can help you identify the most skilful course of action.

Exercise 3.6 — Cultivating Generosity

- *In a relaxed posture, establish a neutral mind through the practice of mindfulness of breathing.*

- *Bring to mind a teacher you feel a strong connection to.*

- *Consider the activities performed by that teacher or by the teacher's spiritual community.*

- *Review your present conditions and take stock of the resources you have available to you.*

- *Can any of these resources be used to help your teacher realise their goals?*

- *Think of the short and long term benefits that would result from your support of these goals.*

- *Develop the desire to offer whatever support you can.*

Practicing Mindfulness in the Presence of the Teacher

By engaging in the offering of practice, service and material support, we have the opportunity to generate oceans of merit and wisdom in a short period of time. This is only possible if you have a strong virtuous connection with your spiritual guide. The stronger the connection, the more powerful the effects from practicing devotion.

To further strengthen this bond, we should take particular care to avoid allowing our relationship to become too ordinary and worldly. This is done by practicing mindfulness whenever we are in the presence of our spiritual guide. Just seeing your teacher should trigger increased awareness of your actions to maintain respect and admiration for everything they represent. We will now examine this practice in regards to your body, speech and mind.

Mindfulness of Your Attitude

The foundation of all our actions is the mind, and therefore we need to be especially mindful of the attitude we develop toward our teachers. In accordance with the lineage, the most beneficial attitude we can have concerning our teacher has four aspects:

1. **Recognising that you are afflicted by a great illness:** Until we recognise that we are sick, we will never truly seek a cure. We therefore need to deeply reflect on how we suffer as a result of the countless afflictions that have conditioned our minds since beginningless time. We cannot afford to be complacent by fooling ourselves into believing everything is fine. When we turn our gaze inward and view ourselves with honesty, we see we are fundamentally dissatisfied with our present situation and this provides the motivation to change. It is this desire for change that allows us to be open to the influence of a teacher.

2. **Recognising that your teacher is like a great healer:** Having achieved the result you seek by actualising the Dharma in their own experience, your spiritual guide is fully qualified to heal your illness. Like a skilled and specialised physician, they are the only one with the capacity to help you. This point emphasises the qualities of the teacher and why we should place our trust in them.

3. **Recognising that without your teacher, there is no cure:** To permanently cure our afflictions, we must uproot every trace of our ignorance. To do this, we have no choice but to rely on a teacher who can provide us with expert advice, potent medicine and effective treatment. This point reinforces the importance of working with a teacher and prevents us from being distracted by false sources of refuge such as the eight worldly concerns.

4. **Recognising that the teachings are the only cure:** The only way to cure an illness is by taking the medicine. Regardless of what instructions we receive from our spiritual guide, we must develop the faith and loyalty to follow that advice to the best of our ability. Even if we find the treatment difficult, we need to persevere and never give up, for only then will we experience the result we are searching for.

With the strengthening of these four realisations, we allow ourselves to be open and receptive, filled with confidence, patient in the face of difficulty and dedicated to maximising benefit. Such a mind naturally appreciates the presence of a teacher and acts as a safeguard to falling into ordinary habitual patterns.

Mindfulness of Your Speech

When in the presence of a spiritual guide it is important to be mindful of both the content of your speech and the way in which you are speaking. With regards to the former, try to remain silent unless you have something meaningful to say, avoiding engagement in pointless chatter. If the teacher initiates a conversation, then respond accordingly but without losing your mindfulness.

You should never openly criticise the teacher in front of other students as this can cause those with weak devotion to lose their faith. If however the teacher requests criticism, it should always be presented in a respectful manner and never out of anger.

Always take great effort to try and understand what your teacher is communicating to you and avoid jumping too quickly to conclusions. To avoid misunderstandings and remove any confusion, don't be afraid to ask questions.

Consider your words carefully before speaking and converse in a manner that is peaceful, relaxed and easygoing. In general, the exchange should be as harmonious as possible.

Mindfulness of Your Conduct

Traditional texts such as *The Fifty Verses of Guru Devotion* detail a variety of methods a student can follow to increase their respect, mindfulness and conscientiousness when in the presence of their teacher. While some of these methods may seem a little strange from the perspective of modern audiences, a good student will try to understand the essence of each one and apply that understanding to the context of their relationship.

In general, we should try to maintain awareness of our position in relation to the teacher and the manner in which we move. When a teacher stands, we should also stand. When they sit we can then sit and if possible, always try to do so below the teacher, never above. This promotes a sense of humility in their presence.

When walking with a teacher as an attendant, it is preferable to walk behind them and to their left as this position is considered respectful in traditional Asian cultures. If the road is dangerous or you need to walk in front, it is best to ask permission.

Restrain your movements as much as possible, limiting them to only what is necessary. Avoid any violent actions such as knocking on doors loudly or slamming them shut. Maintain good posture and avoid being overly casual with your body-language. Handle everything gently and with care, demonstrating mindfulness of your actions and try to anticipate your teacher's needs, taking steps to fulfil them.

If you can maintain your mindfulness at all times, your spiritual guide will become a very special part of your life, cultivating a relationship that will create the necessary conditions for you to mature in your spiritual journey. If however you ignore these guidelines, your relationship will lose its strength and you may find your spiritual guide simply becomes just another person in your life, no longer leading to any significant benefit. For this reason, we must always be vigilant and take great care of this relationship as a precious part of our lives.

EMULATING YOUR TEACHER'S QUALITIES

The more time we spend with someone, the more we are influenced by their behaviour. Whether this is a positive or negative influence will depend on the nature of the qualities we are exposed to. If, for example, you spend substantial time with a person who constantly gossips and speaks nonsense, eventually this behaviour will impact on you. You may find yourself influenced by their habitual patterns and before you know it, they become your patterns as well.

Fortunately the process of influence also works with positive qualities. When you pay attention to a person's constructive patterns of body, speech and mind, those habitual propensities are strengthened in your own mind and they can start to play a more dominant role in your life. This is the basic idea behind *role models*. We model our behaviour on the people who possess the qualities we desire.

In the case of our teachers, if we are not intelligent about which characteristics we emulate, this process can sometimes lead to negative results. This problem comes from an impure view that we project onto our spiritual guides. Due to the strength of our karma, we experience some aspects of our teacher as desirable qualities and some as undesirable faults. Our goal should then be to emulate their qualities while ignoring their faults.

This means that even if your teacher appears to have many faults, as long as they have just one good quality, they can still bring benefit to you. As a result of emulating their good attributes, you may find that aspects you previously perceived as faults, now appear as qualities. This is a sign that you are developing a purer view that is informed by wisdom and when this occurs, more of the teacher's qualities will start to manifest.

It is important to remember that ignoring faults is not about fooling ourselves into thinking they don't exist. It is a recognition that the appearance of faults is relative to the mind perceiving them. For example, if you are attached to sleep, the fact your teacher doesn't sleep much may be seen as a fault. Likewise, if you place particular value on scholastic education, you might construe your teacher's lack of academic study as a fault. By recognising the relative nature of appearances, we can choose not to focus our energy on aspects which will not bring benefit to our minds.

Exercise 3.7 — Reflecting on the Qualities of Your Teacher

- *In a relaxed posture, establish a neutral mind through the practice of mindfulness of breathing.*

- *Bring to mind a teacher you feel a strong connection with.*

- *Consider the qualities you admire most in your teacher.*

- *For each quality:*

    - *Try to remember examples of when your teacher manifested this quality.*

    - *Visualise yourself in similar situations and imagine this quality manifests in you as well. How would you act?*

    - *Strengthen your aspiration to develop this quality in your own mind.*

- *Complete your session by developing the aspiration to achieve all of the qualities of your teacher.*

ESTABLISHING A HEALTHY RELATIONSHIP WITH YOUR TEACHER

Working with a teacher has the potential to be one of the most rewarding experiences you will have in your life. When the teacher-student relationship is developed in a healthy manner, it can have incredible power, but unfortunately, many factors can lead to misunderstanding on both sides. It is therefore essential to be skilful in such a relationship by becoming familiar with the points presented in this chapter. I recommend you keep the following advice close to heart.

1. **Focus on pure motivation:** If you must judge your teachers, I advise that you do so on the basis of their essential aim. If their intention is to help you develop wholesome qualities and dismantle your self-cherishing, you should follow their instructions to the letter. If however their main intention is to cultivate worldly values and accumulate material

possessions, it is not necessary to follow their directives. Spend as much time as you need to determine their intentions, but once you have, try to relax and concentrate on the work of practicing the Dharma.

2. **Always communicate openly and clearly:** When working with a teacher who is from a different culture to your own, it is important to make the effort to avoid unreasonable expectations. Many Tibetan teachers have specific views of how a teacher should behave and it can be difficult for them to adapt to the views held by their Western students. For this reason, it is crucial to emphasise an open and clear line of communication with your teacher and specifically discuss whatever expectations you may have developed. Do not assume you are both on the same page.

3. **Don't run away from hardships:** For a spiritual relationship to bring lasting benefit to the student, the connection with the teacher must be resilient. If the teacher is doing their job, they will constantly challenge the student to re-evaluate their habitual patterns and to transform the way they see the world. This process can be difficult and may lead to many hardships. It is similar to how a cancer patient must endure a long and gruelling regimen of treatments in order to free themselves of their sickness. Regardless of the ratio of good days to bad ones, a patient should see the treatment through. Likewise, even if your relationship with your teacher tests the limits of your patience and capacity, don't give up. If you find yourself overwhelmed and everything feels too hard, don't just run away. Discuss it with your teacher and let them know you are having difficulties. The moment you cut off communication, there is nothing the teacher can do to help you.

4. **Use wisdom to resolve disagreements:** If you are faced with a disagreement, seriously reflect on the subject before making any rash decisions. No matter what level of relationship you are developing, you should always feel free to talk through any issues that may arise. Just remember to do so in a calm and respectful manner. It should not be like a child throwing a temper tantrum, but instead like two adults who care deeply for each other's well being. Ultimately however, you need to learn to rely on your own judgement and to act on the basis of sound observation and a pure motivation. If you feel that what is being asked of you is currently

beyond your capacity, you should respectfully let your teacher know that you are unable to fulfil his request. Develop a sense of equanimity towards the situation and do not focus on it as a fault of the teacher.

5. **Take advantage of every opportunity to learn:** From my own experience, being sceptical and opinionated does not help find a perfect spiritual guide. Having a strong determination to receive teachings, as well as respect and gratitude toward those who share their wisdom, are the types of qualities that carry great benefit. It is usually best to be as non-judgemental as possible and to have very few expectations. Simply develop your appreciation of the Dharma and remember that practicing the teachings is of most importance.

I personally feel you should take hold of every opportunity to receive teachings from authentic lineage holders. Being overly judgmental may result in missing the chance to meet the spiritual guide who is actually best suited for your needs. Rather than basing your opinions solely on a teacher's reputation or status, focus more on your personal experience of their teachings and your own intuition. Through this type of examination, I am confident you will find a teacher who is knowledgeable, humble, honest and kind; who is provocative, challenging and direct; and yet open and flexible. By developing a relationship with such a teacher, we gradually come to realise the level of compassion and wisdom the teacher possesses, even if this may not be immediately obvious.

REVIEW OF KEY POINTS

- In order to receive the blessings of the lineage and the instructions suited to our specific needs, we must rely on a living teacher.

- There are three phases to establishing a strong spiritual relationship with a qualified teacher: (1) choosing a qualified teacher, (2) practicing devotion towards your teacher and (3) emulating the qualities of your teacher.

- Throughout our lives, we will work with different types of teachers that each brings different levels of benefit to our mind. There are four main types we should be aware of: (1) wordly teachers, (2) dharma friends, (3) spiritual guides and (4) vajra masters. There is no limit to the number of teachers you may have.

- Before choosing a teacher, we should examine our own motivations and qualities to ensure that we have the right attitude. In particular, we should cultivate the qualities of (1) impartiality, (2) intelligence and (3) diligence.

- When examining potential teachers, we should be on the lookout for the signs of a false teacher such as: (1) impure intentions, (2) lack of true realisations and (3) being close-minded. We should avoid these sorts of teachers as much as possible.

- There are ten qualities that we should look for in a qualified teacher: (1) maintains ethical discipline, (2) mind is tamed by meditation, (3) afflictions are thoroughly pacified, (4) has more qualities than the student, (5) has enthusiasm for the Dharma, (6) has a strong spiritual education, (7) honestly cares about others, (8) has some degree of realisation, (9) is skilled in communication and (10) unwavering perseverance.

- A spiritual relationship develops over time. The evolution of that relationship can be broken into four phases: (1) babysitter and baby, (2) salesman and customer, (3) siblings in a family, and (4) mother and child.

- Practicing devotion mean using your body, speech and mind in a way that pleases your spiritual guide. There are three main ways to practice devotion: (1) offering practice, (2) offering service and (3) offering material support.

- When in the presence of your teacher, you should cultivate an attitude that sees (1) yourself as a sick patient, (2) your teacher as a great healer, (3) your teacher as the only source of teachings and (4) the teachings as the only cure for your sickness. Try to express this attitude by maintaining mindfulness of your body and speech.

- Even though faults may appear to you, try to focus on the teacher's qualities and emulate them to the best of your ability.

- The key to maintaining a healthy relationship with your spiritual guide is clear and open communication. As long as you are honest with each other, genuine trust can be built over time.

CHAPTER FOUR

Taking Refuge in the Three Jewels
The Foundation of All Paths

In life, we are constantly relying on different things in order to create the results that we desire. When we are hungry, we rely on food to satisfy our appetite. When we are tired, we rely on sleep to feel rested. When we are upset, we rely on the comfort of friends. For every desire we have, there is something we take refuge in. We seek these things out because they provide us with protection from whatever situation or condition we wish to avoid. Although these worldly forms of refuge help us to survive, we need to seek a deeper type of refuge that has the ability to remove the suffering completely.

To use an analogy, consider a mountaineer wishing to climb a mountain. Carefully mapping the approach he will take, he aims to follow the paths of those who have successfully conquered the mountain before him. He also enlists the help of a seasoned guide who is familiar with every aspect of the journey. While planning the climb is a crucial step, it only forms part of his preparations. Before he actually sets foot on the mountain he must gather together the necessary supplies and equipment he will need along the way. He will require food to give him essential energy, clothing to protect him from the elements, an axe to create footholds and ropes to scale difficult cliff faces. Without these supports, there is no possibility of reaching the summit.

Similarly, in our quest to connect with our most sacred truth, we too need to gather the right conditions to ensure our success. So far we have discussed three very important supports: (1) an authentic path to show us the way, (2) an authentic lineage to ensure our path leads to our destination, and (3) an authentic spiritual guide to show us how to safely arrive at that destination. To complete our preparations, we now need to establish the right foundations in our mindstream.

In accordance with the great masters of the Kalachakra lineage, there is no way to achieve enlightenment without first taking refuge in what are known as the *Three Jewels*—Buddha, Dharma and Sangha. Forming the basis upon which we attain all forms of realisation, they are described as "jewels" because they are so incredibly precious and valuable. As we will discuss in more detail below, the essence of taking refuge in the Three Jewels is to develop faith in our own innate capacity, and to use that faith as support for our practice.

Initially people can have difficulty generating this kind of faith. Thinking the connection between the nature of a Buddha and their own enlightened nature is beyond comprehension and does not seem possible. Fortunately this view can be overcome by studying the Three Jewels from different angles to develop a broader perspective that realises the actuality of our potential.

Our deep habituation toward seeing the world through the lens of our self-grasping is an obstacle to the faith we need. Society presents us with many examples of how we constantly compare ourselves to each other; how we look, how we act and who we are as people. We are often critical and judgemental of ourselves and others, which makes our minds very defensive and fragile. The more defensive our attitude becomes, the stronger we cling to a false sense of self and this clinging makes it virtually impossible to see who we really are. To loosen our intense grasping, we need to shift our attention away from the self by developing faith in something beyond the self. In the Buddhist path, that something is the Three Jewels.

CAUSES FOR TAKING REFUGE

In order for the act of taking refuge to have strength in our minds, it is helpful to understand the main causes that motivate our desire to seek refuge in the first place. For every object of refuge, there are two factors: (1) fear of something you wish to avoid and (2) faith in something to protect you from that fear. We will now look at each of these causes in more detail.

Fear

When we think of fear, we usually have an image of being overwhelmed by emotional anxiety and a feeling of helplessness which makes it difficult to deal with the cause of our fear. This is not the kind of fear we are looking to develop here. Our aim is to generate a type of fear that is based on a clear understanding of the nature of our suffering and has the potential to act as a powerful catalyst for spiritual activity. In general, we can speak of three main fears that can motivate someone to seek a valid source of refuge.

1. **Fear of Gross Suffering:** All sentient beings long to be free from suffering but, unfortunately, the reality of our lives is that the experience of suffering is unavoidable. This fundamental fear of pain and anguish motivates many people to seek a source of refuge that can help them live in greater peace and harmony. For some, the scope of their aspirations are limited to this life alone, while for others, their view extends beyond death and considers the potential suffering that could be experienced in future lives as well.

2. **Fear of Samsara:** For those who look deeper into the nature of experience, there is a realisation that our view of happiness is actually a form of potential suffering. The very way in which we interpret our reality constantly sows the seeds for our own dissatisfaction and to make matters worse, we have been doing this since beginningless time. Once we realise we are perpetuating our suffering, we develop a fear of continuing to build our self-made prison. This fear gives rise to a strong desire to completely free ourself from all forms of suffering, whether gross or subtle. Such a motivation longs to cut the endless cycle of existence and to experience lasting genuine happiness.

3. **Fear of Nirvana:** While our personal liberation from cyclic existence ensures we no longer experience suffering, it does nothing for the countless sentient beings who remain in samsara. Recognising the infinite connections of love and affection we have developed with sentient beings over countless lives, it is unacceptable to abandon them to such a fate. With the desire to bring benefit to all sentient beings without exception, a fear of attaining peace merely for ourselves arises. This fear motivates an individual to cultivate the causes to become a fully enlightened Buddha.

If we consider the scope of these three fears, we can see the first focuses on avoiding only immediate forms of suffering. The second has a broader scope which incorporates a much larger understanding of the nature of reality and the third encompasses an even broader view. In the context of the Kalachakra Path, all three fears must be present as a foundation for developing an authentic experience of refuge.

Exercise 4.1 — Developing the Wish to be Free

- *In a relaxed posture, establish a neutral mind through the practice of mindfulness of breathing.*

- *Looking back over your life, bring to mind different examples of physical pain that you have personally experienced, allowing the memories to arise vividly in the mind. Now consider the pain others have experienced. Can you imagine what it would feel like to endure that pain? Develop the strong desire to be free from this sort of manifest suffering.*

- *Again, reviewing your life, look for examples of when you experienced mental anguish and then shift your focus to the many forms of torment other people have encountered. Imagine what it would be like to experience these states of mind. Develop the strong desire to be free of all forms of mental anguish.*

- *Next, imagine you are trapped in a metal cage, carried along by a raging river. You gasp for air as your head is forced under the water, over and over again. As the cage is bashed around by rocks, you are thrown violently in all directions. Try to get a sense for the terror of this situation and what it would be like to have absolutely no control over your experience.*

- *Consider the nature of cyclic existence. Like the cage, it traps you in an endless stream of suffering. The waves of crashing water are like the karma that conditions every moment of your experience, pushing you down into the lower realms and only occasionally giving you time to breathe. Is this how you want to spend your existence? Generate the aspiration to break free from this prison once and for all.*

- *Finally, bring to mind your friends and family. Imagine they are all trapped inside a burning building, crying out for your help. What would you do? Would you abandon them? Or would you do whatever you could to save them?*

- *Just like you, sentient beings are suffering in cyclic existence and just like you they want to be free, but they need your help. Generate a strong aspiration to never give up until everyone is free from suffering.*

- *Rest in the determination to make this happen.*

Faith

To channel our fear into constructive activities, we need to develop faith in our potential to overcome those fears. Without faith, we risk slipping into depression or apathy, which serves no purpose and doesn't help anyone. In this context, we are not speaking of blind faith, but rather a faith based on wisdom. Our aim is to develop a sense of conviction that provides us with a stable foundation for practice. There are three forms of faith that we can use to do this:

1. **Spontaneous Faith:** Spontaneous or vivid faith arises as a temporary feeling of inspiration when we think about the incredible qualities of the Buddhas and Bodhisattvas. It is based on the coming together of conditions that trigger a particular state of mind such as when a person enters a great temple filled with magnificent statues, paintings and holy relics. It can also occur in the presence of our teacher or when we contemplate the lives of the great lineage masters. While this type of faith can be extremely powerful, it is fleeting and will be lost when the conditions change. Therefore it is important to use spontaneous faith as a catalyst for developing deeper and more stable forms of faith.

2. **Reasoned Faith:** When spontaneous faith is combined with logical reasoning it can develop into reasoned faith. This sort of faith recognises the benefit of holding a particular belief and, on this basis, is eager to engage in wholesome actions. When we identify the reasons behind our faith, it becomes stronger and more stable. The greater its stability, the more it is able to withstand any doubts that may arise along the path.

3. **Confident Faith:** Through the act of reasoning, we remove doubt. When we no longer have doubt, our faith becomes unwavering and we are able to fully integrate our beliefs into all aspects of our experience. Because realisations require an openness to experiencing reality as it is, only this sort of faith is a valid foundation for actually accomplishing the path.

As the Buddha once said,

"Oh Shariputra, ultimate truth is realised through faith alone."

Or as the great master Padmasambhava once said,

"The faith of total trust allows blessings to enter you. When the mind is free of doubt, whatever you wish can be accomplished."

Faith is like a seed from which everything positive can grow, whereas an absence of faith will destroy the seed. Faith is considered to be our most precious treasure, as without it nothing truly sublime can come to fruition. When confident faith is present, external conditions can cease to be relevant, as illustrated by the following story of the dog's tooth:

A merchant once travelled from Tibet to Bodhgaya in India to carry out his business. His mother asked him to bring her a holy relic so she could increase the power of her practice. The son, however, forgot all about his mother's wish and returned to Tibet empty handed. Just as he was about to reach his mother's home, he remembered her request and so he found a dog's tooth, wrapped it in silk and prepared to offer it to his mother as one of the Buddha's very own teeth. Instead of giving him the retribution he feared, his mother was over-joyed and proceeded to venerate the tooth as part of her practice. The power of her faith and devotion created all the necessary external conditions and the old dog's tooth was transformed into an object of power. Eventually it became a powerful holy relic, with miraculous pearls emerging from the tooth, as if it really were the Buddha's. The woman died with great peace and joy, with many auspicious signs at her death bearing witness to her liberation. It was the power of her faith that created this attainment.

When the power of our faith opens us to the all-pervasive compassion of the Buddhas, we are blessed by the connection to our own enlightened essence and our own good qualities naturally increase. If we have a small degree of faith this will invoke a small amount of blessings. Great faith on the other hand, will attract a constant stream of blessings. Even today, whenever a student invokes the Buddha or the great masters with sincere faith and devotion, they are bestowed with their blessings.

Exercise 4.2 — A Question of Faith

- *In a relaxed posture, establish a neutral mind through the practice of mindfulness of breathing.*

- *Drawing from your life experience, bring to mind examples of moments where you felt particularly inspired by a person or place. Reflect on the exact conditions of that moment and how they contributed to your reaction. What was it that you found so inspirational? What actions did that inspiration lead you to do?*

- *Consider when you have heard or read an idea and wanted to learn more. As you researched the idea, what effect did this have on your understanding? Did it strengthen your belief in the idea or did it weaken it?*

- *Now think of different beliefs that you hold which you are certain are true. Where does this confidence come from? What factors have contributed to your sense of certainty?*

- *Rest your awareness in any conclusions that may arise.*

THE THREE JEWELS

A spiritual path is a dynamic process of transformation that depends on the interaction between many interdependent components. Just as there is no single cause for any particular moment of experience, so too there is no single object of refuge upon which to rely. Which objects we focus on and how we rely on them will change depending on where we are in our spiritual development.

For this reason, we will examine working with the Three Jewels by applying a multi-level approach. At each level, a different perspective will be highlighted that can be used to reveal increasingly more subtle layers of understanding. When taken as a whole, the three layers create a flexible foundation that provides us with support on our path from beginning to end.

Shakyamuni Buddha—Embodiment of the Outer Three Jewels

The Outer Three Jewels

We begin from the perspective of someone just setting out on the path, whose focus is on identifying which conditions are necessary to effectively practice that path. We can refer to these conditions as the *Outer Three Jewels* as they are generally seen as external supports which we rely on to actualise our potential.

Buddha

The first Jewel is known as the *Buddha Jewel*. At a provisional level, this Jewel refers to the historical Buddha Shakyamuni who manifested in our world and turned the wheel of Dharma for the benefit of all sentient beings. As a source of refuge, the Buddha is a supreme role model who demonstrated how to practice the Dharma and what can be achieved through that practice. Definitively, the Buddha is the perfect manifestation of our Buddha-nature. He is an expression of our innermost capacity and represents the infinite potential we each possess.

We can develop faith in the Buddha by reflecting on his enlightened qualities. While these qualities are infinite, we can generally speak of four main categories:

1. **Enlightened Body:** In accordance with the Mahayana scriptures, the Buddha's supreme Nirmanakaya form was adorned by the *thirty-two major marks and eighty exemplary features* of a noble being. Each of these characteristics was a result of the accumulation of extraordinary merit over the course of three countless aeons. In accordance with the Vajra Vehicle however, due to his perfect realisation of emptiness, the Buddha's form is inconceivable and subsequently there is no limit to the amount of resultant manifestations.

2. **Enlightened Speech:** When the Buddha speaks, his wisdom communicates with all beings in accordance with their specific mind. It is said that if every sentient being within the six realms was to each ask him a question, with instantaneous understanding he would reply to each with a single word. Regardless of where they were located, his response would be in their own language and as though he were standing there next to them.

3. **Enlightened Mind:** Having achieved the perfection of wisdom, the Buddha's omniscient mind has limitless knowledge of all phenomena. Only the mind of a fully enlightened Buddha can know the infinite complexities of cause and effect that contribute to a given moment of experience. Due to the perfection of great compassion, the Buddha's mind is filled with an unwavering love for all sentient beings, curbing any desire to abide in the peaceful state of Nirvana.

4. **Enlightened Activities:** On the basis of the inseparable qualities of his body, speech and mind, the Buddha manifests continuously for the benefit of sentient beings. Having completely perfected all virtuous qualities, he does not need to analyse options or make decisions to know what needs to be done. Instead he is completely free to respond immediately and spontaneously. Whatever conditions are present in any given moment, he does exactly what is needed to bring the greatest benefit to sentient beings. Like a brilliant sun, his rays are always shining.

By studying the enlightened qualities of the Buddha, we learn that suffering is not fundamentally necessary. By recognising his own Buddha-nature, the Buddha was able to eradicate all obscurations and perfect all good qualities. Endowed with the same Buddha-nature, we too have this capacity. It is possible to transcend our limitations to experience complete enlightenment—to achieve the state of Buddhahood. Trusting in this capacity is the essence of what it means to take refuge in the Buddha.

The actual training for taking refuge in the Buddha consists of two precepts:

1. **Abandon sentient beings as ultimate sources of refuge:** Thorough analysis of the nature of cyclic existence generates the realisation that nothing trapped in samsara has the capacity to completely free you from samsara. Although you may receive temporary benefit from relying on sentient beings, ultimately they are not valid sources of refuge. Even the most powerful god is still conditioned by karma and afflictions, and so is fundamentally limited. For this reason, the only valid source of refuge is an enlightened being who has successfully freed themselves from all forms of limitation. We can still turn to worldly beings for help, but we should not consider them to be our ultimate source of refuge.

2. **Honour and respect the symbols of enlightened mind:** In order to strengthen our mindfulness of our own capacity to achieve enlightenment, we should take every opportunity to honour and respect physical symbols of the Buddha such as statues or paintings. Do not confuse this practice for idol worship, as a statue is merely a condition to remind you of the enlightened qualities of the Buddha. By familiarising yourself with these qualities you inspire your mind and develop virtuous aspirations that will eventually produce the result of enlightenment. It is actually this process of transformation that you are honouring. Every time you see the form of a Buddha, you should either physically prostrate in veneration or mentally bring to mind a feeling of deep respect and admiration.

Exercise 4.3 — Exploring Potentials

- *In a relaxed posture, establish a neutral mind through the practice of mindfulness of breathing.*

- *Take a moment to reflect on your present situation in life. Consider different aspects such as where you live, what activities you engage in, who you relate with and who you think you are as person.*

- *Has your life always been the way it is right now? If not, in what ways is it different? Try to develop a sense for the major milestones which have shaped your present experience. Think of the potential possibilities in each of these key situations and imagine what your life would have been like if the scenario had played out differently.*

- *Now consider the Buddha's life story; consider some of the key milestones that influenced his experience. For each point, imagine how your life would be different:*

  - *If you were raised in the sheltered environment of a royal or noble family where all your desires were met.*

  - *If you realised the suffering nature of this life and longed for more meaning.*

  - *If you abandoned all worldly concerns and dedicated yourself to practicing the Sacred Dharma.*

- *If you achieved profound levels of concentration by practicing meditation and used that concentration to observe the nature of reality.*

- *With your understanding of karma, is there any reason you can think of why these situations could not arise in your own experience? What prevents you from creating the causes for these conditions?*

- *Rest in any conclusions that arise.*

Dharma

The second Jewel is the *Dharma Jewel.* In this context the word Dharma refers to any phenomena which can be used to reveal the nature of reality. On the provisional level, the Dharma refers to the teachings of the Buddha as they manifest in the spoken word or in written texts. These teachings represent the methods used to familiarise ourselves with the Sacred Dharma and so are given the name Dharma. On a deeper level, Dharma refers to the actual attainments which manifest in the minds of practitioners as a result of practicing the teachings. These attainments are fully integrated realisations of different aspects of our ultimate nature. They are direct experiences of what we call our most sacred truth—the definitive meaning of reality.

When we actualise our sacred truth, we are free from all forms of suffering, and for this to occur, our minds need to be free from all forms of obscuration. Specifically, this refers to both the afflicted obscurations that condition our existence through our actions and the cognitive obscurations which condition how reality appears to us. The Dharma is both the methods used to purify the mind and the state of the mind after it has been purified.

The Dharma is capable of purifying the mind because obscurations are adventitious in nature—they are not an inherent part of our mind. They exist due to the mind's innate capacity to manifest both wisdom and ignorance. However, once ignorance takes root, it builds up, covering the basic purity of the mind. To prevent the mind from manifesting ignorance, we need to habituate it to abide in wisdom. Trusting in the innate purity of Buddha-nature and the Dharma's capacity to clear away the obscurations that conceal it, is what it means to take refuge in the Dharma.

The actual training for taking refuge in the Dharma consists of two precepts:

1. **Abandon harming sentient beings:** The root of our suffering is the ignorance which grasps onto an inherently existing self and cherishes this self above all else. On the basis of this self-cherishing, we engage in behaviours which reinforce our bias and condition our experience of reality. Since the essence of the Dharma is to dissolve the self-cherishing mind, we need to shift our focus away from the self and towards an attitude that cherishes others. We do this by recognising that all sentient beings long to be free from suffering and to experience happiness. With a mind rooted in love and compassion we choose to abandon all actions which bring harm to sentient beings as a way of helping them achieve their deepest desires. Even if harming sentient beings is unavoidable in some situations, we must always maintain a strong aspiration to practice non-violence.

2. **Honour and respect the symbols of enlightened speech:** Just as with symbols of the Buddha's body, we should also show reverence for symbols of his speech. This specifically means treating all manifestations of the Buddha's teachings as holy objects. We do this because artefacts like books contain wisdom that can be used to remove the causes of suffering. Without these artefacts we would not have the opportunity to access that wisdom, and without it, we would not have the opportunity to experience genuine happiness. It is out of our deep respect for the transformation that is produced by Dharma that we should be mindful when handling any kind of Dharma text. Traditionally this means keeping our texts in places of honour, preferably high up and off the ground. We should also avoid walking over them or stepping on top of them. If possible, keep them wrapped in cloth to protect them from the elements and preserve them for as long as possible. By training the mind in this way, you create the causes to always have access to these teachings and therefore progress along the path.

Exercise 4.4 — Discovering Your Inner Purity

- *In a relaxed posture, establish a neutral mind through the practice of mindfulness of breathing.*

- *Identify moments in your life where you experienced strong anger. Do you always feel this sort of anger? If not, what condition triggered this experience? Likewise what conditions caused it to stop? Based on this analysis what does this tell you about the nature of anger? Are you your anger or is anger something you have?*

- *Choose other afflictive states of mind and analyse them in a similar way. Are any of these afflictions inseparable from who you are as a person?*

- *Rest in any conclusions that arise.*

Sangha

The third Jewel is the *Sangha Jewel*. The term *Sangha* literally refers to a community that supports our practice of the Dharma. At the provisional level, we can identify two types of community—a *Noble Sangha* and an ordinary Sangha. The Noble Sangha consists of those who have actualised a direct experience of the nature of reality in their mindstream. We can call them *noble beings*. They have realised their own sacred truth through their practice of the Dharma and are therefore valid sources of refuge for those who are yet to generate their level of realisation. Any member of this community has the potential to guide us on the path.

It is a great blessing to rely on a member of the Noble Sangha, but we can also rely on the collective support of an *ordinary Sangha*. Such a Sangha is made up of multiple sentient beings at varying levels of development. Individually, they lack the realisation to be a valid source of refuge, but together, they play a key role in providing us with the support we need to progress along the path. The ordinary Sangha inspires us to practice virtue and helps us overcome the obstacles we encounter. By belonging to a spiritual community, we strengthen the importance of Dharma in our lives and reduce the influence of worldly concerns.

Ultimately, the Sangha represents the inseparability of the Buddha's three bodies—Dharmakaya, Sambhogakaya and Nirmanakaya. Each of these is a manifestation of Buddha-nature and represents the way the enlightened mind is experienced by different types of beings. Whereas the Dharmakaya and Sambhogakaya can only be experienced by Buddhas and Tenth Level Bodhisattvas respectively, the Nirmanakayas are accessible to all forms of sentient beings.

When we refer to the Nirmanakaya form of Buddha Shakyamuni, complete with all the marks and signs, this is what is known as a *Supreme Emanation*. This appearance came into the world around the 6th century (BCE) and remained for approximately eighty years before dissolving. Although we did not have the karma to receive teachings from this form directly, the Buddha continues to manifest to this day in an infinite array of ordinary manifestations that we can experience.

The key point we need to understand is that within each and every emanation of the Buddha is the presence of the enlightened mind of a Buddha, complete with all its qualities. They are in fact never separate. To experience the Buddha, we don't have to travel back in time, we simply need to connect with those who have actualised the Dharma in their minds. When Buddha-nature manifests to us, even only partially, we are experiencing the Buddha and through that experience, our mind is inspired to emulate his qualities.

Trusting in the enlightened qualities of our teachers and the potential qualities of our spiritual community is the essence of taking refuge in the Sangha. It is primarily focused on surrounding ourselves with virtuous influences that support our Dharma practice. Without these influences in our lives, we risk falling back into our non-virtuous habits that only bind us further to samsara. Practicing Dharma can be a battle and requires great diligence and strength of mind and so relying on a community that orients our actions towards a common goal is extremely beneficial. Even if we falter along the way, the power of such a community will keep us moving forward along the path.

The actual training for taking refuge in the Sangha consists of two precepts:

1. **Abandon the influence of worldly friends:** When an alcoholic recognises they have a problem and acknowledges the need to break their addiction, they do not surround themselves with people who are constantly drinking. Instead they look for the support of people with similar intentions and who share their same experiences. Similarly, once we recognise the addiction we have to afflictive states of mind, we need to distance ourselves from those who reinforce our afflictions. How much we distance ourselves will depend on the patterns of our relationships with the people in our lives and the strength of our mind at any given moment. If we analyse a relationship and find it is completely fuelled by afflictions, we should seriously consider avoiding that person entirely. If however we find only certain activities reinforce our afflictions, we can avoid engaging in those particular activities. The main point is to be mindful of the influences in our life and to minimise influences which are not conducive to practicing Dharma.

2. **Honour and respect the symbols of enlightened body:** Reflecting on the qualities of the Buddha can be very helpful, but it is not as strong as encountering those qualities in our own experience. When we look around to see where these qualities manifest most clearly, we are drawn towards spiritual guides who are engaged in a spiritual path. These noble beings are a direct manifestation of the Buddha in a form we can experience and work with. In recognition of this, we devote ourselves to them and show them reverence whenever possible. Each time we do, we strengthen our acknowledgement of our own potential to manifest out of compassion for the sake of sentient beings. Even though we may focus on the enlightened qualities of noble beings, we should also be respectful of the symbols that represent those who are dedicated to the Dharma, namely the monastic robes of a monk or nun. When we encounter these symbols, we should develop an attitude of admiration that aspires to dedicate one's own life to the Dharma. This is a technique for training our mind so it does not matter whether the person actually has realisations or not. Seeing the symbols is enough to trigger our mindfulness and that is what will bring us benefit.

Exercise 4.5 — Examining the Influences in Your Life

- *In a relaxed posture, establish a neutral mind through the practice of mindfulness of breathing.*

- *Bring to mind a person you feel is important in your life. Imagine them in the space in front of you. Now consider the nature of your relationship with this person. What sorts of activities do you engage in together? What is the focus of those activities? What states of mind arise when you engage in them? How do they make you feel? What benefit arises from your interaction with this person?*

- *Rest in any conclusions that arise and then allow the person to fade back into the space of the mind. Repeat the process with someone else. Continue in this way until you are ready to end the session.*

- *Based on what you have seen, can you identify any relationships which you feel are not beneficial? What actions could you take to minimise their influence on your behaviour?*

- *Likewise, are there any relationships you feel are very beneficial? What can you do to emphasise these relationships in your life?*

- *Develop a strong determination to be mindful of these relationships.*

The Inner Three Jewels

The next layer of analysis examines our own internal qualities as the source of our refuge and is similar to how a child is nurtured by their parents. In the beginning the child must rely on their parents for everything but as they gather experience, they begin to trust more in their own capacity. The more self-confidence they develop, the less they need to rely on their parents.

Likewise, we use the Outer Three Jewels as a support to build our capacity and eventually we shift our reliance to our own qualities. We can do this through training with the *Inner Three Jewels*—Guru, Yidam and Dakini. These can also be referred to as *The Three Roots* as they represent the root or essence of the Three Jewels.

Guru

The root of the Buddha is the *Guru*. At the provisional level, the Guru or spiritual guide is the inseparability of the Buddha's wisdom mind and form body and is the Buddha manifesting to you, to guide and support you in your practice. That being said, the role the Guru plays in your life is more important than what the Guru is.

The Guru you see is like a mirror of your own potential—a reflection of the capacity of Buddha-nature—but why do we need a mirror? We need a mirror because without one, we cannot see the mud on our face. Once we realise our face is dirty, we have the opportunity to clean it and eventually, when all the mud is removed, our true face is revealed.

In this way, the external Guru is merely a provisional method we use to develop a connection with our internal Guru, which is currently hidden behind layers of obscuration. By practicing the Dharma, we remove these obscurations and our inner Guru begins to manifest in the aspects of inspired intuition and confidence. Trusting our intuition and in the purity of our own nature is the essence of taking refuge in the Guru.

As we will learn later, the training for strengthening our connection to the inner Guru is known as *Guru Yoga*. This powerful technique is designed to increase our awareness of our own enlightened potential. Through the act of making requests to the Guru, they are seen as inseparable from our own Buddha-nature. Followed by a process of empowerment, we visualise our own potential being ripened so it will manifest in our experience. We then rest our awareness in this experience for as long as we can. Each time we do this is like washing our face and looking in the mirror.

Exercise 4.6 — Learning from Your Inner Guru

- *In a relaxed posture, establish a neutral mind through the practice of mindfulness of breathing.*

- *Bring to mind a moment from your life where you reacted very strongly to something that was said or done to you. Focus on the details of the situation and try to identify what you were reacting against. What caught your mind? Why was it so important to you at the time? How did it feel to react in that way? What was the result of your reaction?*

- *Looking back now, is there any part of your reaction you feel was not very skilful? What problems can you identify in how you reacted? How could the situation have been handled differently? What can you learn about yourself from that experience?*

- *Try to identify other examples where you gained insight about yourself after reflecting on your experience. Under what conditions did these lessons arise? What types of situations seemed to lead to the greatest insight? What impact did these insights have on your mind?*

- *Look at different ways your conscience manifests in your experience. Think of examples of where you listened to your conscience and situations where you chose to ignore it. Which is more common?*

- *Rest your awareness in any conclusions that arise.*

Yidam

The root of the Dharma is the *Yidam*. The word *yidam* is a Tibetan word that loosely translates to "connecting the mind." While working with the Guru is mostly concerned with connecting with your definitive nature, the Yidam is concerned with connecting with the ways that nature manifests in the form of enlightened qualities.

At the provisional level, the Yidam is a symbolic form that represents different enlightened qualities. These forms are traditionally presented in the shapes of wisdom deities which should not be confused with worldly gods who are trapped in samsara. They represent the Sambhogakaya realm of experience. Since we currently do not have the capacity to perceive the Buddha in this form, we must rely on paintings and statues instead.

Due to the infinite capacity of our Buddha-nature to manifest an infinite array of qualities, there are also an infinite number of Yidam deities. Each deity highlights a specific collection of qualities. For instance the figure of Chenrezig mainly represents the quality of compassion, whereas the figure of Vajrapani represents the quality of power.

Shri Kalachakra—Embodiment of the Inner Three Jewels

The principal deity of the Kalachakra Path is Kalachakra, usually depicted in union with his consort Vishvamata. When simplified to its essence, Kalachakra represents the *totality of all reality* and therefore encompasses all potential qualities. This means that by practicing Kalachakra you are effectively practicing all Yidams, and also, if you practice with another Yidam, you are practicing with an aspect of Kalachakra. This is one of the unique features of Kalachakra practice.

The Yidam functions as a method for working with the perception we have of ourselves. Normally we cling to an ordinary self with ordinary qualities, perceiving the world in relation to the sense of identity we have created from our experiences. By cherishing this identity, we perpetuate our own suffering and the suffering of those around us. For this reason, we need to abandon this ordinary identity as the root of samsara and adopt a new identity that reflects the true nature of our reality. Developing faith in one's pure identity is the essence of taking refuge in the Yidam.

The practice used to do this is known as *Deity Yoga*. In this method, the practitioner first dissolves their ordinary identity through recognition of its empty nature, essentially connecting them with the purity of their Buddha-nature. Then from this level of reality, they visualise themselves manifesting in the form of whichever deity they are working with. The aim is to recognise one's own capacity to manifest the same qualities as the Yidam. On this basis, the practitioner adopts a pure view of the self that is based on their enlightened nature. The practice is completed by dissolving this identity, to ensure the reality of this form is not grasped onto as existing inherently.

The Yidam is said to be the root of Dharma, as creating the conditions for one's enlightened qualities to manifest is the outcome of practicing the Dharma. In this way, the Dharma is designed to produce the experience of the Yidam. Remember that the visual form of a Yidam is purely symbolic and is used as a skilful means to manifest the qualities. When each quality is manifest, the actual Yidam has been accomplished.

Exercise 4.7 — Deconstructing the Self

- *In a relaxed posture, establish a neutral mind through the practice of mindfulness of breathing.*

- *Consider the details of your physical body, such as its shape, size and colour. What is this body made of? Think of all the different components, down to the molecular level. Imagine placing these components into separate piles. For instance you could make a pile of iron, a pile of calcium, and so forth. Break it down and visualise these piles in the space before you. Is there anything in those piles which you would say is you?*

- *Now consider the various details of your mind. Think of everything you identify with, such as your memories, your thoughts, your preferences and so forth. Individually, is any one of these things you? If you find something that you think might be you, then examine it more closely. Everything in the mind is experienced on a moment to moment basis, which means each moment can be divided into a beginning, a middle and an end. Which part is you?*

- *When you feel you have exhausted all possibilities, then stop your analysis and simply rest your awareness for as long as you can.*

Dakinis and Dharma Protectors

The root of the Sangha is the *Dakini*. When we refer to the external Sangha, we think of the people who are our companions along our spiritual journey. They support us and protect us, helping us to overcome the many obstacles we face. While there is nothing wrong with seeking external supports, we must not neglect the inner resources we also have.

Although our Buddha-nature is buried beneath layers of obscurations, rays of light can still shine through the cracks. These rays of light manifest within our experience in the form of inspiration and inner wisdom. If we can learn to recognise these experiences, we can use them as supports for our practice.

Provisionally, these experiences manifest in the shape of peaceful deities known as *Dakinis* or in the shape of wrathful deities known as *Dharma Protectors*. Even though we use physical representations like paintings and statues to depict such deities, we must not forget they point to a much deeper meaning. While some highly realised beings can experience these deities as external entities, the vast majority of practitioners tend to experience them on a more symbolic level.

Dakinis often manifest in the experience of comfort and support. It is similar to the experience of a child who feels cared for and loved when held in the arms of their mother. When faced with situations where you doubt your own capacity, this feeling acts as a support to your practice. Afflicted doubt cripples our ability to move forward on the path, causing us to second-guess ourselves and waste time. Through the influence of the Dakinis, we remember that confusion is not who we really are and that in fact we already have everything we need to overcome it. Like a mother holding our hand, they give us the boost of confidence we need to succeed.

When afflictive minds manifest they can generate many obstacles that threaten to overwhelm us. Such situations require the strong support of a direct counter-force to overcome them. When we tap into our innate purity, we develop a feeling of inner strength and this is the manifestation of Dharma Protectors. In the context of our spiritual path, relying on Dharma Protectors is vital for challenging our deep seated misconceptions. The further we are along the path, the more our self-cherishing lashes out to protect itself. However, by connecting with the power of the Dharma Protectors, we maintain our course without reverting back into afflicted patterns of behaviour.

Together, the Dakinis and Dharma Protectors are our front line of defence against the countless demons our minds conjure up. When we truly connect with these qualities within ourselves, we stop believing the story our afflictions feed us and begin to trust in our natural capacity for virtue. This trust is what it means to take refuge in the Dakinis and Dharma Protectors.

There are many practices used to connect with Dakinis and Dharma Protectors. They are similar to Deity Yoga in that they involve visualisations, however we do not visualise ourselves as being the Dakini or Dharma Protector. The focus is instead on making offerings and requests to the visualised being as a method of connecting with the feeling of comfort and support, or strength and power. Although the language and imagery may appear as though we are worshipping an external entity, remember that both the Dakini and Dharma Protector are manifestations of our own nature. The request is made from the perspective of a sentient being needing help from the enlightened aspect of themselves.

Exercise 4.8 — Overcoming Obstacles

- *In a relaxed posture, establish a neutral mind through the practice of mindfulness of breathing.*

- *Think back to different examples when you lacked confidence in your ability to do something; moments in which you were filled with doubt. How did this doubt affect you? Were you able to overcome it? If so, how did you overcome it? What conditions existed to help you overcome it?*

- *Now consider different examples of when you were faced with a difficult situation that overwhelmed you. How did it feel? How did you overcome this challenge? From where did you draw your energy? What did you rely on to give you strength?*

- *Reflecting on these examples, can you identify any sources of inspiration that are effective for boosting your confidence and determination?*

The Secret Three Jewels

All refuge practices are provisional in nature, offering us temporary protection from the different fears that arise in our minds. As we work with each object of refuge, we can remove the limitations induced by our fears and eventually transcend them altogether. However, ultimately the aim of taking refuge is to become a fully enlightened Buddha where we overcome even the need to take refuge.

With this in mind, the last layer of our analysis is focused on the final stage

The Tantric Yogi—Embodiment of the Secret Three Jewels

in our spiritual development. This is similar to a child leaving home, having complete confidence in their own abilities and trust in their capacity to overcome the challenges they will face. As adults, they use whatever resources are available to them and achieve their aims primarily through the power of their own determination.

Through the process of maturing and working with the previous two levels of refuge, we arrive at a place in our journey where we are ready to make full use of the unique conditions now manifesting in our experience. Through the use of extraordinarily skilful means, we learn to use these conditions to embrace the many opportunities they create.

When we speak of the *Secret Three Jewels,* we are referring to the subtle energetic body of channels, winds and essences. By working with these three elements, it is possible to produce the conditions for specific states of mind. The subtle body is viewed as a refuge as it is the basis for developing a direct realisation of our enlightened nature. It does this through the interdependent relationship between the mind and the movements of subtle energy in the body.

Channels

At the most subtle level of dualistic mind, there is a strong connection between the mind and energy. The two are often described as being like horse and rider; wherever one goes, the other follows. This is the principle behind the formation of the network of channels and chakras that constitute the structure of the subtle body.

This structure is the energetic equivalent of our karmic propensities and is formed due to the patterns of thought that arise in the mind. As these patterns stabilise, they form the appearance of channels. This is similar to the way a twirling firebrand creates the illusion of a circle, or how the movement of cars at night appears like streams of light when viewed at high speed. Since no physical structure is actually formed, these channels cannot be detected by physical technology, however they can be experienced by the mind of a trained practitioner.

While there are countless branch channels pervading the body, they can be summarised in three: (1) the left channel, (2) the right channel and (3) the central channel. These channels represent the dominant patterns that condition the mind at any given moment. When the mind is operating in the left and right channels, it is functioning on the basis of gross conceptual mind. Depending on the mind's idea of self, the world is divided into phenomena based on attachment and aversion or things we like and things we don't like. When the mind is evenly balanced between the two there is a sense of neutrality. Regardless of which side is dominant, as long as the mind follows the patterns of the left and right channels, reality will be experienced indirectly through conceptual imputations.

To achieve enlightenment, these imputations must be removed so that reality can be experienced as it is. This requires reliance on the central channel. When the mind is flowing in the central channel, the gross mind becomes dormant and a subtle non-conceptual mind manifests. Dualistic appearances of subject and object may still arise, but they are experienced directly in the present moment without imputations layered on top. When we develop faith in the need to cut the proliferation of thoughts, this is what is meant by taking refuge in the channels.

Exercise 4.9 — Awareness of the Present Moment

- *In a relaxed posture, establish a neutral mind through the practice of mindfulness of breathing.*

- *With the eyes open, rest your gaze in the space in front of you.*

- *Allow your awareness to completely flood your senses, becoming aware of whatever arises in your field of experience.*

- *Rest your mind in stillness in the midst of whatever is arising. There is no need to describe what is happening, just observe your experience as nakedly as possible.*

- *Keep your focus on what is happening right now in the present moment. If your mind wanders off to the past or future, then release the distraction and gently return your awareness to the present moment.*

- *Meditate in this way until you tire.*

Winds

The complex network of channels described above is not fixed. It is a dynamic system that is constantly shifting and adapting based on the movements of the mind. In many ways it is like a river flowing through a gorge; wherever the water flows, the appearance of a river arises. If the water encounters an obstacle it will flow around it, changing course and altering the path the river takes. Likewise, the appearances of channels are produced by the flow of the mind. When the mind acts in accordance with its habitual patterns, it maintains a stable structure but if those patterns are disrupted, the structure changes. To understand how these changes occur, we need to understand the patterns that govern how the mind moves. These patterns are known as *winds*.

In total there are ten types of wind, but for our purpose, we can speak of two main groups: (1) the primary winds and (2) the secondary winds. When the winds flow through the channels in a specific way, they gives rise to a variety of appearances. In general, the primary winds are responsible for producing mental appearances whereas the secondary winds are mainly concerned with gross sensory appearances.

As objective appearances arises in the mind, there is a corresponding subjective reaction. When the mind grasps onto this reaction it strengthens the energy and causes the mind to move. If the grasping counteracts the reaction, the direction of the flow is altered and the mind flows in a different pattern.

As long as the mind is moving, dualistic appearances will continue to arise. For this reason, in order to stop these appearances, movement of the mind needs to cease. This is achieved by training the mind to not grasp onto appearances. We can do this by directing the winds into the central channel, which cuts the gross conceptual mind and allows us to work with very subtle levels of experience, then by gradually working with increasingly more intense experiences, we learn how to remain still without grasping onto the experience. Slowly the winds dissolve completely and we maintain the mind in a state of absorption. When we develop faith in the need to cut all grasping onto appearances, this is what is meant by taking refuge in the winds.

Exercise 4.10 — Settling the Mind in Its Natural State

- *In a relaxed posture, establish a neutral mind through the practice of mindfulness of breathing.*

- *With the eyes open, rest your gaze loosely in the space in front of you.*

- *Withdraw your awareness from your senses and bring your focus toward the space of the mind. If you need help to do this, simply generate a thought and observe how it arises from the space of the mind, abides for a time and then eventually dissolves back into the space of the mind.*

- *Resting your awareness in stillness, observe as mental phenomena such as thoughts, mental imagery and so forth arise and dissolve in the mind.*

- *Do not follow after these phenomena, but instead maintain a flow of awareness that is open, vast and vividly engaged in the meditation— free from grasping, and free from distraction.*

- *If your mind begins to move into distraction, return it to stillness and re-establish your awareness of the space of the mind, then continue observing whatever arises.*

- *Meditate in this way until you tire.*

Subtle Essences

At the moment of conception, three components come together: the genetic material of the father, the genetic material of the mother and a stream of consciousness. Due to intense grasping, these three aspects form what is known as a *subtle essence* or drop. Through the influence of the mind, the cell that contains the drop eventually splits and the genetic material is replicated along with the connection to the mind. Over the course of nine months, this process is repeated countless times giving rise to the formation of a human being. By the time a baby is born, the subtle essences have effectively spread out to every cell in the body.

While most winds tend to be localised to only one area of the body, the all-pervading wind completely saturates every cell and provides the mechanism through which the mind is able to influence those cells. You can think of it like the glue that binds everything together. In the mind, this wind correlates to the most primordial concept of an inherent, substantially existent self. Like the wind, this concept is implicit in all dualistic thoughts and therefore pervades all forms of consciousness.

As long as the *all-pervading wind* remains spread throughout the body, the mind will continue to operate from the perspective of dualistic consciousness. This means that even when the winds are brought into and abide in the central channel, there is still more that needs to be done. To fully transcend our consciousness and abide in the sacred truth of our primordial awareness, we must gather all of the subtle essences, as well as the all-pervading wind to dissolve into the central channel.

This process is achieved through working with the channels and winds. Throughout the channel system, there are nexus points where multiple channels branch out into the body. These points are known as *chakras*. When the winds are made to abide in the central channel at the precise centre of these chakras, the mind enters into a state of absorption which draws in the subtle essences from the areas around the chakra. The longer the mind remains absorbed, the more essences are gathered and the more concentrated the mind becomes. Finally, when all of the essences are gathered at the same point, the most subtle layer of dualistic consciousness is dissolved and primordial awareness becomes manifest. Since only the mind of non-dualistic primordial awareness has the capacity to completely eradicate the most subtle obscurations, this is the ultimate realisation of the Kalachakra Path. When we develop faith in the need to transcend all forms of gross, subtle and very subtle dualistic minds, this is what is meant by taking refuge in the subtle essences.

Exercise 4.11 — Merging the Mind with Space

- *In a relaxed posture, establish a neutral mind through the practice of mindfulness of breathing.*

- *With your eyes fully open, rest your gaze loosely in the space in front of you.*

- *As you exhale, expand your awareness into space, releasing any tension and any objects of focus. Allow the mind to become open and vast.*

- *As you inhale, intensify your presence ever so slightly, brightening your awareness of the present moment without contracting the mind.*

- *Repeat this very subtle oscillation, releasing into space and intensifying your awareness. Do not control the breath, but allow the rhythm to flow naturally.*

- *When the two feelings begin to mix, let go of the oscillation and rest your awareness in a mind that is completely free from grasping and vividly aware of the present moment.*

- *Meditate in this way until you tire.*

BRINGING THE THREE JEWELS INTO YOUR LIFE

Studying the outer, inner and secret forms of the Three Jewels provides us with a basic understanding of what the objects of refuge are, the benefits of taking refuge in them and the practices which strengthen each form of refuge. Although at this stage in your spiritual development you may not be working with the deeper forms of refuge, an introduction to them can help give your practice context and demonstrate how the path evolves over time.

When we consider how each type of refuge acts as a support for practice, we can see that the outer refuge of Buddha, Dharma and Sangha is mainly connected to the causal path of the Sutrayana. The inner refuge of the Guru, Yidam and Dakini is closely tied to the generation stage, and the secret refuge of the channels, winds and essences is linked to the completion stage, both of which belong to the resultant path of the Vajrayana. Together they form a complete path that allows you to transition seamlessly through each level of practice, from foundations all the way to full and complete enlightenment.

With this in mind, as we make our first steps along the path, our main focus should be on establishing the presence of the outer Three Jewels in our lives. To help us to do this, we will look at the training to reinforce our faith in the Three Jewels and give strength to our practice.

Three Complementary Precepts

In addition to the six specific refuge precepts already presented above, there are three general precepts that highlight the qualities we need to develop in relation to the Three Jewels. When each quality is present in our mind, our refuge will be strong and our practice will be oriented in the right direction.

1. **Respect, Honour and Veneration:** In order for the Three Jewels to have an impact on our minds, we need to develop a genuine feeling for their presence in our lives. We do this by developing an attitude of reverence for anything that reminds us of their qualities. This is the premise behind why we honour the symbols of the Buddha's enlightened body, speech and mind. The more we look for the Three Jewels in our lives, the more we will see them and the more they will inspire and support our behaviour.

   Nowhere are the Three Jewels more manifest than within one's spiritual guide. If we learn to see our teacher's body as the Sangha, their speech as the Dharma and their mind as the Buddha, every time we see our spiritual guide, we also see the Three Jewels. This attitude brings the Three Jewels out of the realm of abstract concepts and into a reality we interact with directly.

   Identifying your teacher in this way helps maintain a steadfast devotion that diligently works to please the spiritual guide and strives to avoid harming that relationship in any way. By entrusting yourself to the Three Jewels as represented by the teacher, you will begin to realise that all well-being flows from their compassion.

2. **Mindfulness of Blessings:** When we maintain awareness of the Three Jewels in our lives, we receive their blessings in the form of inspiration and confidence. Being mindful of these blessings strengthens our bond with them and allows us to see the incredible opportunities that this life presents us, such as the extraordinary occurrence of having met the Three Jewels and engaging in spiritual practice, instead of being buried beneath the weight of intense negative karma.

   We can apply mindfulness to the presence of the Three Jewels in our lives in something as simple as moving in a particular direction. Take a moment to bring to mind and pay homage to the *Six Buddhas of Primordial Wisdom*: (1) when moving east, think of Buddha Amoghasiddhi; (2) when moving south, think of Buddha Ratnasambhava; (3) when moving north, think of Buddha Amitabha; (4) when moving west, think of Buddha Vairochana; (5) when moving up, think of Buddha Akshobhya and (6) when moving down, think of the Buddha Vajrasattva.

Each of these Buddha figures represents a different aspect of our Buddha-nature and so by recalling them, you reinforce that all your experiences of sights, sounds, smells, tastes, sensations and thoughts are manifestations of that nature. Wherever you go and whatever you do is all dependent on the blessings of these Buddhas.

3. **Gratitude:** A deep sense of gratitude naturally arises when we recognise how the blessings of the Three Jewels pervade every aspect of our experience. When we encounter something that pleases us or brings us joy, we should remember that such an experience is only possible because of the incredible kindness of the Three Jewels.

   We can do this by developing the habit of offering our enjoyable experiences to the Three Jewels. For instance, before eating a meal, bring them to mind and mentally offer the nourishment and pleasure you are about to receive. Likewise, if you encounter a situation that strikes you as beautiful, such as a sunrise or a full moon on a clear night, this too can be offered. No matter what we are doing we can find opportunities to express our gratitude towards the Three Jewels.

   Making offerings is entirely for our own benefit as the Three Jewels do not actually need anything from us. It is simply a skilful support for establishing mindfulness of the role Buddha-nature plays in our experience, while also promoting a mind of non-grasping and generosity.

If you are able to practice in this way, eventually these precepts become second nature. When you are able to maintain your conduct even in a dream, this is a very good sign that the practice has taken root. It shows that you are developing an authentic refuge in the Three Jewels which will protect you and guide you all the way to enlightenment.

Strengthening Your Commitment

Taking refuge in the Three Jewels is considered to be the gateway for entering the Buddhist path. It is the primary condition that distinguishes between a follower of the Buddha-Dharma and a follower from another wisdom tradition such as Christianity or Islam. Whether or not someone has taken refuge depends entirely on the state of their mind. It is an internal realisation, not something that is bestowed by someone else. As authentic refuge is a result of developing strong faith in the objects of refuge, it requires significant reflection on their qualities.

After careful consideration, if you feel confident in your desire to follow the Buddha's teachings, you may choose to participate in a *Refuge Ceremony.* This short ritual is an opportunity to celebrate your commitment to the path by declaring it publicly in the presence of your spiritual guide. At the end of this ritual it is customary for the spiritual guide to give the student a Buddhist name which symbolises the start of a new direction in their life.

In addition to committing oneself to uphold the *Six Refuge Precepts* and the *Three Complementary Precepts*, it is also common for students to take one or more *Vows of Personal Liberation.* These vows are taken for the span of a single lifetime and are mainly concerned with abandoning non-virtuous actions of the body and speech. Since there is a separate ceremony for ordaining monks and nuns, this ceremony generally focuses on what are known as the *Five Vows of a Lay Practitioner*:

1. No killing
2. No stealing
3. No sexual misconduct
4. No lying
5. No intoxicants.

The first four are essentially the same as the first four actions from the *Ten Non-Virtuous Actions* (refer to the subject of karma in Book One). The only difference is that here we are making a strong commitment to uphold these behaviours until our death. As some people are more capable of keeping these vows than others, a student is given the option to take one or more, based on the level of commitment they feel comfortable with. At the very least, a student must commit to the vow of *no killing* as they have already made the commitment to abandon harming sentient beings in relation to taking refuge in the Dharma.

With regards to the fifth vow of *no intoxicants*, the intention of this vow is for the student to abstain from consuming anything which creates the conditions for them to break the other four vows. In the case of the influence of alcohol or drugs, our mental faculties can become so impaired we are unable to make sound decisions and this may lead to acts of non-virtue. It is therefore generally advised to give up these substances. Since the definition of what constitutes an intoxicant can vary, it is considered good practice to follow the specific instructions of the spiritual guide who bestows the vow.

On the basis of the lay vows, you may decide to seek monastic ordination. This is a very important decision and should be made in close consultation with your spiritual guide. While being a monk or nun is an amazing blessing, it is very important to have access to a monastic community that will support you in your training. Taking ordination without this support generally results in monks or nuns abandoning their discipline which carries with it very serious karmic consequences. If you are sincerely interested in this level of commitment, approach your spiritual guide to learn in more detail what is involved.

For those who would like to experience the essence of monastic conduct, there is also a method for taking the root vows for a temporary period of time. These vows are known as the *Eight Mahayana Precepts*. This practice was originally designed for people in positions of power such as kings and queens who did not have the opportunity to dedicate themselves to an ascetic way of life. The vows are normally taken very early in the morning before dawn and last for twenty-four hours. During this time, the practitioner abides by eight precepts which includes the vow to only consume one meal before midday. This method of fasting helps reduce our attachment to food while at the same time creating the conditions for a clear mind that is primed for meditation.

REVIEW OF KEY POINTS

- Taking refuge means to clearly identify the objects most supportive to your spiritual practice and to develop faith in them. In all Buddhists paths, the only valid foundation for achieving enlightenment is the Three Jewels: (1) Buddha, (2) Dharma and (3) Sangha.

- There are two causes for taking refuge in the Three Jewels: (1) fear of something you wish to avoid and (2) faith in something to protect you from that fear.

- Three types of fear can be considered beneficial for motivating spiritual practice: (1) fear of gross suffering such as pain and torment; (2) fear of the conditioned existence of samsara; and (3) fear of abandoning sentient beings by resting in nirvana.

- Faith means to develop conviction about some aspect of reality. There are three aspects of authentic faith: (1) spontaneous faith which inspires the mind; (2) reasoned faith that clears away doubt; and (3) confident faith which is unshakeable.

- Generally speaking, the Buddha is the fully enlightened teacher, the Dharma is the teachings which leads to enlightenment and the Sangha are the community that supports us in our practice.

- Specifically, we can think of the Three Jewels in different ways based on the stage of the path we are currently focused on. From gross to subtle, there are (1) the Outer Three Jewels of Buddha, Dharma and Sangha; (2) the Inner Three Jewels of Guru, Yidam and Dakini; and (3) the Secret Three Jewels of Channels, Winds and Essences.

- In accordance with the Outer Three Jewels, taking refuge in the Buddha means developing faith in our capacity as sentient beings to achieve Buddhahood. The precepts are to (1) abandon sentient beings as an ultimate refuge and (2) honour and respect the symbols of enlightened mind.

- Taking refuge in the Dharma means developing faith in our capacity to remove all obscurations from our mind through practicing the Dharma. The precepts are (1) abandon the harming of sentient beings and (2) honour and respect the symbols of enlightened speech.

- Taking refuge in the Sangha means developing faith in the enlightened qualities of your teachers and the potential qualities of your spiritual community. The precepts are (1) abandon the influence of worldly friends and (2) honour and respect the symbols of enlightened body.

- In accordance with the Inner Three Jewels, the root of the Buddha is the Guru. This means developing faith in your own intuition and the purity of your own nature.

- The root of the Dharma is the Yidam and involves recognising your own capacity to manifest enlightened qualities and developing faith that this is your true nature.

- The root of the Sangha is the Dakinis and Dharma Protectors. This means developing faith in our capacity to overcome all obstacles and reveal our underlying purity.

- In accordance with the Secret Three Jewels, the essence of the Sangha is the Channels. This means developing faith in the need to cut the conceptual mind by relying on the central channel.

- The essence of the Dharma is the Winds, which means developing faith in the need to cut all forms of grasping by dissolving the winds in the central channel.

- The essence of the Buddha is the Subtle Essences, which means developing faith in the need to abandon the dualistic consciousness by gathering the subtle essences into the central channel.

- The Outer, Inner and Secret Three Jewels correspond to the practices of the sutrayana, generation stage and completion stage.

- There are Three Complementary Precepts that should be cultivated: (1) respect, honour and veneration; (2) mindfulness of blessings; and (3) gratitude for their kindness.

- If you want to strengthen your commitment to following the Buddha's teachings, you can participate in a Refuge Ceremony. During this ceremony you publicly take refuge in the Three Jewels while committing to uphold (1) the Six Refuge Precepts, (2) the Three Complementary Precepts and (3) one or more of the Five Lay Precepts.

PART TWO

Entering the Path of a Bodhisattva

CHAPTER FIVE

Overcoming Bias with Love and Compassion

According to the *Karmic Law of Cause and Effect,* for every action we perform with our body, speech and mind, a result will be experienced that is similar in nature to the cause. The nature of an action is influenced mostly by the intention of the mind performing it and so intention forms the connection between an action and a desire. When we want to do something our intention engages us into an action to make it happen. It acts like a magnet drawing our attention toward a particular point and our action then moves us in that direction.

If we change the intention, we change the nature of the action. For instance, consider three people following the Kalachakra Path. The first person wants to find greater peace and harmony in their current life, the second desires to be completely free from the cycle of conditioned existence, whereas the third wants to achieve the state of a fully enlightened Buddha. While all three engage in the same actions of practicing the Kalachakra Path, as their intentions are different, the results experienced will also be different. Only the third person will create the causes for enlightenment.

For this reason, once we have established a strong connection with the Three Jewels through the practice of refuge, we turn our attention toward establishing the most meaningful motivation possible. Such a motivation ensures that every action we engage in from this point onward brings us closer to our ultimate goal of unveiling our sacred truth.

THE IMPORTANCE OF DEVELOPING BODHICITTA

What makes Kalachakra unique among systems of practice is its focus on manifesting the non-dual awareness that knows reality as it is. The only motivation capable of achieving such an experience is known as *Bodhicitta,* therefore, to authentically practice the Kalachakra Path, we will need to establish Bodhicitta in our minds.

Bodhicitta is important in the beginning, in the middle and at the end of the path. In the beginning it defines our actions as causes for enlightenment. Just as the act of taking refuge distinguishes a practitioner of the Buddha-Dharma, generating the sublime motivation of Bodhicitta distinguishes a practitioner of the Great Vehicle (Mahayana) from a practitioner of the Foundational Vehicle (Hinayana). This is the difference between attaining individual liberation and attaining complete enlightenment. Only the Mahayana contains the skilful methods needed to remove the very subtle obscurations which prevent the omniscient mind from manifesting.

Bodhicitta is important in the middle, as it becomes the driving force behind all our actions, imbuing everything we do with the desire to achieve enlightenment for the benefit of all sentient beings. When this motivation arises spontaneously in our mind, we accumulate oceans of merit and wisdom, fulfilling the primary conditions for achieving Buddhahood. Due to its vast scope, our life then takes on incredible meaning, ensuring that we will accomplish not only our own aims but also those of all sentient beings.

Finally, Bodhichitta is important in the end, because it is the result of the path itself. In Tibetan, the term for Bodhicitta is *jangchup kyi sem*. Here *jang* refers to "complete purity", *chup* means "total attainment or mastery" and *sem* means "mind". Together they can be translated as "the complete mastery of a pure mind". In this way, Bodhicitta refers to a mind that is completely free from all obscurations and able to manifest every good quality without limitation. This is the very meaning of Buddhahood.

THE NEED FOR GREAT COMPASSION

At the heart of Bodhicitta is the desire for sentient beings to be free from suffering. When this desire encompasses everyone without preference or bias, it is known as *great compassion*. When great compassion exists in the mind, we naturally do everything in our power to bring benefit. As it is unacceptable that our dear sentient beings endure any further pain, we take the responsibility of creating the conditions to end all their suffering.

When we consider the sheer vastness of sentient beings that exist throughout the six realms, such a desire can seem impossible to achieve. If we lack great compassion, our Bodhicitta will be without strength and we may find ourselves reverting back to emphasising our own welfare. By cultivating great compassion we sustain our resolve, remaining steady when faced with the scope of the task at hand and the difficulties entailed.

Furthermore, the defining characteristic of a fully enlightened Buddha is the attainment of the Dharmakaya wisdom truth body that does not abide in peace but manifests countless form bodies for the benefit of sentient beings. The quality that ensures this form of non-abiding nirvana is great compassion, and without it, a Buddha would be no different from a Shravaka or Pratyeka-buddha Arhat.

Recognising the importance of establishing great compassion, we must ask ourselves what prevents it from arising? The answer is *self-cherishing*. Fully qualified great compassion is completely free from all forms of bias, and therefore anything that creates bias will limit the extent of our compassion.

Bias arises when we relate to the world through the lens of self-cherishing. Grasping onto the five aggregates as an inherently existing self splits our world into two groups. On one side there is "me" and on the other side is everything else that is "not me". Self-cherishing is the mind that believes "me" to be the most important. As a result of this view, we engage in actions that fulfil the desires of "me" or the self. If the self is cold, it seeks warmth; if the self is hungry, it desires food and if the self is threatened, it will lash out in defense. As long as the self-cherishing mind is present, everything revolves around the needs of the self. While these needs may temporarily align to those around us, they are often contradictory, inevitably leading to conflict.

Without great compassion, it is not possible to generate authentic Bodhicitta and without removing self-cherishing, we cannot experience great compassion. Realising this, the Buddha taught methods to expand the heart and counteract our habitual tendency to cherish the self. These methods are considered a vital preliminary for training in the generation of Bodhicitta.

THE ANTIDOTE TO SELF-CHERISHING— THE FOUR IMMEASURABLE QUALITIES

The primary method for removing self-cherishing is through the cultivation of four qualities called *The Four Immeasurables*—love, compassion, joy and equanimity. Each quality develops meaningful connections with sentient beings that chip away the afflicted states of mind that promote self-cherishing. As the barrier between self and others begins to crumble, these qualities strengthen and expand until they eventually become immeasurable in nature.

Quality	Antidote For	False Facsimile
Love	Hatred	Selfish Affection
Compassion	Cruelty	Despair
Joy	Envy	Frivolous Pleasure
Equanimity	Attachment and Aversion	Indifference

Table 5.1 - The Four Immeasurables

The essence of these four qualities is best expressed in the aspirational prayer:

May all sentient beings have happiness and the causes of happiness.
May all sentient beings be free from suffering and the causes of suffering.
May all sentient beings never be separated from the great bliss that is free from suffering.
May all sentient beings abide in equanimity, free from bias, attachment and aversion.

We will now examine each line separately to develop insight into their nature.

Love

The first line expresses the quality of immeasurable love:

May all sentient beings have happiness and the causes of happiness.

In this context, love is not an emotion but the desire for a particular outcome, specifically, the desire for all sentient beings to experience the temporary happiness of pleasurable feelings, as well as the genuine happiness of connecting with their ultimate nature. This aspiration recognises that happiness arises on the basis of specific causes and conditions, and therefore in order for this desire to be met, sentient beings need to create the causes for their own happiness.

This understanding is significantly different from the way that love is commonly portrayed in our popular culture. What we normally view as "love" is often rooted in attachment and as attachment is a major cause for suffering, such forms of love cannot lead to genuine happiness. By learning to distinguish love from attachment, we can use whatever love we have to cultivate genuine love. In general, we can speak of five main types of love:

1. **Possessive Love:** This refers to love which is tainted by covetousness, pride and superficial concerns. It is displayed in a love of objects for vain and egotistical purposes, for no other reason than to satisfy oneself. Because this love is so contaminated by self-cherishing, it contains very little compassion and is predominantly made up of feelings of ownership and attachment. By recognising possessive love, we can learn to abandon it completely and thereby make space for other forms of love to arise.

2. **Romantic Love:** This is the strong emotional form of love we normally refer to when we say two people are "in love." It manifests as attraction, passion and adoration towards another person and is usually mixed with feelings of bliss, pride and strength of focus. As it is generally based on self-centred motivations, it often comes with a sense of possessiveness, expressed as jealousy. All of these factors make romantic love very biased.

   Sadly, romantic love rarely lasts for long. When two people "fall in love", frequently their bond is held together by an attachment to the way the other person makes them feel. When conditions inevitably change, and that feeling is lost, the relationship falls apart. In such a relationship there is little real caring and compassion for the other person.

   If, however, a couple work to cultivate their connection on the basis of compassion, it can open the door to qualities such as thoughtfulness, caring and gratitude. This is a sign that romantic love is dissolving and a more stable form of love is taking shape. In this way, a constructive and loving relationship can develop between two people that helps them grow together in joy and happiness.

3. **Endearing Love:** This form of love evokes feelings of warmth and a sense of closeness toward other living beings, finding them both lovable and endearing. We often experience this type of love when encountering traditionally "cute" things like babies and animals, where there is an instant opening up and affection felt toward them.

   Endearing love can also arise through exposure to another person over time. Through the development of familiarity, we establish a strong bond and we come to naturally care about their welfare, such as with friends and family. Because of its capacity to bring joy, it can often become mixed with an attachment to that joy, as well as a degree of possessiveness.

   When nurtured in a healthy way by focusing on the needs of the other person, this form of love is a wonderful basis for developing connections. However, if the focus becomes too self-centred, endearing love can quickly degenerate into possessive love.

4. **Parental Love:** This is the love a parent feels for their child and is sometimes referred to as "motherly love". It is strong and steady, and often lasts the duration of a lifetime. When this form of love is present, there are usually very few conditions placed on the relationship. Regardless of what the child does, the parent doesn't lose the fundamental compassion and care they feel for them.

   Unfortunately this form of love can be very biased when combined with feelings of ownership, pride and attachment. The stronger the attachment to one's own child, the less love felt toward those who are not and this can lead to actions which bring suffering to others. If this bias can be removed however, parental love can be extended to include a greater number of people.

5. **Unconditional Love:** This form of love is based on a deep understanding of the nature of reality and empathy for the experiences of sentient beings. This highly caring nature values all forms of life, regardless of their shape or size. Throughout our history we can find many inspirational figures who embody unconditional love. For instance the great sages Jesus, Mohammed and the Buddha made compassion and love a central part

of their teachings. Or more recently, Mother Teresa and His Holiness the Dalai Lama, whose immeasurable love for sentient beings meant that even when they appeared to suffer, their hearts remained filled with great joy and compassion.

Fundamental to this form of love is the quality that views all sentient beings as equal to oneself. This generally requires substantial reflection and training to develop, although some exceptional people are born with this quality and feelings of intense caring for others arises naturally. This is usually a sign they have engaged in considerable training during previous lives.

Unconditional love is most powerful when combined with wisdom, making your caring for others genuine, clear and stable. Without wisdom, you may rely on only sympathy or pity which can make it difficult to find a solution that ultimately brings benefit to others. As a consequence, suffering may be the result, causing you to become discouraged and your resolve to weaken. If this occurs, your love is diminished and becomes ineffective. On the other hand, genuine caring combined with wisdom is the defining quality of a Bodhisattva's attitude. It is a bravery that never gives up in the face of hardship.

Of these five forms of love, only unconditional love works as an effective antidote to self-cherishing. It specifically counteracts the affliction of hatred which motivates conflict and fuels the division between sentient beings. Whereas hatred seeks to harm, break connections and reject those who are different, love seeks to nurture and support, embracing diversity and fostering our interdependent nature.

Genuine love is like a mother bird caring for her chicks. She provides them with a soft comfortable nest and shelters them with the warmth of her wings. She is always gentle and protects them until they are ready to fly away. Like a mother bird, we should be kind in thought, word and deed to all the beings of the three realms.

We know we have generated genuine love when we develop a sincere desire for all sentient beings to experience happiness and wellbeing. We know it is stable when we do not lose our desire for their happiness even if they cause us harm or make our lives difficult.

With this type of love, we strive to use our body, speech and mind to bring benefit and to help in whatever way we can. We try to do our best to make every interaction meaningful by avoiding harsh speech and acting in a way that is gentle and pleasant to those involved. No matter how much benefit we may bring, we expect nothing in return, simply being content with the knowledge of others' happiness. If we can generate this level of kindness into every aspect of our life, there will be no room for hatred to take root.

Exercise 5.1 — Meditation on Loving-Kindness

- *In a relaxed posture, establish a neutral mind through the practice of mindfulness of breathing.*

- *Bring to mind your vision of genuine happiness. Imagine having all the conditions you need to truly flourish, both internally and externally. Think of the joy and satisfaction you would experience. Develop great confidence that you have the capacity to achieve this state.*

- *Visualise this inner potential at your heart, manifesting as a radiant white orb of light. Even though this orb is small, it is the source of all virtue and joy. With each out-breath, imagine the orb sends out rays of light into all directions, completely flooding your body with the warmth of peace and harmony.*

- *Now imagine the light extending outwards and filling the room. Bring to mind the sentient beings in your immediate vicinity and imagine the light fills their bodies as well. Imagine they are receiving everything they need to achieve their most heartfelt desires and to experience genuine lasting peace and harmony in their lives. As you do this, think to yourself: "May you be well and happy! May you experience the causes for peace and harmony!"*

- *Repeat this process with each out-breath, expanding the sphere of light and encompassing more and more sentient beings. Imagine them filled with joy and satisfaction and strengthen your aspiration.*

- *Continue in this way until you tire. Finally, release the visualisation and rest in your awareness for a few minutes before ending your meditation.*

Compassion

The next line expresses the quality of immeasurable compassion:

May all sentient beings be free from suffering and the causes of suffering.

The essence of compassion is the desire for sentient beings to be free from suffering. From the perspective of the person experiencing compassion, it is a strong caring for the welfare of another. Just as with the quality of love, suffering does not arise in isolation; it manifests on the basis of causes and conditions and therefore, in order for someone to be free from suffering in the future, they must be free from the causes of suffering.

Love and compassion naturally complement each other, representing two sides of a coin. While love is concerned with what we want sentient beings to experience, compassion emphasises what we hope they don't experience. The main difference is that love desires for sentient beings to achieve their **potential** by going beyond worldly pleasures, to actualise the perfection of peace and harmony through the achievement of full enlightenment. Compassion works with the *actuality* of our lives, with what we are experiencing at the present moment. Love therefore looks to the future, whereas compassion is focused in the present.

Like love, it is easy to confuse compassion with similar ideas. As we discussed earlier, great compassion is the heart of bodhicitta, and so to understand clearly the role that compassion plays in our motivation, it can be helpful to clarify our terms. The following are some aspects that represent different forms of compassion that we can experience:

1. **Empathy:** This is a feeling that reflects how another being is feeling. As it is not a desire, it cannot be considered an authentic form of compassion but it is still a very important component of it. It is difficult to establish the wish for all sentient beings to be free from suffering if we are unable to connect with their suffering. This is why we need to first spend time developing the desire for ourselves to be free from cyclic existence by contemplating our own potential suffering. With empathy, we can then extend that desire to encompass the same wish for everyone else.

2. **Sympathy:** Empathy creates an emotional link between the self and others, and how we respond to that feeling determines whether it is genuine compassion. When we observe suffering but feel helpless or unwilling to do anything about it, we are generally experiencing sympathy. This manifests as pity or sorrow for the plight of the sentient beings concerned and although we feel for them, recognising their pain, we don't know how we can help. This can occur when we watch the news and see the plight of victims of a crime or refugees. While there is a desire for them to be free from their suffering, there is no wisdom regarding what can be done to change their situation. This sort of reaction can build over time and lead to emotional burnout or even depression. As it is not connected to action, it is of limited benefit for both ourselves and for the object of our sympathy.

3. **Gross Compassion:** Genuine compassion is always connected with wisdom. It sees suffering and recognises the potential to be free from it and, on this basis, engages in actions to help those experiencing it. The level of compassion that arises is dependant on the depth of wisdom. When compassion responds to obvious forms of suffering such as poverty, starvation, war or natural disasters, we call it *gross compassion*. It is generally associated with moments of crisis when the suffering is too intense to ignore and often motivates people to volunteer their time to directly help those affected, or to make donations to support volunteer efforts. Unfortunately this type of compassion is biased in the sense that when the crisis is over or ceases to hold our attention, the suffering is forgotten and we return to our usual lives.

4. **Subtle Compassion:** The next level of compassion is based on understanding our potential for suffering. It recognises that as long as we have the causes for suffering in our mindstreams, we are vulnerable to those causes ripening in our experience. Just like a ticking time bomb, we are always on the verge of pain and torment. This type of compassion is known as *subtle compassion* because it is difficult to perceive. Unlike gross suffering that is obviously unwanted, many people fail to see how

their attachment to worldly pleasures conditions their minds to suffering and therefore they don't see the need to do anything about it. This lack of awareness leads them to engage in actions that only guarantee the experience of gross suffering in the future. By developing subtle compassion, we are motivated to help people practice virtue and thereby create the cause for future happiness instead.

5. **Non-referential Compassion:** Although subtle compassion can be incredibly beneficial for sentient beings, it is still limited in scope as it is rooted in a dualistic view of reality. If we could guarantee that sentient beings would never again engage in non-virtuous deeds, there would be no problem, but unfortunately this is not the case. The reality of the situation is that as long as we are under the control of our karma, we will always have the potential to create the causes for suffering which inevitably leads to the experience of suffering. To be completely free from suffering, we need to abandon the dualistic view altogether. The key to achieving this freedom is the realisation of emptiness. When subtle compassion is mixed with this realisation, it becomes *non-referential compassion*. Such compassion recognises the plight of all sentient beings and so is not influenced by bias or limitations. As such, it becomes the basis for compassion to become immeasurable in nature and motivates us to practice the Dharma and attain realisations. Only through actualising the path in our experience can we ever hope to guide others to liberation.

Of these five qualities, the first two are conditions for genuine compassion to arise. Without empathy, there is no connection and without sympathy there is no desire for the object of our compassion to be free from suffering. The last three are then differentiated on the basis of the wisdom we bring to the situation and the corresponding benefits achieved. In order for compassion to be an authentic support for bodhicitta, it must be based on the deepest form of compassion—non-referential compassion. Only non-referential compassion is informed by the wisdom that realises the empty nature of reality and therefore only non-referential compassion can act as an antidote to the root ignorance of self-grasping.

We must be especially careful not to confuse sorrow for compassion. When sympathy has no wisdom it can degenerate into grief which is a more intense form of sadness that weighs heavily on the mind, leading to a pessimistic and apathetic view. Its function is the opposite to that of compassion as it creates the feeling that there is no point to anything and therefore doesn't motivate you into action. It is a self-defeating attitude which forgets about the welfare of sentient beings and allows us to be swallowed by feelings of despair.

The key to avoiding being overwhelmed by such emotions is to develop a profound awareness of the many ways in which we ourselves suffer. By establishing the wisdom that understands the source of our own suffering, we can see the possibility of overcoming it. If we can overcome our own suffering, then so can all sentient beings. This means that no matter what the situation may be, there is always something that can be done, even if it is only to generate the aspiration for sentient beings to be free from suffering. This alone contributes to reducing our self-cherishing which allows us to develop our inner qualities and eventually achieve enlightenment. As we progress along the path in this way we develop the capacity to bring greater benefit to those who suffer.

The practice of compassion can purify us of all our previous negative actions and allow the precious bodhicitta to develop and grow. We must therefore persevere by meditating upon compassion, for what other choice do we have? The image given for meditating on compassion is that of a mother with no arms, whose child is being swept away by a river. How unbearable the anguish of this mother, with such intense love, but helpless to catch hold of her child. Running alongside the river, weeping in heartbreak as her struggling child is carried away by the torrent.

All beings of the three realms are drowning in the ocean of samsara, just like the child in the river. We should open our hearts to the pain they are experiencing and realise we have no means of saving them as we exist now. Meditate upon this and contemplate what actions you can take to help. Have faith in your teacher and the Three Jewels and ask for their guidance in freeing these beings from their suffering.

Exercise 5.2 — Meditation on Compassion

- *In a relaxed posture, establish a neutral mind through the practice of mindfulness of breathing.*

- *Begin by bringing your awareness to your own experience. Consider different examples of the struggles you have faced in your life. This can include experiences of sickness, as well as mental struggles such as anxiety and dissatisfaction. Nurture your desire to be free from these forms of suffering. Imagine your mind is filled with peace and harmony, and all traces of craving, hostility and confusion are removed.*

- *Now turn your attention to a loved one or friend who is currently struggling in their life. Really connect with the person by seeing the world from their point of view and imagining what they must be experiencing. Return back to your own perspective and strengthen the desire for this person to be free from their suffering and its causes. Imagine they find relief from their struggles and develop the freedom to bring greater peace and harmony into their life.*

- *Consider another person who is overwhelmed by afflictive states of mind that causes them to engage in non-virtuous behaviour. Think of the results this type of behaviour will bring them. Again try to see the world from their perspective and relate to their confusion. Allow a strong yearning to arise that wishes this person would encounter an authentic path they can follow to overcome these mental afflictions. Imagine they find a path and begin cultivating the causes for their happiness.*

- *Allow this person to fade into the background and open your awareness to include everyone in the world. Take time to attend to anyone who arises in your mind, including entire groups of people you know are currently suffering. Recognising that we are all deserving of compassion, develop the wish: "May you be free from suffering and its causes! May we all strive to achieve peace and harmony in this world!"*

- *Continue in this way until you tire. Release the visualisation and rest in your awareness for a few minutes before ending your meditation.*

Joy

The next quality to be cultivated is immeasurable joy:

May all sentient beings never be separated from the great bliss that is free from suffering.

The essence of joy is to take delight in the well-being and happiness of others. Cultivation of this quality is generally concerned with two aspects: (1) taking delight in the happiness of others and (2) taking delight in acts of virtue which are the causes of happiness. Each provides a different type of support for your practice.

The first is useful for counteracting the frustration that can arise due to the strength of our habituation to non-virtue. When we concentrate too much on our aspirations for the future, we can sometimes feel as though we are not progressing fast enough and it is easy to become disheartened by the insurmountable work we still need to do. Taking delight in the happiness of sentient beings helps balance out this feeling, inspiring the mind and reminding us why we are working so hard.

With the second, we recognise that the only method for achieving lasting genuine happiness is through the cultivation of virtue, and so whenever we see someone practicing virtue, we are joyfully aware they are creating the causes for their own future happiness. This not only reinforces our sense of purpose, but also strengthens the propensity of those actions in our own mind and we thereby indirectly accumulate merit. The more we rejoice in a particular type of action, the more value we place on it and the more likely we are to perform it in the future.

Even though the practice of rejoicing is essentially the same regardless of the focus, the resulting merit generated will vary significantly based on whose actions you rejoice in. Generally speaking, it is said that by rejoicing in those who are less spiritually developed, you will generate twice the merit that they have created. By rejoicing in those who are equally developed, the merit is equal, and by rejoicing in someone who is more developed than yourself, half their merit is generated. These numbers are of course not meant to be taken too literally, they simply give us an idea of the relationship between object and merit. On the basis of this understanding, we can identify five types of beings who are worthy to rejoice in:

1. **Buddhas:** A fully enlightened being, a Buddha, engages in limitless activities for the benefit of all sentient beings. Not only does their compassion encompass all sentient beings, their capacity is free from all limitations and therefore can manifest in whatever form is needed. By rejoicing in the benefit a Buddha's actions produce, we generate an ocean of merit that strengthens our desire to actualise our own enlightened qualities.

2. **Bodhisattvas:** On a very subtle level we can consider the Tenth Level Bodhisattvas who accumulate immeasurable qualities for the benefit of sentient beings. In particular, we can rejoice in the actions of the *Bodhisattva Kings of Shambhala* who watch over this world and inspire us to practice Kalachakra. On a more gross level, we can consider the *Bodhisattva Lineage Masters* who demonstrated how to practice the Kalachakra Path, inspiring countless people to virtue. This includes rejoicing in the enlightened activities of your own *spiritual guide* who is kinder than all the Buddhas as they work directly with us in a human form. By rejoicing in this way, we strengthen our desire to practice the path and to actualise all attainments.

3. **Pratyeka and Shravaka Arhats:** Even though we are not personally aiming to achieve Nirvana as an end result, those who have attained the state of a fully liberated Arhat are truly extraordinary beings. They have realised emptiness and removed all afflicted obscurations, accomplishing a state that is completely free from gross and subtle forms of suffering. Just consider the enormous virtue required to reach this level of attainment. By rejoicing in this achievement, we strengthen our confidence that liberation is possible.

4. **Ordinary Sentient Beings:** For sentient beings who have not yet entered the path of seeing, we can rejoice in all forms of virtue, whether big or small. Just as the young beggar girl who created the causes for her own enlightenment when she offered a handful of dust with a pure intention to the Buddha, so too sentient beings who perform virtuous deeds are

creating the causes for genuine happiness. By rejoicing in the virtues of these beings, we strengthen our confidence that we are moving closer to the day when all beings will be free from suffering.

5. **Yourself:** We should not forget to also rejoice in our own virtue. Every virtuous deed we perform accumulates more merit and wisdom, bringing us closer to our aim of complete enlightenment. As we do this, we develop our capacity and our ability to bring more benefit to sentient beings, creating further opportunities to rejoice and generate even more merit. When used skilfully, rejoicing in our own virtue is a wonderful way to multiply the effects of our actions. Just be careful to avoid allowing this practice to slip into self-adulation, arrogance or conceit. We rejoice, not because we are an amazing person, but because the virtue we have created will lead to amazing results.

When rejoicing, it is always important to remember why. We rejoice in the actions of enlightened beings, because they inspire us. We rejoice in the deeds of sentient beings because we care about them and want them to be happy. And we rejoice in our own deeds because we want to bring greater benefit to others. When we combine these motivations with a recognition of the interdependent nature of our actions, we ensure our rejoicing will truly be effective.

In addition to the accumulation of vast stores of merit, the practice of rejoicing also has the benefit of cutting through the afflicted mind of jealousy. Joy is like a proud parent who sees their child doing well in school. Instead of being envious of their success or good fortune, we are sincerely thrilled by their achievements as we know they will experience great benefit. There should be no trace of competitiveness whatsoever.

Exercise 5.3 — Meditation on Empathetic Joy

- *In a relaxed posture, establish a neutral mind through the practice of mindfulness of breathing.*

- *Bring to mind a person you know well who possesses the qualities of good cheer and well-being. Someone whose presence inspires you through their attitude, words or deeds. As you think about this person, let your heart open to that joy. Rest in this feeling of sheer delight.*

- *Now shift your attention to someone who has experienced something wonderful in their life. Think of the situation and recall how this event made the person feel. Again, open the heart and share in this sense of delight.*

- *Then bring to mind someone who has obvious virtuous qualities. Someone who inspires you by their generosity, kindness and wisdom. Rejoice in their virtues and take delight in the benefit they have brought to you and to others.*

- *Finally, look back over your own life to instances you felt were inspirational to yourself or others. Consider the virtues you have performed and any effort you have made to cultivate those virtues. Recall all the people that enabled you to engage in these actions and rest your mind in the feeling of both joy and gratitude.*

- *Continue in this way until you tire.*

Equanimity

Finally, the last line of the aspiration emphasises immeasurable equanimity:

May all sentient beings abide in equanimity, free from bias, attachment and aversion.

The Tibetan term which is often translated as "equanimity or impartiality" is *tang nyom*. The word *tang* means "non-attachment or giving up", while the word *nyom* means "even-mindedness". Both of these aspects point to the essence of a mind that abides evenly, free from bias.

Up to this point, the qualities of love, compassion and joy have each worked to weaken the bias of our self-cherishing mind. Through meditating on love, we learn to care for sentient beings regardless of what they do for us, giving up the limitation of attachment. Through meditating on compassion, we learn to care for sentient beings even when they harm us, giving up the limitation of aversion. Through meditating on joy, we learn to take delight in the good fortune of others, giving up the limitation of self-centred jealousy. Now, in order to make these qualities immeasurable, we need to focus on the equanimity that directly dissolves our bias, allowing us to extend our aspirations outward to encompass all sentient beings without exception.

This is achieved by developing an even-mindedness that sees all beings as equal. This state of mind should not be confused with an aloof sense of indifference. The equanimity we are trying to develop comes from the cultivation of love and compassion and is inspired by a profound caring for sentient beings. The attitude is an all-inclusive aspect, just like a great sage who prepares a banquet feast and invites the entire city to attend, regardless of status or wealth.

All forms of bias are rooted in a conceptual judgement that views the superiority of one phenomenon over another. Because these judgements are based on different types of ignorance, the only way to remove them is through cultivating wisdom regarding their nature. It is for this reason that equanimity is primarily developed through analytical meditation where we recognise that all bias is merely a process of mental imputation and that fundamentally, we all have the same nature. We then start to connect more with this nature and less with our projected differences, developing a strong foundation on which to build.

Exercise 5.4 — Meditation on Equanimity

- *In a relaxed posture, establish a neutral mind through the practice of mindfulness of breathing.*

- *Imagine three people in the space in front of you. To the left is a person you feel close to, someone you would call a friend or loved one. To the right is a person you find yourself in conflict with, someone you would call an enemy or adversary. Finally, imagine a third person whom you have only met a few times, someone you would call a stranger. Bring each to mind as clearly as you can, attending to their presence as though they were really there.*

- *Starting with the friend, consider how your friendship developed. What drew you together? How has your relationship evolved over time? Has it always been pleasant or have you had disagreements? What makes your connection to this person stronger than your connection to the other people?*

- *Now turn your attention to the enemy. Have you always had a problem with this person? What is it about this person you find difficult to accept? Why do you think the two of you experience so much conflict? Do you think everyone sees this person in the same way you do? Think of the relationship they have with family and friends.*

- *Now consider the stranger. Could you imagine yourself developing a friendship with this person? What conditions would be needed for this to happen? Likewise, what would it take for this person to become an enemy? Think of the potential changes this relationship could take.*

- *For each person, imagine how your friend could become a stranger or even an enemy. Think of examples from your life where this may have happened. Likewise, imagine how your enemy could become a stranger or even a friend. Again, think of examples. Play with different potential scenarios for how your relationship with these three people could shift.*

- *To end your session, rest your awareness in any conclusions that arise.*

CULTIVATING THE CAUSES OF BODHICITTA

Individually, the Four Immeasurables can be practiced as a method to gradually open the heart and dissolve the self-cherishing attitude. Each quality works in synergy with the others to achieve an extraordinary degree of balance in the mind and if given enough time, the conditions will be created for Bodhicitta to naturally arise.

The Two Supreme Masters, Asanga and Nagarjuna, both recognised the importance of these qualities as the foundation for entering the Mahayana path. They each developed powerful methods for cultivating love, compassion, joy and equanimity that rapidly speeds up the process for realising Bodhicitta. These methods came to Tibet in the form of two main lineages:

1. **Asanga's Vast Lineage of Seven-Point Cause and Effect:** This method focuses primarily on developing a strong emotional bond between the practitioner and sentient beings. It takes its name from six contemplations which act as the causes for the effect of Bodhicitta. The first step is to establish a basis of affection that comes from (1) recognising the intimate nature of our relationships with sentient beings since beginningless

time; (2) contemplating the many benefits we have received from those sentient beings; and (3) developing a sense of gratitude towards them with a sincere desire to repay their kindness. Once a connection has been formed, the practitioner cultivates the qualities of (4) great loving-kindness and (5) great compassion, both of which are distinguished by (6) the altruistic attitude that personally takes responsibility to work for the benefit of sentient beings. When meditated on correctly, this process naturally gives rise to the extraordinary result of (7) Bodhicitta—the aspiration to bring all sentient beings to full enlightenment.

2. **Nagarjuna's Profound Lineage of Exchanging Self for Others:** The second method came through the great Indian master Shantideva based on the teachings of Nagarjuna. Whereas Asanga's method is well suited for emotionally oriented people, Nagarjuna's method emphasises wisdom by considering the nature of our self-cherishing attitude. Through a series of analytical contemplations, the practitioner (1) establishes a basis for equanimity by examining the nature of their relationships with sentient beings; (2) turns away from cherishing the self by analysing the disadvantages of this attitude; (3) turns toward cherishing others by analysing the advantages of this attitude; (4) establishes the determination to abandon self-cherishing completely, concentrating instead on the welfare of sentient beings; and (5) strengthens that determination by cultivating great love and compassion. As this method works to directly cut through the ignorance of self-cherishing, it is very effective for removing bias and establishing the conditions for Bodhicitta to arise.

Through the teachings of the great Indian master Jowo Atisha, both these lineages found their way into the six major traditions of Tibetan Buddhism and over time, it has become customary to draw on the strength of each approach by practicing both lineages as a unified path. This combined lineage is largely recognised as being the most efficient way to develop Bodhicitta. We will now explore this process in greater detail as a support for your own meditations.

Creating a Foundation of Equanimity

Every single being within the three realms, including ourselves, desires above all else to be happy and free from suffering. Despite this undeniable wish, because of our ignorance, we fail to realise that performing harmful actions only perpetuates our suffering and that true happiness will only come from the practise of virtuous deeds. Although nobody wants to experience suffering, we do so all the time.

To fully integrate this truth into our understanding, we need to repeatedly meditate on how all living beings are the same as ourselves in wanting to attain happiness and avoid suffering. This helps to eradicate the attitudes of attachment and aversion we can have toward other beings which lead us to reject them in favour of ourselves. This is not to suggest that everyone is the same in terms of characteristics but, fundamentally, we are all of the same nature and this is the equality we are referring to.

By working with this point on a provisional level, we slowly develop the feeling that we are all in this confusion together and that no matter what the situation, there is always a basis for strengthening our connection to one another. Ultimately, a sense of unity comes from our recognition that our most profound truth is essentially the same. This innate purity binds us together in an infinite web of interdependence. When we recognise this basis of connection, we realise that the suffering of others is not separate from our own and neither is our happiness. We come to see that when others suffer, we inevitably will suffer. Likewise, when they are happy, we too have the opportunity to be happy.

Exercise 5.5 — Connecting to Our Common Aspirations

- *In a relaxed posture, establish a neutral mind through the practice of mindfulness of breathing.*

- *Bring to mind a person who is neither a friend nor an enemy and yet whose background and living conditions are familiar to you. Visualise them in the space in front of you, and spend time attending to them as a person. Consider how, just like you, they wish only for happiness and freedom from suffering. Connect with this fundamental wish and let any differences you may feel about this person fade into the background. Think that even though they play no major role in your life, their happiness is just as significant as your own.*

- *Now, bring to mind someone you feel is an important part of your life and crucial to your well-being. Someone for whom you have great affection. Attend to this person closely, trying to connect with their hopes and fears. Consider how even though you have a loving relationship with this person, there are countless people who feel indifferent toward you and even those who actively dislike you. Think about how this person cannot be a true source of happiness, security or joy. Consider how these qualities must arise from within your own mind.*

- *Then think about a person who seems intent on bringing you harm or depriving you of happiness. Someone with whom you experience conflict. Again, connect with this person on the level of their fundamental hopes and fears. Think about how this person is not a true source of torment or anxiety. Consider how all of the anger and frustration you feel towards this person is in your own mind.*

- *Now open your awareness and allow your attention to wander to different people in your life. Take a moment to connect with their hopes and fears. Strengthen the feeling that we are all fundamentally the same on this level.*

- *As you contemplate these topics, a sense of evenness may arise. If so, rest your awareness in this feeling for as long as you can.*

Establishing a Loving Connection with Sentient Beings

Through the practice of equanimity, we reduce our bias and equalise our relationships with others. From this essential foundation we can work to generate a loving and compassionate attitude toward sentient beings that cares for everyone in an even-minded and consistent way.

Recognising All Beings as One's Mother

The key to developing our affection towards others is to recognise the nature of the relationships we have had with sentient beings over time. When we look at this life it is easy to see the great variety of beings we have encountered. Some people breeze through our lives for only a brief period of time, like the stranger you sit beside on the train, whereas others, like our mother, have been with us since the moment we were born. Some make very little impact on our lives, such as the crowds of people we walk through on the way to work, while others completely change the way we see the world, such as the spiritual teacher who visited for a weekend. If we step back and look at this life as a whole, the sheer number of relationships we have had is enormous.

But this is just one life and only the most recent in a long series of lives that have stretched back to beginningless time in cyclic existence. If we consider the infinite nature of our mindstreams, the number of relationships we have had with sentient beings must also be infinite. In fact, for every sentient being we encounter in this life, we can be sure we have experienced many types of relationships with them and while sometimes they have been enemies or strangers, in many other lives they have been our most loved companions; our mothers, our fathers, our siblings and our dearest friends.

There is great benefit from developing such an understanding as it establishes a basis for building love and compassion, forming the foundation for the mind of Bodhicitta that will ultimately lead us to enlightenment. Whether sentient beings are close to us now or if they have harmed us in the past is irrelevant. Just as the fight we had with our mother when we were five years old is not important, we can still love someone despite difficulties in the past. Our aim is to recognise that our relationships stretch beyond the specific conditions of today and the potential of these relationships is not limited to being only one way.

Once we acquire a sense for this amazing potential, we can direct our attention specifically to the relationship between mother and child. In general, a mother's love for her child is unconditional and she would gladly give her life to protect her offspring. As all sentient beings have been related to us in every possible way, at some point in our continuum of existence, all sentient beings have cared for us in the same way our mother has cared for us in this life.

The relationship with our mother is therefore used as a traditional example of someone who has unconditional love for us. If, however, your relationship with your mother is not particularly inspiring, try to focus on somebody you feel demonstrates the most love and care for your welfare, such as a father, a grandparent or an older sibling. The main thing is to connect with an example of someone who embodies love and compassion in your life.

Being Mindful of their Kindness

The next step is to reflect on the kindness of our mother in this life as a template for the kindness we have received from all sentient beings when they too were our mothers. Kindness means to receive benefit from the actions of another person, whether the act to bring benefit was made consciously or not. The recognition of kindness comes from our own experience. Traditionally we look at four types of kindness we receive from our mothers:

1. **Kindness of producing our body:** Mothers go through incredible hardship during their nine months of pregnancy. Just to bring us into this world they endure physical discomfort and pain, as well as emotional difficulties such as fear of giving birth, worry for their child's welfare and many family pressures. Furthermore, they do all of this with little regard for themselves. As a result of her incredible effort, we receive the benefit of having a precious human body which we can use to achieve enlightenment by practicing the Dharma.

2. **Kindness of giving life without letting us die:** At the time of our birth we were completely helpless and could do nothing for ourselves and if left on our own, we undoubtedly would have died. When we were tiny and fragile, our mother took great joy and delight in holding us close, feeding us with life-giving milk and calming us with her sweet voice. As a result of her protection, we were kept safe and received the benefit of growing up.

3. **Kindness of providing us with material needs:** Our mother has looked after us completely and given us more unconditional love than anyone else in this world. After birth and for many subsequent years, she has continued to care for us, providing food, clothing and shelter as well as attending to our health and education. Mothers not only worry about their children's upbringing, but also the welfare of their grandchildren

and great-grandchildren; there is no end to their concern. If their child is sick, a mother would prefer to be sick herself and if family circumstances were poor, she would willingly go cold or hungry to give what little food or clothing she had to her child. She does not care if her child is ungrateful, she does not know if her child will act harmfully to her in the future or if they have been an enemy from a past life. These things do not concern her as she cares only for her child's welfare. As a result of her kindness, we grew up with everything we needed to make use of our precious life as a foundation for spiritual practice.

4. **Kindness of showing us the ways of the world:** As we grew from babies into toddlers, our kind mother enjoyed showing us how to feed ourselves, teaching us to talk and walk, how to get dressed and how to tie our shoelaces. With infinite patience she taught us how to act in the company of others and showered us with love, no matter how badly we behaved. She took us to school and helped us with our homework and continued to care for us right through our teenage years and even into adulthood. As a result of her kindness, we experience the benefit of having the leisure to reflect on the nature of our existence.

These days, particularly in the West, there are many people who have conflicted relationships with their parents, often blaming them for their own faults. Whilst there can be many reasons for parental difficulties, a view of blame is a limited perspective with which to understand cause and effect. It does not take into account remote or hidden causes that may be traced back to previous lives.

It is not logical to blame our parents for all of our shortcomings as if they were the only ones at fault. If this were the case, different children within a family would all grow up to be the same. The reality of the situation is that our parents are merely a condition for certain experiences to arise and the primary cause for how we relate to those experiences is our own mind.

Discounting rare exceptions, parents try to do the best for their children and provide for them in whatever ways they can. Regardless of how negatively we may view our parents, there are few people who have done more for us. As children, we have received more kindness from our parents than from almost anyone else we have ever met.

We should not fall prey to false logic by blaming all our problems on our parents but at the same time, we must also avoid the other extreme of placing all blame on ourselves. Alternatively, we can humbly acknowledge our negative tendencies but move on to concentrate on cultivating our infinite potential for developing good qualities. It is never beneficial to blame ourselves and feel guilty, nor to blame someone else and remain in a state of anger, as both approaches can cause great harm in the long term. On the other hand, developing strong gratitude toward our parents, especially our dear mother, is extraordinarily beneficial. Such gratitude can then be extended to friends, relatives and then further to every living being such as humans, animals and the many unseen beings who have been our mothers during countless former lives.

By contemplating the kindness of our mothers, we expand our heartfelt connection to sentient beings and this can lead us to a profound sense of unity with all those around us. We do not have to limit our reflections to only the kindness of our mother, we can also look to other loving relationships in our lives, such as with our father, siblings, partners or friends. There is even great benefit in recognising the kindness we receive from people we don't even know, for instance the ones who grow the food we eat, or those who create the homes where we sleep. Every day, countless sentient beings contribute to conditions that ultimately bring benefit to our lives.

If you encounter certain people that are difficult to work with in this way, you should return to developing equanimity. Once your attachment or aversion has diminished, it should be easier to think of examples of their kindness, such as the person who constantly argues with you, making your life miserable. This person is providing you with an opportunity to practice patience and develop your good qualities, and so from this perspective, they are actually showing you great kindness.

Wishing to Repay their Kindness

Reflecting deeply on the kindness of our dear mother sentient beings creates an enormous sense of gratitude towards them. The amount of benefit we have received from them over countless lives is truly amazing and when we recognise this, we are inspired to repay that kindness.

This debt should not be thought of as a burden, but rather as a basis for understanding that our relationships flow in two directions. When one person helps another, there is a natural desire to reciprocate their kindness which strengthens the bond of the relationship, allowing for each to continue to benefit the other in the future. The more we develop this yearning to repay the kindness of our dear mothers, the more open we become to opportunities to bring them benefit.

Exercise 5.6 — Repaying the Kindness of Others

- *In a relaxed posture, establish a neutral mind through the practice of mindfulness of breathing.*

- *Visualise your mother in the space in front of you. Spend some time strengthening the feeling that she is right there with you. Now reflect on the types of benefit you have received from her. Start with your time in the womb and slowly move toward the present day. Think of the sacrifices your mother has made so that you could be clothed, fed and educated. Think of the hardships she had to endure. Consider how this life that you enjoy would not even exist were it not for your dear mother.*

- *Nurture your sense of gratitude toward your mother. Pause and rest in any feelings of affection or closeness that may arise. When the feelings fade, continue reflecting until they return and rest again. Continue in this way until the feeling is very strong.*

- *Now let your mother fade back into the mind and bring your focus to another person you feel close to, perhaps a family member or friend. Consider that this person has not always played this particular role in your life. Since beginningless time they have supported you and nurtured you in exactly the same way as your mother of this life. When you remember the kindness of your mother, let the feeling of connection arise again. Rest in this sensation.*

- *Continue to bring different people to mind and visualise them in the space before you. Recognise the nature of your relationship with them now, and the nature of your relationships with them since beginningless time. Use them as a basis to remind you of the kindness of your mother and then rest in the feelings that arise.*

- *To end the session, imagine you are completely surrounded by sentient beings as far as the eye can see. Imagine that each has been your dear mother, just like the mother of this life. Develop a strong yearning to do whatever is in your power to bring benefit to these beings, to repay the infinite kindness they have shown you.*

Exchanging Self for Others

We have so far explored the nature of our relationship with sentient beings, in particular, cultivating a loving connection between ourselves and all others. We now need to look more closely at the nature of these two entities; the self and others. Usually when we think of the "self", it has a sense of importance, whereas when we think of "others", it carries less weight in our minds. At this point we don't need to question the reasons why this is the case, but simply recognise the existence of this natural bias. This feeling that the self is more important than others is what we have been referring to as "self-cherishing." Once we have clearly identified this experience, we can then begin to analyse its nature.

When practicing exchanging self for others, we are not aiming to convince ourselves that others are the same as the self. The point is to take the feeling we have for the self and transfer that feeling onto others, to put them first in our life and to act for their benefit. This shift in attitude is the driving force behind the motivation of Bodhicitta and is therefore crucial to its development.

The Disadvantages of Cherishing the Self

We first need to consider the many disadvantages that exist because of the attitude that cherishes the self more than others. As the root of all forms of suffering is self-cherishing, the very reason we experience suffering is because we have engaged in actions for the sole purpose of bringing happiness to the self. Take for instance the misery that has been inflicted through the use of weapons. We have encountered these unpleasant conditions because we have harmed sentient beings in the past and the only reason we would cause this harm to others is because we value our own happiness more than theirs.

Self-cherishing is not only the root of suffering, it also destroys the roots of our virtue as it creates the conditions for us to constantly feel the need to protect the self. Instead of living in harmony with those around us, we find ourself under perpetual attack and this leads to afflicted states of mind such as hatred, spite and arrogance. These types of afflictions erode our virtues and prevent us from experiencing any form of lasting happiness.

Viewed from this perspective, it becomes clear that self-cherishing is at the centre of everything we wish to avoid. It is not enough to accept this actuality on an intellectual level, we need to spend time reflecting on the difficulties we have experienced in life and analyse what role self-cherishing has played. When done with conviction, a strong determination to abandon self-cherishing no matter what it takes begins to develop within us

The Advantages of Cherishing Others

By turning the mind away from self-cherishing, space is created in our mind allowing us to reflect more clearly on the needs of others. When we develop a heartfelt concern for their well-being, we engage in actions that will bring benefit to them. This shift in orientation leads us to act with virtue and in doing so, we are also generating the causes for experiencing our own happiness.

Take for example the happiness we experience from having a precious human rebirth. This type of rebirth is the result of practicing ethical discipline, and a large part of ethical discipline is to refrain from causing harm to sentient beings through acts of body and speech. We avoid these types of actions because we understand that sentient beings do not want to suffer and due to our feeling of care for them, it is important to us not to be a cause for their suffering.

We can also observe the people in the world, those whom we interact with directly and those we hear of and learn about. Would you prefer to spend time with people who cherish themselves or people who cherish others? Think of the most egotistical person, consumed by pride and arrogance, using everyone around them for their own personal gain. Now compare this with the Buddha who completely dedicated his life to benefitting sentient beings. While the selfish person creates the causes to suffer for countless aeons, the Buddha achieved enlightenment and continues to bring benefit to everyone. Which result would you prefer?

Recognising the mind that cherishes others is the key to achieving happiness for both oneself and for others and inspires us to cultivate the desire to exchange the self for others. Initially this may seem difficult to achieve, but we begin with the aspiration which creates the motivation to engage in spiritual practice and to cultivate greater wisdom. Eventually, as we realise the empty nature of our reality, there ceases to be the appearance of an inherent self to cherish. We are then completely free to expand our love and compassion to all sentient beings without limit.

Strengthening Love and Compassion

Once we establish the desire to abandon our self-cherishing and to cultivate the mind that cherishes others, we can train our mind using the method known in Tibetan as *tonglen*. *Tong* means "to give" and *len* means "to take" and so together they refer to the practice of giving happiness to sentient beings and taking on their suffering. By cultivating these two aspects in formal meditation, we strengthen love and compassion respectively. When these qualities are strong enough, the aspiration to achieve enlightenment for the benefit of sentient beings naturally arises. It is beautifully summarised in the following verse by Geshe Langri Thangpa:

> *Offer gain and victory to others,*
> *Take loss and defeat for yourself.*

Whenever you feel happiness, cultivate and intensify the feeling, sending it out to all other beings so they too may share in the experience. As you breath out, shower all mother sentient beings with joy and gratitude in the form of loving white light.

Whenever you feel the pangs of suffering or pain, transform it into heartfelt compassion for all the beings that may also be experiencing conditions similar to or worse than yours. Fervently wish them to be free from their pain and take their suffering upon yourself. Draw into your heart all of their sorrows in the form of dark smoke and allow it to dissolve your self-cherishing, transforming your being into openness and radiance.

When we undertake this profound practice, it may be helpful to think of the four types of exchange taking place:

1. **The Exchange of Self-cherishing:** This refers to letting go of the attitude that cherishes the self above all else and replacing it with the attitude that sees others as more important.

2. **The Exchange of What is Cherished:** This refers to letting go of the attitude that sees one's own aggregates as the self and replacing it with a mind that sees the aggregates of others as one's own.

3. **The Exchange of Happiness and Suffering:** This refers to letting go of the desire for one's own happiness and replacing it with the desire to take on the suffering of others.

4. **The Exchange of Non-Virtues and Virtues:** This refers to letting go of the desire to accumulate the causes for one's own happiness and replacing it with the desire to help others produce the causes for their happiness.

In this way, whenever we experience negative thoughts or emotions aris-ing in our own mind-stream, we can use them as a reminder to take upon ourselves all the afflictions and negative karma of others and offer them all our virtue and merit. What better method could we imagine to overcome our own self-cherishing mind?

Exercise 5.7 — The Practice of Taking and Giving

- *In a relaxed posture, establish a neutral mind through the practice of mindfulness of breathing.*

- *With your mind at ease, consider a person you know who is currently undergoing a difficult time; perhaps they are sick or experiencing hardship. Allow their image to arise in your mind and connect with their presence. Recognise that this being has been your mother countless times before and connect with the incredible kindness they have shown you. Allow the desire to repay their kindness to manifest in your mind.*

- *Consider how this person wishes only to be free of their suffering and to experience lasting genuine happiness. Develop the desire to fulfil their wish. Visualise this wish manifesting as a radiant orb of light in the centre of your heart.*

- *As you breath in, imagine drawing out all the pain and sorrow from this person in the form of black smoke. Imagine the smoke being sucked into the ball of light at your heart, where it dissolves completely. Imagine the person experiencing relief from their suffering.*

- *Then, as you breath out, imagine rays of light blazing forth and completely filling the person with joy and bliss. Imagine their mind is set at ease, with no worries or torment of any sort.*

- *Continue in this way, bringing to mind the types of suffering they are experiencing, developing the wish to take those sufferings onto yourself. Likewise, nurture the desire to give them the virtue you have developed so they can experience happiness in the future.*

- *You can stay with this person as long as you like. When you are ready to move on, simply allow the person to fade back into the mind and rest in open awareness until another person arises.*

- *Repeat the meditation as many times as you like.*

We may be afraid that taking on the suffering of others may cause ourselves harm in some way. The only thing, however, that such a practice could ever harm is our self-cherishing mind. If we find this practice difficult at first, we can begin on an aspirational level and slowly build the strength of our conviction. Gradually this can lead to a resolute intention and commitment. Although we cannot be certain that those to whom we direct this practice will receive any benefit, we can be absolutely sure of the benefit we receive ourselves.

REVIEW OF KEY POINTS

- Motivation determines the nature of an action. In order to ensure our practice of the Kalachakra Path leads to enlightenment, we need to establish a motivation that is in the nature of enlightenment. That motivation is Bodhicitta—the desire to bring ourselves and all sentient beings to full enlightenment.

- Bodhicitta is important: (1) at the beginning, where it is the entry to the Mahayana path which leads to enlightenment; (2) in the middle, where it unifies our actions into a single purpose and makes every virtue a source of immeasurable merit, thereby propelling us on the path; and (3) at the end, where it is the ultimate state of Buddhahood, the result of the path.

- The root of Bodhicitta is great compassion which takes on personal responsibility to free sentient beings of their suffering. The bias that is produced by the self-cherishing mind prevents this form of compassion from arising.

- The antidote to self-cherishing is to cultivate the Four Immeasurables: (1) immeasurable love, (2) immeasurable compassion, (3) immeasurable joy and (4) immeasurable equanimity.

- Love is the desire for others to experience happiness and its causes. There are five types of love: (1) possessive love; (2) romantic love; (3) endearing love; (4) parental love and; (5) unconditional love. Of these five, the last two can be considered forms of genuine love.

- Compassion is the desire for others to be free from suffering and its causes. There are five aspects of compassion: (1) empathy; (2) sympathy; (3) gross compassion; (4) subtle compassion and; (5) non-referential compassion. The last three aspects are forms of genuine compassion.

- Joy is the act of taking delight in the happiness and well-being of others. By rejoicing in the virtues of others, we generate merit in the mind. There are five objects which can be used for the practice of rejoicing: (1) Buddhas, (2) Bodhisattvas, (3) Pratyeka and Shravaka Arhats, (4) Ordinary Sentient Beings and (5) Yourself.

- Equanimity is the mind which abides evenly without bias. It is the quality that allows each of the other qualities to become immeasurable.

- There are two lineages which are designed to cultivate the four immeasurables in a very efficient way: (1) Asanga's Vast Lineage of Seven-Point Cause and Effect and (2) Nagarjuna's Profound Lineage of Exchanging Self for Others. Both lineages can be combined to form a unified method: (1) create a foundation of equanimity; (2) establish a loving connection with sentient beings; (3) exchange your self for others through the practice of taking and giving.

CHAPTER SIX

Generating Bodhicitta
The Supreme Mind of Enlightenment

If we look at the whole of the Buddha's eighty four thousand teachings, we can see that from one perspective, they are all skilful means for either causing Bodhicitta to arise within us or strengthening that realisation until enlightenment is achieved. The mind of Bodhicitta, therefore, is the very essence of the path and we should never fall into the misconception that these practices are in any way inferior or just for beginners. As all subsequent practices rely on taking refuge and Bodhicitta as their foundation, without them, there is no path to enlightenment.

In these degenerate times it is difficult to implement the practices in the same way as they were taught during the time of the Buddha and so we need to take care in establishing their essential nature. By becoming familiar with the essence and with the guidance of the pith instructions from an authentic teacher, we can apply the teachings to whatever situation we encounter. This is particularly important in the case of Bodhicitta, as transformation is only possible if we integrate our insight into our experience.

To this end, we will now explore the specific characteristics of Bodhicitta to enhance our understanding of the way to integrate it into our practice. By developing clarity of the role Bodhicitta plays at each stage of the path, we will gain a powerful context for the practices to follow. Then by keeping the essential points in the mind, we will know how to progress from beginning to end without confusion.

With regards to the attitude we should have towards these teachings, it may be helpful to remember the words of the great yogi Padampa Sangye:

Seek the teacher's instructions like a mother falcon seeking her prey, listen to the teachings like a deer listening to music, meditate on them like a simple-minded person savouring food, contemplate them like a northern nomad shearing sheep and reach their result, like the sun coming out from behind the clouds.

Like the falcon, we should be tireless in searching for authentic instructions that help us understand every aspect of our experience. Like the deer, we should fill our minds with the wisdom of those instructions and let all else fade into the background. Like those with a simple mind who are not distracted by intellectual pursuits, we should savour the taste of the instructions by bringing them into our experience and like the nomad, we should not let a single shred of the Dharma be wasted; everything we receive should be put into practice.

By dedicating ourselves to study, reflection and meditation, we will steadily expand the love and compassion of Bodhicitta, coupled with the decline of self-grasping and afflicted states of mind. Do not be content to simply hear and intellectually understand these teachings. Sincerely embrace them as an integral part of your practice and allow them to penetrate your entire experience to the very depths of your heart!

TWO LEVELS OF BODHICITTA

Due to its profundity, Bodhicitta manifests at many levels and depending on the context in which the term is used, it can refer to different aspects. To make sense of the instructions we receive, it is useful to keep its various categories in mind. In general we can speak of two main levels of Bodhicitta: (1) Ultimate Bodhicitta and (2) Relative Bodhicitta. These correspond to the two levels of ultimate and relative truth respectively.

Ultimate Bodhicitta

The term *Ultimate Bodhicitta* is synonymous with Buddha-nature, absolute reality, definitive meaning or sacred truth. While we can use numerous terms, we should always remember they all refer to the same essence, which is the Dharmakaya mind of a fully enlightened Buddha.

In this context, Bodhicitta is the omniscient mind which abides in the sublime emptiness that is filled with all enlightened qualities and is completely empty of all fabrications. This mind is the actual result of the Kalachakra Path and is literally the "mind of enlightenment." To fully realise Ultimate Bodhicitta is to attain the state of Buddhahood and to achieve this we must clear all the obscurations that prevent this state from arising.

Relative Bodhicitta

The method used to reveal Ultimate Bodhicitta is the desire to achieve enlightenment for the sake of all sentient beings. This desire is known as *Relative Bodhicitta* and is what is generally referred to when we use the term "Bodhicitta." This desire usually takes the form of an aspiration prayer, such as:

For the sake of all sentient beings, I will achieve the state of complete Buddhahood.

This aspiration is made up of two key components:

1. **Purpose:** The first is the intentional aspect of the aspiration and is the reason why we want to achieve enlightenment. As we saw in the previous chapter, such an intention is the natural result of developing great love and compassion for sentient beings. When these qualities are present in our mind, we have an overwhelming desire to help our dear mother sentient beings in whatever way we can. We see that they are suffering and we long to free them from it.

2. **Method:** The second is the active component of the aspiration. When we analyse our present capacity, we realise that we are too limited by our afflicted minds to bring lasting benefit to the infinite number of sentient beings that need our help. If we investigate who is capable, only a fully enlightened Buddha has removed all limitations and actualised all enlightened qualities. Therefore, in order to fulfil the purpose of freeing sentient beings from their suffering, the only means is by achieving enlightenment.

While Bodhicitta is usually expressed as an aspiration, to understand how it functions to invigorate our practice, we need to know what Bodhicitta actually is. If you remember from our study of *Buddhist Psychology* in Book One of *Unveiling Your Sacred Truth*, the mind can be divided into primary or secondary minds. The primary mind is the composite of many secondary minds and represents a manifest consciousness. To use an analogy, the secondary minds are like the ingredients for a cup of tea, whereas the primary mind is the experience of the tea itself.

Bodhicitta is considered a primary mind that is produced by specific secondary minds. This means that any consciousness that contains these secondary minds can be labelled "Bodhicitta." Love and compassion, the altruistic intention that takes responsibility for the welfare of all sentient beings as well as the determination to achieve enlightenment to actualise that intention, are all secondary minds. When these four mental factors are present, then so too is Bodhicitta.

This is important to understand because authentic Bodhicitta arises spontaneously from the moment a practitioner enters the Mahayana path until the moment they achieve enlightenment. This is not to say that at every moment a practitioner is explicitly generating the aspiration of Bodhicitta, but by being present implicitly in every action, it acts as a cause for enlightenment. For example when we sit down with a Dharma book, the explicit motivation for reading is to gain knowledge for practice, however the implicit motivation is to achieve enlightenment for the sake of sentient beings. In this way, Bodhicitta becomes the root desire upon which all temporary desires are contained.

This nesting desire of Bodhicitta is also demonstrated in the way we approach achieving our aims. As we have already exchanged our self for others, our main motivation becomes the desire to achieve the aim of others. Through our wisdom however, we realise we cannot achieve their aims unless we actualise our own potential first. Only then will we have the capacity needed to bring benefit to all sentient beings. This is akin to someone on an aeroplane who knows they must put on their own oxygen mask before they can safely help other passengers. Once we recognise this, we can focus on achieving enlightenment as quickly as possible.

Based on this discussion, we can see that the practices presented in the previous chapter are designed to gather the necessary conditions for Bodhicitta to arise. Unfortunately, due to the impermanent nature of this realisation, if the conditions degenerate, Bodhicitta is lost and must be generated once again. It is for this reason that entry to the Mahayana path is marked by the *spontaneous* arising of Bodhicitta, without the need to generate it through meditation. This signifies the full integration of Bodhicitta into your mind where it operates as the implicit basis for all your actions. When we achieve this, we become a valid basis for being called a *Bodhisattva.*

Bodhisattvas experience two types of Relative Bodhicitta:

1. **Aspirational Bodhicitta:** This is the spontaneous desire to achieve enlightenment for the sake of all beings and is the minimum requirement to be authentically called a Bodhisattva. When this type of Bodhicitta first arises, it is fragile and if it is not strengthened through practice, it will degenerate and can eventually be lost. Fortunately it can always be re-generated in the mind by gathering the conditions again.

2. **Engaged Bodhicitta:** When the desire of aspirational Bodhicitta is combined with a specific action, it becomes engaged Bodhicitta. This type of Bodhicitta is a mind that is determined to do something, such as practicing the Kalachakra Path, in order to attain enlightenment for the sake of all beings. There is a sense of immediacy and commitment to your Bodhicitta that motivates you to essentially engage in actions.

The difference between the two can be illustrated by the idea of wanting to set out on a journey and actually taking the steps toward your destination. While aspirational Bodhicitta is a vital component to engaged Bodhicitta, we should not be satisfied with only praying to one day have the ability to lead all beings to enlightenment. Only engaged Bodhicitta will act as a direct cause for achieving enlightenment.

As new practitioners setting out on the path, it takes effort to produce Bodhicitta, but with greater familiarity it will start to arise more naturally. As we purify our minds and clear away obscurations, the effort that is required reduces; however, we will still need to make effort to use our Bodhicitta to complete the accumulations of merit and wisdom. Finally, as Bodhicitta becomes completely spontaneous and free, we will have reached the end of the path and achieved Buddhahood.

GENERATING ASPIRATIONAL BODHICITTA

With clarity regarding the definition of Bodhicitta, the next step is to generate it in the mind. We first train in the aspirational form and then move towards engaged Bodhicitta. Practicing in this way will ensure that our Bodhicitta is well formed and strong enough to act as a firm foundation for our spiritual practice.

Causes for Bodhicitta to Arise

Like all impermanent phenomena, Bodhicitta arises as a result of specific causes and conditions coming together. Therefore, if we wish to experience Bodhicitta in our mind, we need to gather the essential causes. According to Arya Asanga, Bodhicitta is the result of three sets of four: (1) Four Conditions; (2) Four Causes and; (3) Four Strengths. By studying each of these sets, we can identify which causes are currently manifest in our life and which we still need to cultivate.

Four Conditions

The first set of causes describes four conditions which act as inspiration for the desire to achieve enlightenment. It is not necessary to have all these conditions as any one of them is sufficient to trigger the desire in our mind, although some are more effective than others. *The Four Conditions for Arousing Bodhicitta* are:

1. **Seeing the qualities of Buddhas and Bodhisattvas:** The first condition arises when we see or hear the amazing qualities of the Buddhas or Bodhisattvas and we are inspired to become just like these great beings. If we are very fortunate, we may witness the display of such qualities in the form of supernatural powers or miraculous feats. In whatever form these qualities manifest, they generate within us the thought that enlightenment is truly incredible and it is something we aspire to achieve.

2. **Listening to the teachings of the Buddha:** The second condition occurs when we read or listen to Dharma teachings. In this situation

we are introduced to the idea of enlightenment indirectly. By putting the teachings into practice, we realise the possibility of enlightenment which strengthens our faith in our potential. This then gives rise to the desire to actualise that potential and achieve the result of enlightenment.

3. **Seeing that the teachings are in danger of disappearing:** The third condition occurs with the recognition that if the teachings are not actualised in the mindstreams of practitioners, the Mahayana Path will disappear. This situation gives rise to the desire to achieve enlightenment in order to become a qualified lineage holder and preserve the teachings for future generations. For this condition to occur, we must already have respect or faith in the Mahayana teachings and their capacity to bring benefit to sentient beings.

4. **Seeing that it is very rare for someone to generate Bodhicitta:** The fourth condition recognises that we currently live in a degenerate age, and so it is unbelievably rare for people to dedicate their lives to achieving liberation from samsara, let alone full and complete enlightenment. This situation gives rise to the thought of achieving enlightenment to then be able to inspire others to realise their own potential.

These four conditions give rise to the desire to achieve enlightenment, but they are not enough to be considered fully qualified Bodhicitta. For that, they must be combined with the qualities of great love and great compassion.

Four Causes

The next set of causes identifies specific conditions that must be present for Bodhicitta to arise. Lacking any of one of these causes means your Bodhicitta will not be fully formed and therefore will not be as powerful. *The Four Causes for Arousing Bodhicitta* are:

1. **A spiritual lineage:** The first cause is to be born into a life with the necessary conditions for practicing the Dharma, which is commonly referred to as a *precious human rebirth*. If these conditions are not present,

you will never encounter the Dharma and therefore will have no opportunity to practice it.

2. **Being sustained by an excellent teacher:** The second cause is to encounter and work with a spiritual guide who is capable of supporting your Dharma practice. Such a teacher should fulfil the criteria of a qualified spiritual guide as presented earlier. For the teacher to be a cause for developing Bodhicitta, they must be a lineage holder for the Mahayana—following either the Sutrayana or the Tantrayana.

3. **Compassion toward living beings:** The third cause is to have the quality of genuine love and compassion. For these qualities to arise in the mind, the aspiring Bodhisattva must be born in a realm where there is manifest suffering. Without this suffering, there is no way to develop the necessary compassion and therefore Bodhicitta will not arise with any strength.

4. **Not being discouraged by difficulties:** Helping others is not easy, and difficulties can easily overwhelm a practitioner, causing them to lose their altruistic intention. To overcome this, an aspiring Bodhisattva must naturally be courageous, steadfast and mentally strong.

The first two causes deal with external conditions, whereas the second two are mainly internal in nature. While it would be ideal to be born with these causes already present within our life, we should not lose heart if we need to gather them together. If one is missing, we can develop meaningful aspirations and engage in virtuous actions to create the causes for those conditions to manifest in the future. Even if they do not arise in this life, at least we can be sure they will in the next.

Four Strengths

These four causes emphasise the source of our inspiration for the desire to achieve enlightenment. As the name implies, these four causes influence the strength of the resulting desire. *The Four Strengths for Arousing Bodhicitta* are:

1. **Strength of oneself:** This is the strength which arises based on our experience of our potential. When we realise we can remove our ignorance through wisdom or train the mind through meditation, we firmly believe in our capacity to achieve enlightenment.

2. **Strength of others:** This strength arises in dependence on hearing teachings or following the instructions of a spiritual guide. It is mainly derived from the skilful presentation of the material by the teacher or by how strongly you connect with the logic of the teachings.

3. **Strength of cause:** This strength arises on the basis of spiritual practice performed in previous lives. If we are born with an existing predisposition towards Bodhicitta, it takes very little for us generate it again in this life. Sometimes simply hearing certain words such as "enlightenment", is enough to trigger the desire to arise again.

4. **Strength of practice:** Even if we do not have pre-existing habitual propensities for Bodhicitta, there is always the possibility we will encounter the teachings and be introduced to practices for its generation. By relying on these practices we can then lay down the propensities for Bodhicitta to arise in this and future lives. It is never too late to start.

Bodhicitta developed on the basis of the strength of others or the strength of practice uses indirect methods for nurturing the desire to achieve enlightenment. To ensure our Bodhicitta is firm, strong and unwavering, it is necessary to emphasise either the strength of oneself or the strength of the cause. Ideally however, we want to rely on all four.

Actually Generating Bodhicitta

When all the causes and conditions come together, the desire to generate Bodhicitta will naturally arise. Depending on the exact propensities of the practitioner and the particular conditions present, the arising Bodhicitta may take on a slightly different form. In general, we can speak of *Three Ways that Bodhicitta Manifests:*

1. **Like a King:** To rule effectively, a king's first priority is to establish dominion over the kingdom. Only then will he have the capacity to protect his subjects and take care of their needs. Similarly, the wish to firstly attain Buddhahood oneself and then lead all others to their own Buddha nature is called *Arousing Bodhicitta with the Great Wish*. This style of Bodhicitta is exemplified by Buddha Shakyamuni.

2. **Like a Boat Captain:** A boat captain skilfully takes the helm of the ship so all passengers arrives safely together at the desired destination. Likewise, the wish to achieve Buddhahood for oneself and all beings at the same time is called *Arousing Bodhicitta with Sacred Wisdom*. This style of Bodhicitta is exemplified by Lord Maitreya.

3. **Like a Shepherd:** A shepherd walks behind their herd, protectively driving them forward, not resting until each sheep has safely made it home. In the same way, the attitude of those who wish to establish all beings of the three realms in the state of perfect Buddhahood before achieving it for themselves is called *Arousing Bodhicitta that is Beyond Compare*. This style of Bodhicitta is exemplified by the Bodhisattvas Manjushri and Avalokiteshvara.

While some scholars debate the effectiveness of each style, my feeling is that all three are excellent and achieve equally extraordinary results, although generally speaking we could say the aspiration that is like a shepherd is perhaps the most noble and the aspiration that is like a king is probably the most practical. As the style of Bodhicitta that arises is not something we choose, we do not need to develop biases regarding one way over another. Simply observe your natural tendencies and use these categories as a way of focusing your awareness and strengthening your resolve.

There are essentially two ways to generate Bodhicitta: (1) through a ritual, which is mainly used for introducing new propensities for generating Bodhicitta; and (2) through meditation, which is more about cultivating existing propensities.

Generating Bodhicitta through a Ritual

After training the mind extensively in the Four Immeasurables, we may find that aspirational Bodhicitta spontaneously manifests in the mind. This is a sign that we have existing propensities from previous lives, but for those who have never generated this mind before, they may find it helpful to follow the advice of Jowo Atisha:

> *Those who wish to train after they develop Bodhicitta*
> *Accustom themselves with effort for a long time*
> *To the four immeasurables, love and so forth,*
> *Thereby clearing away attachment and jealousy*
> *And produce Bodhicitta through a pure ritual.*

To participate in the *Ritual for Generating Aspirational Bodhicitta*, we need a qualified spiritual guide who is willing to bestow it. Because this ritual involves taking vows and commitments, the student should be willing to hold the spiritual guide as a vow preceptor. This also means that in order for the teacher to give the commitments, they must hold the commitments themselves. A basic understanding of Bodhicitta and a sincere aspiration to generate it is a requirement of the student, as the more enthusiastic they are, the more impact the ritual will have on their mind.

The ritual itself is basically a guided meditation where the vow preceptor leads you in taking refuge, amassing merit through the seven limb prayer, preparing your mind by purifying your attitude, generating Bodhicitta and then familiarising yourself with the precepts that should be upheld. Once you have generated Bodhicitta in this way, you have a working basis to expand upon through the use of meditation.

Generating Bodhicitta through Meditation

Whether you are working with propensities created in previous lives or newly acquired propensities through ritual, the process of generating Bodhicitta basically has three parts:

1. **Cultivating Love and Compassion:** Following the instructions from the previous chapter, we establish a strong connection of love and compassion toward all sentient beings. Through the practice of *Taking and Giving* we can strengthen these qualities until they become truly immeasurable in scope.

2. **Cultivating the Altruistic Intention to Benefit Sentient Beings:** Once we have become acutely aware of the great suffering sentient beings endure, a burning desire to help them arises. We then take upon ourselves the responsibility to repay their infinite kindness and help them to be free from their suffering. The more we nurture this desire, the more unshakeable our determination becomes and we resolve to do whatever is in our power to bring ultimate benefit to our dear mothers.

3. **Generating the Desire to Achieve Enlightenment:** On the basis of this altruistic intention, the question arises, "What can I do?" When we are honest with ourselves, we realise that our limited minds are too overwhelmed by our karma and afflictions to be of any significant benefit. At the most we can help the few beings we encounter in this life, but what about the countless beings in the lower realms or the god realms? To realistically bring lasting benefit to the vast ocean of sentient beings, we need to achieve the omniscient mind of a Buddha. Only then can we know the needs of each being and spontaneously manifest for their benefit.

When we meditate in this way, we gradually build the feeling of resolve and determination that achieving Buddhahood is not only the best solution, it is also entirely possible. Just like the Buddhas and Bodhisattvas of the past, we have everything we need to remove the obscurations from our mind and to actualise our greatest potential. If we develop our faith in this result, the blessings of the Buddhas and Bodhisattvas will enter our hearts and Bodhicitta will absolutely take root.

Exercise 6.1 — Generating the Aspiration for Enlightenment

- *In a relaxed posture, establish a neutral mind through the practice of mindfulness of breathing.*

- *In the space in front of you, visualise your mother from this life and think:*

  "This person, my mother, from the moment I was conceived has taken care of me with great effort. Because she endured hardships such as illness, hunger, and pain, because she gave me food and clothing and cleaned me when I was soiled, and because she taught me what is good and steered me away from evil, I have met the teachings of Buddha and I am now practicing the Dharma. What tremendous kindness!

  Not only in this life, but in an infinite series of lives, she has done this over and over again. While she has worked for my welfare, she herself wanders in samsara and experiences many different forms of suffering."

- *Contemplate these points until a real sense of heartfelt compassion arises for your dear mother. Now extend that love and compassion outward by bringing to mind different sentient beings from your life and think:*

  "From time without beginning, each sentient being has been a mother to me in just the same way as my present mother. Each and every one has helped me and cared for me."

Start with those who are closest to you and then broaden your scope to those who are unfamiliar or who you feel in conflict with.

- *When you feel an evenness of love and compassion for all these sentient beings, develop the determination to repay their kindness by thinking:*

  "All these beings, my parents, not only experience many different kinds of suffering and frustration without intending to, they are also full of potent seeds for future suffering. How pitiable! What is to be done? To return their kindness, the very least I can do is help them clear away what hurts them and make them comfortable and happy."

- *When the wish to help them grows strong and intense, continue by thinking:*

  "What do my dear mothers desire? Just like me, they desire to be happy and to be free from suffering, and yet due to our ignorance we create the exact opposite of this.

  Why do we do this? The cause of our suffering is none other than the self-cherishing thought which, since beginningless time, has been the sole cause for all of the negativity and suffering in our lives.

  The Buddhas and Bodhisattvas recognised the self-cherishing thought as the enemy and strove to abandon it completely. Instead they dedicated themselves to the cultivation of the thought which cherishes others. The result they achieved was perfect enlightenment."

- *With the strong determination to abandon the self-cherishing thought and to dedicate yourself to bringing benefit to sentient beings in whatever way you can, think:*

  "All these parents of mine, who are the focus of my compassion, are hurt directly by suffering and indirectly by the sources of suffering. I shall therefore take upon myself all the suffering of all my mothers and all the disturbing emotions and actions that are the sources of their suffering."

- *With each in breath, imagine drawing into your heart all the negativities and obscurations of your dear mothers in the form of black light. Develop a feeling of great delight that you are able to rid them of their pain and torment. As you do so think:*

  "Without regret I send all my virtuous activity and happiness in the past, present, and future, my wealth and my body to all sentient beings, my parents."

- *Imagine that with each out breath, you send out all your virtue and wisdom in the form of brilliant white light that cleanses and heals all sentient beings, bestowing on them all forms of happiness. Develop a feeling of great delight that they experience this happiness.*

- *Continue in this way using the rhythm of the breath to take in suffering and send out joy and happiness. After meditating like this for a time, think:*

  "While this meditation of taking and giving is extremely beneficial for my mind, it is only a visualisation and my dear mothers are

still suffering. They will continue to suffer until they are completely liberated from the causes of suffering—their karmic propensities and afflicted states of mind.

Right now, I am barely capable of even helping myself, let alone bringing lasting genuine happiness to my dear mothers. To truly benefit them, I must achieve the enlightened state of Buddha Vajradhara.

Therefore I will study, reflect and meditate on the profound Vajra Yoga Path of the Glorious Kalachakra. In this way, I will clear away all my obscurations and be able to bring immeasurable benefit and wellbeing to countless sentient beings throughout the ten directions."

- *Release all visualisations and simply rest your awareness in the feeling of strong determination.*

Strengthening Your Bodhicitta through Conduct

When we first generate the aspiration of Bodhicitta, it has little strength and so can easily dissolve quite quickly. To integrate our aspiration into everything we do, it needs to arise spontaneously as an implicit motivation. Only at that time can it be considered a fully qualified form of Bodhicitta. During the Bodhicitta ritual, the vow preceptor will explain different types of conduct we should follow to ensure that our propensity for Bodhicitta grows stronger rather than declining.

How to Prevent Your Bodhicitta from Declining in this Lifetime

To prevent the deterioration of our Bodhicitta, it is helpful to: (1) contemplate the benefits of developing Bodhicitta; (2) generate the aspiration of Bodhicitta throughout the day; (3) accumulate merit and purify negativities and (4) never abandon any sentient being.

As the great Bodhisattva Atisha said:

If the benefits of the Bodhicitta intention had physical form, any conceivable space would be too small to contain these benefits. The merit from this is far greater than the merit gained from offering as many precious gems as there are grains of sand in the Ganges River.

When the thought of Bodhicitta arises, our name and purpose changes and all the virtue we accumulate is carried by this vast altruistic intention, bearing fruit and growing unceasingly. This is far superior to actions done without Bodhicitta, where results are experienced only once and then exhausted. Furthermore, we should understand that while having relative Bodhicitta is not sufficient on its own to attain Buddhahood, without it, nothing else is of any use, and so the attitude of Bodhicitta is supremely beneficial.

We can reinforce our Bodhisattva commitment by explicitly refreshing our aspiration three times each morning and three times each evening. This strengthens and increases the development of Bodhicitta in our mind-stream and helps to prevent it from declining. We should also strive to accumulate merit and recognise any negative attitudes such as singling out certain sentient beings as being undeserving of compassion, and counteracting them by recollecting our Bodhicitta intention. In particular, we should aim to never forsake a single being and never abandon the courageous wish to accomplish Buddhahood, no matter how great the obstacles we encounter.

Precepts for Generating Bodhicitta in Future Lives

When we commit ourselves to cultivating Bodhicitta, we are speaking of a motivation that spans until the attainment of Buddhahood. As this achievement will most likely take many lifetimes to accomplish, we need to think beyond the conditions of this present life. Since we cannot guarantee we will have the necessary awareness at the time of death to direct our rebirth, we need to familiarise our minds with qualities that will make it easier to generate Bodhicitta in future lives. This will allow us to pick up where we left off in the previous life and continue with our training. The way we do this is through abandoning the four "black" practices and cultivating the four "white" practices.

Abandoning the Four Black Practices that Weaken Bodhicitta

The first set contains four behaviours we should avoid as much as possible as they work in direct opposition to the causes for generating Bodhicitta. Without being mindful of these practices, even if we wanted to develop

Bodhicitta, we might not have the opportunity to do so. *The Four Black Practices* are:

1. **Confusing one's teachers:** As we have seen, our teachers are the source of the teachings and our guides along the path. When we damage our relationship with them through the act of deception, we weaken the strength of our karmic connection and create obstacles to encountering the teachings again in the future.

2. **Making others feel regret about that which is not regrettable:** Similarly, when we intentionally discourage those who are practicing the Dharma by instilling doubt or confusion, we are creating the causes to be deprived of the necessary supports for our practice.

3. **Abusing or slandering those who have correctly entered the Mahayana:** When we disparage a Bodhisattva out of anger or hatred, we establish a negative connection towards the Mahayana in general. This propensity will act as a direct obstacle to developing faith in the Mahayana. Without faith in the path, there will be no desire to generate Bodhicitta.

4. **Using deceit and misrepresentation to manipulate others:** If, while fostering ulterior motives, we intentionally lie or misrepresent reality in order to manipulate sentient beings to serve us, we are actively reinforcing our self-cherishing. This attitude acts as a direct obstacle to developing the wish to benefit others which is a fundamental condition for generating Bodhicitta.

In essence, by abandoning these four practices, we avoid damaging our relationship with the Three Jewels (teachers, teachings and community), the Mahayana Path and sentient beings in general. All these relationships are vital in making certain we will encounter the necessary conditions for reconnecting with Bodhicitta in the future.

Adopting the Four White Practices that Prevent Bodhicitta from Weakening

The next set of practices act as direct antidotes to the above black practices. They not only prevent our Bodhicitta from deteriorating, they also help create conducive conditions for Bodhicitta to arise in future lives. *The Four White Practices* are:

1. **Avoid all forms of lying:** To lie is to deceive, which is the opposite of straightforwardness, kindness and love. By completely avoiding any form of deception, we ensure we are not deceiving our teachers or any other sentient being. Instead, we strengthen our relationships on the basis of honesty and sincerity. This is the antidote to the first black practice.

2. **Helping others practice Dharma:** Rather than causing others to abandon their practice, we should cultivate an unbiased mind that constantly works to establish others in authentic Dharma practices. Without any sort of self-centred motivation, we should encourage them to use whatever methods are most beneficial for them. This is the antidote to the second black practice.

3. **Showing honour and respect to Bodhisattvas:** By venerating those who have cultivated Bodhicitta, we establish a strong connection with the Mahayana Path that the Bodhisattvas embody. This connection forms the basis for encountering these teachings and developing faith in them. This is the antidote to the third black practice.

4. **Maintain an altruistic intention towards sentient beings:** The more we honour and cherish sentient beings, the more we wish to bring them benefit. This attitude assures us of possessing a naturally loving and compassionate disposition in future lives, making it easier to connect with others and develop Bodhicitta. This is the antidote to the fourth black practice.

By developing mindfulness of these four practices, all your actions will gradually align with the nature of Bodhicitta and like the scent of sandalwood which permeates the container in which it is held, Bodhicitta will also permeate your mind. This process strengthens and stabilises our aspirational Bodhicitta so eventually it will arise spontaneously.

Repairing Aspirational Bodhicitta

Due to the power of negative habituation, we may find our aspirational Bodhicitta begins to degenerate. If it does, the loss of strength will reduce the influence it has on our activities. Fortunately, it is relatively simply to restore. First bring to mind the behaviours you think contributed to your Bodhicitta weakening and develop a strong feeling of regret, followed by the desire to avoid these actions in the future. Finish by generating the aspiration of Bodhicitta again, either through reciting prayers or meditating as illustrated earlier. Always remember that it is never too late to generate the mind of Bodhicitta.

Chenrezig—The Buddha of Compassion

TRAINING THE MIND WITH ENGAGED BODHICITTA

The dividing line between aspirational Bodhicitta and engaged Bodhicitta is not always easy to distinguish. We can develop a sense for the distinction by recalling a time when we had a particular ambition, such as wanting to travel to an exotic country. For many years, you held onto the idea, thinking "one day, one day." Finally you make the decision to turn your dream into reality and in that moment you established the conviction to make it happen. From that time on, all your energy is directed towards realising your dream. You investigate the purchase of plane tickets and hotels, and slowly plan your itinerary. You start accumulating leave days at work and save a portion of each week's pay toward your trip; basically you do all you can to manifest your dream.

Similarly, aspirational Bodhicitta sees enlightenment as something far off in the future, whereas engaged Bodhicitta brings it into the present. It is an attitude filled with a sense of drive and purpose which transforms all our actions into supports for achieving our ultimate aim of full enlightenment. When this mind arises, everything falls into context and nothing else is more important than training as a Bodhisattva. When this occurs, even things like eating and sleeping become supports for your training, and therefore causes for enlightenment. This is why engaged Bodhicitta generates vast stores of merit, as every moment, whether you are conscious of it or not, becomes a source of virtue.

Receiving the Bodhisattva Vows

The generation of engaged Bodhicitta manifests in the moment that we take on the commitments of training in accordance with the *Bodhisattva Vows*. These sacred commitments are designed to help us maintain a way of life that is capable of nurturing Bodhicitta and purifying obscurations from our mind-streams. While they can be divided into many categories, the central theme is to cherish sentient beings and to do whatever we can to bring them benefit. A realised Bodhisattva who fully embodies this principle will naturally uphold all the vows on the basis of having received and practiced them in previous lives.

The Bodhisattva Vows are generally bestowed through a short ritual and it is best to at least have a general understanding of the vows to help develop a strong conviction that you have received them. The more aware you are of their details, the more impact the ritual will have on your mind and the more inspired you will be to keep them. To this end, you will find the *Eighteen Root Vows* presented below. There are also *Forty-Six Branch Vows* that will be presented within the next seven chapters. By studying and reflecting on this material, you will have a strong foundation for taking the Bodhisattva Vows.

If however the opportunity arises to receive the Bodhisattva Vows before we have had the chance to study, we should definitely take advantage of such a fortunate situation. As it says in the *Konchok Dala Sutra*:

Regardless of the past deeds of the person, as long as they have strong faith in the Three Jewels and are greatly inspired by the way of the Bodhisattvas, they can certainly receive the Bodhisattva vows.

With great faith in the Three Jewels and the Mahayana Path, every time we receive the vows, we strengthen our Bodhicitta. This then motivates us to continue studying and practicing, bringing greater clarity and making the next time we receive the vows even more powerful.

Another reason to take advantage of participating in a ceremony is that once we have received the vows from a qualified vow preceptor, we can re-take the vows as many times as we like by using the Buddha and Bodhisattvas as our witnesses. Ideally we want to take the vows at least once a day. The following meditation can be used to fulfil this purpose.

Exercise 6.2 — Taking the Bodhisattva Vows

- *In a relaxed posture, establish a neutral mind through the practice of mindfulness of breathing.*

- *In the space in front of you, visualise a vast and open field with an infinite collection of Buddhas, Bodhisattvas and Arhats, as well as your own teachers and the Kalachakra lineage masters. Imagine the ground is completely filled with sentient beings, all in human form and looking to you for help. With this great assembly as witnesses, repeat the following prayer three times:*

> *"Gurus, Buddhas, Bodhisattvas and other holy objects of refuge, please hear my prayer. Just as the previous sublime beings generated Bodhicitta and gradually performed the Bodhisattva deeds, so now do I take the Bodhisattva vows and pledges to train and follow in their footsteps. I vow to generate Bodhicitta and continually practise the Bodhisattva deeds in order to benefit all beings."*

- *After each repetition, strengthen your determination. Then, after the final repetition, develop the certainty that you have now received the Bodhisattva Vows. Nurture a feeling of great delight and gratitude by reciting the following passage:*

> *"Today my human life has become most precious and from now on I have become a son or daughter of the Bodhisattva family. From this time on I will never waste this privilege. Just as a blind man finds a jewel in a rubbish heap, by some remote chance I have come to enter the Buddha's family. I vow to keep my promise. May the gods, demigods and all other beings rejoice as I have taken the Bodhisattva vows in the presence of the Buddhas, Bodhisattvas and all sentient beings."*

- *Complete the practice by reciting this dedication prayer:*

> *"May the precious Bodhicitta arise which has not yet arisen*
> *And may that which has already arisen not degenerate, may it increase."*

The Eighteen Root Vows

In accordance with the combined traditions of Asanga and Nagarjuna, there are *Eighteen Root Vows* that a Bodhisattva should uphold. These vows highlight the core behaviours that will keep your Bodhicitta pure. If you break any of these root vows, you are no longer working for the benefit of sentient beings and therefore have lost your engaged Bodhicitta. As long as you have not completely abandoned sentient beings however, you will not have lost your aspirational Bodhicitta and therefore can still retake the vows either in the presence of a vow preceptor or in the presence of the Buddhas and Bodhisattvas visualised in your mind.

Four Root Vows According to the Tradition of Asanga

According to the tradition of Asanga, any conduct that is not conducive to the pure practice of the trainings of a Bodhisattva can be considered a root downfall. All such downfalls can be summarised by the following four vows:

1. **Claiming to have false realisations:** We should completely abandon seeking praise, gain or respect on the basis of claiming to be a highly realised being or belittling the achievements of others. This vow is broken if we falsely claim to have attained a direct realisation of emptiness. It is a specific form of lying whereby others are deceived into believing we have special attainments. It is not necessary to explicitly claim we have high realisations, simply creating the implication is enough to break this vow.

2. **Not giving material aid or teachings:** When we encounter sentient beings who need our help, we should not be miserly and deprive them of material support, Dharma teachings or spiritual assistance. If our help is requested and we refuse, despite having the means, we are breaking this vow. We should always do our best to practice generosity, and take full advantage when the opportunity presents itself. We should teach those who request teachings by showing them how to meditate or how to develop wisdom by studying.

3. **Not forgiving someone who has apologised:** If someone has harmed us, but offers a sincere apology for their actions, not accepting their apology and instead holding a grudge out of hatred, results in the breaking of this vow. We should always offer sentient beings the opportunity to confess their wrongdoings and to purify their negative karma.

4. **To abandon the Mahayana and present false teachings:** This vow is broken when we reject all or part of the Mahayana teachings as being false or not authentic Buddha-Dharma. For some, the sheer scale of the Mahayana vision is too difficult to grasp and this can lead to the view that some teachings are not Buddhist, for instance, rejecting the teachings of the second and third turning.

In essence these four vows help the practitioner overcome the four main afflictions which act as obstacles for Bodhicitta: attachment, miserliness, hatred and delusion. If we can prevent these afflictions from dominating our actions, we will have a strong foundation for all forms of spiritual practice.

Fourteen Root Vows According to the Tradition of Nagarjuna

In the Tradition of Nagarjuna, the Root Vows are split into three categories which highlight the types of behaviour that different people in different roles should be careful to avoid. Bear in mind, though, that these categories still apply to everyone.

The first set consists of five actions which are closely related to those who hold positions of power such as kings, leaders or elders. Such people are often invested with great authority and therefore must be especially conscious of how they use their power.

5. **To steal the property of the Three Jewels:** We break this vow if we steal anything that was offered or intended to be offered to the Three Jewels. Stealing from others or using material intended for the Sangha for your own purpose undermines people's trust and deprives the Sangha of the support they need to practice the Dharma.

6. **To reject the teachings:** Criticising or claiming that any part of the Hinayana, Mahayana or Vajrayana is not part of the Buddha's teachings will cause us to break this vow. We should not criticise or denigrate any teaching of the Buddha as this will directly cut us off from receiving the benefit of those teachings.

7. **To punish the immoral:** If we force a monk or nun to give up their ordination by forcing them to disrobe or to commit actions which go against their ordination commitments, we are then breaking this vow. We should do whatever we can to encourage people to hold pure ethical discipline and to purify any transgressions they make.

8. **To commit deeds of direct retribution:** Committing any one of the five heinous crimes creates the worst possible negative karma, leading to rebirth in the deepest hell realm without even entering the intermediate

state. Completely consumed by suffering, we would have no opportunity to generate Bodhicitta, nor bring any benefit to sentient beings.

9. **To profess wayward views:** Wrong views include any belief which denies the existence of the Three Jewels, the law of cause and effect, the Two Truths, the Four Noble Truths, the Twelve Links of Dependent Origination and so forth. Holding such wrong views will cause us to break this root vow as we will be unable to benefit even ourselves, let alone others. For example, by denying the law of karma we lack concern for the consequences of our actions and continue to create negative karma and hurt others.

The next set consists of one action which is closely related to those who are charged with caring for or managing a particular region, such as elected officials or administrators.

10. **To destroy a dwelling, town, city, region or nation:** If we completely destroy any place inhabited by living beings we will break this root vow. Destroying a city or country habitat, be it with fire, bombs, black magic or any other means, will kill many living beings. The negative karma that is accumulated by these actions will act as a major obstacle for generating Bodhicitta.

The last set consists of eight actions which are closely related to ordinary people.

11. **To teach emptiness to the untrained:** If we teach the profound subject of emptiness to those who are unable to interpret it properly, or perhaps do not wish to practise it, we will break this root vow. The danger is that some may misinterpret emptiness to mean nothingness or non-existence, falling to the nihilist extreme that denies the relationship between cause and effect. The true meaning of the emptiness of self and phenomena is very profound and difficult to understand. Many believe that the great Acharya Nagarjuna, who strongly propagated this system, was a nihilist, but this was only because they failed to realise the brilliant subtlety of his thought. We should therefore only share the final view of the nature of phenomena with those who are ripe to understand it.

12. **To cause another to give up Bodhicitta:** Convincing someone who is practising the Mahayana to practice the Hinayana path is breaking this vow. We may, for example, tell someone that Bodhicitta is beyond their capacity and suggest they give up this practice and instead follow the Hinayana path of individual liberation.

13. **To make someone abandon the foundational precepts:** We must not cause others to abandon their individual liberation vows, whether they include the 253 precepts of a monk, the 362 precepts of a nun, the eight or five precepts of a layperson, or the practice of the ten virtues. We should never suggest that these are part of a "lesser" system of practice and are not important for Mahayana practitioners. For instance, we should never encourage someone to ignore their vow to not drink alcohol, implying that they are at a lower level than Vajrayana vows and are therefore not important. If we cause others to abandon their vows of individual liberation we are then breaking this vow.

14. **To assert that the Foundational Vehicle does not conquer afflictions:** We break this vow when we disparage the practices of Shravakas or Pratyekabuddhas, saying they are incapable of liberating sentient beings from the suffering of samsara. These comments must be made with the intention of turning a person away from the Foundational Vehicle in order to be considered a downfall.

15. **To praise oneself and belittle others:** Out of jealousy, if we boast about our qualities and seek to criticise or denigrate other Bodhisattva practitioners, we will break this vow. We should be careful to remain humble and to rejoice in the virtues of others.

16. **To exaggerate one's realisations:** Out of attachment, if we falsely claim to have achieved realisations about hidden phenomena, such as emptiness, in order to gain favour or praise from others, then we have broken this vow. In general, you should not speak about your realisations in public. It is a matter for discussion only with your spiritual guide.

17. **To cause a king to inflict a fine:** This vow is broken when through the act of publicly slandering a monk or nun, you cause them to be punished or to have their property seized. Inflicting these sorts of hardships on people can cause them to abandon their vows of individual liberation.

18. **To steal possessions from practitioners:** If you have committed to supporting a meditator in strict retreat and you decide to take back what you have given, or you decide to give your offering to someone who is merely reciting texts or studying, you have broken this vow. The only way to realise emptiness is through training the mind in meditation, therefore by removing our support we prevent those conditions from arising.

Breaking and Repairing Bodhisattva Vows

To break a Root Vow, there must be four conditions present: (1) you must recognise that your behaviour contradicts a vow; (2) you must intentionally desire to break the vow; (3) you must carry out the action to completion; and (4) you must be pleased to have completed the action. Without the presence of all four conditions, you will not lose your engaged Bodhicitta; however if they are, you will need to re-take the vows from a vow preceptor.

Having taken the vows of a Bodhisattva, we should endeavour to keep them as purely as possible. If we do transgress our vows we ought to regret having done so and quickly practise a method of purification. In this way our development of Bodhicitta will constantly progress and we will not amass significant negative karma.

If we break one of the root Bodhisattva Vows, we can restore it in a number of different ways:

- Meditating on emptiness.
- Offering a seven-limbed prayer to the Buddhas and Bodhisattvas.
- Using the four powers of reliance, remorse, remedy and restraint.

Purification is a central part of the Kalachakra preliminary practices, and so the techniques will be discussed in greater detail in the last part of this book. For now, it is enough to realise that through sincere confession and restoration of our vows, we effectively reduce the karmic consequences of our actions. This doesn't mean we won't have to experience any results, but they will not multiply.

Please do not be discouraged or be afraid of maintaining these vows. Whether keeping them is a heavy burden, or something we undertake with ease and joy, depends entirely on our mental attitude. At the very least, we should preserve our desire to bring benefit to sentient beings and for this reason alone, make the effort to maintain our vows as best we can. Even if we falter along the way, the benefit we gain far outweighs any hardship we may experience.

Training in the Six Perfections

When considering the different types of practices a Bodhisattva engages in, there are literally countless variations. This is because there are countless sentient beings who each have specific conditions and therefore specific needs. For their sake, a Bodhisattva works in whichever way will be most beneficial to each sentient being and therefore has knowledge of, and is familiar with, many potential methods.

If we summarise all the Bodhisattva practices, we can identify six trainings known as the *Six Perfections*—(1) generosity, (2) ethical discipline, (3) patience, (4) joyous effort, (5) meditative concentration and (6) wisdom. These trainings encompass all of the activities of a Bodhisattva from the moment they generate engaged Bodhicitta.

At this stage of our discussion we will develop a general understanding of the structure of the Six Perfections and what role each training plays along the path. Then, over the course of the next seven chapters, we will examine each perfection in detail, as well as the skilful means with which to use our training for the benefit of others. Although the teachings of the perfections are based mostly on the Sutrayana, they will provide us with significant insight into how the Kalachakra Path of the Vajrayana uses this structure to efficiently achieve enlightenment.

The Definite Number of the Perfections

When understood correctly, there is nothing within the Mahayana that is not encompassed by the Six Perfections. It is important to have faith regarding this point as believing that something is missing or that "something else" needs to be done will only create doubt. As long as there is doubt, we risk being uncommitted to the path and our practice will lack strength and conviction.

Without conviction, our ability to penetrate deeply into the definitive meaning of the teachings is reduced and enlightenment becomes only a distant possibility. For this reason, we will examine Maitreya's text *Ornament of the Mahayana Sutras*, which addresses the definite number of the six trainings based on five topics: (1) high status; (2) fulfilling two aims; (3) perfecting the complete fulfilment of others' aims; (4) their subsuming the entire Mahayana and (5) the three trainings.

Based on High Status

High status has these excellent qualities:
Wealth, body, companions, the ability to accomplish actions,
Never falling under the power of mental afflictions,
And properly understanding actions.

The first reason Maitreya identifies for there being six trainings, is that they are all that is required to achieve both our temporary and ultimate goals. While our ultimate goal is to lead all sentient beings to enlightenment, to achieve this goal we need to practice a wide variety of methods over a long period of time. If we are fortunate enough to encounter the extraordinary methods of the Kalachakra Path in this life, it is an indicator that we have accumulated significant merit in previous lives. However it is not a guarantee that we will automatically possess the determination and focus necessary to achieve enlightenment in a single lifetime.

The reality of our situation is that we will likely need multiple lifetimes to manifest the final result; therefore, we must not lose the continuity of our practice between lives. If we are not careful, due to the weight of the negative karmas we create, we can easily be reborn in a lower realm, where we will experience aeons of pain and torment, with no chance to practice the Dharma.

To prevent this from occurring, we need to create the causes for achieving a precious human rebirth. Practicing the Six Perfections generates both the causes for our ultimate goal of full enlightenment, as well as the causes for our temporary goal of a higher rebirth. We do this in the following way:

1. **Generosity:** By providing others with what they need, we are born with the resources we need. Food and wealth will be available to us as supports for engaging in the actions we desire.

2. **Ethical Discipline:** By not harming sentient beings, avoiding negative actions and cultivating virtues, we are born with a beautiful human body, bestowed with long life.

3. **Patience:** By treating others with kindness even when they harm us, we create the causes to be surrounded by a pleasant environment and helpful companions. People will naturally be attracted to our beauty.

4. **Joyous Effort:** By striving to finish what we start, we will accomplish everything we desire.

5. **Meditative Concentration:** By taming the mind through meditation, in future lives we will not be overwhelmed by our afflictions and will be able to practice the Dharma effectively.

6. **Wisdom:** By dedicating ourselves to study, reflection and meditation, we will be born with a great interest in learning, an open mind and a sharp intellect. This will allow us to comprehend the profound teachings and to progress along the path.

While these qualities are sufficient to produce an amazing rebirth, there is an added benefit to practicing the Six Perfections within the context of the Kalachakra Path. Because of its unique connection to the Sublime Realm of Shambhala, those who practice the Kalachakra Path will also create the causes to be born into truly extraordinary conditions where the achievement of enlightenment is guaranteed in a single lifetime.

Based on Fulfilling Two Aims

Those who strive for the aims of beings
Work at giving, non-harm, and patience;
And completely fulfil their own aims
With stabilisation and liberation, together with their basis.

The second reason for the definite number of the Six Perfections is that they are all that is required to achieve one's own aim and the aim of others. In this context, generosity, ethical discipline and patience are the causes for achieving other's aim, and meditative concentration and wisdom are the causes for achieving your own aim. Joyous effort is used to achieve both.

The basis for this division is the recognition that no matter how realised we become, in order to benefit others we must have a karmic connection to them, for without it, there is no basis for communication and the mind of others will not be receptive to our influence. As such, practicing generosity creates the foundation for positive relationships as we provide our dear mothers with whatever they need. Relationships are preserved through ethical discipline as we avoid harming them in any way and patience makes certain we don't abandon sentient beings even if they cause us difficulty or harm. These three qualities strengthen the bond between us and others, providing a strong foundation for friendship and a connection that offers the opportunity to benefit them in the future.

The amount of benefit we can bring to a sentient being will depend on the degree of realisation we have achieved, in that the more obscurations we have in our mind, the more limited we are in helping others. Through meditative concentration, we are able to observe subtle modes of experience and generate insight regarding the ultimate nature of reality. Only this insight is capable of permanently clearing away all gross and subtle obscurations so that we can be of real benefit to others.

Based on Perfecting the Complete Fulfilment of Others' Aims

> *Through relieving others' poverty, not harming them,*
> *Being patient with their harm, not being dispirited with what they do,*
> *Delighting them, and speaking well to them*
> *You fulfil other's aims, which fulfils your own.*

The third reason is that the Six Perfections fulfil not only the temporary aims of others, but also their ultimate aim. Through generosity we help them avoid the suffering of poverty. Through ethical discipline we help them avoid the suffering of being harmed. Our practice of patience means we don't retaliate in the face of harm they may inflict on us, and our joyous effort ensures we continually work to benefit their lives. These are all considered temporary benefits that support temporary aims.

Ultimately, on the basis of our Bodhicitta, we will not be satisfied with merely providing sentient beings with temporary happiness. We also want the ability to lead them along a spiritual path so they can remove their own obscurations and break free from the conditioning of their karma. By practicing meditative concentration we achieve a variety of extrasensory abilities allowing us to inspire our students to have faith in the teachings and to be more effective as guides. When this is combined with the force of wisdom, we can instruct our students on the best methods to progress along the path.

Based on Their Subsuming the Entire Mahayana

The entire Mahayana is summed up in
Not delighting in resources,
Reverence, not being dispirited in two ways,
And the yogas free from conceptuality.

In this fourth verse, Maitreya indicates that all of the Mahayana practices are contained within the Six Perfections and therefore to truly practice the Mahayana we must then practice the Six Perfections. Through generosity we abandon attachment to resources and are content with what we have. Without the desire to accumulate wealth, we are able to maintain the precepts and gain respect for our ethical discipline. With patience we avoid being dispirited by inanimate conditions or hardship created by sentient beings, and with joyous effort we are not dispirited by the amount of time it will take to complete the two aims of self and others. Through meditation we learn to calm the mind and withdraw into a non-conceptual state and by training in wisdom we learn how to use that non-conceptual mind as a basis for establishing insight into the nature of reality.

Based on the Three Trainings

The Conqueror rightly presented six perfections
In terms of the three trainings: three are the first,
Two of the six are connected with the final two,
One is included in all three.

Finally, Maitreya demonstrates that all Buddhist practice is contained within the *Three Trainings* of ethical discipline, meditative concentration and wisdom. When these three trainings are divided into six, we arrive at the Six Perfections. Ethical discipline is divided into three: generosity, ethical discipline and patience. Here generosity is considered a pre-condition for ethical discipline to arise, as without it, one is too consumed by worldly concerns to practice discipline properly and patience is a support for ethical discipline as it helps maintain it over time. The last two perfections of meditative concentration and wisdom correspond directly to the second and third trainings. Joyous effort is again used by all the trainings to achieve one's own aim and the aim of others.

The Definite Order of the Perfections

The Buddha had very specific reasons for presenting the Six Perfections in their particular order. As Maitreya wrote in *The Ornament of the Mahayana Sutras*:

> *The second arises in dependence on the first;*
> *Because some abide lower and higher,*
> *Because of being gross and subtle,*
> *In this way, the orders abide respectively.*

The first line of this verse concerns the order in which the Perfections arise in the mind, establishing that the earlier trainings create the foundations for those that follow. When we develop generosity, we are capable of practicing ethical discipline. Through the practice of ethical discipline, we refrain from harming others and are naturally patient if they harm us. When we are patient in the face of adversities we can practice continuously which leads to joyous effort. With perseverance, we attain meditative concentration. Through the achievement of perfect stabilisation of the mind, we are able to experience the ultimate nature of reality.

The second point focuses on the relationship of the Perfections based on superiority. In this context, the earlier trainings are considered lower realisations than the later ones. For instance, the practice of generosity is said to be inferior to the practice of ethical discipline. This simply means that the higher trainings are capable of establishing deeper and more profound realisations, making wisdom the most superior training.

Finally, we can consider the order of the Perfections in terms of their subtlety, where the earlier trainings are coarser than the later ones. This is similar to the idea of higher and lower, only in this case, the emphasis is on the level of reality that each training allows access to. The most subtle layer of reality is only accessible through the perfection of wisdom.

HOW BODHICITTA DEVELOPS OVER TIME

Understanding the Six Perfections on the basis of both their number and order, demonstrates how they work together as a dynamic system of practices that can be used to achieve extraordinary realisations. We will now complete our general discussion of Bodhicitta by examining how training in the Six Perfections progressively purifies the mind, as illustrated by the four levels of development that a Bodhisattva passes through during the process of actualising Buddhahood.

Arousing Bodhicitta by Practicing with Aspiration

After training the mind in love and compassion and generating a fully qualified form of aspirational Bodhicitta, our entrance into the Mahayana Path is established. Within the context of the Five Paths of Attainment (see Book One), we can say we have entered the Mahayana Path of Accumulation. As we progress on the Paths of Accumulation and Preparation, our Bodhicitta is the motivation that inspires our spiritual practice. We still need to remain diligent however, to prevent our aspirational Bodhicitta from weakening. There are four similes used to describe Bodhicitta at this level:

1. **Earth—Aspiration:** When we begin on the path, we rely heavily on Bodhicitta as an aspiration. It is like the earth in the way it provides a solid foundation on which to build a stable practice.

2. **Gold—Stability:** To achieve Buddhahood our aspiration needs to be strengthened so it will remain stable as we progress along the entire path. This is compared to gold which, unlike other metals, does not tarnish and is immutable in the sense that it has the same qualities whether it

is polished or pulled directly from the ground. Likewise, our aspiration needs to remain true, regardless of the conditions.

3. **Waxing Moon—Gradual Refinement:** Through dedicated practice, our Bodhicitta is strengthened and becomes increasingly more profound and rich. Although in the beginning we cannot see our Ultimate Bodhicitta, eventually it will manifest in all its radiance. This process is likened to the tiny sliver of the waxing moon that slowly grows into the dazzling full moon.

4. **Fire—Purifying Obscurations:** To realise even the slightest aspect of Ultimate Bodhicitta, we must make great effort to prepare our minds and clear away our obscurations. Like a burning fire, our practice of the Six Perfections consumes our afflictions and removes the obstacles preventing our Ultimate Bodhicitta from manifesting.

Arousing Bodhicitta Through Excellent and Perfectly Pure Intention

By arousing Bodhicitta at the previous level, we come to the realisation of the emptiness of inherent existence and so have entered the Path of Insight where we are now considered an Arya Bodhisattva. The Path of Habituation then follows where our practice of the Six Perfections steadily refines our realisation of Ultimate Bodhicitta. With the cultivation of each level, more of its boundless nature is revealed until it becomes fully manifest. The similes used to represent the progression of Bodhicitta at this stage are:

5. **Treasure—Generosity:** When we practice generosity combined with the realisation of emptiness we create the causes for inexhaustible wealth and goodness. This is compared to a treasure of such value that it is able to bring great benefit to sentient beings in the future.

6. **Mine of Jewels—Ethical Discipline:** Whereas generosity concerns the giving to others, ethical discipline helps us purify our own mind. Through the power of our realisation of emptiness, we cut through our gross obscurations and allow more of our innate purity to emerge. This is likened to digging in a mine of jewels that is the source of great treasures.

7. **Ocean—Patience:** Through the power of our realisation of emptiness, there is no longer fear of being harmed by sentient beings and therefore patience can grow to become expansive like an immense ocean.

8. **Vajra—Joyous Effort:** As we begin to experience more of our true nature, we naturally strive continuously to improve our realisation of Ultimate Bodhicitta. This unshakeable determination is likened to a vajra which has the quality of being indestructible.

9. **Mountain—Meditation:** Through the power of meditating on emptiness, we completely eradicate all forms of gross grasping and achieve an unwavering stability of mind, similar to a mountain.

10. **Medicine—Wisdom:** Finally, through meditating on the perfection of wisdom we successfully clear away the subtle afflictions that obscured our experience of the fully established nature of reality. This partial experience of the sublime emptiness is likened to medicine which is the cure for all ailments.

11. **Spiritual Guide—Skilful Means:** By then applying that wisdom towards the benefit of others, we further refine our experience of Bodhicitta. This is compared to the spiritual guide who for us, is a source of unimaginable benefit.

Arousing Fully Matured Bodhicitta

Up until this point, our realisation of Ultimate Bodhicitta has been obscured by afflictive obscurations and for this reason, the previous seven stages are considered to be impure stages. Although still on the Path of Habituation, with the complete removal of the afflictions, our Bodhicitta is now considered fully mature and no effort is required to maintain it. The focus then shifts to removing the subtle cognitive obscurations which prevent the omniscient mind from manifesting. Three similes are used to describe this final process:

12. **Wish-fulfilling Jewel—Power:** With the inseparable union of the perfection of wisdom and method, enormous power to bring benefit to countless sentient beings is generated. As such, it is compared to a Wish-fulfilling Jewel.

13. **Sun—Prayer:** By continuing to refine our realisation of sublime emptiness, our capacity finally grows to match our aspirations and whatever prayers we make, we can actually achieve. This is likened to the sun whose light allows all life to flourish.

14. **Melody—Primordial Wisdom:** When our realisation of sublime emptiness is perfected, we abide continuously in primordial wisdom, becoming a Tenth-Level Bodhisattva. This is compared to a melodious song that brings delight to everyone who hears it.

A Tenth-Level Bodhisattva has achieved their own aim of eradicating all adventitious obscurations. To perfectly manifest the result of a fully enlightened Buddha, all that is left is to complete the accumulations of merit and wisdom. There are five similes that refer to their immeasurable activities:

15. **King—Extrasensory Perceptions:** When our realisation of sublime emptiness is combined with the manifestation of extrasensory perceptions, there are no limits to what we can do. We have complete control over our reality and can manifest whatever is needed to guide sentient beings. This is likened to a powerful king who can do whatever he chooses.

16. **King's Treasury—Union of Shamatha and Vipashyana:** When our realisation of sublime emptiness is combined with the union of calm abiding and special insight, there is no aspect of reality we cannot potentially know. Although we have not yet attained an omniscient mind that simultaneously knows all phenomena, there is nothing we cannot know if we direct our minds to it. We are therefore able to guide sentient beings in the exact way that is needed. This is compared to a king's treasure trove from which riches can be distributed to all his subjects.

17. **Great Highway—The Five Paths:** Through joining our realisation of sublime emptiness with the path to enlightenment, we ensure that all our actions will lead to the result of becoming a fully enlightened Buddha, like a great highway that has been travelled by all the Buddhas of the past and will be travelled by all the Buddhas of the future.

18. **Steed—Non-Referential Compassion:** By perfectly joining our great compassion with our realisation of sublime emptiness, we achieve a compassion that is completely free from limitation and completely free from bias. Like a powerful steed, this compassion will carry us through the final phases of refinement until we achieve Buddhahood.

19. **Natural Spring—Recollection of the Teachings:** Once we have fully integrated every aspect of the Buddha's teachings, they are with us every moment so that all our actions become an expression of our realisation, like a natural spring from which water continuously flows, nourishing all who are thirsty.

Arousing Bodhicitta Free from All Obscurations

As we become completely habituated to abiding in the realisation of sublime emptiness, while still manifesting for the benefit of sentient beings, we remove the need to exert any effort whatsoever. We spontaneously manifest as a fully enlightened Buddha and enter the Path of No More Learning. This is the ultimate result that fulfils the two aims of both self and other. Three similes are used to describe this state:

20. **Harp—Enlightened Speech:** A Buddha's speech matures the minds of sentient beings by guiding them to their own enlightened nature. As everyone longs to listen to these teachings, it is likened to the beautiful melody of a harp that captivates its audience.

21. **River—Enlightened Body:** Like the effortless flow of a river shaping itself to the contours of the landscape, a Buddha effortlessly manifests infinite form bodies which fulfil the needs of sentient beings.

22. **Cloud—Enlightened Mind:** With its non-referential compassion that spontaneously manifests for the benefit of sentient beings, the Buddha's mind is like a great rain cloud, nurturing the land and providing the necessary nourishment for all life to exist and flourish. It is the source of limitless manifestations like raindrops falling.

REVIEW OF KEY POINTS

- There are two forms of Bodhicitta: (1) Ultimate Bodhicitta which is the realisation of the essential nature of reality and (2) Relative Bodhicitta which is the desire to achieve enlightenment for the benefit of all sentient beings. Relative Bodhicitta is the method to reveal Ultimate Bodhicitta.

- There are two aspects to Relative Bodhicitta: (1) the purpose which is to free all sentient beings from suffering and (2) the method which is to attain the state of Buddhahood.

- Relative Bodhicitta can be divided into two types: (1) Aspirational Bodhicitta which is the desire to achieve enlightenment for the sake all beings and (2) Engaged Bodhicitta which uses that desire as a motivation for practicing the Dharma.

- The Four Conditions that give rise to the desire to achieve enlightenment: (1) seeing the qualities of Buddhas and Bodhisattvas; (2) listening to the teachings of the Buddha; (3) seeing that the teachings are in danger of disappearing and (4) seeing the rarity for someone to generate Bodhicitta.

- The Four Causes that support the generation of aspirational Bodhicitta are: (1) a spiritual lineage; (2) being sustained by an excellent teacher; (3) compassion toward living beings, and (4) not being discouraged by difficulties.

- The Four Strengths that influence the stability of one's Bodhicitta are: (1) strength of oneself; (2) strength of others; (3) strength of cause and (4) strength of practice.

- The Three Ways that Bodhicitta Manifests are: (1) like a king; (2) like a boat captain, and (3) like a shepherd.

- Bodhicitta can be generated in two ways: (1) through a ritual ceremony bestowed by a qualified lineage holder or (2) through meditation on love and compassion.

- The precepts for aspirational Bodhicitta include: (1) contemplating the benefits of developing Bodhicitta; (2) generating Bodhicitta six times each day, and (3) abandoning the thought of self-cherishing.

- To ensure your Bodhicitta doesn't degenerate in future lives, you should (1) abandon the Four Black Practices and (2) cultivate the Four White Practices.

- When aspirational Bodhicitta becomes stable, you should generate engaged Bodhicitta by first receiving the Bodhisattva Vows from a qualified lineage holder. There are Eighteen Root Vows and Forty-Six Branch Vows.

- To break a vow you must: (1) recognise that your behaviour contradicts a vow; (2) intentionally desire to break the vow; (3) carry out the action to completion; and (4) be pleased by having completed the action.

- Once engaged Bodhicitta has been generated, you should practice the Six Perfections: (1) generosity; (2) ethical discipline; (3) patience; (4) joyous effort, (5) meditative concentration and (6) wisdom.

- The Six Perfections contain everything you need because: (1) they create the causes for higher rebirths; (2) they fulfil not only your own aim but also the aims of others; (3) they help others achieve their temporary and ultimate aims; (4) they contain all of the Mahayana practices; and (5) they contain the three trainings.

- There are four levels of Bodhicitta that develop over time: (1) arousing Bodhicitta by practicing with aspiration; (2) arousing Bodhicitta through excellent and perfectly pure intention; (3) arousing fully matured Bodhicitta and (4) arousing Bodhicitta free from all obscurations.

CHAPTER SEVEN

Releasing Attachment through Generosity

Out of love and compassion, a great doctor develops a desire to bring benefit to their patients, but no matter how pure their motivation, if they haven't acquired the necessary knowledge and skills, they could potentially do more harm than good. Similarly, without putting time and effort into taming our minds and cultivating our good qualities, our capacity to benefit sentient beings will be limited. It is for this reason that the next stage of our practice is to train in the *Six Perfections* of generosity, ethical discipline, patience, joyful effort, meditative concentration and wisdom.

While the Kalachakra Path offers specific techniques for working with each of these qualities, we will first study them in a general context to gain a broader understanding of their purpose, develop greater confidence in the Bodhisattva Path and strengthen our desire to practice engaged Bodhicitta by taking the Bodhisattva Vows. This attitude will then provide a strong support for the formal practice of the Kalachakra Preliminaries that are detailed in the last part of this book.

For each Perfection, we will use a five-point analysis: (1) definition of the quality to be cultivated; (2) reasons to practice this quality; (3) divisions of the quality; (4) how to practice and (5) results of practice.

WHAT IS GENEROSITY?

The quality of generosity, as with all the perfections, is not a physical action but rather a state of mind. It is *the mind that desires to give fully of one's own resources without attachment.* Whether an action can be considered generous depends entirely on the presence of this motivation. If we give out of attachment to personal gain or reputation, we are not cultivating generosity.

As generosity arises in the mind, it does not rely on the actual relief of poverty. If it did, we could not say that the Buddhas had perfected this quality since there are countless beings who live in destitution. Training in generosity is more concerned with how we respond to the reality of poverty and much less about our capacity to satisfy every sentient being on the planet. This comes from the wisdom that knows that the suffering of sentient beings is a result of the karma they have created and therefore to truly solve the problem of their poverty we need to help them create the causes for wealth.

There are two main aspects to the mind of generosity:

1. **Lack of attachment towards one's possessions or body.** Instead of clinging strongly to our possessions and body, we understand they have only arisen due to the kindness of others and we see them as temporary supports for our practice. This attitude works as a direct antidote towards the *self-grasping thought* that holds onto things as being "me" or "mine".

2. **Willingness to give one's resources.** This attitude arises from recognising the needs of sentient beings and our access to resources to fulfil those needs. It takes the form of a desire to then use our resources to bring them benefit. Because its focus is on giving away our possessions, it is a direct antidote to the mind of *stinginess*.

When both these qualities are perfected, we are willing to give whatever we have, including our own bodies, to bring benefit to others. This extraordinary form of generosity is illustrated in a story from one of the Buddha's previous lives, when he was born as a young prince. Walking through the forest with his two brothers, he came upon a mother tigress who had given birth to a litter of cubs. Unable to find food, the tigress had become extremely famished and feeble. Recognising that without food, she would either die or eat her own cubs, the young prince's heart was filled with compassion. As the three continued on their way, the young prince could not stop thinking about the tigress and her cubs. He contemplated how she needed to eat meat to regain her strength but that taking another's life was not acceptable. He then developed the strong aspiration to offer her his body. Saying goodbye to his brothers, he returned to where the tigress lay and without the slightest attachment to his own life, he gave himself to be eaten. Because of this extraordinary sacrifice, an incredibly close bond was formed between these beings. Many lives later this connection would ripen when the tigress and cubs were born as the ascetic yogis who became the Buddha's first disciples after he achieved enlightenment.

For most people, this incredible level of generosity would be extremely difficult to actualise. Such an act would require an extraordinary degree of wisdom and compassion, absolutely no attachment to one's body, with an unshakeable faith in the law of karma and a view which truly understands the nature of death and rebirth. For these reasons, this form of generosity is not generally recommended for anyone other than highly realised Bodhisattvas.

Although we may not yet have perfect motivation, this doesn't mean we have to postpone our practice of generosity. When we know what to look for, there are many aspects of our lives we can use as supports for strengthening the attitude of generosity in our mind. Even if our actions only achieve short-term benefits for this life, they bring us closer to our ultimate aim and so are still completely worthwhile.

REASONS TO PRACTICE THE PERFECTION OF GENEROSITY

It can be helpful to reflect on the reasons for partaking in any practice. Considering the advantages of doing so and the disadvantages of not doing so increases our determination to practice and provides us with the clarity we need for it to be effective.

In the case of generosity, the primary obstacles we need to overcome are those of *attachment* and *stinginess*, which thoroughly permeate our lives through our extreme grasping to our bodies and our possessions. The collection of things we surround ourselves with form the very basis for our sense of identity. The body is seen as the "me" and the possessions are seen as "mine". This clinging is most obvious with physical objects, but we can also see many examples of attachment to mental constructs, such as our country, political views, our jobs and relationships.

A natural result of our clinging is stinginess. We see our favourite jacket or book as an extension of who we are, and so we are less likely to want to share it. It would be like giving a part of yourself away with no guarantee of ever getting it back and this fear of separation can be too hard for many people to accept, so instead we choose to hoard everything we've ever owned, accumulating boxes of "keepsakes" in our home. Even if we don't use them any more, we try to justify our attachment with the thought that we might need them one day.

Herein lies the major disadvantage, for the heart of stinginess relies on the self-cherishing thought that sees it as more important for you to be happy than others. This extends beyond present happiness to future happiness as well. To the mind of stinginess, it is preferable to save one's possessions for a potential situation rather than using them to fulfil the needs of someone in the present. When we do this, we deprive others of temporary happiness and we also create the causes for our own future suffering.

The essence of stinginess is to prevent others from receiving benefit from our possessions, holding onto everything for ourselves and fighting to protect them from others. The karmic result of this mind is to be reborn in the realm of hungry ghosts where we constantly lack the most basic supports for life. Deprived of food and water, our mind is tortured by an endless stream of desires that can never be satisfied. Under such circumstances, there is absolutely no opportunity to practice the Dharma. Even if we are fortunate enough to be born into a human realm, resources will be deficient and what we do have will be in constant danger of being taken away or destroyed.

The influence of attachment and stinginess is like living in a castle of massive stone walls, surrounded by an impenetrable moat. Although the barriers are effective for keeping people out, they also prevent us from leaving, isolating us from the world and destroying our capacity to connect with others. Without that connection, our love and compassion will not grow and we will be unable to actualise our potential. In order to truly realise our Bodhicitta motivation, we must therefore abandon these afflictions.

The best method to do this is through the practice of generosity. By cultivating the desire to give to others, we directly counteract stinginess and weaken our attachment. Rather than holding onto our possessions, we strive to use them to bring benefit and when we see the needs of others are being met, great joy and happiness can be experienced.

If we live our life in this way, as death approaches, we will be content in the knowledge we have made the most of the opportunities we received. By dedicating ourselves to the needs of others, we can be assured we will experience great abundance in our future rebirths. Such resources will enable us to have long and healthy lives where we can continue our practice of generosity, bringing even further benefit to sentient beings.

THE DIVISIONS OF GENEROSITY

Using different sets of criteria, we can divide the practice of cultivating generosity into various categories. If we look at the nature of the practitioner, there is the generosity of lay practitioners living in the world and the generosity practiced by monastics living outside the world. Due to the presence of particular conditions, each is able to give in a different manner. For instance a householder working for wages will be more capable of making material offerings such as food or financial support compared to a monk or nun who has renounced earning an income and therefore is more suited to giving teachings or spiritual support.

It is important to be mindful of the situations in which we find ourselves, as lacking a particular set of conditions doesn't mean we cannot practice generosity in a different way. By studying the various divisions of the practice, we can develop clarity regarding our options which helps us make the most of the opportunities that do arise.

If we divide generosity in terms of benefit received, we can speak of three: (1) the generosity of giving Dharma; (2) the generosity of giving fearlessness and (3) the generosity of giving material wealth. Of these, giving Dharma is the only form of generosity capable of bringing long-term benefit to sentient beings, helping them create the causes for genuine happiness and ultimately enlightenment. The remaining two bring short-term benefit by fulfilling their needs within this life.

Giving Dharma

Of all the sources of wealth in this world, by far the most precious and valuable is the wisdom and realisations we develop through authentic Dharma practice. They provide us with the capacity to clear away our obscurations and provide the basis for helping sentient beings achieve freedom from suffering.

When we share our wisdom with others, we are practicing the *Generosity of Giving Dharma*. This could be the transmission of teachings, bestowing empowerments or simply offering words of advice. Anything that helps sentient beings access the benefits of Dharma can be considered a gift of Dharma.

To ensure the benefit of our gift, we should consider the following points:

1. **Valid recipients:** We should only give Dharma to those with a sincere desire to practice it. If they lack respect towards the teachings or the teacher, they are not a valid vessel for the teachings. In such situations, the teachings can fail to bring benefit to the person, causing them to act in ways that could lead others to lose faith in the teachings. A good way to test the resolve of a student is to wait until they have requested teachings before bestowing them.

2. **Correct motivation:** When giving teachings, we should only do so out of a desire to bring benefit to the people involved. We should avoid all worldly motivations such as accumulating wealth, fame or honour. As the sole purpose of Sacred Dharma is to alleviate suffering, the only valid motivation is compassion.

3. **Without error:** We should only teach the authentic Dharma we have received from qualified teachers and ideally, only what we have practiced and incorporated into our experience. If we have not yet achieved realisations in a subject, we should at least ensure we are transmitting the Dharma without introducing errors, by relying on the teachings of the lineage masters.

4. **Giving proper instruction:** When sharing Dharma, we need to be mindful of the needs of the person. Not everyone is ready for every type of teaching and so we must be careful not to cause confusion by teaching

advanced topics before the necessary foundations have been developed. Knowing which teachings are appropriate for a given situation is an important skill to have before sharing what we have learnt.

5. **Inspiring others to practice:** The manner in which we share the Dharma should be inspiring for those who hear it. The experience should encourage individuals to take what they have heard and put it into practice. Our actions should show reverence to the teachings, making them clear and accessible to the audience and presenting them in a clean and pleasant environment.

In this time of degeneration, effective transmission of the Dharma is difficult. Due to the fact that there are few people with authentic realisations, the chance of introducing errors is high. As the great Kadampa Geshe, Dromptonpa once said:

It is useless for a beginner with neither experience nor realisation to try to help others with the Dharma. No blessings can be obtained from him, just as nothing can be poured out of an empty vessel.

For this reason, if we are not yet in the position to practice the generosity of giving Dharma directly, we can still help others who are. This can be through translating texts or helping your teachers be successful in their Dharma activities, doing whatever you can to help the teachings flourish. This will bring immeasurable benefit to yourself and others.

Giving Fearlessness

As long as we are trapped in cyclic existence we must deal with the impermanent nature of causes and conditions. This means that no matter how happy we may feel now, sooner or later the conditions will inevitably run out, turning happiness into dissatisfaction. Deep down we are aware of this occurrence as it is a pattern we have each experienced over and over again since beginningless time. Due to this familiarity with the suffering of change, we instinctively feel a sense of fear or anxiety over maintaining the pleasure we are fortunate enough to experience.

Of all the things we fear, the strongest is the fear of losing our life. The desire to survive is so powerful in fact that it leads people to engage very easily in non-virtuous acts such as killing, stealing or lying. It seems that in most cultures, when someone's life is threatened, any action can be seen to be justified in order to stay alive.

Recognising this, if we can provide sentient beings with conditions that support their life, we are helping them to live free from fear. This is called the *Generosity of Giving Fearlessness*, and can range from saving a being's life to providing them with a safe place to sleep. Anything in fact that removes fear is considered a gift of fearlessness. Broadly speaking, there are three aspects we can offer protection from:

1. **Animals:** The animal realm is filled with predators that can be extremely dangerous, causing death in only seconds. Making effort to protect others from being bitten by poisonous creatures or eaten by carnivorous beasts is one form of offering protection. This can be as simple as freeing a fly trapped in a spider's web or watching over a herd of sheep. It can also include the creation of animal sanctuaries or safe zones where predators cannot enter.

2. **Humans:** Due to their great intelligence, humans are particularly dangerous. If their minds are dominated by afflictions, intelligence can be used to inflict considerable harm onto other beings. Consider the suffering of animal livestock such as chickens, pigs and cows caused by humans. Making effort to protect those who are in danger of being killed or hurt by humans is a second form of protection.

3. **Inanimate Things:** Finally there are a wide range of problems that arise from interacting with our physical environment, including rockslides, tsunamis, earthquakes, tornados and so forth. By offering people shelter from the elements, we protect them from harm and potential loss of life.

In the case of animals and humans, it is important to act with compassion for both sides. While we should do what we can to protect those who are being abused or harmed, we must never abandon our love for those who are perpetrating the harm. As those who engage in non-virtuous actions are creating the causes for more suffering in the future, they are just as worthy of our compassion. If we can help correct their behaviour, this too can be considered a form of protecting them from suffering.

When we help someone live without fear, their mind is put at ease and they can live in harmony with those around them. For humans, this is especially important as it opens the door to the Dharma, removing the constant battle to stay alive and creating an opportunity to practice.

Giving Material Wealth

The final form of generosity concerns relieving the immediate suffering of sentient beings through the giving of material resources. A direct example of this is to give food to a beggar who is hungry. An indirect example is to offer financial support to someone dedicating themselves to virtue. Whatever form the giving takes, the essence is to use whatever resources you have available to fulfil the needs of others. We call this the *Generosity of Giving Material Wealth*.

For this type of generosity, we can speak of two categories of objects that can be given:

1. **Internal Objects:** These objects are related to the body of the person practicing generosity. It includes donating parts of your body to be used by others, as in the case of donating an organ, giving blood or even sacrificing your life to save another. As we discussed previously, giving your life for the sake of another is extremely difficult and should only be attempted by those who have already attained a high level of realisation. You can however give your body by serving the needs of others, as in serving as an assistant.

2. **External Objects:** All other objects separate from yourself are considered to be external; however, to be a valid basis for giving, you must own the object being offered. This means you should not give away other people's property unless they ask you to. When giving external objects, you can either give up ownership completely and transfer the object to the recipient, or you can let the recipient use the object while still maintaining ownership. Either way, how the object is used should be left to the discretion of the recipient, with no "strings attached" to the gift.

Of these two, external objects are easier to give than internal objects. When the experience of stinginess is strong, work first to lessen your attachment to your possessions. You can start slowly by giving away the things you no longer use, building the strength of generosity in your mind. When the desire to benefit others grows, you can consider volunteering your time to work for others. In this way generosity will eventually overcome your stinginess and self-cherishing.

To illustrate this process we can think of the Buddha and the Miserly King. One day a King approached the Buddha and asked for his advice. He told the Buddha that even though he wanted to help his subjects, he could not bear to be parted from even a single gold coin from his vast treasury. The Buddha told the King that he should not worry and instead of giving away his riches, he should practice by giving with his right hand and receiving with his left, and then he should give with his left and receive with his right. Satisfied with the advice, the King returned to his palace and began to practice by passing a piece of gold between his hands. Through this simple act, the King became familiar with the act of giving and little by little his aversion subsided and generosity was born in his mind.

HOW TO PRACTICE GENEROSITY

Practicing generosity is based on recognising opportunities to counteract one's attachment and stinginess and then taking advantage of those opportunities through the act of giving. It is primarily a mental training that requires both *vigilance* to bring awareness to our actions and *mindfulness* to remember the different aspects of the training. In the beginning, take time to familiarise yourself with the following topics as they will help give shape to your conduct.

Knowing When to Give

Whether an act of generosity will bring long-lasting benefit will depend on how much wisdom we can bring to the act. As each situation will be different, we need to develop our capacity to evaluate what is appropriate to give within a particular context. To help us discriminate wisely, we can consider four general scenarios:

1. **Unpleasant and Not Beneficial:** If giving a gift will not alleviate the recipient's immediate suffering and brings no long-term benefit, we should refrain from giving. It is better to wait until the conditions change so that your gift is not wasted. An example would be to give a TV to someone who is suffering from hunger. This gift will not relieve their hunger, and could potentially lead them to develop attachment to their possessions which will increase their suffering in the future.

2. **Pleasant and Not Beneficial:** If the gift brings the temporary experience of pleasure but is not beneficial in the long-term, it is better to refrain from giving. For example, giving an alcoholic a drink may help them feel better at the time, but feeding their craving may make it harder for them to let go of their addiction.

3. **Unpleasant and Beneficial:** If an object will not alleviate a person's suffering in the short term, but is capable of helping them experience happiness in the future, it is worth giving the gift. For instance, the administration of an unpleasant medical treatment with the result of freedom from sickness. The key here is to consider the tradeoff being made; ideally the benefit to be received later will outweigh the temporary discomfort.

4. **Pleasant and Beneficial:** If giving an object will bring temporary relief to suffering now as well as providing long lasting benefit, it is definitely worth giving, such as giving food to a Dharma practitioner. By nourishing their body, you create the conditions for them to continue practicing the Dharma which then nourishes their mind, helping them create the causes to free themselves from suffering and then in turn others.

In all four scenarios, the deciding factor is how much benefit will be received from the gift. While temporary benefits of pleasure are nice, they are fleeting by nature and so do not solve any long term problems. At most, they offer a brief moment of respite; like a band-aid. To bring lasting benefit to others, we need to think carefully about the karmic repercussions of our gift. Look beyond the physical effects and reflect on how the action will affect both the mind of the person and your mind as the giver.

A Meaningful Motivation for Giving

When offering a gift, it is not the size that is important but the mind with which it is given. To truly make your act of generosity beneficial, it needs to come from a virtuous motivation. You can strengthen this motivation by thinking about the following points:

1. **Purpose:** For the act of giving to be considered a Bodhisattva practice, it should be integrated into your larger motivation of Bodhicitta. You can do this by recognising that through the act of generosity, you are accumulating both merit and wisdom. These accumulations will create the causes for you to achieve Buddhahood and ultimately bring lasting benefit to all sentient beings.

2. **Object:** For the act of giving to be free from attachment, you should cultivate the attitude that sees the object as being on loan from sentient beings. As a Bodhisattva, you should think that you don't own anything and what you do have, has only been borrowed until the time comes to give it back. Developing this attitude helps us let go of our possessive notion that objects belong to us and nurtures the feeling of gratitude towards others who have kindly given to us.

3. **Recipient:** For the act of giving to be free from self-cherishing, you should consider the recipient as though they were your spiritual friend. Our ordinary attitude likes to focus on the benefit we bring to others, leading to a sense of pride about being "a good person." Here it is more important to recognise that through generating a need for help, the recipient of your gift is acting as a support for you to reduce your attachment and stinginess. In this way, it is you who is receiving the real benefit from the act. This will increase your appreciation of sentient beings, strengthening your bond with one another.

Attitudes to Avoid

Having a motivation based on wisdom can cause your merit to increase exponentially, however the opposite also holds true. If your attitude is based on deluded ways of thinking, your merit will be seriously limited and you may even create the causes for further suffering. It is therefore worthwhile to spend time to become familiar with attitudes that prevent our practice of generosity from being effective.

1. **Wrong views:** When we practice generosity on the basis of false assumptions, we automatically limit the potential of the act. The most important wrong view to be aware of is the belief that our act of giving will not bring results. No matter how small our gift, when made with the right intention, it will definitely become a cause for future happiness. To think otherwise disregards the karmic law of cause and effect and makes the action meaningless.

   Another wrong view is the belief that practicing generosity alone is enough to achieve enlightenment. If it were, the Buddha would not have taught the other five Perfections. While focusing on charity is extremely beneficial, it is still provisional in nature and to go beyond merely offering temporary assistance, we need to cut through the root of our suffering and achieve lasting peace and harmony. Generosity is one part of doing this.

2. **Pride:** We must avoid developing pride in relation to our giving. Falling into a competitive frame of mind causes our motivation to deteriorate and we will no longer be authentically practicing generosity. Avoid using acts of generosity as a means of improving your status and showing off, as this kind of thinking reinforces self-cherishing and defeats the purpose of the training. Try to remain humble at all times, recognising that you are truly fortunate to have the opportunity to give.

3. **Discouragement:** After engaging in an act of generosity, we may develop a feeling of remorse, perhaps due to a hardship experienced from no longer having what was given. By regretting a virtuous action we diminish its strength and limit its potential benefits. To avoid generating this form of regret, it is important to give with a joyful mind that recognises the long-term benefits that will come from the act and afterwards rejoice in what we were able to do. No matter how difficult things may become for us, by keeping everything in perspective, our merits will continue to increase.

4. **Bias:** Generosity should never be used as a way of controlling or punishing sentient beings and our decision of who to help should not be based on bias. No matter how a person acts towards us, we should maintain our equanimity and do whatever we can to help them.

5. **Expectations:** Generosity is not like a financial investment or a business deal where we expect to receive greater rewards than what we invest. When we have this type of expectation, it is no longer oriented towards the benefit of others, but on bringing benefit to the self. Always try to give freely without the expectation of results and simply be content with the benefit received by the recipient.

6. **Desire for fruition:** We must be careful not to make temporary aims our primary motivation. Even though generosity creates conducive conditions in future lives, these samsaric conditions should not be the motivation for our actions. Although we can appreciate when such conditions do arise, they are not the driving force behind why we give. Our motivation should go beyond this, to leading all beings to be completely free from samsaric conditions by attaining full enlightenment.

How to Actually Give

Once we have established a meaningful motivation, free of deluded attitudes, we are ready to give our gift. While this attitude ensures our action will bring us benefit, we want to maximise the benefit to the person. Preferably, there will be a direct benefit received, but we should also consider the long-term benefit of forming a virtuous connection to a Bodhisattva.

The manner in which we give determines the overall quality of the experience in the mind of the recipient. If it is a pleasant experience, the connection made will have strength, but if it is unpleasant, they will naturally push away, weakening the connection. When we eventually achieve Buddhahood, the beings we have made strong positive connections with will be the ones to receive the greatest benefit from us. We therefore need to be particularly mindful of our behaviour during the act of giving. The following are general guidelines to consider:

1. **Be pleasant:** Whenever you give a gift, do so with a pleasant demeanour. Your face should be relaxed and calm, not scowling or looking angry and if possible, smile and genuinely enjoy the act. If you have already reflected on the benefits of your actions, appearing happy should come naturally, rather than having to put on a fake display.

2. **Show respect:** Always remember to treat the person with gratitude and respect. It is you who is receiving the greatest benefit, and so it is the recipient who is really demonstrating extraordinary kindness by accepting your gift. Therefore, when you offer the gift, you should bow or present it in a respectful manner that accords to their customs. Avoid showing signs of contempt or arrogance.

3. **Personally give the gift:** If possible you should offer your gifts in person. This will allow you to make a stronger karmic connection with the recipient, as it is a moment of coming together in the same time and place.

4. **Give without harm:** The act of giving should not harm the person in any way. While some gifts may be unpleasant at first, they should be given in a compassionate manner to minimise the pain and suffering of the recipient. Use whatever methods you can to ease their mind and make sure they are as comfortable as possible.

5. **Bear any hardships:** No matter what difficulties you face, you should always be happy to have the opportunity to practice generosity. You should not resent the other person for any hardships you experience as this will damage your karmic connection with them.

By keeping these points in mind when giving, a strong link between you and the person will be established, providing a basis to continue bringing them benefit in the future. In this way, even a brief encounter with a beggar on the street is a wonderful opportunity for accumulating merit and wisdom.

Giving through Visualisation

For those without the material resources to give, using visualisations as a skilful means to reducing attachment and stinginess is another option for

Mandala Offerings are a skilful method for practicing generosity.

practicing generosity. The basic structure for making offerings in meditation is to: (1) choose a recipient; (2) generate offerings and (3) give the offerings. With regard to the type of recipient, we can identify two main approaches:

1. **Enlightened Beings:** To reduce our attachment, it can be very beneficial to make offerings to an enlightened assembly. After visualising the field of refuge in the space before you, bring to mind different examples of things you enjoy or anything you admire or feel attachment to such as good food, beautiful environments or modern technology. Once you have brought the objects of offering to mind, make them vast by imagining them multiplying to fill the entire space around you. With a mind that remembers the faults of attachment and the benefits of generosity, freely give the offerings to the enlightened field, imagining them dissolving into pure white light. Repeat this process over and over again, using whatever objects come to mind.

2. **Sentient Beings:** To reduce our stinginess, working with sentient beings may be more appropriate since it works more directly with our self-cherishing attitude. Here the emphasis is on strengthening our desire to bring benefit to them by fulfilling their needs and desires. Bring to mind those you would like to focus on, which could be an individual you know, or a group of people. Spend some time reflecting on their situation and identify what they need, considering how you could ease their suffering in both the short and long term. Visualise generating these conditions and as you offer them, imagine their suffering disappears, replaced by lasting genuine happiness. Develop great joy in their good fortune. Continue in this way, reflecting on sentient beings in different situations and imagining you are able to fulfil their wishes.

Obstacles to the Practice of Generosity

Even when we are familiar with the teachings on practicing generosity, sometimes when we come to act, we may have difficulty doing so. To help us overcome this, Arya Asanga identified four obstacles we are likely to face and their respective antidotes:

1. **Not being used to the act of giving:** The first problem we may face is that the thought of sharing our wealth and resources may simply not occur to us. When an opportunity for us to give arises, we don't pay attention to it and so fail to develop the desire to practice. This can be remedied by spending time reflecting on the disadvantages of attachment and stinginess and the advantages of generosity. The more time we spend with these reflections, the more awareness we bring to our experience, strengthening our desire to give.

2. **Not having enough objects suitable for giving:** Although we may want to practice generosity, we may feel we lack the resources to do so and consequently, we hold onto our possessions more tightly, fighting against the idea of sharing what we do have with others. While it is important to meet our basic needs, we should be aware that we experience reduced resources due to our past stinginess and attachment. Rather than perpetuating our poverty, by reflecting on the benefits of cultivating generosity, we can work little by little to create the causes for abundance. It is therefore worth making the effort to give what we can even if it means experiencing some initial discomfort.

3. **Greed for attractive objects:** Having access to a wealth of resources creates a danger of becoming attached to some possessions over others. We may be happy to give away things we don't want, but struggle to part with those we find beautiful or attractive. On the basis of this attachment, we strengthen our self-cherishing rather than practicing generosity. We can overcome this obstacle by reflecting on the impermanent nature of our possessions and by considering the suffering generated from attachment.

4. **Desire for wealth in the future:** This obstacle arises when we place too much value in samsaric pleasure, losing sight of our primary goal and being swept away in the desire for temporary happiness. Acts of generosity are then no longer causes for attaining enlightenment, but instead limit us to remaining within cyclic existence. To overcome this we can reflect on the empty nature of positive karmic results such as wealth and pleasure. Understanding their ephemeral and insubstantial nature, we will not hold them as supreme and return our attention to Bodhicitta.

Branch Vows Related to the Perfection of Generosity

As part of our commitment to upholding the Bodhisattva Vows, there are a total of forty-six branch vows that should be maintained to help avoid behaviours that are contrary to the essence of the training. Seven of these vows are specifically related to the practice of generosity. Their essence is to *strive to reduce attachment by focusing on the needs of others*. The vows are to avoid committing the following actions:

1. **Not performing the three kinds of devotion to the Three Jewels:** Having taken the Bodhisattva vows it is necessary to accumulate merit. We should therefore take refuge in the Three Jewels, making physical offerings and prostrations with our body, offering prayers with our speech and offering thoughts of gratitude and devotion with our mind each day.

2. **Allowing desire to remain unchecked:** If we do not restrain ourselves from acting out of delusions or indulging in desires, we will never know true contentment and will constantly grasp at material comforts and the enjoyments of cyclic existence.

3. **Failing to respect one's spiritual elders:** Elders are those who are more experienced Bodhisattvas, having taken Bodhisattva vows before we have. They are objects of respect and therefore worthy objects of offering. Failing to show them due respect will cause us to break this branch vow.

4. **Refusing to reply to questions:** When someone who trusts us sincerely asks us a question and we fail to give the appropriate answer due to laziness or lack of kindness, we will have broken this branch vow. This includes any occasion where we avoid answering questions on the Dharma or other matters.

5. **Not accepting an invitation:** If we decline an invitation without a proper and valid reason, a breach of this vow will have occurred. The vow specifically refers to refusing an invitation due to an attitude of pride or considering ourselves too well-respected to associate with people of lower class. Alternatively, we may think people of a higher position will

look down upon us if we are seen with such individuals. It is acceptable however, to decline an invitation if we have good reason for doing so.

6. **Not accepting gold and other forms of wealth:** When a benefactor sincerely offers gold, silver, money or other precious objects, to decline them with an attitude of malice, anger, laziness, false pride or "holy poverty" means we have broken this branch vow.

7. **Refusing to teach Dharma to those who seek it:** Refusing to teach those who genuinely wish to learn and practise due to lack of interest, would be an infraction of this vow, so long as it is something you are qualified to teach. There are valid reasons for not giving teachings such as being too busy, being unfamiliar with the subject matter, believing there is not suitable time or that the person lacks faith. In these cases it is acceptable not to teach, but refusing to teach the Dharma for any other reason breaks this vow.

Integrating All Six Perfections

To attain the *Perfection of Generosity*, every act of giving should incorporate all six Bodhisattva Perfections: (1) for the *generosity of generosity*, we should make every effort to practice generosity to bring benefit to sentient beings; (2) for the *ethical discipline of generosity*, we should uphold the branch vows related to generosity and ensure we avoid all conduct that promotes attachment or stinginess; (3) for the *patience of generosity*, we should be willing to endure any hardship that arises due to our practice of generosity; (4) for the *joyful effort of generosity*, we should take joy in always striving to fulfil the needs of others; (5) for the *meditative concentration of generosity*, we should maintain our focus on bringing benefit to others by cultivating mindfulness and vigilance; and (6) for the *wisdom of generosity*, we should recognise the illusory nature of the objects being given, the giver of the gift and the recipient of the gift. If all these aspects are present, they will contribute to the two enlightened accumulations of merit and wisdom that are the causes for achieving Buddhahood.

THE RESULTS OF PRACTICING GENEROSITY

The definitive result of practicing generosity is the achievement of the two aims of self and other by attaining full and complete enlightenment. Provisionally, each form of generosity helps purification of the mind and prepares the ground for practicing the subsequent Perfections. Through the practice of *Generosity of Giving Material Wealth*, the mind is cleared of the stinginess that grasps tightly onto objects, not wanting to be parted from them. This then eliminates the behaviour of hoarding material possessions that only serve to reinforce self-grasping. By practicing the *Generosity of Giving Fearlessness*, the minds of sentient beings are put at ease and their lives are prolonged. The *Generosity of Giving the Dharma* protects the mind of sentient beings from deluded states which create the causes for their suffering. Through the first two, we establish sentient beings in the temporary happiness of this life, whereas the third establishes them in the genuine happiness of future lives.

According to Arya Asanga, there are ten aspects which identify the achievement of a perfectly pure form of generosity by a Bodhisattva:

1. **Does not delay:** As soon as an opportunity arises, the Bodhisattva makes a gift immediately without hesitation. They feel a great sense of urgency to fulfil the needs of the sentient being.

2. **Is not influenced by wrong views:** The Bodhisattva is completely free of wrong views such as believing their actions will have no results, that causing harm is Dharma or that generosity alone is enough to achieve enlightenment.

3. **Does not give things that have been stored up:** The Bodhisattva does not wait to save worthy objects of offering to be used in the future as one large offering. They instead use all their resources to bring immediate benefit to sentient beings.

4. **Is free from haughtiness:** The Bodhisattva offers all gifts with a humble mind without rivalry. Their mind is completely free from the pride that thinks they are superior due to their generosity.

5. **Is disinterested:** The Bodhisattva shows no desire for fame or reputation as a result of their acts of generosity. Such aspects are seen as inconsequential and therefore the Bodhisattva shows no interest in them.

6. **Is free of dejection:** The Bodhisattva rejoices in all acts of generosity whether they are performed by themselves or someone else. When they give, their mind is filled with joy in the beginning, middle and end.

7. **Offerings are not meagre:** After carefully considering their options, the Bodhisattva always offers the best and most excellent objects to sentient beings and is happy to maintain a meagre lifestyle if it will benefit others.

8. **Is free of aversion:** The Bodhisattva maintains an equanimous mind that is free from bias and affliction toward the recipients of their gifts. The compassion they feel toward each being is the same regardless of the relationship they have with them

9. **Seeks nothing in return:** At all times the Bodhisattva's mind is filled with compassion toward sentient beings and expects nothing in return for their gift. There is a recognition that everyone wants happiness and therefore they are filled with joy when they can help others achieve their desires.

10. **Does not seek a karmic maturation:** The Bodhisattva looks upon the results of all karma, whether virtuous or non-virtuous, as being completely empty of substance and ultimately worthless. Therefore, they do not cling to positive results such as higher rebirth or an abundance of resources as being anything special. Their focus is always on the transcendental result of full enlightenment for all sentient beings.

REVIEW OF KEY POINTS

- Generosity is the mind that desires to fully give one's own resources without attachment, for the benefit of sentient beings. It has two components: (1) a lack of attachment towards one's possessions or body and (2) a willingness to give one's resources to others.

- Practicing generosity is the antidote to attachment and stinginess. These two afflicted states of mind are the root of self-cherishing and must be overcome in order to achieve enlightenment.

- There are three types of generosity we can train in, depending on our personal conditions: (1) the generosity of giving Dharma; (2) the generosity of giving fearlessness and (3) the generosity of giving material wealth. While the first brings happiness to beings in future lives, the last two bring happiness to beings in this life.

- When sharing Dharma with others, you should be mindful that: (1) the recipient has a sincere desire to practice; (2) your motivation is rooted in genuine compassion; (3) the teaching you share is without error; (4) the teaching is appropriate for the audience and (5) the teaching is given in a manner that inspires the audience to practice.

- When giving fearlessness, the aim is to protect sentient beings from being harmed or killed by: (1) wild animals; (2) humans or (3) inanimate things such as the elements.

- When giving material wealth the aim is to relieve sentient beings of immediate suffering through sharing one's physical resources. This can come in the form of: (1) internal objects that relate to the body of the giver or (2) external objects which are considered possessions of the giver. Either type of object can be given permanently or temporarily.

- Before giving, you should determine if it is wise to do so. Whether or not you should give should be based on long-term benefit rather than temporary pleasure.

- The correct motivation for giving contains three parts: (1) the purpose should be to achieve enlightenment for the sake of all sentient beings; (2) there should be no attachment towards the object and (3) the giver should see the recipient as being like a spiritual friend.

- We should avoid the following attitudes: (1) wrong views which limit the potential for developing generosity; (2) pride which reinforces self-cherishing; (3) discouragement which causes us to regret acts of generosity; (4) bias which prevents us from giving to some beings; (5) expectations which condition how we give and (6) desire for worldly results that are incapable of leading us to enlightenment.

- When actually giving a material offering, you should: (1) be pleasant, (2) be respectful; (3) give the gift personally; (4) do no harm and (5) bear any hardships that arise. This will ensure that your karmic connection with the recipient is strong and will act as basis for you to benefit them again in the future.

- If you cannot make material offerings, you can make visualised ones. You can make offerings to enlightened beings to help reduce your attachment or you can make offerings to sentient beings to reduce stinginess.

- There are four obstacles to practicing generosity: (1) not being used to giving; (2) not having enough objects suitable for giving; (3) greed for attractive objects and (4) desire for wealth in the future.

- There are seven branch vows to avoid with regards to practicing generosity: (1) not performing the three kinds of devotion to the Three Jewels; (2) allowing desire to remain unchecked; (3) failing to respect one's spiritual elders; (4) refusing to reply to questions; (5) not accepting an invitation; (6) not accepting gold and other forms of wealth and (7) refusing to teach Dharma to those who seek it.

- A Bodhisattva with pure generosity has ten aspects: (1) does not delay; (2) is not influenced by wrong views; (3) does not give things that have been stored up; (4) is free from haughtiness; (5) is disinterested; (6) is free of dejection; (7) offerings are not meagre; (8) is free of aversion; (9) seeks nothing in return; and (10) does not seek a karmic maturation

CHAPTER EIGHT

Shaping Behaviour with Ethical Discipline

Training in the *Perfection of Generosity* reduces our self-cherishing attitude, opening the door to work more directly for the benefit of sentient beings. Without this crucial step, our minds have little concern for the suffering of others and are instead more attached to the accumulation of things for our own pleasure. By identifying the benefits of generosity and developing the desire to apply it to our lives, we can then learn how to use our inner and outer resources to alleviate suffering. While our loved ones may initially be the focus of our practice, we can expand our sphere of interest beyond the confines of our immediate family and friends. When we see ourselves as part of a larger context, we gain perspective on the way our behaviour can affect all the people we encounter.

This process of opening naturally leads to the next training—the *Perfection of Ethical Discipline*. While generosity emphasises the act of giving, ethical discipline broadens the practice to include a wider range of actions which provide a virtuous structure for interacting with those around us. By concentrating on the nature of our relationships with others, a foundation of harmony is established, making other forms of training more accessible.

WHAT IS ETHICAL DISCIPLINE?

Ethical discipline is *the mind that desires to abandon doing harm to others as well as the causes of such harm*. It is an attitude that values the wellbeing of sentient beings and is concerned with establishing them in peace and harmony. Based on a caring mind of love and compassion, someone who practices ethical discipline recognises their interdependent nature with sentient beings and so takes responsibility for how their actions will influence them. This mind has two main aspects:

1. **Acceptance:** The Buddhas and Bodhisattvas identified trainings that can not only be used to facilitate abstaining from harming others, but also serve to bring them long lasting benefit. When we recognise the wisdom of adopting the prescribed behaviours presented in the teachings, we can be said to have "accepted a discipline". This acceptance takes the form of an aspiration to uphold a learnt training and then put it into practice.

2. **Determination:** When cultivated, ethical discipline provides us with the capacity to practice virtue and avoid afflictive states of mind. Having identified the value of a particular training we have accepted as being beneficial, ethical discipline draws its power from the commitment to uphold the training and from the strength of determination to manifest its results.

These two qualities of acceptance and determination may be familiar to you as they exemplify the way we distinguished between aspirational and engaged Bodhicitta. We first established acceptance of the training in Bodhicitta by cultivating the qualities of love and compassion and reflecting on the benefits of developing the altruistic intention to achieve enlightenment. Then, by strengthening our determination, we activated our aspiration and committed ourselves to putting into practice the training of a Bodhisattva. As long as we don't abandon that acceptance and determination, we can say the Bodhisattva training is a part of our ethical discipline.

In our study of the Kalachakra Path, we have been introduced to many different types of trainings, and all of them act as a support for building our ethical discipline. Whether they become part of our discipline will depend primarily on our acceptance of them as beneficial and our determination to practice them.

The way ethical discipline evolves is like a tradesperson's tool box. The type of tools they have will depend on the aim they wish to achieve. If the aim is to build a house, you may find a nail gun, tape measure and saw, whereas a plumber fixing a leaky tap would need different tools such as a wrench, plumbers' tape and washers. The presence or absence of tools will directly influence the types of jobs that can be performed.

Similarly, the trainings we choose to emphasise in our lives will directly influence the capacity of our actions. As we are aiming to bring the greatest possible benefit to sentient beings, we should strive to adopt trainings to help us achieve this aim. Ethical discipline is therefore our toolbox and the trainings are our tools. The more diverse the trainings we incorporate into our discipline, the more effective we will be at helping others.

Reasons to Practice the Perfection of Ethical Discipline

Ethical discipline contains the entire path that leads to abandoning all obscurations and manifesting all enlightened qualities. As our Bodhicitta aim is to lead all beings to Buddhahood, all beings need to be established in ethical discipline. To do this, it is necessary for us to take on the discipline for ourselves as only then can we correctly demonstrate the benefits of doing so.

As well as being fundamental to achieving the path, ethical discipline forms a container for all our other practices. Without it, there is no structure to our activities, making it difficult to achieve continuity of practice. It connects our intention to our actions, bringing purpose to our activities and helping us maintain a consistent frame of mind that is conducive to achieving realisations.

Furthermore, practicing ethical discipline helps us remove *fear* from our lives. This type of fear is based on feeling that the self is in danger, causing a restlessness in the mind, preventing us from establishing peace in our lives. Just like a bird who must continually dart its head in all directions on the look-out for predators, we too live in a constant state of anxiety and tension.

To overcome this fear it is necessary to recognise its cause. Since beginningless time, due to the power of our self-cherishing, we have inflicted an endless stream of harm on sentient beings. We have directly contributed to or provided the conditions for their suffering over and over again. This builds a tension between us and our victims. On an instinctual level, as we have inflicted harm on others, we expect others to harm us, just as they have done so on countless occasions. Consequently, a general sense of unease and lack of trust permeates everything we say and do.

As long as this fear is present, perfect meditative concentration will not be possible to achieve. Without a fully stable mind, we cannot experience the ultimate nature of reality directly and therefore enlightenment will not be achievable. The entire path therefore hinges on ethical discipline as a remedy for the fear of being harmed.

The way ethical discipline does this is by shifting the focus from the self, to focusing on the desires of others. To put it simply, as others do not want to be harmed, we do not engage in actions that will cause them harm. We begin to diminish the strength of our self-cherishing, and condition our relationships with others in a positive way. As we are no longer a threat to others, they naturally cease being a threat to us. When the basis of our connection becomes a mutual caring for the welfare of others, it removes tension, allowing the qualities of love and compassion to manifest, bringing about a sense of harmlessness.

The main benefit of practicing ethical discipline is to bring ease to our mind, enabling us to concentrate on virtuous qualities. While this undoubtedly helps us to be effective in this life, it is absolutely crucial at the moment of death. If we can enter the process of transition with a mind that is calm and collected, we can be certain our next rebirth will be beneficial. Facing death with a mind overwhelmed by fear however, we are likely to activate our self-cherishing, potentially leading to a rebirth in an unfortunate realm of experience.

THE DIVISIONS OF ETHICAL DISCIPLINE

Ethical discipline is like a container for the three types of trainings we practice: (1) the training in restraint from non-virtuous actions; (2) the training in gathering virtuous qualities and (3) the training in bringing benefit to others.

These three trainings are sequential in nature as the earlier trainings provide the basis for the later ones. By breaking free from our habituation to non-virtue and developing conduct that restrains our actions of body, speech and mind, we generate the merit that orients our mind toward virtue. Then, through actively working to gather virtuous qualities such as compassion and wisdom, we improve our personal capacity, creating the conditions for bringing benefit to others. Practice of the later trainings is not reliant on mastery of the earlier ones. We just need to be aware of our current level of development and place our emphasis on the training that is most appropriate.

Restraining from Non-Virtues

The first training is the *Training in Restraining from Non-Virtues*. As it forms the foundation for all other practices, this aspect is what is generally thought of when referring to ethical discipline. The primary method used in this training is the practice of keeping vows. Broadly speaking, a vow is a promise to abstain from a particular behaviour. The reason we commit to making such a promise is our recognition that particular behaviours cause harm to others. If we lack the reasoning to directly identify the causes of harm resulting from an action, we trust a valid source of refuge such as the Buddha, who teaches that acting in such a way is harmful and so should be avoided.

On a deeper level, a vow represents a very subtle influence on the mind, forming a non-physical boundary created by the intention to keep our promise. On one side we have behaviours we accept as beneficial and on the other we have behaviours we reject as harmful. This basic sense of right and wrong that guides us in making wise decisions is the "ethical" part of ethical discipline.

It can be noted that the nature of vows to have preference for the practice of virtue over non-virtue illustrates a form of bias. As bias is something we need to abandon, are we then creating a contradiction? It is true that eventually we must completely rid our mind of all forms of bias but the use of vows to restrain our actions is provisional in nature. They are needed while our mind is habituated to the non-virtuous behaviours which obstruct our Buddha-nature from manifesting. As we progress along the path, we integrate the essence of the vows into our experience and rather than needing to control our behaviour, it naturally manifests in virtuous ways. Our use for the vows then becomes increasingly subtle, until they arise naturally.

The Kalachakra Path we are studying belongs to the Vajra Vehicle as taught in Tibetan Buddhism. Within this system, there are three levels of vows used for the training in ethical discipline: (1) the Vows of Personal Liberation; (2) the Bodhisattva Vows and (3) the Tantric Vows. We will now look at the basic structure of each set of vows to gain insight into how they provide us with a foundation for practicing Kalachakra. Details of the first two sets of vows are discussed in other parts of this book and the third is discussed in the third and final book of this series.

The Vows of Personal Liberation

As the name suggests, the Vows of Personal Liberation are concerned with creating the conditions for an individual to break free from the cyclic existence of samsara and achieve the lasting peace of nirvana. The primary method for achieving personal liberation is to restrain the actions performed with our body and speech, which is known as *external conduct*. Through developing a strict discipline based on *non-violence* and the practice of meditation, practitioners of the Vows of Personal Liberation create the conditions to temporarily subdue their afflictions, enabling realisation of the selfless nature of reality and the achievement of liberation from suffering. If we consider the types of practitioners that uphold this type of vow we can speak of two main factions:

1. **Monastics:** A practitioner who abides by the *Monastic Code of the Buddha* (Vinaya) is considered someone who has abandoned the worldly life of a householder. Instead of dedicating their lives to achieving worldly aims, they focus their energy on spiritual practice. There are generally two levels of ordination a monk or nun can take: (1) *novice ordination* consisting of 36 vows and (2) *full ordination* which consists of 253 vows for monks and 364 vows for nuns.

   The bulk of the vows detailed in the Monastic Code are what are known as *prescribed precepts*. They arose out of different guidelines made by the Buddha to correct the behaviour of the monastic population. Most were designed to ensure harmony within the community and to provide a conducive environment for the practice of Dharma. They include how to eat and dress and how to behave in different situations.

2. **Lay People:** A practitioner who abides within the world is considered a householder or lay person. Because they do not live within the context of a monastic community, they do not follow the branch vows of the Monastic Code. They instead concentrate primarily on the five root vows that restrain the body and speech in order to avoid the *natural non-virtues*. This includes aspects such as not-killing and not-stealing. While the conduct is similar to the practice of abstaining from the Ten Non-Virtues, what makes them vows is the promise to abstain from these actions for the remainder of one's present life.

The five root vows can be taken in both a pure or impure form. *Pure conduct* means committing to all five vows combined with the vow of celibacy. Impure conduct means to take any combination of one or more vows without the vow of celibacy. Those who have taken the vows of pure conduct are no longer considered householders as they have abandoned the desire to raise a family. As they do not abide by the Monastic Code nor do they live within a monastic community, they are also not full monastics and so they are considered to be inbetween a householder and a monastic.

The Vows of Personal Liberation are likened to stone as their emphasis is on physical actions which require considerable effort to break. Although they can be easily damaged, it is difficult to lose them completely, however, if they are broken, they are very hard to restore in this lifetime.

The Bodhisattva Vows

Maintaining the Vows of Personal Liberation is the minimum foundation required to create the causes for attaining a fortunate rebirth in the future. The more vows one maintains, the more merit one accumulates and the more conducive the conditions become for the practice of virtue. However, as abstaining from harm is the sole emphasis, the capacity to achieve Buddhahood is not supported. This then requires the motivation of Bodhicitta to be incorporated into our conduct and the expansion of our behaviour to include increased engagement with sentient beings. As we have seen in previous chapters, the Bodhisattva Vows are broken into two parts:

1. **Root Vows:** These are the core vows designed to help ensure that the Bodhicitta motivation is not lost. Their essential nature is to *never abandon sentient beings*. Their focus is therefore to protect our relationship with sentient beings maintaining the strength of our compassion. Based on the approach taken by their lineage, different masters identify particular variations of the vows. In general we can speak of *eighteen root vows—* four vows from Asanga and fourteen vows from Nagarjuna.

2. **Branch Vows:** These vows represent the guidelines a Bodhisattva uses to support their training in the other two forms of ethical discipline. Of the forty-six branch vows, thirty-four are related to the training for acquiring virtuous qualities and twelve are related to the training of bringing benefit to others. These correspond to the practices of *Training in The Six Perfections* and the *Four Methods for Gathering Followers*.

In relation to practice, the Bodhisattva Vows are mainly concerned with maintaining conducive states of mind that act as supports for virtuous actions, known as *internal conduct*. As Bodhisattva Vows are mental in nature, they are more subtle than the Vows of Personal Liberation. This form of practice can then be likened to silver, which when damaged, can be repaired without much difficulty using the right tools. Even though it is easy to give rise to a non-virtuous thought, it is also easy to correct the mistake by giving rise to a virtuous one.

The Tantric Vows

The Bodhisattva Vows function at a gross level of consciousness to ensure our mind abides in virtue as we interact with sentient beings. While they are effective for working skilfully with conventional reality, the accumulation of merit and wisdom they produce is relatively slow when compared to the subtle methods used in Buddhist Tantra. If one were to rely solely on the Bodhisattva Vows, it would take approximately three countless aeons to complete the path—one aeon to achieve the realisation of emptiness, one aeon to remove the afflictive obscurations and one aeon to remove the cognitive obscurations. Using the skilful means of Tantra, it is possible to achieve the same result within the span of a single lifetime.

The Tantric Vows facilitate this process by supporting the development of *pure vision*. This is the capacity of a practitioner to use their experiences as the basis for realising their own ultimate nature. This set of vows consists of both vows and pledges, the difference being that a vow identifies behaviour you promise to avoid, whereas a pledge identifies behaviour you promise to undertake. In total, we can identify three types of precepts used in Tantric practice:

1. **Tantric Commitments:** The foundation for practicing Tantra is the Tantric Commitments or *samaya* which are pledges taken to remind us of the various aspects of our Buddha-nature. By maintaining our mindfulness of them, we develop a close bond to the ultimate nature of reality which can then be used to rapidly clear away ignorance and manifest our primordial wisdom. This is the essence of pure vision. In Kalachakra, there are three sets of pledges: (1) the *Common Pledges of the Five Buddha Families*; (2) the *Uncommon Pledges of the Six Buddha Families* and (3) the *Vajra Pledges of the Kalachakra Completion Stage*.

2. **Root Vows:** For now, we are deeply habituated to seeing the world through the eyes of our ignorance. This ordinary vision limits our perception and prevents us from manifesting our enlightened qualities. Through practicing the Tantric Root Vows, we develop greater mindfulness regarding particular objects so that we can effectively learn how to prevent our ordinary view from arising. There are *Fourteen Root Vows* in accordance with the system of Kalachakra.

3. **Branch Vows:** Depending on the system of Tantra being practiced, there are also a number of Branch Vows regarding what should be avoided, ensuring we have the necessary conditions to practice the path correctly. In the case of Kalachakra, this includes *Twenty-Five Conducts* and *Eight Heavy Infractions*.

Of all the vows, the Tantric Vows are considered the most subtle and are therefore known as the *secret conduct*. This subtlety also makes them the easiest vows to break, but fortunately they are also the easiest to repair. For this reason they are likened to gold which is malleable and shaped with ease.

Practicing All Three Vows Together

Presented as three individual sets of vows, this can create the common misconception that there are three separate forms of conduct, where in fact, each set of vows builds on the preceding set. For instance, to properly practice the Bodhisattva Vows one must practice the Vows of Personal Liberation, as without giving up non-virtuous actions of body and speech, it is impossible to work effectively with the mind. Likewise, to work with the definitive nature emphasised in the Tantric Vows, we must practice the Bodhisattva Vows to ensure we are not dominated by self-cherishing attitudes.

The correct way to view the vows is illustrated by the relationship between the stars, the moon and the sun. On a clear night, the stars shine brightly filling the sky, but they become overshadowed by the rising of the full moon. When the sun comes up, its brilliance completely overpowers the light of both the moon and the stars. Although the sun is the brightest, it doesn't mean the light of the moon or the stars ceases to shine. The Vows of Personal Liberation are like the stars, the Bodhisattva Vows are like the moon and the Tantric Vows are like the sun. Even though a practitioner may emphasise one level of practice over another, if they are skilful they are practicing all three simultaneously.

Another traditional illustration of the differences between the sets of vows is to consider a poisonous plant. One approach is to identify the plant as poisonous and so avoid it completely—this is the approach of the Vows of Personal Liberation. A second approach is to recognise that under the right conditions, the poison can be mixed with other substances to form a powerful medicine— this is the approach of the Bodhisattva Vows. The final approach is to recognise that if used skilfully, the poison itself can be used directly, just like the feathers of a peacock which are produced from the consumption of poison—this is the approach of the Tantric Vows. As we progress along the path, we develop the capacity to work with our poison in increasingly more skilful ways.

Gathering Virtuous Qualities

The *Training in Gathering Virtuous Qualities* consists of all the virtuous practices we perform in accordance with the teachings. In order for our actions to contribute to the aim of achieving enlightenment, we should ensure the actions are virtuous in the beginning, in the middle and at the end. This means at the start of each practice we should generate the *virtuous motivation* of Bodhicitta. As we engage in a *virtuous action* we should maintain mindfulness and aware-ness of what we are doing and when we are finished, we should use a *virtuous dedication* to direct our merit so it becomes the cause for all sentient beings to be completely free from suffering.

The Kalachakra Master Lama Lobsang Trinlé
was known for his pure ethical discipline.

In relation to the Kalachakra Path as practiced in the Jonang-Shambhala Tradition, there are ten specific virtuous actions we should strive to practice:

1. Contemplation on the Four Convictions of Renunciation
2. Practicing devotion to the Guru and Lineage Lamas
3. Taking refuge in the Three Jewels
4. Cultivating the Four Immeasurables and generating Bodhicitta
5. Purifying the mind with Vajrasattva Recitation
6. Accumulating merit with Mandala Offerings
7. Making supplications to the Guru
8. Recitation of the Innate Kalachakra sadhana
9. Meditation on the Three Isolations
10. Practice of the Six Vajra Yogas

Within these ten actions is everything we need to clear away all obscurations, manifest all virtuous qualities within our mindstreams and achieve Buddha-hood within a single lifetime. We should therefore familiarise ourselves as much as possible with these practices so we can integrate them into our experience.

Bringing Benefit to Sentient Beings

The last form of training within the practice of ethical discipline is the *Training in Bringing Benefit to Sentient Beings*. This consists of using the qualities we have already developed to bring benefit to eleven types of beings in eleven ways:

1. **Supporting meaningful activities** in order to benefit those who need immediate and direct support.

2. **Providing proper instruction** in order to benefit those who do not know how to achieve what they desire.

3. **Showing gratitude for benefit received and then repaying it** in order to benefit those who need material or spiritual assistance.

4. **Offering protection from danger** in order to benefit those who are living in fear.

5. **Dispelling sorrow** in order to benefit those who are living in misery.

6. **Furnishing objects that are needed for subsistence** in order to benefit those who are living in poverty.

7. **Providing a safe abode** in order to benefit those who currently have no place to stay.

8. **Complying with others** in order to benefit those who desire friends or agreeable companions.

9. **Giving encouragement** in order to benefit those who desire to practice something that will lead them to nirvana or enlightenment.

10. **Suppressing misconduct** in order to benefit those who are currently following a wrong path or need to reverse the direction of their focus.

11. **Displaying miraculous powers** in order to benefit those who are in need of extraordinary or miraculous help.

In addition to these actions, we should also make particular effort to conduct ourselves in a manner that inspires others to practice the Dharma. This includes: (1) avoiding untamed actions of the body such as unnecessarily jumping around or other frantic movements; (2) avoiding untamed actions of speech such as speaking with idle or harsh words; and (3) avoiding untamed actions of the mind such as craving the eight worldly dharmas or developing attachment to laziness.

HOW TO PRACTICE ETHICAL DISCIPLINE

Training in ethical discipline is a very broad topic that encompasses all the provisional methods we use to achieve enlightenment. Furthermore, the entire path is contained within the three Bodhisattva disciplines of avoiding non-virtue, cultivating virtue and benefiting others. The methods for cultivating virtue and bringing benefit to others will be discussed further in the coming chapters, so for the moment, we will concentrate on the discipline of avoiding non-virtue through working with vows.

The training in avoiding non-virtue consists of two steps: (1) establishing a commitment to practice a particular discipline and then (2) maintaining that discipline. By applying the vows in this way, we shape our mind to be supportive for the achievement of both the provisional and definitive results of the practice.

Committing Yourself to an Ethical Discipline

A vow is established in the mind when we develop a firm determination to live our life in accordance with that vow. It is a conscious decision that arises as a result of considering the advantages of keeping a particular form of discipline and the disadvantages of not keeping it. The strongest form of vows are those in which we take the time to carefully consider, reflecting deeply on the role an ethical discipline will play in our practice and why it is important.

Each set of vows uses different methods for generating this quality of determination. In the case of the Bodhisattva Vows we are encouraged to study them before committing to them, whereas the Vows of Personal Liberation and the Tantric Vows are usually given without specific knowledge of what they are. This approach can seem counter-intuitive until we understand the logic behind the practice.

The first set of vows we need to establish are the *Vows of Personal Liberation*. They are taken on the basis of faith in the Three Jewels which is developed through reflecting on the disadvantages of cyclic existence and the advantages of liberation. This analysis leads to the result of *renunciation*, which is a strong desire to break free from samsara. It is renunciation which drives us to seek a spiritual refuge and to place our faith in their guidance. Like a sick person who has searched for a qualified doctor to provide them with a cure, they do not need to know exactly what is in the medicine prescribed, only that they need to take it.

The second set of vows is the *Bodhisattva Vows* and their basis is the engaged aspiration of Bodhicitta. As the duration of these vows lasts from the moment they are taken, until the achievement of enlightenment when their essence becomes spontaneous, we potentially need to hold our Bodhicitta commitment for billions of lifetimes. To do this, we must have an unshakeable faith that fully understands such an immense commitment. If the path forward is unclear, we will have difficulty believing in the possibility of enlightenment, therefore before taking the vows we are encouraged to study the path in as much detail as possible. The more familiar we are with the training, the more our confidence will grow, providing us with the necessary determination.

Finally, we have the *Tantric Vows* which are taken on the basis of an extremely powerful form of Bodhicitta. This motivation arises when a Bodhisattva's love and compassion become so intense they cannot bear the idea of sentient beings suffering for even one moment longer. Due to this profound sense of urgency, they seek the most skilful methods for achieving Buddhahood as quickly as possible. Great faith is then developed in the practice of the Vajrayana which can produce this result within the course of a single human lifetime. As we are already expected to hold both the Vows of Personal Liberation and the Bodhisattva Vows, at the time of taking the Tantric Vows, we should already have a strong foundation of renunciation and Bodhicitta. When these two aspects are combined with reflection on the advantages of practicing Tantra, we develop a very strong determination to take the corresponding Vows. Our determination should be so strong, we are willing to do whatever it takes to achieve our own aim and the aim of others.

Ideally, we would first spend time developing the necessary determination for the level of discipline we are currently focused on. We would then seek a qualified teacher to bestow on us the corresponding vows. Due to these degenerate times however, this process can be difficult and the opportunities for receiving vows are few and far between. For this reason, we need to be skilful with how we take our vows.

If the situation arises to receive vows from an authentic teacher, you should always take the opportunity. Sometimes people are afraid to take vows, whether out of concern over their ability to maintain them or perhaps anxiety regarding their knowledge of them. Choose to focus instead on the present, strengthening your aspiration and do not worry about what may or may not come to pass in the future. Simply rejoice in the chance to create powerful karmic propensities and try not to view vows as being a burden. Think of them as a blessing you aspire to maintain and if your aspiration is sincere, the benefit you will receive will be immeasurable.

Furthermore, remember that working with vows is not black and white. Developing pure ethical discipline is a process that takes time to master and the key is maintaining your aspiration to uphold the vows. As we are not yet perfect, we will falter and make mistakes, but we should not give up, continuing to practice with determination for however long it takes.

Once you have taken on a higher ethical discipline such as the Bodhisattva Vows or the Tantric Vows, it is important to not speak about them in public to those who do not have faith in your path. Not only is there the possibility of spiritual pride arising about your discipline but there is also the danger that those hearing your words will misunderstand the purpose behind the conduct and consequently speak negatively about you. In order to protect these people from generating extremely non-virtuous karma, it is better to keep your discipline a private matter between you and your spiritual guide.

Safeguarding Your Discipline

After you have received a set of vows from a qualified vow preceptor, your practice of ethical discipline shifts to maintaining those vows as purely as possible. By studying your vows, you become aware of the behaviours that should be abandoned. You can then apply your knowledge to cultivating the *Five Types of Mindfulness*:

1. **Mindfulness of the Past:** This is the practice of reflecting on the actions you have committed in the past. This can be done as a daily review of your behaviour or as a general contemplation based on your understanding of karma. Either way, the aim is to recognise damage to your vows and then take the appropriate steps to purify any negativity. This is followed by restoration of the purity of your discipline in accordance with the level of vow you are working with.

2. **Mindfulness of the Future:** This is the practice of analysing your daily patterns in order to identify any potential situations where you are likely to break your vows. By meditating in this way, you will strengthen your mindfulness of the present and will be more likely to avoid any transgressions or faults.

3. **Mindfulness of the Present:** This is a present-moment awareness that is vigilant for any infractions that may occur. If your vows are damaged in any way, you should take immediate steps to purify the negativity and restore your discipline.

4. **Mindfulness that is Practiced in Advance:** Make the effort to meditate regularly on the benefits of keeping your vows and the faults of breaking them. Doing this will strengthen your determination to keep your vows purely and heighten your mindfulness, protecting your discipline.

5. **Mindfulness that is Practiced Concurrently:** The stronger your determination, the more mindful you are of your discipline. This will provide you with a natural awareness of what you should or shouldn't do in any given situation, weakening your habitual tendencies to engage in non-virtue.

This practice will enable you to maintain a continuous flow of mindfulness, protecting your discipline at all times. By holding your vows in such a way, you generate an extraordinary amount of merit that will propel you along the path.

Branch Vows Related to the Perfection of Ethical Discipline

Of the forty-six branch vows, there are nine specifically related to the practice of ethical discipline. The essence of these vows is to *dedicate oneself to spiritual practice for the benefit of sentient beings.* By making our discipline the heart of our activities, we bring meaning to our lives and help relieve the suffering of others. The vows are to abandon the following forms of conduct:

1. **Abandoning those who are immoral:** If we refuse to forgive or help those whose discipline and moral self-control have lapsed then we will break this vow. We should recognise such people need advice and try to help them relieve their guilt and amend their conduct if they wish. We should not treat them with contempt or ignore them for it is those who are overwhelmed by their afflictions that we should generate the most compassion for.

2. **Not training oneself in a way that engenders faith in others:** Out of a desire to inspire others to practice virtue, we should always try to maintain an external conduct which accords with the Vows of Personal Liberation. This is the foundation of our practice and we should never abandon it.

3. **Engaging in few activities for the sake of sentient beings:** Even though we train in the Vows of Personal Liberation, we must do so in a manner which accords with the Bodhisattva Vows. This means our Bodhicitta motivation always takes precedence. Unlike practitioners of the Foundational Vehicle, Bodhisattvas should always keep the welfare of sentient beings in their minds and therefore if they have taken monastic vows they should not abide by those rules which discourage working for the benefit of others.

4. **Failing to act with sympathy:** A Bodhisattva's discipline is always contextual, meaning we must be able to adapt to changing situations. If we are endowed with great wisdom and can determine that breaking the Vows of Personal Liberation would bring benefit to sentient beings, we should do so. For instance, if we are witness to a social injustice in which a person in power consistently abuses or inflicts harm on sentient beings and we are in a position to act with authority, it is our responsibility to remove that person from power. Even though this is a form of taking what was not freely given, we must act to prevent the harm of sentient beings. This includes the harm that the perpetrator inflicted on themselves through the creation of non-virtuous propensities in their mind. We should only engage in these actions of body or speech when there is absolutely no other alternative. If we do, we must always maintain a mind filled with compassion towards the sentient beings we are acting against.

5. **Persisting in wrong forms of livelihood:** Once we have generated Bodhicitta, we must stop all forms of livelihood that are based on five wrong attitudes: (1) *hypocrisy* that gathers wealth through misrepresenting oneself to others; (2) *flattery* that praises others in order to acquire their

wealth; (3) *intimidation* which tries to persuade others to give you their wealth by making hints; (4) *oppression* which threatens harm to others so they will give you their wealth; and (5) *seeking rewards* where you try to acquire wealth by giving small gifts in the hope of larger returns. Due to circumstances, it may not be possible to abandon these forms of livelihood immediately. If this is the case, we should develop a strong aspiration and take steps to change our situation so we can abandon them in the future.

6. **Engaging in mental excitation and excessive merriment:** In general, we should avoid indulging in frivolous activities such as entertainment, sports and drinking as they can cause the mind to be filled with agitation, ignorance or lack of mindfulness. Being agitated in this way is an obstacle to practising Dharma and achieving any kind of stable concentration as it increases our attachment. If we are constantly joking, singing, dancing, and drinking, we cannot concentrate, we will distract others and we are likely to fall prey to negative acts such as deriding others. Furthermore, such activities waste time which could be used constructively for Dharma practice. It is acceptable to sing, listen to music, laugh and joke if we have a good purpose for doing so. If, with compassion and love, we wish to relax or make others feel relaxed and happy, then singing, joking and the like can be useful. This vow mainly refers to doing these things under the sway of agitation and ignorance.

7. **Regarding samsara with complacency:** Because the mind of Bodhicitta is focused on achieving the benefit of sentient beings, it is possible to develop the misconception that Bodhisattvas should not strive for nirvana and instead should be happy to remain in samsara. This is a wrong view in that to remain in samsara means to be under the dominance of afflictions, while to attain nirvana means to be completely free from them. It is impossible for a Bodhisattva to achieve enlightenment without removing all of their afflictions and therefore, even though liberation is not the aim of a Bodhisattva, we should strive for the discipline which helps us abandon the afflictions.

8. **Failing to dispel a bad reputation:** Recognising that external behaviour can have a huge impact on the minds of sentient beings, we must do whatever we can to avoid developing a bad reputation or drawing unnecessary criticism. If people lose faith in us as practitioners, our connection will be damaged, making it more difficult for us to bring them benefit. This does not mean we should abandon actions we know to be virtuous because the deluded minds of others find them displeasing. For instance, even though some people may not appreciate the benefits of long-term retreat, this is not a reason to stop. We should instead be more determined to demonstrate the benefits so their minds can be cleared of misconceptions.

9. **Failing to apply a distressing measure:** If a person's negativities of body and speech can be overcome through forceful methods, but we instead elect to use flattery to help them save face, we are breaking this vow. We should make every effort and use all our skill and wisdom to find suitable methods to help those who perform negative actions such as breaking their vows or harming others. Wherever possible, we should teach them ways to purify negative karma such as the four opponent powers. By practising such methods ourselves, we lead by way of example.

Integrating All Six Perfections

To achieve the *Perfection of Ethical Discipline,* we must integrate all Six Perfections into our practice: (1) for the *generosity of ethical discipline,* we should practice discipline for the purpose of bringing benefit to sentient beings; (2) for the *discipline of ethical discipline,* we should always train in the three forms of discipline, upholding our vows and striving to practice the Kalachakra Path; (3) for the *patience of ethical discipline,* we should not be discouraged by the hardship that may come from practicing, such as giving up what we are attached to; (4) for the *joyful effort of ethical discipline* we should always strive to cultivate virtue and rejoice in having the opportunity to practice the three forms of discipline; (5) for the *meditative concentration of ethical discipline,* we should maintain a constant awareness of our actions, ensuring we behave in a way that accords with the precepts we have chosen to uphold; and (6) for the *wisdom of ethical discipline*, we should always maintain awareness of the illusory nature of the agent who performs the action, the action being performed and the object that is the focus of the action, as none of these exist inherently. By integrating the Six Perfections in this way, you can be sure your practice of ethical discipline will lead you quickly to the state of a fully enlightened Buddha.

THE RESULTS OF PRACTICING ETHICAL DISCIPLINE

Ultimately, the result of practicing a Bodhisattva's ethical discipline is leading all sentient beings, including oneself, to achieving the complete enlightenment of a Buddha. On the provisional level there are general and specific results. Generally, because we dedicate ourselves to not harming sentient beings, we do not need to fear them and therefore our mind abides in a state of contentment. This sense of joy and ease carries us through to the death process. As our mind will not be clouded by delusions at the moment of death, we can face it without fear, naturally giving rise to a favourable rebirth in a realm where other Bodhisattvas are manifesting. This means we have the chance to meet again with the Dharma and continue our practice of discipline, maintaining the continuity of our practice all the way to enlightenment.

When we examine the individual types of ethical discipline, we can speak of three specific results. By practicing the *Discipline of Restraining from Non-Virtue*, the result is the achievement of great mental stability. Because of our ethics, we remove the causes for fearing sentient beings, enabling us to live in harmony with those around us and experience less anxiety which disturbs the mind. This result is the foundation for later achieving meditative concentration.

By practicing the *Discipline of Acquiring Virtuous Qualities*, we actively clear obscurations from our mind and create the conditions for enlightened qualities to manifest in our experience. The more qualities that manifest, the more capacity we have to bring benefit to sentient beings. These qualities allow us to accumulate vast stores of merit and wisdom, thereby creating the conditions for manifesting as a fully enlightened Buddha.

Finally, with the practice of the *Discipline of Benefiting Sentient Beings*, we establish powerful karmic connections with sentient beings that can be used to continue bringing them benefit in the future. These connections provide the basis for us to influence others' behaviour and to guide them along the path. This discipline also clears away the self-cherishing thought that limits our potential.

According to Arya Asanga, a Bodhisattva who has achieved pure ethical discipline can be identified by the following ten characteristics:

1. **Discipline is adopted properly:** The Bodhisattva naturally adopts an ethical discipline with the desire to abandon worldly concerns and dedicates themselves to achieving enlightenment.

2. **Free from regret:** The Bodhisattva clearly recognises the benefit of practicing ethical discipline and is free from faint regret which is unconcerned with engaging in non-virtue or unwarranted regret that is displeased by virtue.

3. **Free from laziness:** Through the act of maintaining their discipline, the Bodhisattva develops great perseverance in all their actions and avoids falling into laziness.

4. **Embraced by mindfulness:** The Bodhisattva possesses a constant awareness of their ethical discipline through the perfected practice of the five forms of mindfulness described earlier.

5. **Dedicated correctly:** The Bodhisattva recognises the limitation of worldly pursuits and therefore does not dedicate themselves to trying to achieve benefit in samsara. They are completely dedicated to achieving enlightenment through pure spiritual practice.

6. **Embraced by excellence of conduct:** By following the precepts of their ethical discipline, the Bodhisattva's actions are always excellent and provide a worthy example for others to follow.

7. **Embraced by excellence of livelihood:** The Bodhisattva never engages in wrong forms of livelihood that bring harm or torment to sentient beings. They instead engage constantly in actions which promote virtue and bring benefit to others.

8. **Has abandoned the two extremes:** The Bodhisattva has completely abandoned the extreme of self-gratification where the mind is consumed with desire for sensory pleasures and the extreme of self-mortification where the mind and body are made to suffer as a form of ascetic practice. They instead practice in a balanced way that avoids these two extremes.

9. **Has abandoned all forms of wrong views:** Having dedicated themselves to pure ethical discipline, the Bodhisattva gains direct insight into the nature of reality and has therefore cleared away all misconceptions which obscure their capacity and distort their practice.

10. **Acceptance has not become ruined:** The Bodhisattva's determination to practice the three forms of Bodhisattva discipline is unwavering. They become so habituated to these practices that no matter how many lives it takes for them to achieve their aim, they will never abandon them.

REVIEW OF KEY POINTS

- Ethical discipline is the mind that desires to abandon doing harm to others as well as the causes of such harm. It has two aspects: (1) acceptance of a particular training as being beneficial and (2) determination to practice that training.

- The main affliction we are trying to overcome with ethical discipline is the fear of retaliation that comes from non-virtuous actions which harm sentient beings. By focusing on cultivating harmonious relationships with others, we remove the fear and our minds are able to settle.

- The ethical discipline of a Bodhisattva can be divided into three types of trainings: (1) the training in restraining from non-virtuous actions; (2) the training in gathering virtuous qualities and (3) the training in bringing benefit to sentient beings.

- Training in Restraining from Non-Virtues consists of working with vows in order to shape one's behaviour of body, speech and mind in a way that is conducive to the path. There are three sets of vows that are used within the Kalachakra Path: (1) the Vows of Personal Liberation; (2) the Bodhisattva Vows and (3) the Tantric Vows. All three vows should be practiced as one system with the higher vows incorporating the lower vows.

- Training in Gathering Virtuous Qualities consists of engaging in spiritual practices which help us habituate our minds to virtue. There are ten practices which are the focus of the Kalachakra Path: (1) Four Convictions of Renunciation; (2) Devotion to the Guru and Lineage Lamas; (3) Taking Refuge; (4) Generating Bodhicitta; (5) Vajrasattva Purification; (6) Mandala Offerings; (7) Guru Yoga; (8) Deity Yoga; (9) Three Isolations Meditation and (10) the Six Vajra Yogas.

- Training in Bringing Benefit to Sentient Beings consists of working for the benefit of eleven types of sentient beings: (1) those who need immediate and direct help; (2) those who do not know how to achieve what they desire; (3) those who need material or spiritual assistance; (4) those who are in fear; (5) those who are in misery; (6) those who are in poverty; (7) those who need a place to stay when travelling; (8) those who want friends or agreeable companions; (9) those who desire to practice something that will lead them to nirvana or enlightenment; (10) those who are on a wrong path and need to reverse direction, and (11) those who need extraordinary, miraculous help.

- Working with vows consists of two main steps: (1) establishing a commitment to practice a particular discipline and then (2) learning how to actually maintain that discipline.

- There are nine branch vows for practicing ethical discipline. They include avoiding the following behaviours: (1) abandoning those who are immoral; (2) not training oneself in a way that engenders faith in others; (3) engaging in few activities for the sake of sentient beings; (4) failing to act with sympathy; (5) persisting in wrong forms of livelihood; (6) engaging in mental excitation and excessive merriment; (7) regarding samsara with complacency; (8) failing to dispel a bad reputation; and (9) failing to apply a distressing measure.

- A Bodhisattva with pure ethical discipline has ten aspects: (1) discipline is adopted properly; (2) free from regret; (3) free from laziness; (4) embraced by mindfulness; (5) dedicated correctly; (6) embraced by excellence of conduct; (7) embraced by excellence of livelihood; (8) has abandoned the two extremes; (9) has abandoned all forms of wrong view; and (10) acceptance has not become ruined.

CHAPTER NINE

Having Patience in the Face of Difficulties

Training in the *Perfection of Ethical Discipline* is mainly concerned with learning to use our actions of body, speech and mind in a wise and useful way. By shaping our conduct in a virtuous manner, we create the causes of future happiness for ourselves and others. This process is like a farmer planting seeds in a field; we invest our time and energy now so that one day we can reap a bountiful harvest.

One of the biggest problems we face in our practice is that we do not get to start with a clean slate. Our minds are completely filled with non-virtuous propensities, providing the causes for a wide range of suffering. Just like trying to plant in a field full of stones which inhibit the seeds from growing, our non-virtuous propensities generate considerable hardship and obstacles that prevent us from achieving our aims.

Without the skills to work with the ripening of our negative karma, it becomes difficult to maintain our discipline and instead of cultivating virtue we are likely to slip back into our old non-virtuous habits. This is why we require the next training of the *Perfection of Patience*, which is vital for giving us the strength of mind needed to face the many challenges and difficulties we will encounter on the path. If patience is absent, we are easily derailed, leaving little chance for our virtue to ripen.

WHAT IS PATIENCE?

Patience is *the mind which is able to abide in equanimity as a response to the experience of suffering.* This quality acts as a direct counterforce to the perpetuation of our karma by not reacting to suffering with non-virtue. Alternatively, it responds with a sense of ease and compassion, providing the basis for virtue to arise. We can think of patience like a person standing in the middle of a rushing river; although the water crashes into their legs, they hold their ground and are not carried away by the current.

The essential nature of patience is to refrain from three types of actions:

1. **Anger:** This is the afflicted mind of aversion that rejects a particular experience and labels it as suffering. Anger exaggerates the negative qualities of the perceived object and then mistakenly blames it as the primary cause for the suffering. As a type of mental reaction, it conditions the mind to continue to respond in this way to similar experiences in the future.

2. **Retaliating to harm:** On the basis of anger, we can develop the desire to inflict suffering back onto the person or thing we perceive to be causing our experience. For instance, if someone hits us we respond by hitting back, or if our feelings are hurt by abusive words, we retaliate with insults. It is an eye-for-an-eye mentality that generates non-virtuous propensities in our mind while also inflicting harm on others, which is the exact opposite of the ethical discipline we are trying to cultivate.

3. **Holding a grudge:** This is the mind which does not let go of anger. It is like a loop where the feeling of suffering is replayed over and over again in the mind, each time reinforcing our anger and weakening our connection to the person we blame for our experience.

By actively refraining from these actions, we protect our mind from their destructive effects and give ourselves the opportunity to build virtuous propensities. Our aim is not to stop the external world from harming us, but to recognise that the causes of our suffering occur within our own mind and therefore to end the experience of harm, we need to focus internally on the real enemy—our anger. By cutting the root cause, whatever conditions arise, there will be no suffering to experience.

As we progress along the path, the quality of our patience will evolve based on the methods used to generate it. In the beginning, our patience is mainly derived from careful consideration of the advantages and disadvantages of reacting with anger. Using discriminating wisdom, we build a resistance to anger, allowing us to experience the quality of patience. Once we realise the empty nature of dependent phenomena, we see the illusory nature of our experience so that it no longer has the power to influence us. Patience then arises as a natural result of our view. By habituating ourselves to this realisation, the bias that desires happiness and fears suffering is weakened. At this point we attain a profound sense of equanimity towards all experiences and anger no longer has any capacity to affect us. Finally, with the realisation of the sublime emptiness that is the absolute nature of reality, we are completely free of dualistic limitations and there is nothing to be afraid of.

REASONS TO PRACTICE THE PERFECTION OF PATIENCE

To achieve enlightenment, our mind needs to be completely habituated to virtue. This habituation is known as the *accumulation of merit*. When combined with the *accumulation of wisdom*, all the causes for manifesting the state of a fully enlightened Buddha will have been gathered. As these accumulations are so important to our ultimate aim, we must do everything in our power to protect them from degenerating.

There are two aspects which can cause the loss of the merit we generate: (1) not dedicating our merit and (2) anger. While it is easy to dedicate our merit, overcoming anger is considerably more challenging; however, by reflecting deeply on its nature, we will come to understand the destructive effect it has on our mind. As we weigh up the disadvantages of anger versus the advantages of patience, the determination to practice patience is developed, giving us the ability to protect the merit we create through our practices of generosity and ethical discipline.

So how is it that anger is so destructive? Within a single moment, anger can destroy vast stores of merit, which is why the traditional texts liken it to a forest fire that completely consumes everything in its path. What makes anger so dangerous is its explosive energy that can very quickly motivate non-virtuous actions, while also creating powerful conditions preventing virtue from ripening. This means the effectiveness of our virtue is reduced and our mind becomes habituated to an afflicted relationship with reality.

The degree of impact anger will have on your mind depends on its intensity and the object at which the anger is directed. Because of its afflicted nature, anger breaks connections with its object of focus—the more intense the anger, the stronger the separation. If you've ever had a major fight with a friend or family member, you will know how powerful connection breakdowns can be.

Often when we separate ourselves from one person through anger, we also become separated from the people we associate with them. For instance, after a difficult breakup or divorce, friends and even family can be forced to take sides. Although we may hold no ill will towards other members of the network, on a subconscious level a degree of aversion can exist due to their association with the object of our hatred. As we cannot avoid the nature of interconnection, anger has the potential to influence a vast array of relationships in a short period of time.

This effect becomes especially dangerous when our anger is directed toward a powerful object such as a Bodhisattva like our spiritual guide or vajra master. As these beings work solely for the benefit of sentient beings, harming them out of anger indirectly brings harm to everyone they are serving. The larger the network of beings associated with the object of our anger, the more destructive the effect will be. Since we cannot tell who is a Bodhisattva, we need to be very careful about allowing anger to dominate our minds.

Regardless of the object of our anger, once it takes root in our mind, it is impossible to have genuine Bodhicitta. As long as anger is present, love and compassion will be suppressed and without love and compassion, Bodhicitta withers and dies. Enlightenment cannot manifest without Bodhicitta, and instead self-cherishing and bias will grow, causing us to create oceans of non-virtuous karma binding us to cyclic existence.

By practicing patience however, we strengthen our tolerance toward the experience of suffering which reduces the intensity of our anger and defuses our reactions before they have a chance to inflict damage on ourselves or others. When anger is restrained, qualities like love and compassion can manifest, naturally leading to the practice of virtue. Friendly and supportive relationships develop easily and are accompanied by a feeling of peace, where not only do we feel content, but so do those around us. By living our lives in such a way, we can die without regret and achieve a higher realm rebirth characterised by harmony and beauty.

THE DIVISIONS OF PATIENCE

The key to preventing anger from arising is developing a strong awareness of why it is never an appropriate response and by identifying and becoming familiar with the conditions that trigger it. Initially the strength of our determination is needed to build a resistance that serves as a counter-force for our habitual reactions. In time however, we can form constructive habits and the aspects that once triggered our anger completely lose their power.

In regards to our practice of patience, we can speak of three general categories which can arouse a response of anger: (1) when someone inflicts harm on us; (2) when we experience suffering as a result of our own actions; and (3) when we are faced with doubts about our capacity to know reality. Each of these situations has the potential to give rise to feelings of frustration or even full blown hatred. Whereas the first situation deals specifically with suffering that arises in dependence on others, the last two are more concerned with the suffering experienced when practicing Dharma.

Patience that Bears the Harm Inflicted by Others

The self-cherishing mind is extremely fixated on protecting anything we consider to be "me" or "mine". This includes our physical body and possessions as well as our characteristics, our likes and our dislikes. It even extends outwards to those we feel a close connection with such as our friends, family and partner. All these things form what is commonly referred to as our *personal identity*.

When another sentient being threatens an aspect of this identity, the self-cherishing mind feels discomfort and fear. It immediately perceives the perpetrator as an enemy and a feeling of bias is subsequently developed against them. On the basis of this bias, the self-cherishing mind feels happy when the enemy suffers and is dissatisfied when they experience happiness. To counteract this, we must develop the *Patience that Bears the Harm Inflicted by Others*.

We do this by contemplating nine topics known as the *Four Points* and the *Five Conceptions* as presented in the *Stages of a Bodhisattva* by Arya Asanga. Try to reflect on each of these topics and use examples from your own life to generate the conviction to abandon the mind which holds beings as enemies and wishes harm upon them.

The Four Points

The first set of topics deals with the suffering that we experience. By analysing its nature and the damage our impatience toward the experience of suffering has on our mind, we can reduce the strength of our anger and establish a greater sense of equanimity. We should contemplate these points whenever we experience intense, continuous or prolonged suffering due to the actions of others.

1. **Suffering is the fault of my own karma.** All conditioned experience is the result of karmic propensities that have been stored in the mind. They are formed in relation to the actions we have performed in the past and while a sentient being can contribute to the conditions for a propensity to ripen, they are not the primary cause of our experience. Whether we experience their actions as suffering depends entirely on the state of our mind, therefore it is inappropriate to think of them as an enemy who is causing our suffering. The true enemy is the self-cherishing mind that motivated our non-virtuous deeds in the first place. This is the mind that must be abandoned.

2. **Impatience or anger is a cause for suffering.** If we react to suffering with impatience or anger, we generate non-virtuous propensities that will ripen in the form of suffering in the future. As karma expands, it is certain the results of these actions will be significantly worse than the harm we are currently experiencing. How foolish it is to harbour ill will toward another, when it is ourselves creating the greater harm. If we really desire happiness, we need to abandon impatience and anger.

3. **Suffering is the basic condition for all sentient beings.** All impermanent phenomena which arise out of causes and conditions have the nature of suffering. Because sentient beings are unaware of this fact, they cling to appearances and inflict harm on others. Having met the Dharma we are

able to recognise the nature of cyclic existence and therefore cannot use a lack of awareness as an excuse. Just because someone inflicts harm on us out of ignorance doesn't mean we should act under the same ignorance. As we have been exposed to wisdom, we have a choice which they do not have.

4. **A Bodhisattva is dedicated to the welfare of others.** A spiritual practitioner who dedicates themselves to their own personal liberation recognises that to achieve states of deep meditative absorption, it is necessary to establish one's mind in an equanimity that is free from attachment and aversion. Although such a practitioner strives only for their own welfare, they know the importance of practicing patience. How much more important must patience then be for someone practicing for the welfare of all sentient beings? If we sincerely wish for sentient beings to be free from suffering, how can we possibly consider inflicting harm on them?

The Five Conceptions

The second set of topics focuses on sentient beings who inflict harm on us. By analysing the conditions of these sentient beings and our relationship to them, we can defuse the strength of any arising anger and strengthen our connection to them. When we embrace these conceptions as a result of meditating intently on them, we will happily endure the harm inflicted upon us by friends, enemies or strangers.

1. **Seeing that the being has been close to you in previous lives:** This is not the first time you will have encountered the being presently causing you harm. In the past, this being has been your closest loved one, sharing innumerable experiences and due to their infinite kindness you have received immeasurable benefit from them. Having recognised your long history together, you understand that they only harm you now because their mind is confused. Even though they are mistaken in their behaviour, it is not a valid reason to abandon them. As we have all made mistakes, we should cultivate compassion for their present suffering and do whatever we can to help them.

2. **Seeing that the being is a mere collection of aggregates:** When you consider the nature of the person doing you harm, recognise they are merely a collection of aggregates that have come together due to causes and conditions. There is no inherently existent person causing you harm. Just as we would not feel anger toward the wind for blowing or the sun for shining, why should we be angry at an illusory being acting in accordance with their karma?

3. **Seeing that the being is impermanent:** This being who was born and presently exists in your life is only a temporary and impermanent phenomenon that is subject to death. The time will therefore come when this being no longer manifests in your experience. Knowing this, what benefit is there in harming something that is naturally impermanent and insubstantial?

4. **Seeing that all sentient beings abide in a state of suffering:** For all those abiding in cyclic existence, life is filled with the three forms of suffering—the suffering of pain, the suffering of change and all-pervasive suffering. Just like us, these beings wish to be free from suffering. When they inflict harm upon us, it is proof that their minds are overwhelmed with delusion as they are convinced their actions will bring them happiness, when they instead only perpetuate their suffering. With a heart of great compassion, nurture the desire to bring them benefit and not bring them harm.

5. **Regarding all beings with an attitude of love and compassion:** Having cultivated great love and compassion, you have generated the extraordinary mind that seeks to achieve enlightenment for the benefit of sentient beings. The person inflicting harm on you is one of the sentient beings you have promised to protect and to benefit however you can. It therefore makes no sense to want to harm them.

You can meditate on these topics individually or in sequence depending on what you feel will be most effective for you. It is a good idea to establish the logic behind each contemplation and then use either set as a glance meditation to keep the topics fresh in your mind. When you become familiar with them, the moment angry thoughts arise, you can refer to the contemplations that serve best as a remedy.

Patience that Endures Suffering

The second form of patience we need to develop is the *Patience that Endures Suffering*, which specifically refers to the suffering that arises as a result of our conviction to practice the Dharma. It is a misconception to think that Dharma practice will be easy and will always make us feel good. The Dharma has the purpose of removing obscurations and such a process is not necessarily a pleasant one.

We experience hardship as an immediate result of our practice because the Dharma actively purifies our mind. As we clear away obscurations, our negative karma often ripens in the form of mild suffering during this life and although we may think our present suffering is intense and unbearable, when compared to the suffering we would have encountered in future lives, it is significantly weaker.

It can be helpful to remember that our ability to work with suffering is a strong indicator that Dharma is taking root in our mind, so rather than seeing hardships as something to be avoided, we can view them as ornaments, or like battle scars to remind us of how far we've come. These experiences constantly test our resolve and strengthen our determination. The more resilient we become, the further we can progress along the path.

The following topics explore the different types of suffering that arise while practicing, and by reflecting on them we can maintain mindfulness of the need to cultivate patience :

1. **Supports:** For those who have abandoned the householder's way of life to dedicate themselves to monastic discipline, there are four supports which are used: (1) monastic robes; (2) alms food; (3) beds and seats and (4) medicine. To develop patience in this context is to endure the hardship that comes from having too little of these supports, having the wrong quantities, being given these supports in a disrespectful manner or when they are of a poor quality.

2. **Worldly conditions:** Until we break free from cyclic existence, we are dominated by causes and conditions and therefore we will inevitably be faced with nine forms of suffering: (1) loss of material things; (2) being held in disrepute; (3) being blamed for things you haven't done; (4) experiencing physical pain; (5) the perishing of that which is perishable; (6) constant separation from that which disappears; (7) continuously aging; (8) enduring sickness and (9) experiencing death. When we recognise these sufferings as an unavoidable part of worldly existence, we learn to accept their presence and develop the patience needed to endure them.

3. **Physical behaviour:** Throughout the day, we transition between four basic positions: (1) walking; (2) standing; (3) sitting and (4) lying down. Any one of these positions can lead to suffering if performed for too long or if used at inappropriate times. By using each of these activities as a support for our practice, we can develop the patience to endure whatever hardships arise.

4. **Embracing the Dharma:** When we accept an ethical discipline to abstain from non-virtue, to cultivate virtue or work for the benefit of others, maintaining that discipline will result in the experience of varying degrees of hardship. Activities such as making offerings to the Three Jewels, studying the teachings, reflecting on their meaning and meditating on the experience, all require time and energy. Performing such actions can often be difficult, but we should never stop striving to do so.

5. **Mendicant's way of life:** For those who wish to dedicate themselves to living without a home, there are seven aspects which will present challenges: (1) your physical appearance will be unattractive; (2) your clothing will be unattractive; (3) you will be considered an outsider for acting in a way that is contrary to worldly conventions; (4) you will have to rely on others for your livelihood; (5) having abandoned hoarding worldly possessions, you will need to seek things like robes and supplies; (6) you will not experience sensual pleasures due to having taken vows of celibacy; (7) you will refrain from attending different forms of frivolous entertainment and (8) refrain from behaving in a way that

involves idle laughter or amusement. By recognising these sufferings as part of the sacrifice you are making in order to practice the Dharma intensively, you develop the patience which is happy to endure different forms of austerities.

6. **Fatigue from striving:** After dedicating oneself to virtuous activities, it is common to experience feelings of exhaustion or fatigue. Even when we feel tired or mentally drained, we should never abandon striving to maintain our discipline. Developing patience toward fatigue is based on recognising the preciousness of this human life and its impermanent nature. Knowing that in the future, we may not have the opportunity to practice, we are unwilling to relax our effort.

7. **Acting on behalf of others:** Working to benefit the eleven types of sentient beings can lead to many types of hardship. To develop patience in the face of these sufferings, we need to strengthen our love and compassion toward sentient beings to prevent our self-cherishing from dominating our mind.

8. **Regular activities:** For those who live according to worldly conventions, there are many sufferings that result from trying to maintain a household. This includes the daily activities that must be completed in relation to one's profession and commitment to a family.

Regardless of the situations in which we find ourselves, rather than allowing hardship to discourage our practice of the Dharma, we can strive to transform our activities into causes for enlightenment, bringing meaning to the suffering we endure. It can be a worthwhile exercise to examine our personal routine and when we identify hardships, try to think of constructive ways to bring them into the context of our spiritual journey.

Patience that is Gained by Reflecting Upon Reality

The last form of patience is concerned with a subtle form of suffering that arises on the basis of not knowing the nature of reality. When we begin spiritual practice we are essentially facing the unknown. The Dharma draws our attention to particular aspects of reality, providing us with a way to familiarise ourselves with it. As we have never experienced this reality before, we must rely on our faith in the teachings to guide us. Lacking clarity regarding what we are doing will cause us to have doubt when faced with the challenges of establishing a different view and this manifests in a form of discomfort that can discourage us from practice.

Failing to develop a tolerance for this type of suffering can cause the gradual degeneration of our faith and a loss of strength in our determination. An aversion toward our practice can often develop and eventually we may abandon it altogether. Without practice we cannot overcome our habituation to ignorance, therefore it is important to learn how to clear away our uncertainty and develop an unshakeable conviction in why we are practicing.

According to Arya Asanga, there are eight subjects we should develop certainty about. By spending the time to study, reflect and meditate on them, we can develop mental clarity which can help us practice with confidence and enthusiasm.

1. **The virtuous qualities of the Three Jewels:** Having strong faith in the Three Jewels as our objects of refuge is the foundation of practicing the Buddhist path. If we are unsure about why the Three Jewels are worthy objects of refuge, what their qualities are or why they are important to our practice, our Dharma practice will remain vague and weak, lacking any real power to guide us. The more we understand the role the Three Jewels plays in our life, the more support we can draw from them.

2. **The nature of reality:** This specifically refers to developing a direct realisation of the Two Truths of conventional and ultimate reality. Achieving this realisation requires considerable faith in what we are trying to achieve and why it is key to achieving enlightenment. This realisation is especially difficult as it directly threatens the perception of the inherently existent self that is the basis of our samsaric existence, and due to our self-cherishing attitude, damaging that self is uncomfortable and fearful. We can overcome this form of suffering by studying

the different aspects of our philosophical view to develop a conceptual model that accurately represents the nature of reality. With this model as our foundation, we can meditate without reservation until we experience this reality directly.

3. **The great power of the Buddhas and Bodhisattvas:** When we first learn of the Buddhas' and Bodhisattvas' amazing qualities, it can be difficult to imagine that one day we could be exactly like them. Even when we have great admiration for these extraordinary beings, we may lack the confidence in our own Buddha-nature. We can dispel this doubt by studying our deepest and most profound potential. When we understand how the path works to transform the ground into the result, we develop faith in our fundamental capacity.

4. **Causes:** Until we completely clear our obscurations, we are subject to causes and conditions. Our spiritual path is based on an understanding of these causes to skilfully manifest a desirable outcome. When we are unaware of the causes that contribute to a particular phenomenon or experience, we lack the ability to work with them. Therefore the more we comprehend the causal factors that influence us, the more choice we have for transforming our experience.

5. **Results:** Likewise, recognising the karmic consequences of our actions provides a powerful method for restraining our behaviour in the present. When we are unsure of what results an action will bring, it creates doubt regarding what we should or should not do. This uncertainty robs our practice of conviction, making it considerably more unstable.

6. **The goal to be achieved by oneself:** In the case of a Bodhisattva, achieving full enlightenment will allow them to be of greatest benefit to sentient beings and fulfil their goal of leading those beings to Buddhahood. In order for this goal to have strength in our mind, we need confidence in the reasons why it is necessary to remove both the afflictive and cognitive obscurations. Realising that only by becoming a Buddha will we achieve our deepest aspiration, we will not be satisfied with anything less.

7. **The means of achieving that goal:** Having a clear goal is a crucial step, but without understanding how to get from where we are to where we want to be, this will be impossible to achieve. When we lack clarity regarding the path leading us to enlightenment, we second guess our actions and fail to commit to our practice. Like a dog chasing its tail, we run around in circles, never making progress. Therefore, studying the stages of the path and understanding the intermediary realisations that support each phase is fundamental to achieving our goal.

8. **The field of that which needs to be known:** The Buddha gave a vast amount of teachings during the period of his life that followed his enlightenment. Familiarity with the full breadth of his view enables us to comprehend the interconnected nature of his teachings and how everything he taught fits together. When we lack an understanding of the completeness of the teachings, we tend to develop a narrow view that focuses on only one aspect of reality. This limits our capacity to realise the definitive meaning of the Buddha's teachings, restricting the benefit we can bring to sentient beings. Although we may personally find some instructions more effective than others, due to the diverse needs of sentient beings, we should still be aware of the many approaches available.

These eight subjects cover a considerably vast field of knowledge and as we are not expected to know everything all at once, this list identifies where we can begin our investigation. We first develop a general understanding by simply introducing ourselves to key concepts which we can use to create a foundation for our behaviour. Over time, we shape and fine-tune this understanding while simultaneously testing it against our experience. As we do so, we clear away our doubts and develop the clarity needed. In this way, our knowledge of reality grows alongside our capacity to work with it.

HOW TO PRACTICE PATIENCE

The practice of patience involves the development of three forms of awareness: (1) awareness of the destructive nature of anger; (2) awareness of the beneficial nature of suffering and (3) awareness of the wisdom presented in the teachings.

Each provides the method for developing the corresponding type of patience described above.

Maintaining Vigilance Against Anger

When we contemplate the destructive nature of anger, we recognise how counter-productive it is to our aims and why it is so important to avoid it at all costs. As we develop a meaningful desire to be free from it, this aspiration provides us with an opposing force we can use to weaken our anger and develop patience.

The key to training with anger is to recognise when it has arisen and to then purify it as soon as possible. This requires us to be extremely vigilant whenever we interact with sentient beings, particularly those we know very well and who can be skilled at exposing our areas of vulnerability. Because of their familiarity, they often know how to "push our buttons" and act as triggers for anger to arise.

No matter how much we prepare for the experience of anger, in the heat of the moment we can still find ourselves doing or saying things we later regret. Due to the strength of our habits, this is to be expected. Instead of beating ourselves up about it, we should recognise that dealing with our destructive behaviours is a process where we need to be diligent. Generate courage by contemplating the benefits of patience and draw strength from knowing such training fits into your greater goal of achieving enlightenment.

Finally, be diligent in purifying any anger that arises so its negative effects do not expand in the mind. Develop a strong feeling of regret for the actions you performed by recognising your faults and acknowledging them to be unwise. Remember your faith in the Three Jewels and refresh your determination to cultivate virtue and bring benefit to sentient beings by engaging in a spiritual practice based on love and compassion. Finish your purification by establishing a strong resolve to not engage in these destructive actions again.

Using Suffering as a Basis for Growth

Our normal attitude toward suffering is to see it as something to be avoided. We go to incredible lengths to prevent it from occurring, but it inevitably does anyway. The Buddha recognised that suffering is a natural consequence of the mistaken way in which we see the world and until we change our view, we will continue to experience that which we don't want. For this reason, instead of avoiding suffering at all costs, we can try to find a way to transform it into something useful that will help us progress along the path. This can be done by contemplating the following benefits of suffering:

1. **Suffering motivates us to achieve liberation:** When we are stuck in a destructive habit, we often don't notice the damage we are doing to ourselves. Due to our lack of awareness, we simply don't see any reason to change. Sometime it takes a crisis of intense suffering to bring awareness to our problem and to jolt us out of our complacency. Suffering can therefore give us perspective and help us identify what is truly important in our lives. It energises and motivates us to develop renunciation of the causes of our suffering which is the basis upon which all spiritual practice is built.

2. **Suffering destroys arrogance:** Another reason we fail to address the problems in our lives is because we don't look for help. When we allow our ego to become puffed up with pride and arrogance, we develop a false sense of security that leads us to think we know everything. Suffering deflates this pride by showing us that we are vulnerable and through its humbling effect, we begin to search for answers and open ourselves to asking others for guidance. Without this willingness to learn, there can be no progress on the path.

3. **Suffering encourages conscientiousness:** Understanding the karmic law of cause and effect, we see that our present experience is the result of our past actions and our future experience will be the result of our present actions. This principle highlights the fact that we are the creators of our own experience so that when we suffer, we become interested in why we suffer. This leads us to investigate its causes and to the realisation that we do not *have* to suffer, which encourages us to practice a path where we consciously abandon those causes of our suffering.

4. **Suffering strengthens our desire for happiness:** The only way we can recognise happiness is in relation to our suffering. The stronger the suffering, the more obvious the experience of happiness becomes. This is why it's so difficult to practice Dharma in the god realms. Surrounded by so much pleasure, these beings lack even the most basic reference point for understanding their potential for suffering. This prevents them from seeking a deeper, more profound level of happiness.

5. **Suffering provides us with a basis for empathy:** Without experiencing something for ourselves, it is difficult to relate to those who have. For instance, imagine trying to explain the experience of seeing to someone who was born blind. Likewise, because we experience a range of suffering in our own lives, we can empathise with the suffering of others, using it as a basis for developing love and compassion. Without some degree of shared experience, such connection would be impossible.

Each of these five points provide us with an opportunity to bring meaning to the suffering we experience and while suffering itself has no good qualities, our attitude toward it can have an extraordinarily beneficial effect on our mind. Once we learn how to view our suffering, the hardships that arises as a result of our practice transform from being obstacles into supports for our spiritual development.

Removing Uncertainty through Study

Doubt arises because we lack certainty in what we are doing. The only way to reduce it is to study the teachings and build familiarity with how everything fits together. We do this by first developing an essential model for the path and then adding in the details. Just like a sculptor working with clay, a general shape is established which is slowly refined until the finished form is achieved.

How much study an individual needs to undertake depends largely on their current level of spiritual maturity. For some, an introduction to a particular teaching is enough for faith to immediately develop. This is a sign of strong propensities which have been built from practice in previous lives. For such a person, once they have been reminded of what they need to do, they can concentrate on practicing the teachings and achieving realisations.

For those who are not yet at this level, knowledge needs to be converted into certainty and faith to be able to practice effectively. In the beginning, keep it simple by starting with the essential and then build complexity as needed. By focusing on the essence and bringing it into your experience, you can cultivate a taste for the practice and determine if there are any doubts. If there are, acquire new information through study and reflect on the new material, addressing the concerns you have. Once doubt has been cleared, continue to practice. This cycle can be repeated as many times as needed, until you no longer encounter doubts.

It is not uncommon for people to postpone their practice until some fictional time in the future when everything will be perfect, however, as we can develop the ability to transform any condition into a support for practice, we can instead work with bringing the Dharma into our lives right now. It is a dynamic process that involves constant revision and adjustment, but if we don't give ourselves the chance to actually experience the Dharma, it will become just another intellectual exercise with little benefit for our mind.

Branch Vows Related to the Perfection of Patience

There are four branch vows that relate to training in patience. Their essence is to *avoid damaging relationships with sentient beings due to anger,* by focusing on protecting the harmony of those relationships. The vows are as follows:

1. **Not retaliating to harm:** There are four disciplines used to cultivate patience and self-restraint. They are (1) not responding to anger with anger; (2) not responding to physical harm with physical harm; (3) not responding to criticism with criticism; and (4) not responding to arguments with arguments. We should maintain mindfulness of these four conditions in which anger arises and make effort to restrain our reactions.

2. **Ignoring those who have been angered:** We must not add fuel to the anger of others by neglecting or ignoring those who are angry with us. Rather than closing ourselves off, we should try to communicate and dissipate their anger. If we cause a problem for others or suspect them of

harming us, and then because of pride, laziness, malice or other afflictions do not clear the air by apologising when we have the opportunity, we then incur a downfall of this vow.

3. **Refusing to accept an apology:** If others harm us and then confess or apologise in a genuine way, but due to malice or resentment we do not accept their apology, we will have then broken this branch vow. This vow is similar to the third root vow except that the four conditions mentioned previously are not required here to break it.

4. **Allowing anger to remain unchecked:** If we become angry with someone and make no effort to try to control our impulses of anger, but allow them to continue unchecked, this vow is breached.

Integrating All Six Perfections

In order to achieve the *Perfection of Patience*, we need to practice while maintaining awareness of all Six Perfections: (1) for the *generosity of patience*, we should practice patience out of a desire to free sentient beings from the sufferings inflicted due to anger; (2) for the *ethical discipline of patience*, we should act in accordance with the branch vows related to patience while also upholding the various trainings; (3) for the *patience of patience* we should accept the hardships that arise as a result of practicing the Perfection of Patience; (4) for the *joyful effort of patience*, we should always strive to strengthen our patience, regardless of the difficulties we face; (5) for the *meditative concentration of patience*, we should always be mindful of anger and suffering, bringing awareness into our actions; and (6) for the *wisdom of patience*, we should always remember the illusory nature of the suffering we experience, the being who inflicts the suffering and the being who experiences the suffering. In this way, our practice will lead to the Perfection of Patience that is free from all forms of grasping and abides in perfect equanimity.

THE RESULTS OF PRACTICING PATIENCE

As a result of our practice of patience, we create the causes to achieve enlightenment. Our mind can abide in a state of ease in both this and future lives as we do not strike out at people in retaliation. Having established resilience, we are able to face whatever hardships arise without fear or doubt and because our mind is calm and collected, we do not engage in non-virtuous activities which only perpetuate our own and others' suffering. We are alternatively concerned with cultivating virtue and bringing happiness to everyone we meet. Whenever suffering does arise in our experience, we view it as a support for our practice and as a basis for feelings of sympathy toward sentient beings.

As Arya Asanga has said, a Bodhisattva who achieves pure patience can be identified by nine characteristics:

1. **Does not retaliate:** No matter what harm may be done to them, the Bodhisattva never retaliates out of anger. They instead gladly endure hardships for the benefit of sentient beings.

2. **Does not develop an angry mind:** The Bodhisattva's mind abides in an equanimity that is free of the bias of attachment and aversion. There is never any animosity or malice towards those who inflict harm.

3. **Does not hold a grudge:** Because the Bodhisattva does not grasp onto anger in any way, it is not perpetuated in their mind. While it may occasionally manifest due to causes and conditions, it quickly dissolves and leaves no trace.

4. **Is ready to assist even after being harmed:** The Bodhisattva is always poised to help sentient beings, regardless of how they behave toward them. If the opportunity arises to bring benefit, they will take it.

5. **Is willing to reconcile with those who have harmed them:** If the Bodhisattva sees that their relationship with a sentient being has been damaged, they will seek to repair it. No matter how severe the harm to them, they will always be willing to forgive the perpetrator.

6. **Never rejoices in the suffering of others:** The Bodhisattva's mind is free of the ill will that wishes their enemies to suffer. They instead hold an even level of compassion toward all beings, wishing them to be free from suffering and its causes.

7. **Strong shame and abashment towards impatience:** If the Bodhisattva ever experiences impatience in the face of extreme difficulties, they feel a strong sense of moral shame and the desire to purify their impatience immediately.

8. **Strong feeling of compassion:** The Bodhisattva's compassion extends to all sentient beings and they sympathise with their struggles on a very profound level.

9. **Free of attachment to the desire realm:** Because they are keenly aware of the endless struggles that sentient beings endure in the desire realm, the Bodhisattva holds no attachment toward its pleasures.

REVIEW OF KEY POINTS

- Patience is the mind which is able to abide in equanimity as a response to the experience of suffering. Training in patience consists of (1) refraining from anger; (2) refraining from retaliation and (3) refraining from holding grudges.

- The main reason to practice patience is to remove our habituation to aversion which causes us to engage in non-virtuous activities and to prevent our virtuous propensities from ripening.

- Patience can be divided into three types: (1) the patience that bears harm inflicted by others; (2) the patience which endures suffering and (3) the patience which is gained by reflecting on reality. The first type focuses on protecting our relationship with sentient beings while the last two help us overcome the hardships we face while practicing the Dharma.

- To develop the Patience that Bears the Harm Inflicted by Others, we need to contemplate the disadvantages of anger from two perspectives: (1) from the perspective of how anger affects our mind and (2) from the perspective of how anger affects our relationship with others.

- To develop the Patience that Endures Suffering, we need to strengthen our awareness of the many types of suffering we experience as a result of our practice. These are divided into eight: (1) suffering from gathering the supports for practice; (2) suffering from worldly conditions; (3) suffering from physical behaviour; (4) suffering from embracing the Dharma; (5) suffering from living like a mendicant; (6) suffering from fatigue; (7) suffering from acting on behalf of others and (8) suffering from our regular activities.

- To develop the Patience that is Gained by Reflecting on Reality, we need to remove doubt about eight areas of knowledge: (1) the virtuous qualities of the Three Jewels; (2) the nature of reality; (3) the great power of the Buddhas and Bodhisattvas; (4) causes; (5) results; (6) the goal to be achieved; (7) the method to achieve that goal and (8) the field of all that is to be known.

- You can train in patience by developing awareness of (1) the destructive nature of anger; (2) the beneficial nature of suffering and (3) the wisdom presented in the teachings.

- There are four branch vows for the training in patience: (1) not retaliating to harm; (2) ignoring those who have been angered; (3) refusing to accept an apology and (4) allowing anger to remain unchecked.

- A Bodhisattva with pure patience has nine aspects: (1) does not retaliate; (2) does not develop an angry mind; (3) does not hold a grudge; (4) is ready to assist them even after being harmed; (5) is willing to reconcile with those who have harmed them; (6) never rejoices in the suffering of others; (7) strong shame and abashment towards impatience; (8) strong feeling of compassion and (9) is free of attachment to the desire realm.

CHAPTER TEN

Cultivating Joyful Effort to Achieve Your Aims

In any journey, the key to arriving at our destination is taking more steps forward than backwards—a simple equation that also holds true for spiritual practice. Recognising that afflictive emotions such as anger and hatred only serve to send us in the wrong direction, we train in the *Perfection of Patience*. This cuts the flow of our habitual negativity and gives us the opportunity to nurture virtuous propensities. When we we exert ourselves correctly, virtue begins to hold sway and the momentum of our practice shifts in our favour.

The energy needed to create this shift is generated through the practice of the *Perfection of Joyful Effort,* which is like the motor on a boat, propelling it upstream. As the motor grows in power, our habituation toward virtue is reinforced until eventually it becomes so strong that there is no longer any danger of falling backwards. With less resistance in our mind, the effort we need to exert is reduced and as we approach our destination, virtue becomes effortless, arising naturally and spontaneously.

WHAT IS JOYFUL EFFORT?

Before we participate in any activity we must first develop an intention to do so. We then strengthen that intention with grasping until it leads to an action. This focusing of energy is known as *effort,* and can be directed to any kind of action whether virtuous or not. When we speak of *joyful effort,* we are referring to a very specific type of effort that acts as a catalyst for realisations. It can be defined as *the mind which takes delight in exerting effort to practice virtue.*

This special form of effort is a key condition for maintaining ethical discipline. Without it, spiritual practice becomes difficult and lacks the conviction necessary to attain realisations. There are two aspects to joyful effort that we need to familiarise ourselves with:

1. **Feeling joyful:** The first aspect is a sense of delight in making the effort to practice. This joy comes from understanding the nature of one's practice and the benefit it will bring. When we see that our actions can produce truly extraordinary results, we are filled with a sense of satisfaction and contentment. This feeling is important for strengthening our desire to repeat the action again in the future. If it is lacking, our practice can feel boring or tedious.

2. **Striving for virtue:** The second aspect is making the effort to practice virtue. In this context, *virtue* refers to any action which is based on authentic wisdom. Through cultivating virtue, we clear away ignorance, bringing ourselves closer to reality. By striving to practice virtue, we concentrate our energy on the causes of genuine happiness, creating the conditions for joy to arise.

When both aspects are present in our practice, we effectively energise our mind creating a positive reinforcement loop. The more effort we make, the more joy we experience, while the more joy we experience, the more effort we make. This feedback builds a momentum which allows the mind to overcome its habitual tendency towards ignorance.

How we use the energy we create is a crucial part of any successful practice. Recognising that every activity we engage in drains us both physically and mentally, we need to be skilful in where we invest our time and effort. The training in joyful effort is specifically designed to direct our energy toward virtuous activities in a self-sustainable way so that not only does it motivate us to practice more, it also helps refresh our interest and maintain our engagement.

REASONS TO PRACTICE
THE PERFECTION OF JOYFUL EFFORT

The biggest obstacle to cultivating joyful effort is *laziness*. This is the quality of mind that is attached to non-virtuous activities. Because we have perpetuated our ignorance for countless lifetimes, we are deeply habituated to activities which either prevent us from cultivating virtue or actively reinforce afflictive ways of thinking. This situation is similar to being stuck in quicksand which binds us, keeping us trapped and slowly pulling us down, causing us to suffer.

When we begin to practice, laziness manifests as all kinds of excuses that prevent us from even starting. It is a mind which procrastinates and postpones practicing until the conditions improve in some way. For instance, if we are raising a family we may tell ourselves that with all that needs to be done for the children, there's no time left to practice. Or we may have a demanding job and think we will make the time to practice when we've earned enough money to be comfortable. Whatever the excuse, the end result is a failure to see the potential for practice in each moment of our experience. By taking the path of least resistance, we continue to relate to the world in the same way we have always done, missing the potential for transformation.

Through training in joyful effort, we concentrate on the benefits of practicing virtue and develop the strong aspiration to overcome our limitations. Supported by the power of Bodhicitta, we establish a determination to do the best we can. Although our circumstances may not be perfect, we still recognise the numerous opportunities to practice and we realise that there is no benefit to be gained from doing nothing.

Once we have overcome our initial procrastination to practice, laziness manifests in the form of *boredom*, which is the mind that is unsatisfied with its present conditions and longs for change. It arises primarily due to the nature of our training as in order to habituate our mind to virtue, we need to practice over and over again until it becomes second nature. This repetition can cause the untamed mind to become restless and when the mind lacks stability, it defaults to whatever activities will stimulate it. Many people, for example, relieve their boredom by eating, watching TV, listening to music or socialising with friends. Whatever the distraction, this form of laziness cuts the continuity of our practice, preventing us from achieving realisation. Rather than penetrating the depths of our experience, we sit on the surface, treading water, causing our practice to become weak and unstable, and making it easy to abandon if conditions become difficult.

When we develop perseverance through training in joyful effort, we actively strengthen our connection to virtue and increase our positive qualities. It is these qualities that bring joy to our mind and are the provisional attainments which help us gain confidence and feel transformation is possible. When we notice we are a little bit more loving, compassionate or disciplined, we are encouraged to continue our practice. Taking joy in this process shifts our attention away from our negative habits, keeps us working enthusiastically toward our goals and gives us the chance to establish virtuous habits and progress along the path.

Any activity which is concerned with creating conditions for a future experience will, by its nature, require perseverance to complete. Complex activities take considerable time and effort as they involve many "moving parts" that need to be correctly placed before the final result can be achieved. This requires the ability to maintain determination from the very beginning through to the end. The greatest challenge to this is the laziness which manifests in the form of self-doubt and discouragement. The longer the process takes, the harder it is for the mind to sustain its intention and if we lose sight of our purpose, we abandon the activity before it is completed.

Joyful effort keeps us focused and helps us avoid these types of laziness. Instead of collecting pieces of incomplete realisations, we develop a momentum that can carry us through to the perfection of each quality. This is achieved by working skilfully with short-term activities that contribute to long-term goals. By taking baby-steps, we remain attentive to the present and don't get bogged down by what may come in the future. Our aim is to habituate ourselves to finishing what we start no matter the size of the task. As we make progress, a confidence that one day we will achieve our ultimate aim of enlightenment then develops.

In this way, the perseverance of joyful effort is a fundamental quality in the beginning, middle and end of our practice. It is the thread which ties together all of our actions on the path, connecting the ground with the result and making it possible to manifest our greatest potential. If we strive diligently to perfect this one quality, every other quality naturally manifests as a result of our practice.

THE DIVISIONS OF JOYFUL EFFORT

The only way to counteract laziness is to cultivate perseverance by developing a resistance to laziness and an attraction to practicing virtue. As the second naturally arises from the first, we will examine the three types of perseverance we need to suppress and remove our laziness: (1) armour-like perseverance;

(2) perseverance of right conduct and (3) perseverance of perpetual enthusiasm. These forms of joyful effort provide a basis to reverse the flow of our habitual tendencies, enabling us to progress quickly along the path.

Armour-Like Perseverance

Bodhisattvas are sometimes referred to as *compassionate warriors*, as they battle against their self-cherishing mind and its army of afflictions. They are internal warriors who recognise that the real enemy is within the mind and therefore dedicate their lives to practicing the Dharma. They are tireless and filled with courage, never wavering from their determination to bring lasting benefit to sentient beings.

Using the sort of language that refers to war, fighting and enemies may seem like an unnecessary analogy, which contradicts a Bodhisattva's conduct of compassion and their desire for peace and harmony. While it is true that we should cultivate an equanimous mind of love for all sentient beings, we should also never accept or underestimate the force of afflicted minds such as hatred, attachment or ignorance. They are the very causes for the suffering of all beings and if they are not directly confronted, they will continue to bind us to cyclic existence. From the wisdom that sees the harm we endure as a result of our afflictions, we must do everything in our power to combat and remove them.

The first form of perseverance arises from this warrior-like determination to never give up until all sentient beings are freed from suffering. In order to develop this, we need to bring a sense of urgency to our mind and strengthen our desire to achieve enlightenment. In times of war, the stakes of life and death are high and people do whatever they think is necessary to survive. Unfortunately, without realising where the real enemy lies, they end up killing each other and create unimaginable suffering for themselves. A Bodhisattva has the same willingness to fight, but directs all their energy on the real source of conflict. There is no anger toward anyone, no wish to harm others; only the strength of mind that will not back down, regardless of the afflictions thrown at them. This sort of determination creates an armour that offers protection in the face of adversity, allowing for a greater capacity to complete our actions and achieve our goals. This is known as *armour-like perseverance.*

We can identify this type of perseverance in worldly examples such as olympic athletes, scientific researchers or entrepreneurs. Setting themselves ambitious and challenging goals which they believe to be important, they may become discouraged by the hard work and extended time required to bring their dreams into reality. Those who can accept such factors as the nature of their goal are those who are most likely to succeed. They lock on to their desired outcome and do not let anything deter them from it. If such determination can be established for worldly activities, imagine the benefit from directing it to the achievement of enlightenment.

The key to developing such determination is having a clear vision of why enlightenment is necessary, and reflecting deeply on Bodhicitta to make it the driving principle in our lives. This doesn't mean we have to become monks or nuns, living in secluded hermitages, but simply that we need to strive to bring our Bodhicitta into each and every action we do. Facing each challenge like a stepping stone that brings us closer to our aim, no matter the time it takes, no matter how insurmountable the odds may seem, we should never give up. There is no choice, we must fight for our freedom.

The purpose of cultivating this form of courageous thought is to counteract the discouragement that can arise when we consider the enormous scale of what enlightenment entails. The scriptures speak of three countless aeons to accumulate the necessary merit and wisdom needed to attain Buddhahood. They also speak of the infinite number of sentient beings who continually suffer. While both of these statements can produce overwhelming feelings of disheartenment, what is the alternative? If we do nothing, we are guaranteed to continue suffering just as we have since beginningless time, but if we strive to achieve enlightenment, at least we are working towards a future in which genuine peace and harmony can manifest. No matter how small the step, as long as it moves in the right direction, we can be confident that one day we will arrive at our destination.

When we accept the journey we have embarked upon, it is far more beneficial to concentrate on the day-to-day victories we achieve rather than worrying about all that is still left to do. Each person we help, each minute spent meditating, each virtuous thought, every aspect of our practice becomes a basis for developing

*Manjuvajra—The Great Kalachakrapada who persevered
to recover the teachings of Kalachakra from Shambhala*

joy. In this way, a Bodhisattva can move through life filled with happiness and contentment. While there will definitely be difficulties and hardship, these too are an important part of the journey. If we embrace the process, there is nothing to stop us from achieving our goal.

Never be discouraged by the profundity, time, or magnitude of your goal, as illustrated to us in the stories of the great teachers, Buddhas and Bodhisattvas and do not doubt your ability to achieve what they have demonstrated. By acting with diligence and perseverance, they became the great beings that they are and although we may not yet be at their level, as we are their disciples, what other choice do we have but to follow in their footsteps? Just as they faced great hardship, we too will experience similar struggles from which we can also recover.

At this moment we have found a precious human birth, we have met an authentic spiritual teacher and we are receiving their pith instructions. We have this incredible opportunity to really practice the Dharma and should therefore try to accept any hardships or burdens—even risking our own lives for the Dharma without care for our flesh or blood, rather than falling prey to discouragement or lack of confidence.

Perseverance of Right Conduct

The second form of perseverance is related to how we engage in the practice of maintaining our discipline. As we spoke about previously, all the practices of the path are contained within the three trainings of: (1) restraining from non-virtue, (2) cultivating virtue and (3) benefiting others. Therefore, to achieve our aims we must develop what is known as the *Perseverance of Right Conduct*, which is simply the habituation to virtuous activities. This type of perseverance is established by cultivating three forms of diligence:

1. **Diligence to avoid afflictive emotions:** The afflictions are the root cause of our suffering and therefore we must do all we can to prevent them from dominating our mind. Through the use of vigilance and mindfulness we constantly stand guard to prevent the afflictions from arising. This attitude is similar to a security guard protecting a precious jewel, who must remain alert, never resting for even a moment.

2. **Diligence to accomplish virtue:** To successfully cultivate virtue, we need to practice five qualities: (1) we must exert effort in a *persistent manner* that repeatedly engages in virtuous activities with body, speech and mind; (2) we must practice *with devotion*, acting immediately with joy and inspiration, taking full advantage of the opportunities that present themselves; (3) we must *be unshakeable* in our determination to overcome whatever hardship arises as a result of practice; (4) we must *make effort without turning back*, no matter how difficult the situation may become; and (5) we must *be free from arrogance*, not allowing ourselves to become haughty about our practice.

3. **Diligence to benefit sentient beings:** The root of all happiness is the mind which cherishes others. To fulfil our desire to bring benefit to them, we should cultivate a form of diligence that is constantly mindful of the needs of others and looks for opportunities to help them however we can. Sometimes this means acting directly by helping sentient beings through charity, while at other times it is acting indirectly to cultivate the qualities that will allow us to benefit more people in the future.

It is easy to waste an entire human life by prioritising worldly aspects over our practice of the Dharma. We often plan to practice but tell ourselves we will "start tomorrow" and then we put it off until the next day and then the next. Then one day we wake up and find we no longer have the capacity to properly practice the Dharma. The constant "busyness" which keeps us imprisoned in repetitive worldly activities is a form of laziness, making us act according to wrong or distorted priorities. The perseverance of right conduct is the antidote for this type of laziness.

We should therefore try to abandon worldly activities and take action today. Doing the best we can, we should strive to reduce our self-cherishing and serve the people around us. Once we feel this wish to practice, we do not procrastinate or allow laziness to override it, but start working with the Dharma immediately!

Perseverance of Perpetual Enthusiasm

The final form of perseverance is most easily described as a constant hunger for practicing Dharma. It is known as the *Perseverance of Perpetual Enthusiasm* as it fuels our desire to accumulate merit and wisdom. It is a mind which always strives to acquire more Dharma knowledge, cultivate further virtues and achieve greater realisations.

When this perseverance takes root, we are no longer satisfied by doing a few good works, a small retreat or a couple of prayers. One part of our mind is always thinking about the next practice or good deed and there is never a feeling that enough has been done. At no time can we become complacent, for until the state of enlightenment has been reached, past negative actions and propensities still need to be removed and wholesome qualities need to be strengthened. We should instead work to make our practice powerful, diligent and consistent, just like the waves of a great ocean, carrying the boat to shore.

While intelligence alone is not enough to achieve our goals, when accompanied by joyful effort, it will create the conditions for an extraordinary practitioner. By making the effort to understand the Dharma and persevering in the face of difficulty, joy will gradually develop and hardship will naturally subside.

HOW TO PRACTICE JOYFUL EFFORT

The training in joyful effort is based on working with the conditions that influence our desire to practice virtue. When we successfully remove the conditions inhibiting our practice and gather the conditions which support it, we naturally exert the effort required to maintain the practice.

Keep in mind that perseverance and diligence are mental phenomena and as they arise in the mind, this is where the training focuses. While external conditions contribute to our capacity to practice, they are always secondary. The primary conditions are the mental factors we work with through meditation.

Eliminating Unfavorable Conditions

As we have discussed throughout this chapter, the main obstacle to maintaining our practice is laziness. It can manifest in three ways: (1) the laziness of procrastination; (2) the laziness of distraction and (3) the laziness of discouragement. For each of these forms of laziness, we need to apply specific antidotes.

The Laziness of Procrastination

Procrastination occurs when despite knowing the great benefit of practicing the Dharma, we do not want to practice at this moment. We postpone our practice to attend to something we believe is more urgent or important. Essentially, it arises because we fail to prioritise our practice, mistakenly thinking we have plenty of time and therefore it is reasonable to put it off until later.

The antidote to this type of laziness is to meditate on impermanence. You can find a more detailed presentation on this topic in Book One of this series, but we can summarise the material into three basic contemplations:

1. **Developing the certainty that you will definitely die:** Right now you have a precious human body that is the result of many different causes and conditions coming together. When these conditions separate, your life is no longer sustainable and you will die. Nobody can escape death and from the moment we are born, we move closer to that inevitable moment. Therefore abandon the thought that thinks you are invincible and dedicate yourself to the practice of Dharma.

2. **The uncertainty of when your death will occur:** Although we may accept the certainty of our death, we have no idea when it will occur. Death can happen at any moment so what guarantee do you have that you will not die today? Our bodies are extremely fragile and almost anything can become a cause to end our life. If we are not prepared when death does come, we will have no chance to use the process for practice and we will instead be consumed by suffering. We should therefore not waste the little time we have left and practice Dharma immediately.

3. **Recognising that only Dharma will help you at the time of death:** When death arrives, you will be separated from everything in this life. All of your possessions, your friends and family, even your precious body will be lost. None of the things you hold dear will be of any benefit to you when you die. The only things that will carry through into your

next life are the karmic propensities you have created in your mind. If you procrastinate and spend your time cultivating non-virtue, you will experience great suffering, however, if you dedicate yourself to Dharma, you will ensure your happiness in this and future lives. There should be nothing more important to you than practicing Dharma.

The more we reflect on these points, the less attraction we have towards worldly concerns. An intense fear of wasting this life then develops which counteracts our laziness and drives us to take full advantage of our present conditions. We should nurture the feeling that this life is unbelievably precious and rare, filled with truly extraordinary opportunities. Like a person with their hair on fire, we cannot afford to waste anytime whatsoever.

The Laziness of Distraction

Distraction arises from attachment to sensual pleasures. As we do not recognise our potential for long-lasting genuine happiness, we only pay attention to things that bring us temporary satisfaction. This narrow view prevents us from seeking a higher aim and consumes our lives with meaningless activities. We may think we are creating the causes for our happiness, but they are actually the causes for future suffering and this fundamental mistake distracts us from practicing the Dharma, binding us to cyclic existence.

The antidote to this type of laziness is to contemplate the suffering nature of cyclic existence and to seriously consider the potential of the mind. When we meditate on the results produced by practicing the Dharma, we find no reason to fixate so heavily on temporary pleasures. With a broader view, we are able to recognise the great benefit of striving to achieve genuine happiness.

Through dedicated study, the more familiar we are with how the ground, path and result can produce enlightenment, the more confidence we develop, giving strength to our conviction and practice. Such faith keeps us focused on our goal and prevents us from becoming sidetracked by distractions.

The Laziness of Discouragement

Self-doubt is a subtle form of laziness that inhibits our effort before we even start. This is caused by a lack of awareness regarding our potential. When we hear of the incredible results of practicing the Dharma, we often compare them with our own current conditions and for many, it is difficult to imagine ever being able to achieve the perfection of the Buddhas. The destination is remote and the path seems to overflow with insurmountable obstacles so it is no wonder we can be so easily discouraged.

If we entertain this type of doubt, it can rapidly grow in our mind to become a cause for abandoning Bodhicitta. The antidote for dispelling this form of laziness is to contemplate the nature of three types of discouragement that commonly arise:

1. **Discouragement about the goal:** Doubting your capacity to achieve enlightenment requires meditation on Buddha-nature. The Buddha taught that every single sentient being possesses the nature to also become a Buddha and so you too are part of that Buddha family. You therefore have the exact same ground that can be purified by practicing the path, to produce the exact same result. All that is needed is the exertion of effort in practicing virtue and you will definitely achieve complete enlightenment.

2. **Discouragement about the means to attain the goal:** Not only must you develop faith in your own innate capacity, but also faith in your capability to walk the path. This can be done by meditating on the suffering you have endured in relation to worldly activities. Consider everything you have gone through in this life and the countless lives before, and what you have to show for it. Now you have this incredible opportunity to practice the Dharma and create the causes for genuine happiness, shouldn't you at least try? Although at first it will be difficult, with time it will become easier and through hard work and determination, you will definitely progress along the path.

3. **Discouragement about having to take limitless rebirths:** This form of discouragement arises when we mistakenly believe a Bodhisattva must endure the sufferings of samsara for countless aeons. While it is true that a Bodhisattva continues to take rebirth until all sentient beings are free from suffering, this does not mean they suffer themselves. Like the great Arhats of the Foundational Vehicle, Arya Bodhisattvas completely cut

their afflictive tendencies and can therefore abide in samsara without being affected by it. Understanding this, it does not matter how long they need to stay in samsara; it is enough to know they are benefiting sentient beings.

In all these situations, we can see that discouragement arises out of our ignorance regarding some aspect of our experience. For this reason, a general antidote for removing the laziness of discouragement is to make the effort to study the path and to develop a crystal clear awareness of how all the parts fit together. By doing this we know exactly what we are doing at any given moment so we do not give in to discouragement.

Gathering Favourable Conditions

Once we have effectively cleared the different forms of laziness, we are in a good position to generate truly vast amounts of merit. Cultivating the following four virtuous qualities can help us in this effort: (1) aspiration; (2) steadfastness; (3) joy and (4) relinquishment. These qualities give us the power to persevere in the face of difficulty and establish a solid foundation for our practice.

The Power of Aspiration

All action begins with desire. Usually when we speak of desire, it is something we want to avoid because of its potentially afflictive nature. In this context however, we are referring to our desire to practice virtue, which is known as an *aspiration*. As long as we are on our spiritual path, aspirations are an essential part of our practice as they keep us moving in the right direction.

Having a strong aspiration to practice the Dharma means we are sincerely interested in practice, and understand its value while wanting to maintain our discipline. If we lack this basic aspiration we can slip into apathy or a general lack of enthusiasm; for this reason, we should reflect on the nature of the *Karmic Law of Cause and Effect*. When we comprehend how karma functions, we realise the ways in which individual practice contributes to our achievement of full enlightenment. Focusing on the resultant benefits strengthens our aspiration until it becomes strong enough to motivate us to actually engage in virtuous actions.

The Power of Steadfastness

Spiritual practice requires us to be resolute in our determination and steadfast in the face of obstacles. Even after developing a strong aspiration to do something, we may find that soon after beginning, conditions are no longer enjoyable and we encounter difficulties. This can often throw us for a loop and cause us to give up and change our aspiration. Behaving in this way means we are repeatedly changing our direction and consequently will make little progress along the path.

To develop the steadfastness needed to stay the course, we can analyse whether we have the capacity to complete an action before we start. If we have uncertainty about our ability to finish, it may be better not to begin and instead concentrate on actions we are confident of completing. With each task we see through to the end, our confidence increases which gives us greater fortitude and allows us to tackle larger projects with certainty. The best type of activity is one that challenges us and yet is still feasible to complete. Working on something impossible will only end up being an exercise in frustration. If we can be wise about where we invest our energy, we build our conviction and subsequently achieve a great deal.

The Power of Joy

Armed with the power of aspiration and steadfastness, it becomes relatively easy to focus our energy on virtuous activity. To strengthen these qualities, we can use *joy* which is the mind that is delighted by the thought of virtuous activity and is also filled with pleasure when engaged in the activity. This blissful feeling creates an insatiable mind that is motivated to practice continuously. Such insatiability gives us enthusiasm and keeps us coming back for more.

While being attached to worldly pleasure creates an obstacle for practice, having a strong desire for the joy that comes from virtue functions as a support to achieving enlightenment. This is because the joy of this kind is a form of genuine happiness that comes from acting in accordance with reality. Since it is not based on ignorance, it connects us to our deeper nature. We can strengthen the joy we feel by actively rejoicing in any virtue we perform, as this not only multiplies the effect the virtue has on our mind, it also conditions us to enjoy the same action again in the future.

The Power of Relinquishment

Generally speaking, training in joyful effort is about making a continuous and vigorous effort, but we need to be careful to approach this training in a balanced way. If we do too little, we will never overcome our laziness, but if we do too much we can overexert ourselves, leading to physical and mental fatigue. The wise way to practice joyful effort is to then maintain awareness of our energy levels and know when to rest.

For the most part, it is preferable to work steadily over a long period of time rather than sporadically. Try to work for some time each day on your project, as much as you can until you feel fatigue setting in. If you need to sleep, then sleep and if you need to eat, then eat. Do whatever you need to do to replenish your energy and regain your clarity of focus so you can eventually complete your project.

To make the most of your time, it is good to identify a number of secondary activities that help "recharge your batteries". For instance, going for a walk can be a wonderful way to get some exercise as well as a change of scenery. Reading a book or listening to teachings can also be very beneficial. If you can, try to find a way to bring virtue into each activity so that even when you are resting, you are still creating causes for enlightenment. Once you have successfully energised your body and mind, you should return to your primary activity immediately. Be vigilant to avoid laziness taking hold.

Being Intent on Making Effort

Having removed the conditions which inhibit our practice and then cultivated the conditions which support it, we move to training in joyful effort by practicing ethical discipline. This consists of two aspects: (1) preventing the afflictions from dominating the mind and (2) destroying the afflictions by applying their remedies. While the first emphasises developing wisdom through study and reflection, the second is mainly concerned with our conduct. Without both of these aspects, our progress will be slow.

Furthermore, it is important to develop a discipline that has the correct balance between study and practice, without taking an extreme approach that focuses too heavily on one over the other. If we spend all our time studying and never practicing, we may become very learned, but fail to tame our mind. This leads us to engage in non-virtuous actions, filling our minds with the causes for suffering. Likewise, spending all our time practicing without any study may lead to a lack of clarity regarding what we are practicing, creating confusion and decreased effectiveness.

Using Effort to Make the Mind Serviceable

As we are now, our mind and body are unserviceable. Although we may want to do something virtuous, we are either unable to do so physically or the power of our afflictions overpowers us. Through the training in joyful effort, we purify the mind by maintaining our discipline. This naturally brings our body and mind into alignment, giving us greater control over what we do and providing us with enough strength of mind to make meaningful choices in our lives.

In the beginning, it is necessary to exert large amounts of effort in order to break existing habits. Over time, the effort required is reduced as we gain greater control. Like a well trained pet, the body and mind need only a little effort to make them do what you want them to do. If you persevere, you will gain complete mastery over your body and mind and at that point, no effort will be required. You simply need to form the desire and your mind and body respond accordingly. This is what it means to perfect joyful effort.

Branch Vows Related to the Perfection of Joyful Effort

Three of the forty-six branch vows are related to the training in joyful effort and their essence is to *always strive to use your time for virtue*. By not giving in to laziness, we ensure our practice continues to grow and develop. The vows are to avoid the following behaviour:

1. **Gathering a following out of desire for gain and honour:** If we gather a circle of followers and other people for the self-centred purpose of gaining respect, fame, profit, praise or security, we will have broken this branch vow. Instead of striving for worldly concerns, we should exert effort on the basis of a meaningful and virtuous motivation.

2. **Failing to dispel laziness, and the like:** The three types of laziness include idleness, attraction to useless or negative actions and a lack of confidence or discouragement. They prevent us from acting within our capabilities. If due to laziness we sleep excessively through the day but do not make an effort to eliminate this habit, we are then breaking this branch vow. Note that laziness is not just inactivity, it also applies to actively engaging in useless or negative activities which make our spiritual practice degenerate.

3. **Engaging in idle speech with a sense of attachment:** If we waste our time by gossiping about famous people, politics, war, relationships, divorce, crimes and so forth with an attitude of attachment or desire, we are then breaking this vow. We should always strive to use our speech in a meaningful way to bring benefit to others.

Integrating All Six Perfections

The *Perfection of Joyful Effort* is achieved through working simultaneously with all six of the Perfections: (1) for the *generosity of joyful effort,* we should practice joyful effort out of a desire to inspire others to cultivate virtue; (2) for the *ethical discipline of joyful effort,* we should uphold the branch vows and specifically do whatever we can to overcome our laziness; (3) for the *patience of joyful effort,* we should not be discouraged by the hardships which arise as a result of striving to be diligent; (4) for the *joyful effort of joyful effort,* we should always strive to exert effort so we can bring benefit to sentient beings; (5) for the *meditative concentration of joyful effort,* we should be mindful of our habituation toward laziness and be vigilant in preventing it from dominating us; and (6) for the *wisdom of joyful effort,* we should constantly remind ourselves of the illusory nature of the agent who is performing actions diligently, the actions performed by that agent and the object for whom the actions are being performed, as none of these exist inherently from their own side. When practiced skilfully in this way, joyful effort will quickly ripen and become perfect.

THE RESULTS OF PRACTICING JOYFUL EFFORT

There is no way to manifest enlightened qualities without making effort to remove our obscurations, therefore through the power of training in joyful effort, all our temporary and ultimate aims can be realised. It is joyful effort that builds the momentum that will carry us to the end of our journey. By practicing *Armour-Like Perseverance*, our mind will be free from discouragement and will remain strong and stable in the face of whatever hardship arises—we will never tire of practicing virtue. Through the practice of *Perseverance of Right Conduct,* our afflictions will subside, setting our mind at ease and we will never waver from our practice of virtue. Finally, by practicing *Perseverance of Perpetual Enthusiasm*, the very experience of practicing virtue will be joyful, making it easy to practice at all times.

According to Arya Asanga, when a Bodhisattva has achieved pure joyful effort, they can be described as having the following characteristics:

1. **Appropriate:** The Bodhisattva always exerts effort to maintain mindfulness of the afflictions arising in their mind. Immediately recognising their nature, they diligently apply the antidote which is most appropriate to the situation, preventing afflictions from gaining strength.

2. **Experienced:** The Bodhisattva is experienced in the sense that they have fully familiarised their mind with practicing the Dharma. By continuously applying effort, they understand exactly how to practice at all times and never doubt their ability to do so with confidence and determination.

3. **Free of laxness:** Until their attainment of Buddhahood, the Bodhisattva maintains the mind of a novice, recognising that there is always more to learn. They are never satisfied with their progress nor are they content with the depth of their spiritual qualities and so do whatever they can to improve and develop their understanding.

4. **Well informed:** Recognising wisdom as the key to overcoming ignorance, the Bodhisattva strives to establish mental clarity regarding all forms of phenomena. They seek sources of wisdom whether these be exalted beings or their own inner capacity and there is no subject the Bodhisattva does not wish to learn.

5. **Practices according to context:** Based on their profound and vast knowledge, the Bodhisattva knows exactly what to practice at any given moment. They are extremely aware of the state of their mind and of what will bring the greatest benefit to the varying situations that arise. Specifically they understand where they are in terms of spiritual development and therefore are able to practice in accordance with a path.

6. **Perception of signs:** The Bodhisattva exerts a great deal of effort to practice meditative equipoise on the nature of reality and can subsequently observe, maintain mindfulness of and achieve the signs of calm abiding and special insight. Through this effort, the Bodhisattva comes to know reality as it is.

7. **Free of dejection:** Having studied extensively and inspired their mind through reflecting on the meaning of the teachings, the Bodhisattva is never discouraged by the hardships that arises due to practicing the Dharma. Recognising the great potential they possess, the Bodhisattva always strives for what is superior and is never satisfied with incomplete realisations.

8. **Not deficient:** The Bodhisattva strives to create the conditions to support authentic meditative practice. This includes guarding the three doors of body, speech and mind, regulating one's intake of food, being mindful of sleeping patterns and so forth. They do whatever is in their power to orient everything they do toward attaining realisations.

9. **Balanced:** Understanding that it is impossible to maintain a practice that is either too tight or too loose, the Bodhisattva exerts effort to establish the perfect balance. They act with care to avoid becoming listless, while also avoiding straining themselves too much. They are relaxed, yet persistent, and steadily apply effort in a continual manner.

10. **Dedicated to Great Enlightenment:** No matter what action the Bodhisattva engages in, they never fail to dedicate the merit generated. This ensures that all their actions contribute to the accumulation of merit and wisdom and therefore become the causes for achieving Buddhahood.

REVIEW OF KEY POINTS

- Joyful effort is the mind which takes delight in exerting effort to practice virtue. It consists of two parts: (1) the joyful feeling that arises when one engages in spiritual practice and (2) the determination that values virtue and strives to practice it as much as possible.

- The main obstacle to joyful effort is the laziness that is attached to non-virtuous activities. In the beginning it distracts our mind, preventing us from starting our practice. In the middle it breaks the continuity of our practice and weakens our resolve. At the end it discourages us from following our actions through to completion.

- Joyful effort acts as an antidote to laziness. In the beginning it focuses our attention on the benefit of practice and helps us cultivate determination. In the middle it helps maintain our continuity by giving us strength to face obstacles. At the end it clears away doubt and ensures we have the confidence we need to finish what we start.

- There are three types of perseverance that are cultivated in the training of joyful effort: (1) armour-like perseverance; (2) perseverance of right conduct and (3) perseverance of perpetual enthusiasm.

- Armour-like Perseverance is the attitude of a compassionate warrior who refuses to give up the fight against the enemy of self-cherishing and other afflictive states of mind. It is an unwavering determination that is steadfast and resolute.

- The Perseverance of Right Conduct is the joyful effort exerted in the practice of the three trainings of ethical discipline. It relies on cultivating three forms of diligence: (1) diligence to avoid afflictive emotions; (2) diligence to accomplish virtue and (3) diligence to benefit sentient beings.

- The Perseverance of Perpetual Enthusiasm is the attitude that yearns to practice Dharma and is never satisfied with the achievements that one makes.

- There are four aspects to practicing joyful effort: (1) eliminating unfavourable conditions; (2) gathering favourable conditions; (3) establishing a mind intent on practice and (4) making your body and mind serviceable.

- To eliminate the unfavourable condition of laziness we need to work with each type of laziness: (1) remove the laziness of procrastination by meditating on impermanence; (2) remove the laziness of distraction by meditating on suffering and (3) remove the laziness of discouragement by meditating on the nature of the goal, the method to achieve the goal and the time it will take to do so.

- To gather favourable conditions we need to cultivate four virtuous qualities: (1) a strong aspiration to practice; (2) an unwavering steadfastness in the face of difficulties; (3) the feeling of joy in all virtuous activities and (4) the relinquishment that knows how to rest when fatigued.

- To establish a mind intent on practice we should: (1) develop the wisdom that prevents the afflictions from dominating the mind and (2) engage in conducts that destroy the afflictions by applying their remedies.

- The body and mind will naturally become serviceable through the prolonged and consistent training in exerting joyful effort.

- There are three branch vows that relate to the training in joyful effort: (1) gathering a following out of desire for gain and honour; (2) failing to dispel laziness, and the like; and (3) engaging in idle speech with a sense of attachment.

- A Bodhisattva with pure joyful effort has ten characteristics: (1) appropriate; (2) experienced; (3) free of laxness; (4) well informed; (5) practices according to context; (6) perception of signs; (7) free of dejection; (8) not deficient; (9) balanced and (10) dedicated to great enlightenment.

CHAPTER ELEVEN

Using Meditation to Observe Reality

When we first begin training in the Six Perfections, our main challenge is to create the conditions which enable us to calm our mind. Due to afflictions such as attachment and aversion, our minds are restless and distracted, racing from object to object, just like a monkey leaping from tree to tree. Within this constant state of turbulence and confusion, our true nature is hidden from us and only the wisdom that knows the nature of reality can remove these obscurations created by ignorance. To effectively generate this wisdom, we need to train the mind.

The root of our suffering is the mind of ignorance that grasps onto reality as existing in a way that it does not. From this root comes attachment which perceives the qualities of an object to exist inherently as part of that object and due to that attachment, we develop the mind of aversion. Until these branch afflictions are made dormant, we cannot work directly with the root. As aversion depends on attachment, by targeting our attachment, we automatically reduce our aversion and for this reason our training begins with *generosity*.

With the weakening of our attachment, the mind is less susceptible to being pulled and scattered in all directions and becomes more receptive to abiding in virtue. Through the training of *ethical discipline*, we work with our conduct to further reduce the power of the afflictions and to strengthen the quality of our mind. Sowing the seeds of virtue places us in greater harmony with those around us, reducing the causes for distraction so that our mind no longer feels threatened and we are able to rest peacefully.

Due to the vast stores of negative karmic propensities we have built in our mind, maintaining this peace is not easy. Sooner or later as the conditions come together, these propensities ripen in the form of suffering. We train in *patience* to give us the strength of mind to maintain our equilibrium in the face of hardship and adversity.

The state of mind that results from these three trainings is one of equanimity, resting peacefully in a state of virtue. For such a mind, the gross afflictions have largely subsided and it becomes poised to train in the *Perfection of Meditative Concentration*. The focus of this training is to use meditation as a method for refining the quality of the mind to enable the experience of increasingly more subtle layers of reality.

WHAT IS MEDITATIVE CONCENTRATION?

The Sanskrit word for "meditative concentration" is *samadhi,* which means to abide single-pointedly in virtue and refers to optimal states of mind used as a basis for observing reality. The various forms of samadhi depend on the subtlety of the mind and where that mind is directed. Each form is like a different type of lens. Some enable us to see short distances, whereas others allow us to see much further. Altering the quality of the lens changes the types of phenomena we can observe. The types of samadhi a Bodhisattva can develop are too numerous to list here, but they can all be summarised into two main categories:

1. **Shamatha:** The essence of *Shamatha* is to rest single-pointedly on a virtuous object without distraction. As long as the mind abides in this form of samadhi, afflictive states of mind like attachment and aversion are completely dormant. What distinguishes the levels of samadhi within this category is the degree to which very subtle forms of ignorance remain active.

2. **Vipashyana:** The essence of *Vipashyana* is to clearly distinguish the different aspects of reality without superimposing conceptual fabrications. When the mind abides in this form of samadhi, it can know reality as it is and is therefore able to develop insight into its nature. These types of samadhi are differentiated based on the types of phenomena that they focus on, for instance, the development of the samadhi that clearly distinguishes the empty nature of dependent phenomena, or the samadhi which clearly distinguishes the basis of that emptiness—the definitive meaning of suchness.

In order to experience the samadhi of Vipashyana, it is necessary to first establish a preliminary samadhi of Shamatha. As long as our afflictions are active, concepts fill the mind and project on top of reality, obscuring its true nature. Only by cutting the conceptual movements of the mind can we observe reality as it is.

Once the samadhi of Shamatha is achieved, the practice of vipashyana can be used to remove the remaining layers of subtle ignorance. This has the effect of refining our samadhi and allowing us to experience even more subtle levels of reality. Learning to abide in these highly concentrated states of mind shifts our perspective of reality and our relationship to appearances is drastically altered. Rather than viewing the world through the lens of ignorance, we begin to see through the eyes of wisdom.

REASONS TO PRACTICE THE PERFECTION OF MEDITATIVE CONCENTRATION

A mind that lacks concentration is scattered in nature. Thoughts arise like the churning and swirling of bubbles in boiling water. When we grasp onto these thoughts, a chain reaction is triggered, causing further propagation of thoughts until eventually our mind is full of an endless sea of concepts. This unceasing movement prevents the mind from resting in one place for any significant period of time.

One traditional example used to illustrate an untrained mind is a butter lamp in a drafty room. As the wind blows, the candle flame flickers and lacks strength, casting shadows which make it difficult to see anything clearly. When the wind is subdued, the flame becomes stable and burns brightly, its light filling the entire room and allowing us to see without obscuration.

When the mind is overrun with concepts, it casts many shadows preventing us from seeing the full picture of reality and this lack of information leads us to create misconceptions that distort our understanding even further. As our confusion grows, our capacity becomes extremely limited as we are separated from the full potential of our experience. This lack of wisdom and method makes it difficult for us to be of any real benefit to sentient beings.

Through training in meditative concentration, we cut the grasping that fuels our afflictions and as our afflictions cease, the generation of thoughts naturally dissolves. This process allows us to experience the foundational consciousness in a more precise and unmediated way. As the resultant mind has less limitations than gross consciousness, it functions as a perfect staging ground for investigating the many aspects of reality and developing transformative wisdom.

Developing stability in deep states of concentration enables us to manifest clairvoyant or extrasensory capacities and although these powers are not the goal of our training, they are extremely helpful for bringing benefit to others. As the great master Atisha said in his *Lamp for the Path to Enlightenment*:

Just as a bird with undeveloped
Wings cannot fly in the sky,
Those without the power of higher perception
Cannot work for the good of living beings.

The merit gained in a single day
By one who possesses higher perception
Cannot be gained even in a hundred lifetimes
By one without such higher perception.

Those who want swiftly to complete
The collections for full enlightenment,
Will accomplish higher perception
Through effort, not through laziness.

Meditative concentration is pivotal to making significant progress along the path as not only does it expand our awareness of what is possible, it also provides us with the chance to achieve lasting transformation by targeting the root of our delusions. Recognising it as fundamental to our spiritual journey, we need to be dedicated to familiarising ourselves with these phenomenal states of mind.

THE DIVISIONS OF MEDITATIVE CONCENTRATION

As previously discussed, meditative concentration can be divided infinitely based on the countless number of potential objects of focus for single-pointed awareness. For our purposes, we will examine three types of concentration that function as a support for our development on a spiritual path. These are the states of mind that need to be mastered in order to attain full enlightenment.

The Concentration of Abiding in a State of Ease

If we divide the experiences of sentient beings based on the levels of concentration they can manifest, we speak of three realms: (1) the desire realm; (2) the form realm and (3) the formless realm. An awareness of the type of concentration that corresponds to these realms can assist us to find the most effective state of mind for achieving the results we seek.

Desire Realm Concentrations

Desire realm concentrations are a partial or unstable realisation of Shamatha. There are *Nine Attentional States* that correspond to the varying degrees of concentration experienced by those who train in meditation:

1. **Placing the Mind:** This is a concentration where we focus our attention on an object by exerting effort. Because it is extremely unstable, we have to repeatedly re-establish the connection and the mind spends more time in distraction than actually on the object.

2. **Continuous Placement:** As the mind becomes more stable, the periods of time spent engaged with the object become longer. In this concentration we can maintain our awareness of the object for anywhere between a few seconds to several minutes. While discursive thoughts start to diminish, considerable effort is still needed to bring the awareness back to the object when we become distracted.

3. **Patched Placement:** Eventually, the balance between awareness and distraction reverses. We can now hold our focus for longer periods and we are more aware when that attention is lost. Occasionally we lose our object of meditation completely, however we can re-establish the connection with considerable ease.

4. **Close Placement:** This is a concentration where our attention is so strong, we no longer lose our object and even if our main focus moves away temporarily, a part of the mind still remains aware of the object. At this point, gross discursive thoughts have dissolved, allowing us to work with subtle mental experiences.

5. **Disciplining:** As the mind withdraws from sensory stimuli and turns inward, we experience a process of dissolution similar to that which occurs when we fall asleep. As we go deeper here, there is a risk of simply slipping into unconsciousness. This concentration therefore dispels subtle laxity and dullness by intensifying awareness and emphasising the vivid clarity of the mind.

6. **Pacifying:** Like a pendulum reversing direction, if we intensify our attention too much, we risk generating the conditions for subtle excitation to arise. This concentration finds a very subtle balance between excitation and laxity, allowing us to remain in a state of continual focus for at least an hour. At this stage, the mind is incredibly stable and vividly clear.

7. **Fully Pacifying:** By dwelling in the previous concentration, the mind settles into its natural state. Subtle obstacles may occasionally arise but they are quickly remedied and the mind is brought back into balance. Both the intensity and duration of distractions become minimal.

8. **One-Pointed:** After thoroughly familiarising ourselves with the practice of meditation, we reach a state of concentration that abides single-pointedly on the object of meditation, with only a small amount of effort required at the beginning of the session. Once engaged with the object, it is possible to abide continuously with it for up to three hours.

9. **Equanimity:** This state of mind is the pinnacle of what can be achieved with the desire realm concentrations. Having become so familiar with our object of meditation, we can enter into single-pointed focus without effort and the mind can abide continuously on the object for approximately

four hours, completely free of gross and subtle obstacles. This concentration is also known as "access to Shamatha" as it brings you to the threshold of the form realm concentrations.

While none of these states are considered fully-qualified forms of Shamatha, they are all extremely helpful for strengthening the mind and facilitating our practice. As we master each state, our mind becomes increasingly more stable and clear, and we are more effective in whatever activities we decide to attend to.

Form Realm Concentrations

After attaining the ninth attentional state, by continuing to familiarise ourselves with this level of concentration, we can eventually experience a major shift in our subtle energetic system. This marks the transition between the desire realm and the form realm of experience. It is characterised by five qualities:

1. **One-Pointed:** The mind remains completely absorbed on its focus, with no movement or distraction of the awareness.

2. **Pliancy:** The physical body becomes extremely light and pliant making it possible to sit for indefinite periods of time without experiencing discomfort. When the body is at ease, the mind is filled with bliss.

3. **Effortless:** With physical pliancy also comes mental pliancy. The mind becomes so flexible it can maintain its attention on whatever is desired without effort.

4. **Free from afflictions:** Although the root afflictions are not removed, they are temporarily made dormant for as long as we remain in a state of absorption. This gives us an incredible opportunity to practice the Dharma without the distortion of afflicted states of mind.

5. **Free from sensory perceptions:** When we are absorbed in the form or formless realm concentrations, we are completely withdrawn from all gross sensory consciousness. This means we no longer experience sights, sounds and so forth through our physical body as we are completely focused in the mental sphere of experience.

Once we have entered the first form realm concentration, we are said to have "achieved Shamatha". Our minds are now completely efficient so they can be used to develop profound insight into the nature of reality, and while this realisation is very powerful, it can still be refined further to even greater levels of subtlety. This process of refinement leads to four levels of concentration:

1. **Examination and Analysis:** At this stage, all the afflictive states of conceptual mind are dormant, leaving only virtuous and neutral states of mind that can be used to analyse different aspects of reality.

2. **Joy and Bliss:** In this state, the capacity to form intentions ceases and the mind abides in a perpetual state of blissful absorption with the object of analysis.

3. **Inhalation and Exhalation:** Without the movements of conceptual mind, the flow of energy becomes incredibly subtle, causing the grasping onto subjective feelings of bliss to dissolve, thereby revealing a more direct manifestation of the object of focus.

4. **Free from Eight Defects:** Finally, the mind arrives in a state of concentration that is free from the eight defects of: (1) physical suffering; (2) mental suffering; (3) analysis; (4) examination; (5) joy; (6) bliss; (7) inhalation and (8) exhalation. At this point the breath completely stops and the mind abides in a state of of unwavering equanimity upon the object.

Of these four, the first is very useful for gross levels of vipashyana in which we actively explore different types of phenomena. Once an aspect of reality has been clearly discerned, the following three concentrations can be used to thoroughly familiarise the mind with the experience. Because the last is free of all but the most subtle forms of grasping, it is considered the best basis for refining our realisations.

Formless Realm Concentrations

The form realm concentrations are a good basis for vipashyana as they maintain a very subtle relationship between subject and object. This allows us to direct our mind towards different aspects of reality with a minimal amount of conceptual interference. As we progress into ever more subtle levels of concentration however, objective appearances completely dissolve and we are left with a purely subjective experience of nothingness, known as the *formless realm*. Because it lacks any sense of focus, it is generally not considered effective for developing insight into the nature of reality, as it is simply too subtle. There are four levels of absorption related to this realm: (1) infinite space; (2) infinite consciousness; (3) neither existence nor nonexistence and (4) nothing whatsoever. As these concentrations use up huge stores of merit, for a Bodhisattva whose aim is to benefit sentient beings, they should be avoided as they only serve to postpone our spiritual practice.

The Concentration of Accumulating Good Qualities

Through the persistent training in meditative concentration, the qualities of the mind are naturally refined, giving rise to a number of accomplishments which can be used to bring benefit to sentient beings. When these states of mind are combined with the trainings of the Foundational and Great Vehicles, we arrive at two main types of accomplishments: (1) common and (2) uncommon.

Common Accomplishments

The first set of accomplishments is shared with the Shravaka and Pratyekabuddha practitioners of the Foundational Vehicle, as well as with the non-Buddhist traditions that train in meditative concentration. They arise as a result of abiding in the form realm concentrations. In general, we can speak of *Five Mundane Forms of Higher Perception*:

1. **Knowledge of Miraculous Feats:** This power gives a Bodhisattva the ability to move between different realms of experience and thereby bring benefit to the sentient beings who abide in those realms.

2. **Knowledge of the Minds of Others:** This power enables the Bodhisattva to perceive the mental states of sentient beings, allowing them to specifically tailor their teachings to suit the minds of their audience.

3. **The Divine Ear:** This is a form of clairaudience which allows the Bodhisattva to mentally hear what is happening in distant realms of experience. This power can be used to receive teachings from the Buddhas and Bodhisattvas in the pure realms.

4. **Knowledge of Past Lives:** This is the power to remember the people, places and events a Bodhisattva has had strong karmic connections to in the past, enabling them to retrieve their experiences to make use of them in the present.

5. **The Divine Eye:** This is a form of clairvoyance that gives the Bodhisattva the ability to perceive how a being's karma could potentially ripen. It can be used to predict future states of experience.

On the basis of the higher perceptions, a Bodhisattva can perform *Eight Common Siddhis*:

1. **The Siddhi of the Celestial Realm:** The Bodhisattva can separate their mind from their body and travel to other realms of experience. This is commonly known as *astral projection.*

2. **The Siddhi of the Sword:** This power prevents the Bodhisattva from being harmed by an enemy. It is effectively a form of *invincibility.*

3. **The Siddhi of the Pill:** Through the blessing of certain pills, it is possible to prevent sentient beings from perceiving the Bodhisattva, essentially a form of *invisibility.*

4. **The Siddhi of Fleet-Footedness:** Through the blessing of their boots, the Bodhisattva can travel great distances in an instant. This power can also be used for *levitation.*

5. **The Siddhi of the Vase:** After blessing a vase or chest, the Bodhisattva is able to multiply anything placed inside. For instance, if water was placed inside the vase, it would produce limitless water.

6. **The Siddhi of the Yaksha:** This is the capacity to command spirits and demons. Such beings can then be used to accomplish tasks that would normally take considerable time to complete.

7. **The Siddhi of the Elixir:** This power allows the Bodhisattva to have an extremely long lifespan as well as to maintain their youth and beauty.

8. **The Siddhi of the Balm of Magical Sight:** After blessing a balm and smearing it on the eyes, the ability to see through physical matter is received. This can be used to detect objects buried under the earth or within rocks.

Although the common siddhis make a practitioner very powerful, within the context of the Bodhisattva Path, they must only be used to inspire and support sentient beings. They should only be viewed as useful tools that expand our capacity to bring benefit, never as an end in and of themselves.

Uncommon Accomplishments

The second set of accomplishments is specific to Bodhisattvas training in the Six Perfections. As these practitioners progress along the Path of Habituation, they eventually establish a fully matured form of Bodhicitta. From the eighth stage, they begin to manifest the *Ten Enlightened Powers*:

1. **Power Over Life:** As a result of their perfection of generosity, a Bodhisattva gains full control over the length of their life. This power permits them to remain as long they are needed to bring benefit to sentient beings.

2. **Power Over Material Things:** With perfected generosity, they also gain control over all forms of matter and can therefore materialise whatever objects they wish, merely by thinking of them.

3. **Power Over Actions:** As a result of their perfection of ethical discipline, they have complete mastery over their body and mind and so can perform whatever action is needed of them.

4. **Power Over Birth:** Due to perfect discipline, a Bodhisattva may manifest as many births as are necessary to fulfil their wishes. They can also choose the exact time and place when each birth will occur.

5. **Power Over Aspirations:** Through the perfection of patience, a Bodhisattva gains the capacity to fulfil the aspirations of sentient beings by manifesting countless worlds filled with countless emanations.

6. **Power Over Prayer:** Due to the perfection of effort, whatever a Bodhisattva prays for will become manifest. They can bring extraordinary benefit to sentient beings by shaping their aspirations to suit the needs of others.

7. **Power Over Mind:** As a result of their perfection of meditative concentration, they attain mastery over all states of absorption. This enables them to abide in whatever state they desire for however long they chose.

8. **Power Over Miracles:** Also due to their perfection of meditative concentration, they can manifest miracles in all forms without any limitation.

9. **Power Over Wisdom:** Having perfected wisdom, they come to know all phenomena of the past, present and future without attachment and without limitation.

10. **Power Over Dharma:** With the perfection of wisdom, the Bodhisattva knows exactly what teachings will bring the greatest benefit to sentient beings and can therefore transmit the Dharma at the exact moment when needed and in a way that is completely free from distortion.

When a Tenth Level Bodhisattva uses these powers to bring limitless benefit to sentient beings, they produce vast amounts of merit that clears even the most subtle forms of cognitive obscurations. Through this process of extraordinary refinement, eventually they achieve the supreme accomplishment of a fully enlightened Buddha.

The Concentration of Acting on Behalf of Sentient Beings

When a Bodhisattva achieves meditative concentration through the union of Shamatha and Vipashyana, they have attained direct realisation of emptiness. From their entry to the Path of Seeing, up to the Path of No More Learning, for the sake of sentient beings, a Bodhisattva trains in producing emanations.

An *emanation* is an appearance that arises in the mind of a sentient being as a result of the influence of another being's mind. We already possess this skill, just in an extremely limited form. When we encounter other sentient beings in our day to day life, our mind projects a particular self-image which is perceived by those around us. This is not something we do consciously, it is more like an instinctual habit and usually, due to our intense self-grasping, we can only manifest one form. When we realise emptiness, our self-grasping dissolves, giving us the ability to manifest many forms. Then as we refine our realisation and approach Buddhahood, we have the capacity to emanate limitless forms within countless realms.

Each of these emanations is manifested in order to fulfil the specific needs of sentient beings and is not limited to complex organisms like humans or animals. For instance, a Bodhisattva could manifest as a tree to provide shade for those suffering from the heat of the sun. They could also manifest as water for those who are thirsty or as a bed for beings that need to rest. The possibilities are truly limitless.

By skilfully using their emanations, an Arya Bodhisattva fulfils the needs of each of the eleven types of sentient beings described in the chapter on ethical discipline. The more emanations they master, the more sentient beings they can support, increasing the merit they generate.

HOW TO PRACTICE MEDITATIVE CONCENTRATION

Training in meditative concentration is based on formal meditation techniques to develop familiarity with progressively more subtle states of mind. As we learn to abide in equipoise within these states, we gain the qualities and capacities described earlier.

The process to do this has four stages: (1) gathering the conditions for meditation by withdrawing from distractions; (2) establishing single-pointed concentration with shamatha meditation; (3) analysing the nature of reality with vipashyana meditation and (4) meditating on the union of Shamatha and Vipashyana.

Withdrawing from Distractions

Up to this point, training in the Six Perfections has involved substantial engagement with sentient beings. While working on our relationships with those around us, our focal point has been disciplining our mind to reduce our afflictions of attachment and aversion. As we move into the next phase of our training, we need to temporarily isolate ourselves from sentient beings to experience deep states of meditative absorption.

This is necessary due to the nature of the practice, as meditative concentration is achieved through a process of withdrawal. We currently experience the world from the perspective of a desire realm being whose mind operates at a gross level, conditioned mostly by our five senses. To achieve Shamatha, we must completely withdraw from the desire realm and abide in the subtle mental sphere of the form realm.

Living an engaged form of life requires interaction with sentient beings which keeps our awareness tethered to the desire realm. To overcome this and develop meditative concentration, we need to temporarily abandon this way of life by living in solitude, far removed from worldly distractions. There are three benefits to doing this:

1. **Excellent offering to the Buddhas:** To seek solitude with Bodhicitta as our motivation means we are actively working to create the causes for achieving enlightenment. This is a worthy offering for the Buddhas and pleases them more than making infinite offerings of food and wealth.

2. **Renounce Samsara:** By living in solitude we withdraw our interest from the eight worldly concerns. This strengthens our renunciation and stops us from energising our attachments.

3. **Quickly achieve concentration:** Without the external distractions of living in a village, suburb or city, it is much easier to focus inwards on the mind. This promotes a continuity of practice, helping us to establish meditative concentration in a relatively short period of time.

Once the desire to live in solitude is established, we need to find a place located at a reasonable distance from a major settlement. It should be far enough to be free from disturbance but close enough to access supplies, as well as being safe, without the danger of wild animals and so forth. It should not be toxic to your health, allowing you to maintain an illness free state. If possible, it is also beneficial to be surrounded by a small group of people with similar motivation, who are dedicated to similar practices. When you have found such a place, special effort should be made to cultivate the right attitude. There are five points to consider:

1. **Free from expectations:** Try to avoid setting expectations for how you want your meditation practice to evolve. Your mind should also be free from desire for things such as clothing and food.

2. **Be content:** No matter what conditions you encounter, cultivate a mind that is content with what you have. This reduces the development of desires which will only distract your mind.

3. **Give up activities:** While in solitude, abandon worldly activities and concentrate your energy on your spiritual practice. When developing single-pointed concentration, you should avoid anything which promotes discursive thinking.

4. **Maintain your discipline:** Keep all your vows as purely as possible since maintaining your discipline enables the mind to naturally be at ease. Achievement of results will then occur much more quickly.

5. **Cut all thoughts of desire:** Recognising the roles craving and desire play in the proliferation of thoughts, contemplate subjects like impermanence and suffering to cut their influence on your mind. This form of renunciation is vital for achieving a form realm concentration.

Gathering these conditions will give you a strong basis for establishing meditative concentration. Until you achieve the single-pointed concentration of Shamatha, you should remain in isolation, working diligently day and night.

Establishing Single-Pointed Concentration

The next step to perfecting our meditative concentration is to establish its basis of *Shamatha*. Under the guidance of your teacher, an object of focus on which to meditate should be chosen. While there are literally countless objects that can be used as a basis for developing single-pointed concentration, in general the Buddha taught four classes of virtuous meditation objects: (1) the all-pervasive object; (2) the pacification of behaviour; (3) the objects of the learned and (4) the purification of afflictions.

The All-Pervasive Object

The first class is based on achieving Shamatha by using the nature of the mind as the object of meditation. As all phenomena arise within the mind, by becoming familiar with the mind's nature, we also become familiar with the nature of all phenomena. We can work with this object using the support of analysis in order to identify the nature of the mind, or simply by resting in that nature which is always present.

Another very common way of working with the mind is through the use of a virtuous mental image such as a Buddha-figure or meditational deity. Every feature of these highly symbolic forms is embedded with meaning and so when they are held in the mind, they act as a reminder of their deeper significance. Due to their complexity, initially it may take some time to develop the image clearly, but once stability has been achieved, they can be an effective foundation for achieving Shamatha.

The Pacification of Behaviour

The second class works with six objects which are the antidotes for the root afflictions. These meditations can be particularly helpful for those with a strong tendency toward a certain affliction that will often act as a major obstacle for the achievement of Shamatha. For all but the last object, the instruction is to firstly use analytical meditation to provide the antidote for the selected affliction. Through this meditation, a state of mind free from that affliction is established and this state is the actual object of meditation. Once it manifests, rest in the awareness of that experience. The six afflictions and their antidotes are:

1. **Attachment:** To counteract attachment, meditate on perceiving the physical body as being ugly and disgusting. This combined with extensive contemplation on its impermanent nature, naturally decreases the experience of attachment replaced with the feeling of equanimity. Rest your awareness in that feeling.

2. **Hatred:** To counteract intense hatred and aversion, meditate on loving-kindness toward sentient beings. After reflecting deeply on the benefit you have received from others, develop an immeasurable love for all

beings regardless of their relationship to you. Rest the awareness in the feeling of connection that arises.

3. **Ignorance:** To counteract the stupor of ignorance, meditate on the subject of dependent origination. Study and analyse the nature of cyclic existence from many angles until a confidence arises regarding the truth of how reality exists. Rest your awareness in the feeling of certainty.

4. **Jealousy:** To counteract the jealousy which arises because of aversion towards the happiness of others, meditate on equalising yourself and others. Contemplating how all sentient beings wish to be free from suffering and desire lasting genuine happiness, counteracts the self-cherishing mind and strengthens the desire for all beings to be happy. Rest your awareness in the feeling of joy that arises from reflecting on the happiness of others.

5. **Pride:** To counteract the pride that sees oneself as more important than others, meditate on exchanging the self for others. Contemplate the disadvantages of cherishing the self and the advantages of cherishing others and practice taking on their suffering for yourself and giving them your happiness. Rest your awareness in the state of equanimity that arises from this process.

6. **Equal Afflictions or Discursive Thoughts:** If all your afflictions are similar in strength, meditate by focusing on the tactile sensations related to the flow of the breath.

The Objects of the Learned

The third class of objects is related to using one's study and reflection as an object of meditation. Here the focus is on learning topics such as the five aggregates, the eighteen elements, the twelve sense bases and the twelve links of dependent origination, as well as a full examination of what to adopt and what to abandon. This is an analytical approach to achieving Shamatha that requires careful reflection on different subjects until a conclusion or sense of certainty is reached. When this occurs, rest your mind in that feeling and familiarise yourself with your understanding of the Dharma.

The Purification of Afflictions

This last class uses meditation on the concentration itself as the object. It mainly concerns identifying the faults of a mind that lacks the qualities of a particular concentration and comparing it with a mind endowed with those qualities. This contemplation generates a desire to achieve the concentration, which is then used as the object to meditate on. It is very similar to the worldly vipashyana described below in that it abandons a lower state of concentration in order to achieve a higher state.

By practicing diligently with any one of these objects, you will progress through the nine attentional states and arrive at the threshold of the desire realm. There you will achieve physical and mental pliancy by thoroughly familiarising yourself with the state of single-pointed concentration. Once an authentic realisation of Shamatha is established, you are ready to move on to practicing with Vipashyana.

Analysing the Nature of Reality

Using the power of single-pointed concentration, reality can be observed intently in order to develop insights into its nature. This is known as *Vipashyana* or insight meditation. Within the Buddhist system, we can identify four styles of vipashyana that are used by different types of practitioners to explore different aspects of reality:

The Vipashyana of the Non-Buddhists

This form of vipashyana is practiced to refine one's realisation of Shamatha in order to achieve progressively more subtle stages of absorption. Since it does not result in liberation from samsara, it is considered a mundane path. Within a Buddhist context, this form of vipashyana is used as a way of achieving the fourth of the form realm concentrations which is the subtlest level of mind still capable of analysing reality.

The vipashyana of non-Buddhists relies on the use of seven mental processes: (1) *precisely discerning characteristics* to determine the positive and negative qualities of each stage of experience; (2) *developing conviction* to orient the mind toward the higher stages of experience; (3) *thoroughly separating* yourself from the coarser levels of experience to abide in a higher state of concentration; (4) *gaining joy* in the higher concentrations by increasing physical and mental pliancy; (5) *closely examining objects* to determine if the mind is free from the afflictions of the lower concentrations; (6) *engagement* where the necessary antidotes are applied to remove any afflictions of lower concentrations; and (7) the *result of engagement* which is the mind that rests in a state free from the afflictions of the lower concentrations. Through applying these processes to your experience, the mind is effectively turned away from coarse phenomena and toward increasingly more peaceful states of mind.

The Vipashyana of the Foundational Vehicle

The next form of vipashyana is practiced in accordance with the teachings of the *Foundational Vehicle*. It is specifically suited for practitioners wishing to achieve personal liberation from samsara. Their focus is on abandoning the root ignorance which grasps onto an inherently existent self and the main method used is contemplation on the *Four Noble Truths*: (1) the truth of suffering; (2) the truth of the origin of suffering; (3) the truth of the cessation of suffering and (4) the truth of the path leading to cessation.

Each of these truths can be divided into four, producing sixteen aspects in all. For the truth of suffering there is (1) impermanence; (2) suffering; (3) emptiness and (4) selflessness. For the origin of suffering there are the aspects of (5) origination; (6) cause; (7) condition and (8) production. For the cessation of suffering there is (9) cessation; (10) peace; (11) excellence and (12) emergence. For the path there are the aspects of (13) path; (14) reasoning; (15) accomplishment and (16) total freedom.

Through carefully observing their experience, a practitioner at this level establishes each realisation in their mind and abides single-pointedly in that realisation by thoroughly familiarising themselves with it. Unlike the vipashyana of non-Buddhists which only temporarily suppresses the afflictions, this method actually cuts their root cause and therefore prevents the affliction from ever arising again.

The Vipashyana of the Great Vehicle

For the Bodhisattva practitioners of the *Great Vehicle*, realising the *selflessness of persons* is not sufficient to remove the subtle cognitive obscurations which are the cause for perceiving reality as inherently existent. Out of their great compassion, Bodhisattvas meditate on the *selflessness of phenomena* to realise the nature of all dependent arisings and thereby attain full enlightenment.

The main method for doing this is to meditate on emptiness and while there are different approaches used within each tradition, they generally involve the careful analysis of appearances on the basis of various logical arguments. For instance, there is the logic of *one and many*, which states if a single entity cannot be found to be inherently existent, it is then impossible for many entities to be inherently existent. Using the example of a hand, we see it is made up of many parts, such as fingers, palm, flesh, muscles and bones. Other than these parts, there is no hand to be seen, proving that the appearance of a hand is only a mental imputation that is projected on the basis of its parts. This understanding holds true for all phenomena perceived by the dualistic mind.

Another powerful logic is that of *dependent origination* which states that anything which arises in dependence on causes and conditions by definition cannot be inherently existent. Consider the example of the reflection in a mirror. It can only arise in dependence upon the qualities of the mirror and the condition of someone standing in front of it. Take away the conditions and the appearance of a reflection cannot arise. The characteristics of the reflection can also change by altering the qualities of the mirror. Similarly, as all the appearances we experience rely on the coming together of various causes and conditions, they do not inherently exist, just like the reflection in the mirror.

The basic structure of this form of vipashyana is to identify the object of negation and to then use it to work through the different logics. As you contemplate its empty nature, the appearance of the object will eventually dissolve back into the mind, leaving you with an absence of the object. Rest the mind in this space-like awareness until such time as the appearance returns as a result of your habitual tendencies. The more familiar you become with this process, the more your grasping weakens. Without grasping, the afflictions cease to arise and the conditioning of karma is eventually purified.

The Vipashyana of the Vajra Vehicle

The Vajra Vehicle recognises that the use of logic to establish emptiness is a very powerful tool, but is a comparatively slow method for developing a direct realisation of emptiness. As it relies on the gross conceptual mind, the result is still a concept that takes on the aspect of emptiness, and although it is a very subtle concept, it is not emptiness itself. To actually realise emptiness it is necessary to abandon concepts altogether.

For this reason, the methods used in the Vajra Vehicle tend to emphasise a non-conceptual approach. The focus is turned inward to the mind which provides the basis for all experience but when searching for the solid, inherently existent mind, it cannot be found. It instead naturally arises as being an emptiness filled with potential that is neither one thing in particular, nor is it nothing. This nature is experienced as a profound sense of peace and bliss.

The main characteristic which differentiates this approach is an absence of trying to fabricate or generate a particular state. There is no judgement concerning what should be accepted and what should be abandoned. Everything is unified within the realm of experience and, therefore, everything becomes an instance of the mind that can be used to realise its underlying nature. When we directly examine the range of our experiences, we find that even afflicted states of mind have a pure nature. They are not separate from the mind and by closely examining the process in which they arise, dwell and dissolve, we can experience that pure nature directly.

After observing the nature of objective experience, the focus then shifts to the subject itself. By examining the nature of the knower, the misconception of self-grasping is cut, also severing the root of ignorance. When the process of knowing is experienced as being empty, we recognise the indivisibility of awareness and emptiness. In this way, the Vajra Vehicle establishes the selflessness of phenomena and the selflessness of the person without needing to resort to conceptual analysis.

Unifying Shamatha and Vipashyana

Neither Shamatha nor Vipashyana in isolation is sufficient to achieve enlightenment. The nature of Shamatha is to rest single-pointedly—not altering or changing anything, it simply abides peacefully. This means that even though afflictions are temporarily subdued, they are not eradicated and therefore Shamatha alone is not enough to achieve liberation.

Vipashyana has the nature of clearly knowing how reality exists. As the wisdom that knows reality as it is acts to prevent ignorance from arising, it is capable of breaking the chains which bind us to cyclic existence. Without the root of ignorance, we cease to generate new karma and eventually our mind is purified of all obscurations. While this is enough to liberate us from suffering, it does not create all the conditions needed to become a fully enlightened Buddha.

Although the minds of both a Buddha and an Arhat abide continuously in a state of peace, what differentiates them is that a Buddha manifests limitless form bodies, whereas an Arhat does not. This difference is produced as a result of completing the accumulations of merit and wisdom. Fundamental to this process is the ability to simultaneously rest the mind in a genuine state of samadhi while still engaging in activities; this is known as the *Union of Shamatha and Vipashyana.*

When Shamatha is first achieved, the mind withdraws from the gross levels of consciousness and abides in the unconfigured aspect of the foundational consciousness. It is able to maintain this single-pointed quality because the mind has become so subtle; however, as soon as we emerge from the meditation, the mind is once again engaged in sensory information, losing the quality of its concentration. Likewise, when we first realise emptiness, the mind rests in complete absorption of that truth. Upon arising from the meditation, we no longer have direct experience of emptiness but instead a memory of that experience.

The training of unifying Shamatha and Vipashyana aims to mix the experience that arises during meditation with the experience that arises in post-meditation. When mastered, we can maintain the same degree of absorption at any given moment regardless of the activity we are engaged in. The key is to condition the mind in such a way that whenever Shamatha arises, so too does the mind of Vipashyana, making the two co-emergent.

According to the sutra tradition, this union is achieved by alternating between analytical meditation and placement meditation. First you analyse a subject with discriminating wisdom and then rest your awareness in the conclusion. When the insight fades, return to conceptual analysis. During this process, the mind constantly shifts between the movement of Vipashyana and the stillness of Shamatha. This effectively mixes the two and imbues both with the capacity to trigger the other. With diligent practice, the point is reached where the actual process of analysis is enough to manifest the pliancy of Shamatha. When this occurs, a continuous flow of concentration can be maintained, whether the conceptual mind is active or not.

From the perspective of the tantric tradition, the union is achieved by understanding the relationship between two aspects of the mind—awareness and appearances. Like waves on the ocean, the mind constantly generates appearances which grab the attention of awareness and set it in motion. The Shamatha aspect of our practice is when awareness abides in stillness, free from grasping onto whatever appearances arise. The Vipashyana aspect is when that awareness knows that the arising appearances lack any inherent existence. In this way, the practice of meditating on the nature of the mind automatically incorporates both aspects of Shamatha and Vipashyana and therefore leads to the realisation of their union. From this perspective, whether you are in formal meditation or not is irrelevant as all experience offers the same opportunity to realise the nature of the mind.

Branch Vows Related to the Perfection of Meditative Concentration

There are three vows which relate to the training in meditative concentration. Their essence is to *strive to achieve meditative concentration for the benefit of beings*. By establishing the union of Shamatha and Vipashyana, we cut the roots of our ignorance and actualise the state of a fully enlightened Buddha. For this reason, we should abandon the following behaviours:

1. **Failing to pursue single-pointed concentration:** As we need to develop concentration, if through malice, pride or laziness we refuse to seek instruction and advice on how to develop it, or refuse to practice after receiving instruction, we break this vow. We should make an effort to listen, study and meditate in order to develop single-pointed concentration.

2. **Failing to eliminate the hindrances to meditative concentration:** There are five obstacles to single-pointed concentration that need to be overcome: (1) laziness; (2) forgetting the meditation instructions; (3) dullness and agitation; (4) under-application and (5) over-application. Not making an effort to overcome these obstacles when they arise causes you to break this branch vow.

3. **Regarding enjoyment of the states of meditative absorption as a good quality:** When we achieve high states of meditative absorption, the mind experiences an enormous amount of bliss. If this bliss becomes an object of attachment, it can become a major obstacle for achieving enlightenment as rather than striving to use our concentration to remove ignorance, we spend our time blissed out in meditation. If the bliss itself becomes the main purpose of our practice, we will have broken this vow. We must always strive to make use of our concentration as a means to accumulate wisdom and bring benefit to sentient beings.

Integrating All Six Perfections

To achieve the *Perfection of Meditative Concentration*, we will need to incorporate all six of the Perfections: (1) for the *generosity of meditative concentration*, we should guide sentient beings in how to meditate and help them achieve states of concentration; (2) for the *ethical discipline of meditative concentration*, we should maintain the branch vows and dedicate ourselves to practicing meditation in solitude; (3) for the *patience of meditative concentration*, we should not abandon our practice until we have achieved stability in the union of Shamatha and Vipashyana; (4) for the *joyful effort of meditative concentration*, we should strive day and night to familiarise the mind with meditative states; (5) for the *meditative concentration of meditative concentration*, we should practice meditation with mindfulness and vigilance, not allowing ourselves to become distracted; and (6) for the *wisdom of meditative concentration*, we should recognise that the person meditating, the act of meditating and the object being meditated upon, are all completely empty of inherent existence. In this way, perfect meditative concentration will arise in the mind.

THE RESULTS OF PRACTICING MEDITATIVE CONCENTRATION

When we abide in a particular meditative concentration, whether Shamatha, Vipashyana or their union, we abide in a state of mind that manifests specific qualities. The ultimate form of meditative concentration is then the vajra-like concentration of a fully enlightened Buddha and is the state of *Non-Abiding Nirvana* that is the produced result of practicing the path.

On the provisional level, we can speak of a number of different states that act as stepping stones to achieving full enlightenment. These are the various attainments we establish by dedicating ourselves to our practice. Through achieving the *Concentration of Abiding in a State of Ease*, we gain mastery over our body and mind and can move effortlessly between the levels of subtlety. Through the *Concentration of Accumulating Good Qualities*, we develop extrasensory perceptions and powers, enabling us to work more skilfully with sentient beings. This naturally gives rise to the *Concentration of Acting on Behalf of Sentient Beings*, where our capacity to emanate forms grows exponentially, giving us the ability to bring benefit to limitless beings.

As it states in the *Stages of the Bodhisattva*, a Bodhisattva who has achieved pure meditative concentration will exhibit the following characteristics:

1. **Lacks grasping onto the joy of the absorption:** The Bodhisattva recognises the limitations of the meditative concentrations of the three realms. As such, they do not grasp on to the feelings of joy and bliss that arise when abiding in these states.

2. **Lacks afflictions:** Because the Bodhisattva abides in a continual state of absorption, the afflictions are dormant and unable to affect the Bodhisattva's behaviour.

3. **Has a pure form of preparation:** Through the practice of Shamatha and Vipashyana, the Bodhisattva achieves a union which forms a genuine foundation for experiencing the empty nature of reality directly.

4. **Has attained a pure main stage:** The Bodhisattva is considered a noble being due to attaining a direct realisation of emptiness. From that moment onwards, all their actions are pure and become the causes for attaining enlightenment.

5. **Has attained a pure level that is higher and superior to the main stage:** Through their perfect training in the Six Perfections, the Bodhisattva achieves a fully-matured form of Bodhicitta that abides in the sublime emptiness that is filled with all enlightened qualities, allowing them to bring limitless benefit to sentient beings.

6. **Has mastered entry, abiding in and arising from states of single-pointed concentration:** The Bodhisattva can generate whatever state of mind they require without the need for effort.

7. **Able to use states of concentration without attachment:** Even though the Bodhisattva has completely turned away from abiding in states of absorption, they can still use them as a skilful part of their practice.

8. **Has gained mastery over extrasensory perception:** The Bodhisattva has fully trained the mind so they are no longer limited to experiencing reality through the senses. They have developed a fully qualified yogic perception which forms the basis for a wide variety of accomplishments.

9. **Has eliminated all forms of mistaken views:** On the strength of their special insight, the Bodhisattva knows reality as it is and is no longer dominated by mistaken views such as grasping onto the aggregates as a self.

10. **Has abandoned the two obscurations:** Because the Bodhisattva has realised the empty nature of all phenomena, they have removed the afflictive obscurations as well as the more subtle grasping of the cognitive obscurations. This creates the cause for the Bodhisattva to experience all objects of knowledge.

REVIEW OF KEY POINTS

- Meditative concentration is the mind which abides single-pointedly in virtue. There are two forms of concentration: (1) the concentrations of Shamatha which emphasise resting single-pointedly on a virtuous object and (2) the concentrations of Vipashyana which know reality as it is free from conceptual overlays. We must first develop Shamatha before we can develop Vipashyana.

- The primary obstacle for developing meditative concentration is the scattered mind which is constantly lost in the proliferation of thoughts. These thoughts are energised by grasping and are the basis upon which the afflictions develop.

- Through training in meditation, the mind is trained to abandon grasping which cuts the proliferation of thoughts and allows a non-conceptual awareness of reality to arise.

- The Concentration of Abiding in a State of Ease refers to the progressively more subtle layers of single-pointed concentration that are achieved through the practice of Shamatha meditation. They are divided based on the realm of experience to which they belong. In general, we can speak of three types of concentration: (1) desire realm concentrations; (2) form realm concentrations and (3) formless realm concentrations. While desire realm concentrations are too scattered, formless realm concentrations are too subtle. The optimal focus is achieved in the form realm.

- The Concentration of Accumulating Good Qualities refers to the various accomplishments produced as a result of abiding in deep states of meditative concentration. There are the common accomplishments which include the Five Mundane Forms of Higher Perception and the Eight Common Siddhis. These accomplishments can be achieved by anyone who achieves Shamatha. The uncommon accomplishments refers to the Ten Enlightened Powers which are produced on the basis of unifying Shamatha with Vipashyana. These are unique to practitioners of the Bodhisattva Path.

- The Concentration of Acting on Behalf of Sentient Beings refers to the capacity to emanate form bodies for the benefit of others. It is a skill which is developed by Arya Bodhisattvas who have had a direct realisation of emptiness.

- The training in meditative concentration is divided into four stages: (1) gathering the conditions for meditation by withdrawing from distractions; (2) establishing single-pointed concentration with shamatha meditation; (3) analysing the nature of reality with vipashyana meditation and (4) meditating on the union of Shamatha and Vipashyana.

- The branch vows related to meditative concentration are: (1) failing to pursue single-pointed concentration; (2) failing to eliminate the hindrances to meditative concentration; and (3) regarding enjoyment of the states of meditative absorption as a good quality.

- A Bodhisattva with pure meditative concentration has ten characteristics: (1) lacks grasping onto the joy of the absorption; (2) lacks afflictions; (3) has a pure form of preparation; (4) has attained a pure main stage; (5) has attained a pure level that is higher and superior to the main stage; (6) has mastered entry, abiding in and arising from states of single-pointed concentration; (7) able to use states of concentration without attachment; (8) has gained mastery over extrasensory perception; (9) has eliminated all forms of mistaken view; and (10) has abandoned the two obscurations.

CHAPTER TWELVE

Developing Wisdom through the Zhentong View

When the Buddha began teaching in India, the science of samadhi had already been practiced by a long tradition of yogis and yoginis. The training in Shamatha was therefore not a Buddhist creation. The great contribution that came from the Buddha was to use the concentrations of Shamatha as a basis for investigating the nature of reality. He recognised that abiding in the subtle realms of bliss would not bring true freedom from samsara and without cutting the root of ignorance, eventually the afflictions would return, breaking the practitioner's concentration. If, however, these advanced states of absorption were combined with profound wisdom, the concentrations of Vipashyana could be generated to ultimately achieve liberation. In this context, training in the *Perfection of Meditative Concentration* is predominantly concerned with refining the quality of the mind. It is essentially *how* the mind experiences reality.

What the mind actually perceives largely depends on the degree of wisdom we bring to our experience. With only a little wisdom, our view will be narrow and limited, only allowing us to see partial aspects of reality. If we spend time to accumulate knowledge and apply it to our experience, our view widens and we gain insight into a reality that is much more expansive and profound.

To this end, the training in the *Perfection of Wisdom* revolves around establishing a philosophical view we can then use to achieve full enlightenment. Although wisdom is the last of the Six Perfections, it is not a practice we should leave until the end of the path. Wisdom is needed at every stage of our journey and so the sooner we begin to cultivate our awareness of these topics, the greater the benefit we receive.

WHAT IS WISDOM?

The term *wisdom* is used to refer to a *mind which is able to clearly discriminate the characteristics of reality.* It is our capacity to make sense of the world and interpret what we experience. On the basis of such wisdom, it is possible to know phenomena. This knowledge informs our actions and helps us develop meaningful intentions that can shape our present and future experience. The mind of wisdom can be understood as having two aspects:

1. **Awareness:** This is the basic quality of mind that knows phenomena. The types of phenomena we are able to know depends on the subtlety of our awareness. When awareness is distracted and dull, the amount it can know is limited. As we train with meditation, our awareness becomes stronger and more vivid, allowing us to perceive phenomena that was previously hidden from us. We can think of awareness like a torch; the brighter it shines, the more we can see.

2. **Discrimination:** This is the quality of mind that differentiates between different appearances in the mind. Because it requires isolating appearances into separate phenomena, it is based on grasping and is therefore provisional in nature. We use discrimination to develop conceptual models which explain how a phenomenon exists.

Through these two qualities, we develop a *view* that represents how we experience reality. This view will always be relative to the level of awareness at which the view was established. For instance, when our awareness operates at a gross level, mediated by sense faculties and focused on external phenomena, we develop a view that corresponds to that level of experience. When we train our mind in meditation, we become familiar with more subtle levels of experience and our view changes accordingly. In this way, views are not static but extremely dynamic and constantly change based on context.

REASONS TO PRACTICE
THE PERFECTION OF WISDOM

Wisdom has one purpose: to remove ignorance. To understand the need to cultivate wisdom, we need to know why ignorance is such a problem. For this reason, we will now examine how ignorance develops and the way wisdom counteracts it.

While there are many different ways to be ignorant, the two types of ignorance directly responsible for our suffering are (1) innate ignorance and (2) discriminating ignorance. The first can be described as a basic unknowing that comes from a lack of focus. It is referred to as *innate ignorance* because it occurs in co-emergence with the ultimate nature of conventional reality. We can think of it as the potential for unawareness to arise. This is possible because the nature of ignorance is emptiness and therefore it is not inherently fixed in any way—there is always the potential for us to be distracted by the display of our own mind.

On the basis of innate ignorance, we develop *discriminating ignorance*. This is a mistaken perception that arises because we do not realise that appearances are of the same nature as our mind. The most subtle form of this type of ignorance is the basic discrimination of self-awareness, this feeling of "I am". The moment this form of grasping arises, all appearances are perceived in relation to this concept of self and so the dualistic mind is born.

As the mind becomes accustomed to seeing the world from the perspective of a self, adventitious obscurations begin to accumulate. Unaware of this process as it unfolds, we do not see the effect our grasping has. The longer we abide in this form of ignorance, the more it dominates our experience, and soon we cannot even remember a time when this was not our reality. This is one of the major problems with ignorance. Because it arises out of unawareness, we don't recognise it until it is too late. Only when our needless suffering is pointed out to us, do we begin to recognise the need to remove our ignorance. This profound habituation to seeing the world from a dualistic perspective is known as *cognitive obscuration*.

Due to the strength of these obscurations, our mind grasps onto different appearances as being either internal or external. We then build a sense of identity around the self, conditioning how we relate to what we view as other. With this type of discrimination, we develop the mind that cherishes the self above all else and from that mind arises confused and afflicted ideas known as the *afflictive obscurations*. At the root of all afflictions is a mind full of bias, inequality and desire.

While the cognitive obscurations provide the basis for accumulating karma, afflictive obscurations shape our grasping in a way that results in suffering. Through wisdom, we can learn how to stop perpetuating the mind which supports these obscurations. The means of doing this is twofold: (1) realise the nature of reality then (2) habituate oneself to that realisation.

We use our capacity to discriminate between phenomena in order to establish an awareness of how reality actually exists. As long as that awareness is present in the mind, our misconceptions will not arise. We train in this wisdom to become habituated with it so that it permeates every moment of our experience. By establishing an unwavering mindfulness that is never distracted from the truth of reality, we remove the potential for ignorance to arise again.

THE DIVISIONS OF WISDOM

In accordance with our Bodhicitta motivation, we practice the Six Perfections to achieve two aims. We strive to achieve our own aim of complete enlightenment in order to fulfil the aim of others—freedom from suffering. To do this, we need to accumulate both merit and wisdom.

There are three types of wisdom needed to achieve these aims: (1) the wisdom that realises the nature of ultimate reality; (2) the wisdom that knows the five branches of learning and (3) the wisdom that accomplishes the aims of sentient beings. All three provide the knowledge we need to remove our obscurations and manifest the two enlightened bodies of a Buddha. The first type of wisdom gives rise to the Dharmakaya truth body of a Buddha and the last two contribute to the manifestation of a Buddha's countless Rupakaya form bodies.

The Wisdom that Realises the Nature of Ultimate Reality

The entire path comes down to one thing—removing all ignorance so our pristine nature can fully manifest. The method used to achieve this is the cultivation of the wisdom that knows reality *as it is*. By abiding in this wisdom, we completely cut through our ignorance and unravel the conditioning of our karma, ultimately freeing ourselves from the suffering of cyclic existence.

Such a wisdom is unbelievably profound and difficult to realise. Recognising that different sentient beings had varying levels of spiritual maturity, the

Buddha knew that skilful means were necessary to effectively guide others to the truth. For this reason, he chose to train his students in a gradual manner that concentrated on the needs of each individual. The Buddha's approach was illustrated in the *Sutra Teaching the Great Compassion of the Tathagata*:

O child of lineage, jewellers, for example, take an unpolished jewel from a jewel-mine. They thoroughly wash it with a strong solution of soda and wipe it with a haircloth. However, they do not cease effort with just that; after that, they wash it with a strong solution of quicksilver and rub it with wool. However, they do not cease effort with just that; after that, they soak it in the juice of a great herb and thoroughly clean it with a fine cloth. Having been polished, the jewel—free from defilement—is called a cat's eye gem.

Just so, O child of lineage, the Tathagata also, upon recognising the impure basic constituent of all sentient beings, causes sentient beings who greatly enjoy cyclic existence to be discouraged through discourse on impermanence, selflessness, uncleanliness, and disquiet, introducing them to the disciplinary practices of superiors.

The Tathagata does not cease effort with just that; after that, he causes them to understand the Tathagata's own mode through discourse on emptiness, signlessness, and wishlessness. However, a Tathagata does not cease effort with just that; after that, he causes sentient beings of various natures to enter the land of a Tathagata through discourse on the irreversible wheel of doctrine, discourse on the complete purification of the three spheres. Having entered and upon realising the suchness of a Tathagata, they are called the "unsurpassed boon."

In this passage we can identify a three-fold method. Firstly the Buddha shows his students how to cut their attachment to cyclic existence and then how to clear the grasping that binds them to it. Finally, he shows them how to abide in the enlightened state of Buddha-nature by thoroughly purifying their experience. For each of these stages, the Buddha taught specific discourses that emphasised what the student needed to hear in order to progress along the path.

If we collect these discourses into groups, we establish the *Three Turnings of the Wheel of Dharma*. Each turning focuses on a particular subject matter which is suitable for practitioners at a particular stage of development. This framework is clearly stated in the *Sutra Unravelling the Thought*:

Initially in the area of Varanasi in the Deer Park called "Sage's Propounding," the supramundane victor thoroughly turned a wheel of doctrine for those engaged in the hearer vehicle, fantastic and marvellous which none—god or human— had previously turned in a similar fashion in the world, through teaching the aspects of the four noble truths. Furthermore, that wheel of doctrine thoroughly turned by the supramundane victor is surpassable, affords an occasion [for refutation], requires interpretation, and serves as a basis for controversy.

Based on just the naturelessness of phenomena and based on just the absence of production, the absence of cessation, quiescence from the start, and naturally passed beyond sorrow, the supramundane victor turned a second wheel of doctrine for those engaged in the great vehicle, very fantastic and marvellous, through the aspect of speaking on emptiness. Furthermore, that wheel of doctrine turned by the supramundane victor is surpassable, affords an occasion [for refutation], requires interpretation, and serves as a basis for controversy.

However, based on just the naturelessness of phenomena and based on just the absence of production, the absence of cessation, quiescence from the start, and naturally passed beyond sorrow, the supramundane victor turned a third wheel of doctrine for those engaged in all vehicles, possessed of good differentiation, extremely fantastic and marvellous. This wheel of doctrine turned by the supramundane victor is unsurpassable, does not afford an occasion [for refutation], is of definitive meaning, and does not serve as a basis of controversy.

By relying on the Three Turnings, the Buddha provided a path for purifying coarse, subtle and very subtle obscurations which limit our capacity and prevents us from manifesting as a fully enlightened Buddha. Within this path, the first two turnings are considered provisional whereas the last turning is recognised as being definitive in nature. This is indicated very clearly in the Buddha's own words.

Arya Asanga—Great Pioneer of Yogachara Madhyamaka
who propagated the sublime teachings of the Bodhisattva Maitreya

Unfortunately, due to an attachment to their views, there are those who reject some of the Buddha's teachings, claiming that the Second Turning is definitive while the Third Turning is provisional. As the Third Turning teaches experience to be "mind-only", they reason that this automatically places it within the philosophical tenets of the Cittamatra school which is widely accepted as being more limited than the middle-way philosophy of the Madhyamaka school.

This conclusion shows a lack of understanding as to the import of the Third Turning. The Buddha taught each turning as a progression from ignorance to wisdom with each higher stage incorporating the teachings of the previous stages. According to the sutra, the First Turning is suited for those "engaged in the hearer vehicle", the second for those "engaged in the great vehicle" and the third for those "engaged in all vehicles". This means that the Third Turning is suitable for those who have already matured their mindstreams through the practice of the previous two vehicles.

Although it is true that the Third Turning presents teachings which became central to the Cittamatra school, this does not mean they are exclusively Cittamatrin. To authentically understand the definitive nature of the Third Turning, we must hold the Middle Way view as a foundation. The existence of individuals who misinterpret a teaching is not a valid reason to label it as provisional. If it were, the fact that some interpret the Middle Way as being nihilistic would mean that it too is provisional. This would lead to the absurd conclusion that none of the Buddha's teachings are definitive.

The first and second turnings are considered provisional as they both present reality in a way that is incomplete. In the First Turning, that which is empty of self is presented as being not empty of self—everything is viewed from the perspective of the conventional truth of cause and effect. In the Second Turning, that which is not empty of self is presented as empty of self—everything, including the ultimate truth, is viewed as being empty of self. Only in the Third Turning is that which is empty of self presented as empty of self and that which is not empty of self presented as not empty of self—instead of mixing the two truths together, they are clearly distinguished. This is the criteria for whether a teaching should be considered definitive or not. Understanding this, we rely on the clear descriptions of the Third Turning as our guide for developing a view of the ultimate nature of reality.

To give context to our system of practice, it is first necessary to develop some familiarity with the core concepts we can use to discuss the nature of reality. While there are many ways to understand the different aspects of our experience, we will follow the advice of Jetsun Taranatha, who recommended studying the *Five Dharmas*, the *Three Natures* and the *Seven Types of Emptiness*. These doctrines are primarily expounded in the *Sutra of the Definitive Commentary on the Intention* and the *Sutra of the Descent into Lanka*, both of which belong to the *Ten Sutras of Definitive Meaning* that are part of the *Third Turning of the Wheel of Dharma*.

The Five Dharmas

If our purpose is to understand the nature of reality, we should begin by clarifying what we mean by the term "reality". In this context, we are referring to two aspects of our experience: (1) everything we are *actually* aware of and (2) everything we could *potentially* be aware of. A phenomenon is considered to be "real" if the possibility exists for it to be known. In this system, if there is no possibility to know a phenomenon, there is no reason to posit it as real.

When the Buddha investigated the limits of what can be known and what cannot, he found there were only five types of phenomena that could potentially manifest to the mind. He spoke about these dharmas in the *Sutra of the Descent into Lanka:*

> *The Buddha told Mahamati, "The distinguishing characteristics of the five dharmas, the modes of existence, the forms of consciousness, and the two kinds of no-self include name and appearance, projection, pure wisdom, and suchness. As practitioners cultivate these and reach the realm of personal realisation of Buddha knowledge, they transcend views of eternity and annihilation and existence and nonexistence and dwell in the bliss of meditating on what is present and what appears before them. Mahamati, because they are unaware that the five dharmas, the modes of existence, the forms of consciousness, and the two kinds of no-self are perceptions of their own minds, fools imagine their external existence, but not the wise."*

What the Buddha is suggesting is an extremely pragmatic approach to understanding reality. Rather than looking outwards to an external world you have never actually experienced, focus inwards on what is arising in the mind. That is your reality and knowing it thoroughly will bring you everlasting peace and harmony. To this end, he identifies five dharmas we need to understand: (1) appearances; (2) names; (3) projections; (4) suchness and (5) pure wisdom.

Appearances

These are the objective appearances which arise in the mind and are perceived as having shapes or features. There are five types of consciousness which correspond to the different types of sensory appearances: (1) the appearance of shape and form to a *visual consciousness*; (2) the appearance of sounds to an *auditory consciousness*; (3) the appearance of smells to an *olfactory consciousness*; (4) the appearance of tastes to the *gustatory consciousness*; and (5) the appearance of sensations to the *tactile consciousness*.

Names

On the basis of these appearances, we construct the notion of an external reality inhabited by sentient beings. When appearances arise, the mind recognises patterns of experience and isolates them from other patterns through the power of designation. For instance, when we see a "round bulbous" appearance which holds what appears to us as "water" and "flowers", we refer to it by the name "vase". By using names in this way, we draw lines around different types of appearances, separating them as being distinct parts of our reality. The names themselves are part of the conceptual mind of the *gross mental consciousness*. Over time, these concepts accumulate and form a detailed description of our experience, describing both the external world of objective experiences and the internal world of subjective experiences. Our entire notion of who we are is based on this vast network of concepts.

Projections

Once an appearance has been named, the mind becomes involved with the appearance by creating a conceptual relationship between the two. Whenever the appearance arises, the mind projects onto it a collection of concepts, eventually fusing the two together. When this occurs the mind perceives the appearance as a self-existent object that actually possesses the projected attributes. It is at this point the *deluded consciousness* takes shape. If a mind projects attributes onto appearances which do not accord with the way reality truly exists, that reality will be distorted and lead to suffering.

Suchness

While names and appearances can be experienced, neither of them can be found to exist independently from their own side. The more we examine the nature of these phenomena, the more we find they only arise in dependence on momentary causes and conditions. Through careful analysis, they all eventually dissolve back into the mind and we are left with an innate experience that transcends mistaken projections—this is known as *suchness*. It is what remains after the conceptual mind has ceased.

Suchness can be described by way of five qualities: (1) it is *pure* in that no matter what temporary phenomena may appear to arise, its nature is never stained or altered in any way; (2) it is *pervasive* in that all relative experiences arise on the basis of suchness; (3) it is *self-existent* in that all the qualities of suchness are innately present, and do not arise on the basis of causes and conditions; (4) it is *permanent* in that there is never any moment where the qualities of suchness do not arise; and (5) it is *truly established* in that it is the object of experience of an undistorted pristine awareness.

Pure Wisdom

Suchness is the very ground upon which all experiences arise. As suchness is completely free from any form of limitation, it has the potential to function as the basis for both ignorance and wisdom. When the conceptual mind relates to suchness through a network of mistaken and deluded projections, then suchness arises as the *foundational consciousness*. This type of mind accumulates karmic propensities and conditions the nature of experience.

Through the infinite compassion of the Buddhas, they have provided us with teachings we can study and meditate on to develop a correct understanding that is free from mistaken projections. With this knowledge, we can remove the deluded consciousness and dissolve our karmic propensities so that the true nature of the foundational consciousness is revealed and we experience the reality of suchness. To abide in the non-dualistic union of suchness and correct knowledge is the very meaning of achieving the Dharmakaya of a Buddha. Such a state is completely free from obscurations and prevents the adventitious stains of ignorance from ever arising again.

The Three Natures

By studying the Five Dharmas, we can identify a basic model for how ignorance takes hold and what is required to clear that ignorance. If we further analyse the relationships between the five types of phenomena, we can speak of *Three Natures* or modes of existence. These natures represent the *ground* to be purified, the *path* used to purify that ground and the *result* of that purification. From the perspective of Kalachakra these natures are represented by the realities of external, internal and enlightened other. As it says in the *Sutra of the Definitive Commentary on the Intention*:

> *Gunakara, there are three natures of phenomena. What are these three? They are the imputed nature, the other-dependent nature, and the thoroughly established nature.*

> *Gunakara, what is the imputational nature of phenomena? It is that which is imputed as a name or symbol in terms of the own-being or attributes of phenomena in order to subsequently designate any convention whatsoever.*

> *Gunakara, what is the other-dependent nature of phenomena? It is simply the dependent origination of phenomena. It is like this: Because this exists, that arises; because this is produced, that is produced. It ranges from: "Due to the condition of ignorance, compositional factors [arise]," up to: "In this way, the whole great assemblage of suffering arises."*

> *Gunakara, what is the thoroughly established nature of phenomena? It is the suchness of phenomena. Through diligence and through proper mental application, Bodhisattvas establish realisation and cultivate realisation of [the thoroughly established nature]. Thus it is what establishes [all the stages] up to unsurpassed, complete, perfect enlightenment.*

We will now look at each of these natures in greater detail to gain a sense of how they relate back to the Five Dharmas.

The Imputed Nature

The first level of reality we need to familiarise ourselves with is the *imputed nature*. This is the reality formed by the interplay between appearances and names. It is the layering of concepts that build as a result of grasping onto appearances as existing in the way they appear to the mind. The Buddha likens this nature to defects which arise when the eyes are affected by cataracts. When a person's eyes are obstructed, they see things which are not actually there. These mistaken perceptions have never existed independently and as soon as the cataracts are removed, this truth can be seen. There are two types of imputed natures:

1. **Apprehended:** These are the imputed natures that represent all objective appearances. They range from the appearances of the various sense faculties, as well as the mind itself, when taken as an object of attention. While they all appear to exist as separate entities, they arise in the mind as a result of causes and conditions coming together. They are effectively the artefacts of a mind experiencing reality through the lens of delusion.

2. **Apprehender:** This second category represents the subjective appearances we identify with as being a self. It is the feeling of being a substantially existent entity that possesses a variety of attributes. These imputed natures are merely concepts that establish a relationship between what is apprehended and the mind which is perceived as apprehending them.

With these imputed natures, we have the basis for a dualistic mind that sees reality as an interplay between subject and object. If however we investigate this relationship, we see that everything we relate to as being a part of the self is actually made up of objective appearances. What makes them subjective is merely our grasping onto them as being "me" and "mine". The distinction itself is imputed and therefore lacks any essence of its own.

As an example of how imputation manifests, we can take the appearance of a hand. If you look at your hand right now, you will see the appearance of various shapes and colours. This particular pattern of shape and colour is familiar and you know it by the name of "hand". But if we look for the actual hand, which part is the hand? Is the thumb the hand? Are any of the fingers the hand? What about the palm or the back? Are any of these the hand? If none of those parts are the hand then, where does the hand exist?

The aim of this analysis is to clearly distinguish between what is "name" and what is "appearance". The more we investigate the nature of our imputations, the more arbitrary the process becomes. This not only applies to the words we use to label things, but also to the layers of meaning connected to those words. Just like a house built of sand, they are unstable and subject to change. We can interpret the world in a particular way on one day, and have a completely different perspective the next.

The Dependent Nature

When we analyse the imputational nature of our experience, we find that all the concepts we use to make sense of the world have no essence, such as when we search for "hand", we cannot find it. However, if we were to dissolve the imputation of "hand" , the mere appearance which acts as the basis for imputing "hand" still remains. This is the *dependent nature.* It is what arises as a result of causes and conditions and is the basis upon which all imputations are made. Within the category of dependent natures we can speak of two types:

1. **Impure:** The moment the mind imputes a "self", it will also impute an "other". This means that a mind operating under the influence of an apprehender imputed nature, will automatically experience reality from a dualistic perspective. Because this view is the basis upon which mistaken projections are formed, it is referred to as being *impure.*

2. **Pure:** By thoroughly investigating all three natures, it is possible to clear the false imputations of an inherently existent self. When we do this, we experience the dependent nature without the distortion of conceptual overlays. Appearances will still arise, but they are not conditioned in relation to the self and therefore naturally arise, abide for a time and then dissolve back into the mind. Since it is free from distortion, it is referred to as being *pure.*

Whether impure or pure, both these dependent natures are connected to how we understand the dynamic relationship between awareness and appearances. Whereas the first is an interpretation based on ignorance, the second occurs as a result of wisdom. When awareness grasps onto appearances, an impure view arises, but if it abides in non-grasping, a pure view will then arise.

Subsequently, the dependent nature of experience is not fixed. How it manifests depends on the view that is present at any given moment so that if we change the view, we change the perception. The Buddha likens this to a pristine clear crystal which, when placed in a red light, appears to be a ruby. Placed under a green light, it looks like an emerald and under golden light, it appears to be gold. By changing the colour, the crystal changes appearance. This is the nature of the foundational consciousness which is a neutral base, that can be interpreted in an infinite number of ways.

By contemplating the dependent nature, we come to realise that all phenomena perceived by a dualistic consciousness are empty of inherent existence. They instead exist as a dynamic process of constantly changing conditions that shape the quality of experience. When we develop greater awareness of this nature, we can influence the way our experience arises, creating the possibility for genuine peace and harmony in our lives.

The Thoroughly-Established Nature

Once the mind has been purified through the recognition that the imputational nature does not exist within the dependent nature, the reality of suchness can manifest. This is the ultimate level of reality and provides the basis upon which the dependent and imputational natures arise. There are two ways to view the thoroughly-established nature of suchness:

1. **Immutable:** This is the actual nature of suchness as experienced by a non-dualistic mind, completely free from all forms of imputation. Without the conditioning of conceptual fabrications, the mind abides in a sublime state, filled with infinite qualities. It is called *immutable* because the awareness is free from grasping and therefore never moves from the blissful experience of the present moment.

2. **Undistorted:** When suchness is experienced from the perspective of a pure view, it is known as *pristine wisdom.* This mind is actually a dependent nature as it maintains a very subtle dualistic separation that provides a reference point for making distinctions regarding appearances. What differentiates this nature from ordinary imputational natures is that there is no conception of the self being real, and therefore there is no ignorance. All phenomena are experienced as pure manifestations of suchness.

When the dualistic mind completely dissolves, awareness and appearances become inseparable and are said to be *non-dual,* like water into water, they thoroughly mix. While awareness abides in stillness, its spontaneous radiance gives rise to countless appearances. Regardless of the shape these appearances take, they are never experienced as being separate from suchness. Everything is instead seen as deities of ultimate pristine wisdom.

Upon examination, all three natures can be condensed into two. The dependent nature can be experienced as either an imputational nature or a thoroughly-established nature depending on the view that is present. Imputational natures correspond to the deceptive truths of conventional reality, whereas the thoroughly-established nature corresponds to the definitive truth of ultimate reality.

The Seven Types of Emptiness

Recognising that we currently experience the dependent nature on the basis of an impure view, it begs the question, what can we do about it? How do we purify our view to experience suchness in an undistorted way? The answer is *emptiness.*

Our confusion is a result of the accumulation of many mistaken projections and as they only exist as imputations, they completely lack any substantial essence. Unfortunately, due to our habituation to these concepts, it is very difficult to cut through the layers of obscurations they generate. By realising the emptiness of different types of phenomena, we can peel back these layers and thereby purify our perception of reality.

Depending on which layer of reality we are working with, there are different types of emptiness we need to consider. In the *Sutra of the Descent into Lanka*, the Buddha states:

> *Mahamati, briefly, there are seven kinds of emptiness: (1) the emptiness of characteristics; (2) the emptiness of self-existence; (3) the emptiness of phenomena; (4) the emptiness of non-phenomena; (5) the emptiness of ineffability; (6) the great emptiness of the ultimate truth of Buddha knowledge and (7) the emptiness of mutual exclusion.*

Of these seven, one is related to the reality of imputed natures, three are related to dependent natures and three are related to the thoroughly-established nature. Clearly understanding these relationships provides us with a methodology we can use as a path for practice.

The Emptiness of Imputed Natures

Although our focus is on developing the wisdom that realises the ultimate nature of reality, we cannot ignore the fact that we live in a world where conceptual imputations play a major role. Ultimately imputations do not exist in the way they appear, but on a provisional level, they can still be very useful for supporting our spiritual practice.

If the imputed nature of the objects we perceive is not analysed, it is still possible to use them to perform functions. For instance, when an appearance of something arises that looks like a chair, we can use it as a basis for sitting and so it performs the function of a chair. If we didn't recognise that it was a suitable place to sit, then we wouldn't label it "chair". Knowing how to discriminate between the functions of different appearances in order to achieve what we desire is known as *conventional wisdom*.

The support for this type of wisdom is a particular type of emptiness known as the *emptiness of mutual exclusion*. This is the realisation that a particular phenomenon is absent in relation to another, such as recognising that in a room filled with monks, there is an absence of elephants. We could also recognise that where there is light, there is an absence of darkness, or where there is short, there is an absence of long. This type of emptiness is useful as the basis for making discriminations about the characteristics of a particular phenomenon. These distinctions allow us to manipulate reality in many skilful ways.

Take for example a situation in which you perceive a person in need of help. Without the ability to discriminate between the person and the characteristics of the situation, you would be unable to act for their benefit. All virtuous activity performed along the path relies on discriminatory knowledge based on this form of emptiness. Without it, everything becomes mixed up and unclear, leading to further confusion.

We should not forget however that developing conventional knowledge is provisional in nature. It is only useful while we are dominated by grasping onto imputations. As we eventually need to transcend these imputations altogether, the Buddha warns us to avoid this type of emptiness. We cannot allow ourselves to become complacent with knowledge that does not directly liberate us from cyclic existence. Our main focus should therefore be on developing a deeper wisdom through contemplation of the remaining six forms of emptiness.

The Emptiness of Dependent Natures

By analysing the absolute nature of imputed phenomena, we can develop a wisdom that knows how conventional reality actually exists. To purify our view, it is first necessary to develop awareness of three types of emptiness, which provides the basis for clearing specific misconceptions that serve to perpetuate our confusion.

The first is the *emptiness of characteristics*. This refers to the recognition that the basis of imputation is empty of the imputations we project onto it. For example, the dependently arising appearance of a shape in the visual consciousness provides the basis for imputing names such as "apple", "red", and "food". If however we search for these labels in the actual appearance we cannot find them. Developing familiarity with this form of emptiness helps us remove the mistaken belief that appearances and names are the same entity.

Although it is relatively easy to recognise that names are imputations, it is much harder to recognise that the appearances themselves are also imputational in nature. When an appearance arises, we immediately have the sense that it exists from its own side, manifesting as a result of its own characteristics. This is the mind that grasps onto the self-existence of the appearance. Even though we may accept that the label "apple" doesn't exist in the appearance, the appearance still seems to have qualities that make it appropriate to be labelled "apple"; it maintains a certain "appleness". To dispel this misconception, we need to familiarise ourselves with the *emptiness of self-existence*, which involves thoroughly investigating the dependent nature of the appearance.

Let's take the example of a table. What is the basis for imputing the name "table" on a particular appearance? If we consider the meaning of table, we could say, four legs and a top. What happens if we take away one of the legs? Is it still a table? Yes, although probably not a very functional table and so we may now call it a broken table. If we were to remove another leg, is it still a table? How many legs do we need to take away before we stop calling it a table?

What this shows is that the appearance, as a valid basis of imputation, is dependent on various causes and conditions coming together. When the conditions are present, they function as a basis for imputation and when the conditions dissolve, the imputation is no longer valid. This proves that the basis does not exist from its own side; for if it did, it would always function as a basis for imputation.

These first two forms of emptiness provide the foundation for realising the empty nature of objective phenomena. By working with them, we cut our grasping onto external reality, creating the opportunity to explore the more subtle nature of our subjective experience. It is our grasping onto this internal reality that is the actual root of the ignorance that binds us to cyclic existence.

In order to dissolve self-grasping, we need to consider the *emptiness of phenomena*. This is the emptiness that recognises that there is no substantial, inherently existent self that exists within the psycho-physical aggregates. After identifying the mind of self-grasping, we then investigate whether the perceived self is the same or different from the aggregates. By conducting a thorough investigation of the aggregates, we come to the conclusion that this perceived self cannot possibly exist.

For these meditations to have the strength to cut our habitual tendencies, they must be joined with the single-pointed concentration of Shamatha and Vipashyana. Only then can we experience the emptiness of phenomena directly. If we are able to familiarise ourselves with this reality, our habit of grasping onto the aggregates as a self dissolves and the dependent nature can be seen to be completely empty of the imputed nature.

The Emptiness of the Thoroughly-Established Nature

With the wisdom that realises the emptiness of dependent natures, grasping onto appearances ceases to occur and phenomena are no longer seen as inherently existing entities, but as illusory manifestations of the mind. This realisation is enough to end cyclic existence; however, to achieve perfect enlightenment, there is still work that needs to be done.

The next step on our journey is to familiarise ourselves with the thoroughly established nature of suchness. By learning how to experience reality from the perspective of suchness, the very subtle traces of our karmic habituation are removed and we achieve the enlightened state of a Buddha, free from all forms of limitation. For this to occur, we need to transcend the mind that sees reality from the perspective of a dualistic consciousness.

The first obstacle to achieving this is the mistaken belief that the foundational consciousness is the ultimate nature of reality. To overcome this obstacle, we need to realise the *emptiness of non-phenomena* which is the emptiness that recognises that the dualistic appearances of dependent natures do not exist from the perspective of suchness. Suchness is non-dual in nature, free from the reference point of a subject who experiences objects.

We can think of this as being similar to a person dreaming. Within the reality of the dream they engage in various activities and subsequently experience feelings of happiness and sorrow. One day their dream becomes lucid and everything they then experience takes on an illusory nature. As they realise they are only dreaming, they don't grasp onto the dream as real and can experience it without any need for suffering. Upon waking, they recognise that as a dream, none of the world they just experienced ever existed as anything other than their own mind.

Likewise, the appearances of a dualistic mind are illusory and dreamlike in nature. When we grasp onto them as real we experience suffering, but if we let go of our grasping, they cease to condition our experience. However, whether we grasp onto appearances or not doesn't change the fact that we are still dreaming. By realising suchness, we effectively awaken to the reality that none of these distinctions have ever existed from the perspective of the thoroughly-established nature.

When we realise this form of emptiness, we develop the desire to transcend our dualistic perspective which requires the removal of the very subtle grasping that binds the conceptual mind together. To understand how this is possible, we need to consider the space-like awareness that is the result of analysing imputed natures.

By investigating the reality of any given phenomenon, we will eventually come to the realisation of a mere absence of that phenomenon. When we rest our mind in this absence, the mind is free from grasping onto the phenomenon being investigated. It is said to be a non-affirming negation, in that nothing is explicitly affirmed as a result of negating the object of analysis. It is simply recognised to be non-existent.

There is the danger at this stage of grasping onto the mere absence as being inherently real. As the absence is all that remains, we can think that it must be all that exists. This type of thinking prevents the mind from experiencing suchness, by locking it into a deconfigured aspect of the foundational consciousness, effectively creating a wall in the mind. Fortunately the appearance of an absence is simply another dualistic appearance and therefore it too can be analysed, leading to a realisation of the emptiness of emptiness.

When we realise the emptiness of a mere absence, we have removed all explicit grasping onto appearances. The last step is to remove the implicit grasping as well. For something to be an absence, requires an implicit conception of that which is absent. For example, if I recognise there is an absence of elephant in my room, it requires awareness of what an elephant is. Likewise, when we realise the absence of inherent existence, there is an implicit awareness of the concept of inherent existence. Even though our focus may be explicitly engaged with one type of phenomenon, there can still be multiple implicit connections. This is simply the nature of our conceptual mind, where concepts are linked to more concepts.

Therefore, to realise the thoroughly-established nature of reality, we must realise the *emptiness of ineffability*. This is the fact that suchness is completely devoid of all concepts, both explicit and implicit. Because this form of emptiness by definition transcends concepts, we cannot use conceptual methods to produce it. We must instead rely on nonconceptual meditative techniques such as the meditation of the *Yogacara Madhyamaka* or the completion stage practices of the *Six Vajra Yogas*.

Cutting the conceptual movement of the dualistic mind topples the last remaining barriers so that the brilliance of suchness can shine through. The full radiance of the thoroughly-established nature is not immediately experienced however, it takes time to dissolve the habitual propensities that have been building since beginningless time.

Just like a large building being demolished, the dynamite reduces it to rubble, but the debris still needs to be removed. Only when the site is clear can something new be built. Likewise, realising the emptiness of dependent natures is the dynamite which destroys the foundations of our dualistic mind, causing it to collapse. Abiding in suchness removes the very subtle grasping which binds the conceptual mind together. Without these bonds, the propensities completely dissolve.

Resting this mind in a state completely free from all forms of conceptual fabrications is known as *the great emptiness of the ultimate truth of Buddha knowledge*. It is the primordial wisdom that knows suchness as it is. This form of emptiness is not a mere absence as when it is experienced by a mind set in meditative equipoise, it is an endless field of enlightened qualities—an infinite realm of possibilities. This state is none other than our Buddha-nature and is the wisdom that realises the ultimate nature of reality—the actual perfection of wisdom.

The Wisdom that Knows the Five Branches of Learning

Once a Bodhisattva transcends their dualistic mind by developing the wisdom that realises the ultimate nature of reality, they no longer operate at the level of conceptual constructs. This means they do not engage in decisions to do "this" or "that", as all of their actions are completely spontaneous, like the rays of a brightly shining sun.

Whether a sentient being can experience those rays of sunshine depends on whether they are in the vicinity of the sun. Even though the sun always shines, if there are clouds in the sky the warmth of the rays cannot be felt. For this reason, Bodhisattvas make extraordinary efforts to build connections with sentient beings so that when they achieve enlightenment, they will be able to bring lasting benefit to everyone.

The method for establishing these connections is through teaching the Dharma. However, in order to be an effective teacher, both knowledge and skill are required. This is why Bodhisattvas dedicate themselves to studying the *Five Branches of Learning* until they achieve Buddhahood:

1. **The Inner Science:** This field of knowledge encompasses all Dharma teachings and through its study, it is possible to know the nature of reality and generate genuine causes for peace and harmony to arise. As Bodhisattvas, we study the inner science to remove our own obscurations and to also guide others to do the same. Due to the infinite variations of karma that sentient beings possess, we need to study the methods that will be of benefit to others as well as those which will benefit our own mind. It is therefore important to develop a non-sectarian approach that establishes a broad view that can incorporate the needs of everyone. If an idea could potentially bring benefit to a particular type of mind, it is worth learning.

2. **The Science of Logic:** As we move along the path, doubt can become a major obstacle to achieving realisations. When we lack certainty, it is easy to develop wrong views which prevent us from seeing the truth of our reality. Through the science of logic, we learn to use reasoning as an antidote for this type of doubt. If our understanding is based on reasoning, the formulation of our ideas will be clear and precise, making us more effective teachers who can guide our students in overcoming their own doubts.

3. **The Science of Grammar:** Knowing what to say is one thing, but knowing how to say it is another. Communication is a key part of guiding others effectively. Without the ability to communicate in a way

that connects with our audience, the meaning of what we are saying will be lost. By studying grammar, we learn how to work with sounds and words to give shape to ideas. Then through subjects like poetics, we learn to inspire the mind of others with words, transcending the mere delivery of information and connecting with a deeper level of experience. This also includes learning a variety of languages to open communication with people living in diverse cultures.

4. **The Science of Medicine:** It is difficult to learn when our mind and body are out of balance, giving rise to sickness that becomes an obstacle to both concentration and achieving one's aim. Studying the science of medicine enables us to provide relief from such suffering. Knowledge of both the gross physical body and the subtle energetic body means we know how to diagnose and treat imbalances in these systems. This offers patients temporary relief and gives them the opportunity to practice the Dharma in order to establish a more long-term solution.

5. **The Science of Crafts and Occupations:** Practicing Dharma requires specific conditions and at least some degree of leisure time in which to practice. This leisure is created when our basic needs of food, shelter and so forth are fulfilled. Once these immediate needs are met, the mind can turn its attention to what is truly important. We therefore need a particular occupation to meet the needs of the society in which we live. When we do this, the society supports us, providing us with what we require to survive. As Bodhisattvas, we should try to focus on occupations which help people meet their worldly needs, but also their spiritual needs. For instance, by learning how to build statues of the Buddha, we create the conditions for people to become familiar with the marks and signs of an enlightened being, laying down powerful karmic propensities in their mind and supporting their Dharma practice. We should obviously avoid any occupation that directly harms sentient beings in any way.

Of these five, the first provides the knowledge for achieving one's own aims and the aims of others, and the last four provide the supporting conditions for helping others. Contained within these five branches is all the wisdom that is known in the world. We do not need to know everything to free ourselves from our afflictions, but the more we know, the greater our ability to help others. As they are the focus of our practice, we should endeavour to learn all we can to guide them effectively along the path.

The Wisdom that Accomplishes the Aims of Sentient Beings

Through our study of the five branches of learning, we acquire a wealth of knowledge that can potentially bring benefit to sentient beings. Simply knowing something however, is not enough. We also have to know when to use that knowledge. The only way to truly know how to respond to a given situation is through experience.

Consider the difference between someone freshly graduated from university and someone who has been practicing their trade for many years. What effect does their experience have on the decisions they make? A person with more experience will generally be more resilient to change as they have gained mastery over their skills and know how to apply them in any situation which may arise. They can adapt in a way that a novice cannot.

This is the basic principle behind the Buddha's enlightened activities. The reason a Buddha can manifest in exactly the form that is needed, is because they have attained complete mastery over all forms of activity. Fuelled by their great compassion, Bodhisattvas exert enormous effort over a long period of time to gain the necessary experience. By thoroughly habituating themselves to helping the eleven types of sentient beings, they fully integrate their behaviour to the point where they no longer have to think about it. When the need arises, they simply act.

This is the wisdom we need to develop to achieve the *Non-Abiding Nirvana* of a fully enlightened Buddha. Without it, the mind will abide single-pointedly in suchness and will not manifest any form bodies. This is the result achieved by an Arhat of the Foundational Vehicle and is equivalent to the seventh stage of an Arya Bodhisattva. Rather than resting in Nirvana, a Bodhisattva traverses the last three stages by manifesting countless emanations and working for the benefit of others.

HOW TO PRACTICE WISDOM

When we begin our spiritual journey, our view is considerably limited, but as we progress along the path, it begins to expand, becoming both vast and profound. To achieve this broadening of scope, we need to practice three basic activities:

1. **Study:** To overcome even the most basic ignorance, we first need to acquire new information to counteract our misconceptions. We do this through studying the Dharma, either by listening to teachings or reading books. The aim should be to correctly receive the teachings in an undistorted way and have the ability to clearly identify what we are being taught and understand its basic intent.

2. **Reflection:** Once we have learned something new, we need to reflect on its meaning. We should contemplate the subject from as many angles as possible to build a robust understanding. Particular attention should be paid to any doubts which arise as they can become obstacles for developing certainty in our practice.

3. **Meditation:** Once we have removed doubt through reflection, we can rest our mind in our realisation of the teaching. This transforms a teaching from being a mere collection of ideas to being a direct and lived experience. By developing familiarity with this new state of mind, wisdom is integrated into our mindstream and effectively blocks corresponding ignorance from arising.

This process should be repeated at every stage of the path. No matter what the practice is, we first learn about it, then clear our doubts and finally we bring the practice into experience. Once we have a basic realisation to work with, we can refine it through further study, reflection and meditation. By working skilfully in this way, we eventually clear all our obscurations and perfect all our good qualities.

Based on the view presented in the Third Turning, we need to remove the mistaken projections of our conceptual mind in order to realise our most sacred of truths—the sublime emptiness of suchness. This is achieved through a four-step process: (1) reverse the grasping of imputed phenomena; (2) release the coarse grasping of relative appearances; (3) release the subtle grasping of the conceptual mind; and (4) rest the mind in suchness.

In the coming chapters we will explore the specific practices used in the Kalachakra Path to accomplish these stages. For now it will suffice to focus on a general overview of how this process is achieved within the traditions of the Great Vehicle. Keep in mind that even though the different traditions place their emphasis in different areas, they all provide methods for achieving these stages and therefore they all have the same capacity to produce enlightenment.

Reversing the Grasping of Imputed Phenomena

The first stage of practice is to counteract the ignorance that does not know the causes for suffering, or the causes for happiness. Because we lack the wisdom to clearly distinguish between virtue and non-virtue, we grasp onto the causes of suffering believing they will lead us to happiness. To progress along the path, this grasping needs to be reversed and our mind oriented toward the practice of virtue. This reversal is achieved by cultivating wisdom regarding three types of grasping:

1. **Permanence:** Grasping onto the permanence of phenomena fuels our attachment to conditions, creating the causes for inevitable suffering when those conditions change. As long as we remain attached to the *Eight Worldly Dharmas,* we will never create the time to practice sacred Dharma and experience its benefits. The antidote for this type of grasping is to cultivate *the wisdom that realises the impermanent nature of phenomena.* As our awareness of impermanence grows, our attachment naturally diminishes.

2. **Suffering:** We grasp onto suffering when due to our ignorance, we think the causes for suffering are the causes for happiness. To overcome this ignorance we need to cultivate *the wisdom which understands the karmic law of cause and effect and the suffering nature of cyclic existence.* Familiarity with these topics allows us to develop the capacity to clearly distinguish between the genuine causes for happiness and causes for suffering.

3. **Self-cherishing:** This is the ignorance which grasps onto the self as being more important than others. As it is the root of all bias, it limits our capacity by keeping our attention firmly fixed only on ourselves. While this restricted vision can be used to realise the selflessness of persons, it cannot realise the selflessness of phenomena and therefore is unable to clear the cognitive obscurations. The antidote to self-cherishing is to cultivate *the wisdom that cherishes others*. We do this by meditating on *love and compassion* and generating the altruistic intention of *Bodhicitta*.

Releasing the Coarse Grasping of Relative Appearances

Based on the wisdom generated in the previous stage, we develop a mind with little attachment, that is focused on practicing virtue and is motivated to benefit sentient beings. Such a mind is ripe to gain insight into the empty nature of dependent phenomena. This realisation is the direct antidote to the self-grasping which binds us to cyclic existence and perpetuates our suffering.

There are two main approaches for realising emptiness: (1) the scholar's approach of conceptual analysis or (2) the meditator's approach of observing the nature of the mind. Within the Jonang Tradition, emphasis is generally placed on the latter and as this method will be discussed extensively throughout the rest of the path, we will now examine the logical reasonings of the scholar's approach.

There are many different logics used to cultivate the wisdom that realises the emptiness of self and they can be summarised into five main reasonings: (1) the reasoning based on nature; (2) the reasoning based on causes; (3) the reasoning based on existences; (4) the reasoning based on everything and (5) the reasoning based on interdependence.

To meditate on emptiness from this approach, we first need to identify the *object of negation*. We are not trying to negate appearances, only our mistaken projection of them being inherently existent and so the object of negation should always be a form of grasping. It is recommended to begin with the mind that grasps onto the appearance of an inherently existent, substantial and permanent self, as this is the root cause of our suffering. To identify this mind, reflect on how the self appears to you. Considering times when you have felt threatened or filled with pride can be helpful, as self-grasping is particularly strong in these moments and so can provide a clear target for your attention.

Once the object of negation has been identified, select a reasoning to work with. Whether you refer to one in particular or make use of all five is up to you as long as you are methodical in your analysis. If your conclusion is to have an impact on your mind, you need to have a strong certainty that the object of negation cannot possibly exist, therefore take your time and explore every possibility.

Reasoning Based on Nature

The first reasoning is known as the *Neither One nor Many Reasoning*. It investigates whether or not the inherent nature of a singular object can be established. If it cannot, it stands to reason that multiple objects also cannot be established, as multiple objects consist of many singular objects. You cannot have ten apples if you do not first have one apple. On the subject of inherent nature Nagarjuna writes:

> *If they are natureless,*
> *What transforms?*
> *If there were nature,*
> *How could there be transformation?*

In the first part of this verse, Nagarjuna identifies a wrong view held by many. Because we grasp onto the inherent existence of objects, we believe they have an enduring nature from one moment to the next. In the case of ourselves, we have a sense that the person we are today is the same person born many years earlier and although we recognise we have undergone many changes in our lives, we still feel like the same person.

Nagarjuna refutes this idea by asking the question, "If nature were to exist inherently, how can it transform into anything else?" The nature of any given thing is defined as the qualities which are inseparable from that phenomenon and without them, the phenomenon cannot exist. For instance the nature of fire is heat, and so, if there is no heat there is no fire. If a nature is inherent, those qualities must always be present, but if they are always present, how can they transform? When we look closely at a phenomenon, we observe that it constantly changes, therefore we come to the conclusion that it must lack an inherent nature.

Another way to analyse whether a singular entity can be established as existing inherently is to search for its nature within the appearance. If we use the self as our object of analysis, we can see that the self appears to be present within the aggregates of body and mind. By investigating whether the self is the same or different from the aggregates, we come to see that it is neither. As Nagarjuna writes:

> *If the aggregates were the self,*
> *It would have to arise and cease.*
> *If it were different from the aggregates,*
> *It would not have the characteristics of the aggregates.*

The first part of this verse indicates that a self that is inherently the same as the aggregates, would necessarily be exactly the same. As the aggregates constantly change, the self too would constantly change, which contradicts the notion of it existing inherently.

If on the other hand the self were inherently different from the aggregates, it would be completely different from the aggregates in every way. This means that the self would lack all of the aggregates' attributes, including its dependent nature. Such a self could never be produced by anything and therefore could never exist—like a sky flower or the son of a barren woman.

Reasoning Based on Causes

The second reasoning, sometimes referred to as the *Diamond Slivers Reasoning*, analyses the causes for producing an inherently existent object. If we truly believe that an object exists inherently from its own side, its cause must also be inherent in nature. In such a scenario there are four possibilities: (1) the object arises from itself; (2) the object arises from another; (3) the object arises from both itself and other; or (4) there is no cause. With regards to the first option, Nagarjuna writes in his *Root of the Middle Way*:

If, the cause, having ceased,
Passed completely into the effect,
Then a previously arisen cause
Would, absurdly, arise again.

In this verse, Nagarjuna points out the absurdity that would occur if an inherently existing effect were to have the same nature as an inherently existent cause. Since the definition of a cause is that it gives rise to an effect, to say the effect is the same as the cause, means that the resulting effect would also be the cause. The cause would therefore be permanent and would continuously arise, which doesn't make sense as it has already arisen.

Let's take the example of a cup. We know that the cup has not always existed as it is an impermanent phenomenon that came into existence at some point in time. For it to exist inherently as a cup, it must have an inherent cause that brought it into existence. If its cause is the same as the cup, which is its effect, the mere presence of the cup would give rise to another cup. For every moment that the cup endured, it would be giving rise to a cup. But is this what happens? Is this how the cup exists?

Regarding the second possibility, Nagarjuna states:

Moreover, if an effect is not related to its cause,
How can it be given rise to?
The cause gives rise to the effect
Neither by seeing it nor by not seeing it.

If an inherent cause is inherently different from an inherent effect, the two would be totally unrelated. Such a cause would have no capacity to function as a cause, because of its inability to give rise to the effect. If the cause gave rise to an effect "by seeing it", there would be a moment where both the cause and the effect existed at the same time. In such a situation, there would be no need for the cause to give rise to the effect, as it has already arisen. For instance, imagine a seed existing at the same time as its sprout. As the sprout is already there, how could the seed be considered a cause? It is equally absurd to think that a cause can give rise to an effect "by not seeing it". This would mean that a totally unrelated cause could give rise to a totally unrelated effect. The consequence of this would be that anything could potentially give rise to anything else. For instance, darkness could give rise to brightness.

Having already proven that the cause cannot inherently exist in itself or in another, the option of it being both self and other is also impossible. We are then left with the fourth possibility which is also logically absurd. If an effect could be experienced without a cause, there would be nothing stopping it from arising in every moment nor would there be any reason for it to arise in the first place. As this clearly contradicts how reality manifests, it should be rejected.

Reasoning Based on Existences

The third reasoning is known as the *Refutation of Existent or Non-Existent Production* and concerns the nature of results. There are two absurdities that arise when we consider a result as being either inherently existent or inherently non-existent. As Nagarjuna writes:

> *If an effect is inherently existent,*
> *To what could a cause have given rise?*
> *If an effect is inherently nonexistent,*
> *To what could a cause have given rise?*

Firstly we consider that if a result is inherently existent it would have to already exist at the time of the cause. If this were the case, there would be no reason for the cause as the result already existed. Secondly, if a result is inherently nonexistent, it would always be non-existent which means that no matter what the cause, the result would never arise. Both of these arguments prove that results are dependent phenomena that rely on cause and conditions in order to arise.

Reasoning Based on Everything

The fourth reasoning looks at the relationship between causes and effects. It is known as the *Refutation of Production from Four Alternatives*. These four are: (1) one cause producing multiple results; (2) one cause producing one result; (3) multiple causes producing multiple results and (4) multiple causes producing one result.

If the relationship of cause and its result is taken to exist inherently, both sides of the relationship would have to exhibit the same nature. It is impossible for something which is inherently unitary to transform into something that is inherently plural, as these two properties are mutually exclusive. Therefore one cause would have to produce one result and multiple causes would have to produce multiple results. This leaves us with only two alternatives, neither of which is tenable.

For a single cause to inherently give rise to a single result, both the cause and the result need to also inherently exist. As this has already been proven to be impossible, we cannot establish a case where one cause gives rise to one result. If we can't establish one, then we can't establish many, therefore the third alternative of many causes producing many results is also not possible.

Reasoning Based on Interdependence

The fifth reasoning is considered the *King of Reasonings*, proving that all dependent phenomena lack inherent existence due to the very fact that they are dependent arisings. In the *Root of the Middle Way*, Nagarjuna writes:

> *That which is dependent origination*
> *Is explained to be emptiness.*
> *That, being a dependent designation,*
> *Is itself the middle way.*

In the first two lines, Nagarjuna is equating all dependent arisings to objects which possess the property of self-emptiness. This means that wherever you find a dependent arising, you will also find it is empty of inherent existence. From the perspective of the Three Natures we could say that all dependent natures are empty of their imputed natures.

Nagarjuna continues by stating that the imputations of "dependent origination" and "emptiness of self" are both dependent designations. For something to be considered dependent, it must be self-empty. For it to be considered self-empty, it must be dependent. This illustrates the very nature of how the middle way view understands self-emptiness to be the balance between eternalism and nihilism.

He goes on to say:

There does not exist any thing
That is not dependently arisen.
Therefore there does not exist any thing
That is not empty.

To understand this verse, we must remember the perspective from which we are speaking. Dependently arisen phenomena appear to the mind of a dualistic consciousness; they do not appear to the meditative mind that abides in a non-dualistic awareness of suchness. Therefore, this verse is referring to the reality of a dualistic mind. For such a mind, there are no entities which are not dependently arisen and therefore there is nothing that is not empty of an inherently existent nature.

Releasing the Subtle Grasping of the Conceptual Mind

As a result of our thorough analysis of the nature of relative appearances, we eventually arrive at a view that clearly realises that all imputed phenomena are empty of inherent existence. However, for this view to function as an antidote to our self-grasping, it needs to be combined with the single-pointed concentration of Shamatha.

There are two types of training based on practicing Shamatha: with or without a sign. Practicing *with a sign* is to place our attention on a specific object of meditation, such as the breath, a mental image or even a mere absence. These objects are considered to be conceptual in nature as they involve an implicit relationship between a subjective observer and the objective appearance being observed.

In order to experience suchness free from dualistic projections, it is necessary to completely stop our conceptual mind. This is achieved by practicing Shamatha *without a sign*, where the mind learns to rest in its own nature, free from grasping and free from distraction. As we become habituated to this mode of meditating, conceptual proliferation naturally ceases and the mind enters a non-dualistic experience of suchness.

At this stage, an important distinction needs to be made. The realisation of selflessness and suchness are not the same thing. Realising selflessness does not automatically establish the realisation of suchness, however through the realisation of suchness, you also realise selflessness. To understand how this works, we can think of suchness as being like a jewel wrapped in fancy paper. When we meditate on the selflessness of dependent natures, it is as though we are analysing the qualities of the paper. We can spend considerable time establishing a view of the way the paper exists, but this misses the point. Eventually, we need to remove the paper so we can experience the actual jewel. It then becomes very obvious that the jewel is not the paper, nor is the jewel the absence of the paper—the jewel is the jewel.

Recognising this, yogic practitioners first develop a degree of mental stability by training with conceptual signs such as the breath or mental images. Using this stability, they then meditate on the selflessness of dependent phenomena to reduce their grasping and establish a view that is conducive to realising suchness. On the basis of this view, with the use of non-conceptual methods, the focus then becomes realising suchness.

Abiding in Suchness

The process for achieving an attainment of suchness involves a gradual withdrawal from all manifest appearances. First the gross sensory appearances dissolve and one abides in the gross conceptual mind. As that mind becomes increasingly more subtle, all objective appearances dissolve and only subjective appearances remain. By cultivating the view that realises the emptiness of dualistic appearances, we cut through the most subtle layers of our grasping and experience the non-dualistic mind of suchness.

When the dualistic mind becomes dormant in this way, the spontaneous nature of suchness begins to manifest in the aspect of pure appearances known as empty-forms. Unfortunately, due to the power of our karmic conditioning, it is difficult to maintain this absorption and eventually we will revert back to our dualistic mind of subject of object. Like a ball tied to an elastic, we quickly snap back to what is familiar.

To remove this habituation to ignorance we need to become habituated to the wisdom that realises the empty nature of suchness. This is not the self-emptiness of dependent natures, but the sublime emptiness that is filled with all enlightened qualities. It is achieved by gradually mixing the different aspects of our experience with the pure appearances of suchness. If we stabilise our experience of empty-forms, they cease to act as a basis for dualistic perception. With all gross and subtle experiences fully integrated, we can abide indefinitely in the immutable thoroughly-established nature that is the ultimate truth of suchness.

Branch Vows Related to the Perfection of Wisdom

The training in wisdom is supported by eight branch vows. Their essence is to *always strive to expand your awareness of the different aspects of reality* and so we should apply ourselves as much as possible to studying, reflecting and meditating on Dharma. The specific vows are to avoid the following behaviours:

1. **Rejecting the teachings of the Foundational Vehicle:** A Bodhisattva must always remember that the Great Vehicle is built on the teachings of the Foundational Vehicle. Even if we don't engage in their specific practices, we still need to study them so we can guide those for whom the teachings are suitable. It is therefore not right for a Bodhisattva to hold or proclaim a view that studying and practicing the Foundational teachings is not necessary. To do so is considered a breach of this vow.

2. **Failing to pursue the teachings of the Great Vehicle:** Having already taken the Bodhisattva Path, if we dedicate our time to practicing the Foundational Vehicle at the expense of our Bodhisattva practices, we will have broken this vow. Our core practice should always be in accordance with the Great Vehicle. This vow may also be broken if we decide to abandon an authentic teacher or teaching after already establishing a stable and sure path to enlightenment.

3. **Studying Non-Buddhist teachings more than Buddha's teachings:** Once we have committed ourselves to achieving enlightenment for the sake of all sentient beings, we should dedicate the bulk of our energy to putting the Buddha's teachings into practice. If we prioritise worldly

knowledge or Non-Buddhist teachings we will have broken this vow. There is however no fault in studying them as a means to support your Buddhist practice.

4. **Delighting in the study of Non-Buddhist texts:** With a specific purpose in mind it is sometimes helpful to study Non-Buddhist texts. If however we allow ourselves to become attached to and completely involved in Non-Buddhist subjects, taking great pleasure in them, we will break this branch vow. If this does occur, we strengthen our attachment to worldly knowledge and fail to create the causes to transcend conventional reality.

5. **Denigrating the teachings of the Great Vehicle:** We break this vow if we denigrate any Mahayana teaching or teacher, suggesting that they are of no benefit and will not help others. Appearing similar to the second root vow, this vow specifically relates to the practice and teachings on wisdom and emptiness. We should always try to cultivate a sense of devotion towards the vast and profound nature of the Mahayana teachings.

6. **Praising oneself and disparaging others:** A breach of this vow occurs when, motivated by pride or anger, we praise ourselves and denigrate others. This is the same as the root vow, except the four conditions are not required to break it. It is acceptable for a Bodhisattva to speak in such a way to help those dominated by wrong views to overcome them. Such an act must always be motivated by pure love and compassion.

7. **Failing to pursue learning:** If through pride or laziness we fail to attend Dharma teachings, discussions or other Dharma activities, we will break this branch vow. It refers mainly to the realisation of wisdom, for which one needs to study diligently. We should always make the effort to deepen our understanding whenever we have the opportunity.

8. **Showing disrespect toward a Dharma Teacher or the Dharma:** This vow is broken if we knowingly deride, make fun of or otherwise act disrespectfully towards someone who teaches the Dharma. Even if the person relies only on the literal meaning, out of respect for the meaning of the words, we should still respect a teacher who is kind enough to share the Dharma with us.

Integrating All Six Perfections

The *Perfection of Wisdom* is achieved through training simultaneously with all six Perfections: (1) for the *generosity of wisdom,* we should guide sentient beings in the cultivation of wisdom; (2) for the *ethical discipline of wisdom,* we should strive to uphold the branch vows related to wisdom while also striving to study, reflect and meditate on the teachings; (3) for the *patience of wisdom,* we should happily bear any hardships which arise as a result of cultivating wisdom; (4) for the *joyful effort of wisdom,* we should diligently apply ourselves to practice and bring wisdom into every moment of our experience; (5) for the *meditative concentration of wisdom,* we should cultivate the concentrations of special insight so we can realise the ultimate nature of reality; and (6) for the *wisdom of wisdom,* we should cultivate wisdom from within the realisation that the person who is studying, the act of studying, and the teachings that are studied are completely empty of inherent existence. We should specifically learn to discriminate between the different natures of our experience and to correctly realise their corresponding forms of emptiness. If we practice in this way, we will surely reach the perfection of wisdom which abides inseparably within suchness.

THE RESULTS OF PRACTICING WISDOM

As a result of cultivating *The Wisdom that Realises the Nature of Ultimate Reality,* it is possible to completely clear the two obscurations and reveal the pristine nature of suchness. This is known as the *separative result,* as this is when adventitious defilements are separated from your experience of reality. When this result arises, your Buddha-nature is able to manifest fully in a way that is completely free from all forms of limitation and conditioning.

To ensure our Buddha-nature manifests in the form of a fully enlightened Buddha, we must complete the accumulations of merit and wisdom. In reliance on *The Wisdom that Knows the Five Branches of Learning* and *The Wisdom that Accomplishes the Aims of Sentient Beings* we accumulate vast quantities of merit and create the conditions to effectively transmit the teachings to others, causing them to engage in virtue, inspiring them to practice the Dharma and giving them the confidence to overcome their ignorance.

By dedicating ourselves to these actions, we produce the *liberative result* of a fully enlightened being, with all the marks and signs, whose sole purpose is to bring benefit to limitless sentient beings. It is said to be "liberative" because it is the basis upon which all sentient beings will be liberated from their suffering. Whereas the separative effect is the result of the cessation of grasping, the liberative effect is the result of training the mind on the path. Both are required to actually manifest as a Buddha.

According to Arya Asanga, a Bodhisattva who has achieved the *Perfection of Wisdom* can be identified by the following ten characteristics:

1. **Correctly grasps the complete extent of reality:** There is no aspect of reality that the Bodhisattva does not know. They are familiar with the full range of experiences whether in samsara or nirvana and are not content with only provisional knowledge.

2. **Correctly grasps the true nature of reality:** Due to their thorough habituation to the sublime truth of suchness, the Bodhisattva clearly perceives all appearances as pure appearances manifesting within suchness.

3. **Correctly grasps causes:** They are able to distinguish the true causes of suffering and the true causes of happiness, recognising that even though they have never existed as anything other than suchness, for the mind of a sentient being, they appear to exist.

4. **Correctly grasps effects:** Similarly, the Bodhisattva clearly distinguishes the difference between provisional forms of happiness and definitive peace and harmony. Knowing this, they dedicate their life to achieving genuine happiness for themselves and others.

5. **Understands the error of grasping:** The Bodhisattva has abandoned grasping onto dualistic appearances as inherently real. Recognising their illusory nature, they are never separated from their realisation.

6. **Understands the absence of error:** Their awareness is free from gross obscurations and therefore they are able to see reality in an unmistaken way.

7. **Understands which actions should be carried out:** Through their clear understanding of the Dharma, they know exactly how to behave to cultivate virtue, actualise their qualities and bring benefit to sentient beings.

8. **Understands which actions should not be carried out:** The Bodhisattva also knows which behaviours act in contradiction to the Dharma. Recognising that they will only bring suffering, they abandon them completely.

9. **Complete understanding of the process by which afflicted entities cause affliction:** Like a skilled doctor, the Bodhisattva knows exactly how cyclic existence works and how it gives rise to suffering. Because they are so familiar with its causes, they know exactly what needs to be abandoned.

10. **Complete understanding of the process by which purifying entities bring about purification:** Based on their clear understanding of the path, the Bodhisattva knows exactly how to practice in order to remove afflicted states of mind. They know the function of each method and how to apply them in the most skilful way.

REVIEW OF KEY POINTS

- Wisdom is the mind that can clearly discriminate the characteristics of reality. It consists of two aspects: (1) awareness that knows phenomena; and (2) discrimination which differentiates characteristics.

- There are two types of ignorance: (1) innate ignorance which is a mere unknowing; and (2) discriminating ignorance which is an active misconception. Discriminating ignorance gives rise to the two types of obscurations: (1) cognitive obscurations; and (2) afflictive obscurations.

- Wisdom can be divided into three types: (1) the wisdom that realises the nature of ultimate reality; (2) the wisdom that knows the five branches of learning; and (3) the wisdom that accomplishes the aims of sentient beings. The first wisdom achieves one's own aim of freedom from suffering, while the second and third achieve the aim of others by making enlightenment possible.

- The Wisdom that Realises the Nature of Ultimate Reality was presented by the Buddha in the collections of teachings known as the Three Turnings of the Wheel of Dharma. The first two turnings present provisional trainings while the third focuses on the definitive meaning.

- According to the Third Turning, all phenomena fall into five categories known as The Five Dharmas: (1) appearances; (2) names; (3) projections; (4) suchness; and (5) pure wisdom. By knowing these five, we can identify the mistakes that we make with regards to our perception of reality.

- The relationships between the Five Dharmas can be understood by way of The Three Natures: (1) the imputed nature; (2) the dependent nature; and (3) the thoroughly-established nature.

- Imputed natures can be divided into two: (1) apprehended natures; and (2) apprehender natures. They represent the objective and subjective aspects of our experience respectively.

- Dependent natures also have two aspects: (1) impure natures; and (2) pure natures. These represent whether reality is interpreted on the basis of ignorance or wisdom.

- The thoroughly-established nature can be divided into: (1) the immutable nature which is the actual nature of reality; and (2) the undistorted wisdom that knows reality as it is.

- The path to realise the ultimate nature of reality relies on seven forms of emptiness that can be used to clear the misconceptions which obscure reality. They are: (1) the emptiness of characteristics; (2) the emptiness of self-existence; (3) the emptiness of phenomena; (4) the emptiness of non-phenomena; (5) the emptiness of ineffability; (6) the great emptiness of the ultimate truth of Buddha knowledge; and (7) the emptiness of mutual exclusion.

- The Wisdom that Knows the Five Branches of Learning is concerned with the study of five fields of knowledge: (1) the inner science; (2) the science of logic; (3) the science of grammar; (4) the science of medicine; and (5) the science of crafts and occupations.

- The Wisdom that Accomplishes the Aims of Sentient Beings is concerned with developing first-hand experience in the application of wisdom in order to bring benefit to others. It is the main cause for developing the capacity to act spontaneously.

- Wisdom is cultivated through three activities: (1) study which acquires information; (2) reflection which develops certainty by clearing doubts; and (3) meditation which familiarises the mind with virtuous states.

- There are four steps to cultivating the wisdom that knows reality as it is: (1) reverse the grasping of imputed phenomena; (2) release the coarse grasping of relative appearances; (3) release the subtle grasping of the conceptual mind; and (4) rest the mind in suchness.

- The branch vows related to the Perfection of Wisdom are to avoid the following: (1) rejecting the teachings of the Foundational Vehicle; (2) failing to pursue the teachings of the Great Vehicle; (3) studying Non-Buddhist teachings more than Buddha's teachings; (4) delighting in the study of Non-Buddhist texts; (5) denigrating the teachings of the Great Vehicle; (6) praising oneself and disparaging others; (7) failing to pursue learning; and (8) showing disrespect toward a Dharma teacher or the Dharma.

- A Bodhisattva with pure wisdom has ten aspects: (1) correctly grasps the complete extent of reality; (2) correctly grasps the true nature of reality; (3) correctly grasps causes; (4) correctly grasps effects; (5) understands the error of grasping; (6) understands the absence of error; (7) understands which actions should be carried out; (8) understands which actions should not be carried out; (9) complete understanding of the process by which afflicted entities cause affliction; and (10) complete understanding of the process by which purifying entities bring about purification.

CHAPTER THIRTEEN

Bringing Benefit to Those Around You

An aspiring doctor looking out into the world perceives the incredible degree of pain and distress experienced by beings due to sickness, disease and injury. Arising from feelings of compassion, they develop the desire to do something to help alleviate such suffering. In the beginning, due to a lack of knowledge and skill, their capacity is limited and despite their good intentions, trying to treat the illness of others would only aggravate the situation. To truly make a difference, they need to exert the effort to train in the practice of medicine.

During their education, the doctor-in-training studies disease and infection; developing the ability to recognise the external symptoms, they learn to apply the corresponding remedies. Treating the symptoms alone may provide their patient with temporary relief, but without the wisdom to identify the root cause of sickness, the symptoms are likely to return and the doctor will be unsuccessful in curing their patient.

Realising they have only skimmed the surface of the aid and benefit they could potentially provide, the doctor continues their training, striving to develop a greater understanding of the nature of sickness. While they examine the obvious manifestations, their investigation goes deeper to include more subtle influences within the body. The more levels of knowledge they master, the more effective their treatment becomes. When their training is completed, as a fully qualified doctor, they can offer lasting relief and healing to their patients.

All Bodhisattvas can be considered doctors-in-training with the job of relieving suffering in whatever form it takes, whether it be obvious, subtle or very subtle. What differentiates a Bodhisattva from a medical doctor however, is the recognition that physical suffering is a symptom of mental suffering. The mind is primary and so to offer truly lasting relief, they must work with the mind to find treatments and solutions.

Training in the *Six Perfections* provides us with the methods to become skilled doctors. They teach us how to connect with the limitless potential of our mind and thereby achieve liberation from suffering. Through our practice, we accumulate the wisdom needed to expand our capacity to actually be of benefit to sentient beings, but this process takes time and is not an easy one. Due to the strength of our compassion, we may be tempted to focus our attention on working with others before we have completed our training. Having a genuine desire to help others is a wonderful quality, but we must be careful to avoid a perspective that is too short-term in nature. Unless we can confront the root of the problem, our time will be spent treating symptoms and applying band aids, without making true progress. For this reason, we must be skilful.

OVERVIEW OF THE FOUR WAYS TO GATHER A FOLLOWING

The Buddha understood that only the Dharma has the capacity to ultimately liberate sentient beings from their suffering. Therefore the greatest gift he could offer that would be of the most benefit, was to teach the Dharma. As aspiring Bodhisattvas, we should follow in his footsteps, channelling our efforts to master the Dharma to establish within us the capacity to share it with others. To help us do this effectively, the Buddha taught four methods known as the *Four Ways to Gather a Following*:

1. **Generosity:** When someone likes and trusts us, they are more receptive to our influence. It is therefore necessary to build positive relationships with those we encounter. We can do this through the practice of generosity. While the general effect of generosity is to fulfil the immediate needs of others, the relationship that is subsequently formed is our primary interest.

   Our goal here is to cultivate meaningful connections where sentient beings see us as their benefactors or supporters. For such a relationship to be authentic it must be based on genuine compassion and a sincere desire to help them. If our intentions are self-centred or manipulative, the connection will be unstable and fail to serve its purpose. Generosity needs to come from the heart. When it does, people naturally want to be near us and will be open to what we have to say.

2. **Agreeable Speech:** Once a connection is made, communication becomes possible. Agreeable speech refers to any form of communication that is appealing, truthful, relates to Dharma and is meaningful. Through offering advice in this way, we can transmit beneficial knowledge from our mind to the minds of others. This is sometimes referred to as "planting seeds" as we are helping to establish the potential for realisations to arise.

   The purpose for using agreeable speech is to cultivate enthusiasm for the Dharma in the minds of those who listen to it. As a student becomes more familiar with the teachings, they begin to see and experience the benefit that comes from putting them into practice. Once this understanding takes hold, the desire for change manifests. When this occurs, we must always check that our motivation is pure before imparting advice. If our minds are clouded by self-cherishing or desire for worldly concerns, our advice is unlikely to lead to any long-term benefit. What may appear as agreeable speech, could in fact do more harm than good.

3. **Beneficial Conduct:** Simply transmitting the Dharma is not enough. For the seeds which have been planted to ripen, they must be nurtured through practice. The next method is to engage in the beneficial conduct which encourages others to practice the Dharma they have received. This can take the form of bestowing vows of ethical discipline or providing pith instructions that indicate how to practice the teachings.

   Whichever form beneficial conduct takes, the result is that it shows students how to apply the teachings to their own experience. When they recognise the teachings as instructions for practice, they can then use the Dharma as a mirror into their lives. By looking closely at their own habitual patterns, they gain insight into the nature of reality to overcome their ignorance, ascertaining the cure for their suffering.

4. **Sameness of Purpose:** For our advice to carry any weight in the minds of our students, we must be able to demonstrate its application in our own lives. Simply put, we need to practice the Dharma we teach. Having a sameness of purpose is a recognition that our advice is rooted in personal experience, for only then can we authentically guide other beings along the path.

The purpose of this method is to provide a role model that continually inspires others to practice. No matter how profound a teaching may be, without someone to demonstrate its capacity, it is difficult to be dedicated to its practice. When our students see authentic qualities manifesting in our actions, they witness the possibilities and are motivated to make the effort to train.

In summary, within these four methods are the ways Buddhas and Bodhisattvas work for the benefit of others. As the aspiration of Bodhicitta is for all sentient beings to be free from suffering, the only way this will happen is for them all to cut the roots of their ignorance. This entails practicing the Dharma and sincerely following the teachings—there must be a belief in its benefits, generated from recognising its effects in the lives of others. Hence, through generosity, the Buddhas and Bodhisattvas demonstrate their qualities and attract sentient beings to them, enabling them to transmit the Dharma and guide their students toward freedom from suffering.

A DETAILED EXPLANATION

We will now examine each of these methods in greater detail based on the teachings of Arya Asanga in *The Stages of a Bodhisattva*. As an extensive presentation of the practice in generosity has already been presented earlier in this book, here we will address the last three methods for gathering a following.

Agreeable Speech

For our speech to be beneficial to sentient beings, we can consider it on two levels. Firstly, the *manner* in which we speak needs to accord with worldly conventions otherwise it will be rejected by those listening. Secondly, the *content* of our speech needs to accord with the Dharma so it has the capacity to bring benefit. From these two levels we can identify three types of speech:

Speech that is Friendly

How we speak impacts greatly on the receptivity of our audience. Coming across as angry and wrathful is likely to instill fear in our audience, acting as an obstacle to their understanding of what we are saying. While wrathful actions have a place in training students, it is generally best to maintain a friendly, welcoming expression and to refrain from frowning which signals to people to stay away.

Another important point to consider is the cultural background and social expectations of a particular audience. Failing to take these factors into account can lead to false perceptions and misunderstandings. For example, when we greet people, we should do so in a way that is culturally acceptable and shows both respect and care. By taking advantage of opportunities such as these, we cultivate positive connections that keep the lines of communication open.

Speech that Pleases

Sentient beings are for the most part social creatures. We constantly react to the feedback we receive from the people around us and based on those reactions, we distinguish between those actions which are desirable and those which are not. We grow accustomed to this behaviour from a very early age, learning that some actions bring praise and others criticism. As we enjoy the feeling that comes with praise, we seek to repeat the corresponding actions while avoiding those that incite criticism.

A Bodhisattva recognises this habit and uses it as a way to reinforce positive behaviours. When sentient beings engage in virtuous actions, they should be congratulated and made aware that they have done something beneficial. As this skilful means works with our attachment to praise, it is considered provisional in nature. By temporarily feeding this attachment, students eventually become habituated to virtue, naturally reducing their attachment so they no longer need praise to motivate them.

Speech that Contains the Dharma

The primary purpose of using agreeable speech is to transmit the wisdom of the Dharma to bring temporary and ultimate benefit to the sentient beings receiving it. This requires us to be skilful in what we teach and to whom. Sentient beings will be at different stages of spiritual development and due to the complexity of our karmic propensities, no two are exactly alike. For these reasons, to effectively share the Dharma with others, we need to develop our capacity to identify the level of teaching most appropriate for a given audience. Such an ability takes time to develop and comes mostly from experience. To assist us in this process, there are a number of general guidelines we can follow: (1) correcting the attitudes of students; (2) the qualities of the teaching; (3) the qualities of the teacher and (4) the manner of presenting the teaching.

Correcting the Attitudes of Students

The first is to recognise that certain attitudes a student may have will obstruct the benefit a teaching can provide. To help them overcome these attitudes, we should strive to teach in accordance with the *Four Reliances:* (1) rely on the words, not the teacher; (2) rely on the meaning, not the words; (3) rely on the definitive meaning, not the provisional meaning; and (4) rely on primordial awareness, not consciousness. This involves encouraging students to cultivate four attitudes that directs their attention, assisting them to penetrate the most profound levels of truth. These four are:

1. **Focus on listening to the Dharma correctly:** In today's degenerate times, finding authentic sources of Dharma can be difficult. Many teachers have only partial qualities and so are limited in the benefit they can provide to their students, but this does not mean they cannot offer what Dharma they do have. Too much emphasis on our teachers being "high lamas" with fancy titles creates the risk of closing us off to receiving wisdom from unlikely sources. The greatness of a being is based on their mind, not on their reputation or status. Students who learn to correctly listen to teachings can evaluate for themselves whether or not it is authentic. Rather than focusing on the source, we need to focus on what is being taught.

2. **Focus on the meaning:** Another difficulty many students face is grasping too strongly to the form a teaching takes. They develop particular tastes for what a "good teaching" sounds like and tend to reject any teaching that doesn't fall into that category. A more beneficial attitude is to concentrate on the meaning of what is said regardless of the form it takes. If the meaning is authentic, everything else can be considered irrelevant.

3. **Focus on the teachings of definitive meaning:** The Buddha taught an extraordinarily vast amount of teachings during his short time on this planet. As he always taught in accordance with the needs of his students, some of his teachings were meant as provisional stepping-stones for understanding more profound truths. Relying too heavily on these teachings can generate uncertainty and confusion. Students therefore need to develop the capacity to recognise when something is provisional in nature or when it presents a definitive truth. Of the two, we should always strive to focus on the definitive meaning for this is what will ultimately set us free.

4. **Focus on putting the teachings into practice:** Whatever Dharma we receive, we should never be satisfied with intellectual understanding. In order for the Dharma to transform our lives, we need to reflect on what we study and integrate it into our mind through meditation. Even the wisdom of a single line of teaching can be brought into experience.

The Qualities of the Teaching

The following aspect concerns choosing an appropriate teaching for your audience. There are five qualities to be considered:

1. **Correct:** The subject matter should be something you have established a correct understanding of as a result of study, reflection and meditation. Although it is not necessary to have a perfect realisation of the material, it is important to have an understanding of the intent of the teaching in order to clearly communicate it to the audience.

2. **Fitting:** Just because you know something, doesn't mean you should teach it. The subject matter should be of interest to your students. A teaching can be considered particularly fitting if it has been specifically requested or your own teacher has asked you to teach it.

3. **Not jumbled:** To teach a subject effectively, it is necessary to have clarity regarding how different aspects of the teachings relate to one another. If points are jumbled in the mind, it will lead to a confusing teaching that will not be beneficial.

4. **Conforms to Dharma:** Every teacher has a different style based on their interpretation of the subject matter. This allows us to adapt the teachings to fit a specific time and place, contextualising the material and making it relevant for our audience. Regardless of the form our presentation takes however, it needs to be in accordance with the Dharma as presented in authoritative scriptures. While the form can change, the meaning should always be preserved.

5. **Appropriate:** A teaching should always be chosen in accordance with the level of understanding present within the audience. For instance, if the audience lacks faith, teaching the foundational subjects may generate inspiration. Knowing those you speak to enables you to tailor your teaching to their needs.

The Qualities of the Teacher

With a topic in mind, the next step is to ensure you generate an authentic motivation for giving the teaching. As our intention determines the karmic consequences of our actions, if we want our teaching to become a support for others to achieve enlightenment, our attitude needs to possess the following aspects:

1. **Amicable:** Before giving a teaching, our mind should be free from manifest afflictions. Giving a teaching when angry or confused will only distort the information and limit its potential benefit. We should instead feel loving-kindness toward those who are receiving our teachings.

2. **Seeks to benefit:** Our only purpose for giving teachings should be to bring benefit to the others. Even if our skills are limited, sharing what we understand with the desire to help, ensures the activity will create the causes for happiness in the future.

3. **Compassionate:** With our aim to help others, we should feel compassion toward our audience and be willing to offer whatever explanations are required to dispel their confusion. This means happily answering questions and repeating ourselves if necessary.

4. **Without consideration for gain:** We do not teach for our own benefit. Our focus should always be on the effect our teaching has on the mind of those listening. Any other outcomes resulting from the process are secondary and should not influence our actions.

5. **Without praising one's own qualities or disparaging others:** Teaching the Dharma is not a competition. We do not need to win over students nor do we need to convince them to abandon other teachers. By concentrating on what we know, students can determine for themselves which teachings they find most beneficial. It is best to remain humble and respectful to ensure the act of teaching does not become tainted by self-cherishing.

The Manner of Presenting the Teaching

With a gathering of students, the appropriate subject matter and the correct attitude, the final aspect is the manner in which the Dharma is presented as this will determine the overall experience of the audience. The following points should therefore be kept in mind: (1) the teaching should be held at an appropriate time and place which is conducive for concentration and minimises distraction; (2) we should demonstrate great respect and devotion toward the Dharma we are teaching; (3) our presentation should be logical and orderly, ensuring each topic is easy to follow; (4) we should use words that clearly communicate the meaning of the teachings; (5) to the best of our ability, those words should bring gladness and joy to the minds of the students, inspiring them to put the instructions into practice; (6) the teachings should fulfil the student's needs so they are satisfied, but still challenge them to consider new ideas; and (7) we should instill confidence by encouraging students to continue studying.

Beneficial Conduct

Through agreeable speech, we transmit the theoretical understanding a student can use to shape their worldview. To convert their knowledge into experience, it is necessary for them to apply it to their lives. Anything we do to encourage this and influence their practice of the Dharma is considered a form of *beneficial conduct*. Our intent here is not to transmit new ideas, but more to indicate how the information they have received can be applied to practice.

The function of beneficial conduct is to cause sentient beings to engage in spiritual practice. We do this by assisting them to form meaningful aims that orient their lives towards genuine happiness and then providing them with instruction for reaching those aims.

Causing Others to Adopt Meaningful Aims

We perform actions with our body, speech and mind to fulfil a desire for something we don't have. Spiritual practice is no different. There needs to be a recognition of some aspect within our present experience that we want to change, for only then are we likely to exert the effort to make it happen. For this reason, the foundation for practice is to first establish a meaningful motivation that represents the future we hope to achieve.

We can have motivations which are provisional and those which are definitive. Provisional motivations are like temporary milestones that provide us with something immediate to hold our attention to prevent us from feeling overwhelmed. The definitive motivation is the ultimate aim we can achieve, that of full enlightenment.

Part of our beneficial conduct is assessing the capacity of students to establish them in a practice that suits their current needs. We can identify three levels of capacity that correspond to the cultivation of three types of practice: (1) the practice of virtue; (2) the practice of ethical discipline and (3) the practice of a liberative path.

Establish in Virtue

The first level of practice is suitable for those dominated by afflictive states of mind such as hatred, attachment and ignorance. As a result of living non-virtuous lives, they experience a constant fear of being attacked, of having their possessions taken away or of being incarcerated. They often find themselves in situations where they have to fight for survival and consequently develop a "kill or be killed" attitude. In society, these types of beings are usually labelled as *criminals*.

Through our beneficial conduct, we establish them in a motivation that desires a virtuous livelihood, as this will allow them to acquire, preserve and increase their wealth by engaging in actions that accord with the Dharma. Our aim is to show them the possibility of earning a living without the need to kill, steal or lie.

As a result of embracing a virtuous livelihood, we can help sentient beings experience a greater degree of peace and harmony in their lives. With their basic needs met, their mind is put at ease, providing them with more leisure time that can be channelled into cultivating spiritual qualities.

Establish in Ethical Discipline

The second level of practice is suitable for those concerned with what will happen after their death. Living a virtuous livelihood, they have acquired the time to reflect on their mortality and have asked themselves what is truly important in life, which generally leads them to a greater interest in spirituality.

For such a person, their main motivation is to be reborn into the pleasurable states of the higher realms such as those of the heavenly gods. Recognising the way to achieve such a rebirth is through the practice of ethical discipline, our beneficial conduct emphasises helping sentient beings abandon their worldly attachments so that they can themselves take ordination as a monk or a nun. This can be done by bestowing the vows for the level of discipline that they are capable of upholding.

As a result of establishing sentient beings in ethical discipline, we help them focus their energy on the cultivation of virtuous qualities. This propels them into higher realms as well as providing them with the basis for engaging in spiritual paths that can ultimately lead them to liberation from suffering and full enlightenment.

Establish in a Liberative Path

The final level of practice is suitable for those open to the transformative aspects of spiritual practice. While those within the previous levels work within the system to establish desirable conditions, at this stage they recognise the system itself is broken, as no matter where they are reborn, they are not completely free and suffering still continues. By contemplating this suffering nature, beings develop a strong desire to completely transcend the system, seeking liberation.

The beneficial conduct for such a being is to help them enter into a spiritual path that has the potential to lead them to liberation. This includes any of the three vehicles of Buddhism: (1) the Foundational Vehicle; (2) the Great Vehicle and (3) the Vajra Vehicle. Whereas the first is capable of leading them out of suffering, the last two are designed to also perfect their qualities and achieve complete enlightenment. Which path we assist others to practice depends on their spiritual development.

The Manner in Which to Bring Them to These Aims

After identifying the level of practice a sentient being is aiming for, we can then provide instruction for achieving that aim. An *instruction* can be understood as advice that indicates how to perform an action which is given to a group of practitioners or as personal counsel to a single individual. For instance, instructions can be received on how to do a prostration or how to meditate on impermanence. This is distinct from a teaching which explains the theory and purpose behind a particular practice. Similar to the way we give a Dharma teaching, there are two main guidelines for giving instruction: (1) the mind that gives instruction and (2) how the instructions should be given.

The Mind that Gives Instruction

Whenever a student requests advice, we should cultivate a virtuous attitude that is conducive to bringing benefit to the student. Before giving instructions you should check for the following qualities:

1. **Compassion:** Make sure you give instruction out of a sincere desire for the sentient being to be free from suffering. If you genuinely care for their welfare, your advice will usually be more effective.

2. **Diligence:** When a student approaches you, you should feel delight in having the opportunity to work for their benefit. There should never be a sense of weariness or aversion toward offering advice.

3. **Humble:** Offer advice with a mind free from conceit, pride and haughtiness. Remember that your knowledge has arisen as a result of the kindness of your teachers and the advice you have received from them. As you are simply passing on what you have been given, there is no reason to consider yourself superior in any way.

4. **Selfless:** When giving advice, your mind should be free of desire for personal gain and instead concerned with the needs of the student and establishing a strong desire to benefit them.

5. **Loving-Kindness:** Cultivate a warm and affectionate heart that feels connected to the person receiving your advice. Think of yourself as a loving parent taking care of their child.

How Instruction Should be Given

Having cultivated an appropriate attitude, your instructions should then be appropriate for the needs of the student. To do this, consider the following points:

1. **Irreproachable:** No matter what level of practice a student is engaged in, our instruction should always be virtuous in nature. We should never advise them to engage in actions under the influence of afflictive states of mind.

2. **Not misdirected:** Our instruction should be clearly identified as provisional or definitive as this will prevent students from developing attachment to a particular practice. We should avoid portraying provisional methods as being definitive which may cause students to become complacent and prevent them from progressing to deeper levels of realisation. For instance, incorrectly teaching that the path is complete after achieving Shamatha.

3. **Systematic:** Instruction should be given in a gradual and systematic way, allowing students to build the necessary skills needed to accomplish the intended results of their practice. Skipping steps or failing to prepare them properly can cause them to practice incorrectly and impact their ability to attain realisations, ultimately wasting their time.

4. **Reaches everywhere:** Our instruction should be given freely to all who request it. We should be unbiased in our guidance and not withhold instruction from those we don't like, in favour of those we do.

5. **According to circumstances:** Each student is unique and therefore they should be guided in accordance with their needs. While teachings are generally given to everyone, instructions should be tailored to meet the specific minds of our students. This is similar to a doctor adjusting a patient's medication to fit their body's chemistry.

Sameness of Purpose

Sacred Dharma is an expression of realisation. It arises from a state of mind that knows reality as it is and is therefore able to communicate that reality to others and provide methods to replicate the experience. To authentically transmit that wisdom, it is necessary to have some degree of realisation into the nature of the subject matter being presented. If our purpose is to bring benefit to others, it is important to develop a personal practice that reflects the advice we give.

By aligning our purpose with the purpose of our students, we effectively demonstrate the conviction we have in the teachings that we ourselves have received. We show our students that just like them, we too seek happiness and freedom from suffering, that we also turn to the Dharma as our refuge and just like them, we put the teachings into practice. In this way, students can see that as we are not hypocritical, they can develop faith in our teachings and such faith allows them to draw benefit from our guidance.

Four Alternatives between Purpose and Practice

Working with the sameness of purpose concerns the way our external behaviour appears to our students. For it to be inspirational, it needs to reflect what they themselves are practicing. This however does not mean our inner practice needs to be the same as theirs. To illustrate the different ways we can work for the benefit of others, we can consider four alternative scenarios: (1) same purpose, different practice; (2) different purpose, same practice; (3) same purpose, same practice; and (4) different purpose, different practice.

Same Purpose but Different Practice

In this situation, although we may have been practicing for many years and have developed considerable realisations, we do not engage in the activity of teaching. Even though our practice is quite advanced, we do not display our qualities but present ourselves as being of equal status to those who are less spiritually developed.

The benefit of doing this is to prevent drawing attention away from the Bodhisattvas who are actively engaged in teaching the Dharma. Displaying our qualities might cause students to lose faith in their teachers, so rather than taking on a teaching role, you work in a supportive capacity to facilitate the study of Dharma taught by others.

Different Purpose but Same Practice

The best way to teach some practitioners is by example. Even if we hold a higher purpose such as achieving enlightenment, we may practice in a way that accords with a more spiritually immature practitioner. For instance, while our ultimate motivation may be Bodhicitta, we may purposefully choose to live an ordinary virtuous life to demonstrate how to live harmoniously in society.

This particular type of practice is more suitable for those who have entered the Path of Habituation and have the ability to manifest emanations. Practicing in such a way prior to having reached this level, we essentially delay our realisations and therefore it is not recommended. Once we become skilled at sending out and gathering back emanations however, we are free to manifest whatever is needed to demonstrate to others how to practice.

Same Purpose and Same Practice

In this scenario, we actively demonstrate the practices we advise others to undertake and is what is usually meant when referring to training in *sameness of purpose*. The idea is that we only teach those practices we have personally experienced through study, reflection or meditation. If for example you have only studied a practice, you would only present it for others to study, you wouldn't give instruction on how to practice it.

The benefit of this form of practice is that you become a role model for others. Everything you do becomes a demonstration of the path, providing inspiration and encouragement for others to practice. As your actions are consistent with your purpose, you instill confidence in your teachings and can be sure that others will receive at least the same degree of benefit you have received yourself.

Different Purpose and Different Practice

The final situation involves a Bodhisattva who from a lack of mindfulness with respect to how their actions affect their students, acts in a way that contradicts the advice they give. As a result, students can become confused and lack faith in the advice they receive. Even if the guidance is correct, they may fail to put it into practice and therefore are not benefited in any way. For this reason, teaching in this way is not recommended.

An example of this would be someone from one spiritual tradition giving advice to someone in another, such as a Buddhist instructing a Christian on practicing Christianity. As the Buddhist does not speak from experience, their advice seems false and is unlikely to be taken seriously. This does not mean however we cannot benefit from dialogue between traditions. It simply means we shouldn't speak for traditions to which we do not belong, but stick to what we know and only offer our perspective to those who request it.

HOW TO PRACTICE BENEFITTING OTHERS

The training for bringing benefit to others is performed differently according to our stage of spiritual development. Initially this practice can be quite limited, but as we progress along the path, our scope broadens to eventually becoming limitless. We will now look at three types of Bodhisattva and how each works for the benefit of others. They include: (1) the Impure Bodhisattva; (2) the Pure Bodhisattva; and (3) the Fully-Matured Bodhisattva.

The Practice of an Impure Bodhisattva

An impure Bodhisattva is a Bodhisattva who operates under the influence of afflictive obscurations. This includes *ordinary Bodhisattvas* who have just entered the Mahayana path and *Arya Bodhisattvas* who have achieved a direct realisation of emptiness. Both types bring benefit to sentient beings by working with the three doors of their experience:

1. **Body:** We restrain our body through the use of ethical discipline which minimises the harm we do to others and also demonstrates how to practice virtuous behaviour. In this way, we accumulate merit and become role-models for the Dharma.

2. **Speech:** In the beginning, we focus on restraining our speech to prevent harming others. Once we have accumulated some degree of wisdom, we share our understanding with others as a Dharma friend.

3. **Mind:** We dedicate ourselves to cultivating virtuous qualities by practicing the Dharma. This removes our afflictive obscurations and expands our capacity to benefit others through our body and speech.

For ordinary Bodhisattvas, the main emphasis should be on working with the mind by training in the *Six Perfections*. It is important to maintain our ethical discipline at this stage but we shouldn't be overly worried about the amount we are benefiting others. Our attention should be on realising emptiness as quickly as possible to cut the flow of karmic conditioning. Once we achieve the state of an Arya Bodhisattva, we enter a process of purification where our focus shifts to the removal of afflictive obscurations. This is when the *Four Methods to Gather a Following* becomes more central to our practice. With our realisation of emptiness, we are free to engage in a much wider range of activities without the danger of accumulating negative karma. As a result we are significantly more qualified to guide others on the path.

The Practice of a Pure Bodhisattva

A pure Bodhisattva has mastered the Six Perfections and has completely eradicated the afflictive obscurations. From the seventh bhumi onwards, such a Bodhisattva is free from karmic conditioning and will never be uncontrollably reborn in samsara. Only the cognitive obscurations remain to be purified, which condition the Bodhisattva's mind to perceive dualistic appearances.

At this point the Bodhisattva's practice is entirely concerned with the *Four Methods to Gather a Following*. Using their extraordinary capacity of mind,

*The Bodhisattva Chenrezig—Manifesting limitless emanations
for the benefit of sentient beings*

their time is spent manifesting emanations to bring benefit to sentient beings throughout the six realms. What differentiates the practice of a pure Bodhisattva from that of an impure Bodhisattva is the presence of seven qualities which allow them to accumulate vast oceans of merit in relatively short periods of time. These qualities are split into two groups: (1) the greatness of their minds and (2) their freedom from afflictions.

Greatness of Mind

The greatness of a pure Bodhisattva's mind is rooted in three qualities enabling them to act without limitations:

1. **Freedom from Bias:** Having removed all self-cherishing, the pure Bodhisattva lacks any desire for personal benefit and so completely dedicates themselves to benefitting others. Their compassion encompasses all sentient beings without exception.

2. **Clearly Realises Entities:** Without the afflictive obscurations distorting their perception, the pure Bodhisattva can know all entities directly and therefore is able to be extraordinarily skilful in their actions.

3. **Practices Continually:** As all laziness has been eradicated, the pure Bodhisattva abides in a perpetual continuity of practice. This is achieved through the extensive use of emanations which constantly manifest and dissolve in the space of the Bodhisattva's mind.

Freedom from Afflictions

The next set of qualities illustrates the quality of experience from the perspective of a pure Bodhisattva:

1. **Serene delight:** Having achieved complete pliancy of body and mind, the pure Bodhisattva is never burdened by their practice. They can exert themselves continually while maintaining a mind filled with delight and free from regret.

2. **Free of adversity:** All the pure Bodhisattva's practices are free from afflictive states of mind and therefore they never harm sentient beings in any way. They avoid following mistaken doctrine and so are also free of afflictive behaviour.

3. **Filled with devotion:** The pure Bodhisattva's mind is suffused with their Buddha-nature and faith in the teachings. Without doubt of any kind, they no longer need to rely on external forms of refuge.

4. **Without attachment:** All forms of attachment have dissolved and the mind of the pure Bodhisattva can abide in a state of equanimity toward all phenomena.

The Practice of a Fully-Matured Bodhisattva

A fully-matured Bodhisattva is one who has completely habituated their mind to the practice of the *Six Perfections* and the *Four Methods to Gather a Following*. By the strength of their habituation they can now engage effortlessly in these practices until they reach Buddhahood. Their practice is distinguished by three qualities:

1. **Intensity:** The fully-matured Bodhisattva's mind manifests virtuous activities spontaneously without the need to exert any effort.

2. **Steadfastness:** During every moment of every day, the fully-matured Bodhisattva completes the accumulation of merit and wisdom.

3. **Complete Purity:** The fully-matured Bodhisattva has perfected all qualities and they achieve the state of complete purity, the final stage before attaining Buddhahood.

Branch Vows Related to Benefitting Others

In total there are twelve branch vows related to the practice of bringing benefit to others. They can be divided into three groups. The first four act as reminders of our duty to stay committed to working for the benefit of others:

1. **Failing to assist others:** This branch vow is broken if we fail to provide counselling, teaching, protection, shelter, guidance and so forth when we have the opportunity and capacity to do so, but instead decline to help due to anger, laziness or other afflictions. This especially applies to situations where we have promised to help.

2. **Failing to care for the sick:** When we have the opportunity to look after a sick person or animal and we fail to do so due to anger, laziness or other afflictions, we are then breaking this vow.

3. **Failing to assist those who are suffering:** This vow is broken if we refuse to help those we see suffering for a variety of reasons. This includes the suffering of the blind, the deaf, the handicapped, those who are exhausted or afflicted by obstacles, those under the influence of malicious thoughts and superstitions and those derided by others.

4. **Not indicating what is proper to others:** If through anger or laziness we fail to skilfully guide those who are wrongly involved in self-centred pursuits motivated only by concerns for this life, who lack consideration for others and are unaware of the Dharma, we are then breaking this vow.

The following six vows indicate how we should train in benefitting others:

5. **Failing to return a benefit received from others:** This branch vow is broken if, motivated by ill-will or laziness, we fail to repay the kindness of others who have helped us and shown us generosity.

6. **Failing to dispel the grief that others are experiencing:** If, due to malice or laziness, we do not work to alleviate the grief of relatives, friends and others who are stricken with misfortune, poverty, depression and so forth, we will then break this branch vow.

7. **Failing to provide food and the like to those who seek it:** If someone asks for charity and we refuse their requests due to ill will or laziness, we are breaking this vow. If, however the aid will cause harm or there are other good reasons not to give, it is appropriate not to respond to their requests.

8. **Failing to assist one's followers:** We break this vow if we fail to give teachings to or do not look after the welfare of the people who trust in us.

9. **Failing to comply with the wishes of others:** If we fail to act agreeably toward others due to laziness or ill will, we break this branch vow. We should at all times avoid arguing with or harming friends, relatives and

others with whom we associate. We should instead show consideration and endeavour to respond to their needs and aspirations, as long as they do not bring harm to themselves or others.

10. **Failing to praise those who deserve to be praised:** We break this vow if, due to ill will or laziness, we do not praise the knowledge or virtuous qualities of others. We should encourage and nurture the good qualities of others and do our best to show an interest in them.

The last two emphasise our responsibility to put an end to negativity:

11. **Failing to suppress those who engage in misconduct:** If, due to laziness or ill will, we do not act to expel, punish or deflate the pride of those who would benefit from this kind of direct treatment, we will then commit a downfall of this vow. Some situations require forceful action to stop harm and we should apply whatever means are deemed necessary by the circumstances.

12. **Failing to use one's miraculous powers:** We should use whatever wrathful or miraculous powers we possess if doing so will benefit other living beings. If we do not use them when appropriate, we break this vow. We should be extremely cautious, however, not to make a display of such powers if it does not serve great benefit, as Bodhisattvas should never show their miraculous powers without a good reason.

THE RESULTS OF PRACTICING IN THIS WAY

Whereas the Six Perfections are designed to habituate us to the wisdom that realises the ultimate nature of reality, the Four Methods to Gather a Following are designed to habituate us to manifesting for the benefit of others. Together they produce the two enlightened bodies of the Buddha—the Dharmakaya truth body and the Rupakaya form bodies. While the qualities of a Buddha are immeasurable, we can summarise them as follows:

1. **Unsurpassed True and Complete Enlightenment:** By practicing with diligence in all the trainings, the Buddha has removed all obscurations, both afflictive and cognitive.

2. **Unparalleled Qualities:** On the basis of abiding in the sublime emptiness that is filled with all possibilities and in a state free from all limitations, the Buddha's infinite qualities spontaneously manifest for the benefit of sentient beings.

3. **Worthy of Being Venerated:** After fulfilling the needs of limitless sentient beings with unobstructed emanations, the Buddha is worthy of being venerated by all who abide in samsara and nirvana.

4. **Foremost of All Beings:** By striving to practice in accordance with a true spiritual being, they have perfected the liberative results and now manifest as a fully enlightened Buddha. They are the perfection of method and wisdom.

5. **Possessing a Body Adorned by the Marks and Signs:** By practicing every possible type of virtue, the Buddha manifests a supreme Nirmanakaya form with the *Thirty-Two Major Marks of a Great Being* and the *Eighty Secondary Signs.* Every aspect therefore represents the purity of their mind.

6. **Abides in the Seat of Enlightenment:** The Buddha's mind abides continuously at the seat of enlightenment—the immutable, thoroughly-established nature that is sublime emptiness. Even though they constantly manifest form bodies for the benefit of sentient beings, their mind never sways from this vajra state.

7. **Achieves the Supreme Meditative Concentration:** From the supreme meditative concentration of immutable bliss, the Buddha accomplishes all meditative concentrations and can manifest any state of mind with ease.

8. **Possesses the Four Forms of Purity:** Through constantly striving in the purity of practice, the Buddha manifests four forms of purity—the *Nirmanakaya* purity of the physical support, the *Sambhogakaya* purity of mental objects, the *Svabhavikakaya* purity of the mind, and the *Jñana-Dharmakaya* purity of primordial wisdom.

REVIEW OF KEY POINTS

- The Four Methods to Gather a Following are: (1) generosity; (2) agreeable speech; (3) beneficial conduct; and (4) sameness of purpose.

- There are three forms of Agreeable Speech: (1) speech that is friendly; (2) speech that is pleasing; and (3) speech that contains the Dharma.

- When teaching the Dharma, you should (1) correct your students' attitudes so they are prepared to receive the Dharma; (2) select an appropriate teaching for your audience; (3) adjust your attitude before teaching; and (4) present the teaching in an appropriate manner.

- Beneficial Conduct should be used to (1) cause sentient beings to adopt a meaningful aim; and then (2) provide those beings with instruction for the way to practice.

- There are three types of practice students should aim for: (1) the practice of virtue; (2) the practice of ethical discipline; and (3) the practice of a liberative path.

- There are four alternatives for how to relate one's purpose to one's practice: (1) same purpose, different practice; (2) different purpose, same practice; (3) same purpose, same practice; and (4) different purpose, different practice. The first three are considered part of the training in Sameness of Purpose while the last should be avoided.

- The Four Methods to Gather a Following are practiced differently depending on your spiritual development. There are three levels of practice: (1) the practice of an impure Bodhisattva; (2) the practice of a pure Bodhisattva; and (3) the practice of a fully-matured Bodhisattva.

- The four branch vows that remind us of our duty to benefit others are to avoid: (1) failing to assist others; (2) failing to care for the sick; (3) failing to assist those who are suffering; and (4) not indicating what is proper to others.

- The six branch vows that indicate how to benefit others are to avoid: (1) failing to return a benefit received from others; (2) failing to dispel the grief that others are experiencing; (3) failing to provide food and the like to those who seek it; (4) failing to assist one's followers; (5) failing to comply with the wishes of others; and (6) failing to praise those who deserve to be praised.

- The two branch vows which emphasise our responsibility to remove negativity are to avoid: (1) failing to suppress those who engage in misconduct; and (2) failing to use one's miraculous powers.

- The result of perfecting the training in the Four Methods of Gathering a Following are: (1) unsurpassed true and complete enlightenment; (2) unparalleled qualities; (3) worthy of being venerated; (4) foremost of all beings; (5) possessing a body adorned by the marks and signs; (6) abiding in the seat of enlightenment; (7) achieving the supreme meditative concentration; and (8) possessing the four forms of purity.

PART THREE

Preparing the Mind for Tantra

CHAPTER FOURTEEN

How to Practice the Kalachakra Path

The Jonang-Shambhala Tradition represents the unification of two great lineages—the sutric lineage of *Zhentong Madhyamaka* and the tantric lineage of *Kalachakra Tantra*. Both are fundamental to Jonang practitioners, providing extremely efficient methods for achieving profound realisations. To understand how enlightenment can be achieved through following this system, this chapter will examine the methods used and how to put them into practice.

Although the Jonang have a robust philosophical tradition, it is not their main focus. Since the time of Khunpang Thukje Tsondru, the Jonang have always placed emphasis on practice and the need to experience the primordial awareness of the ultimate nature of reality. With the clear objective of realising Buddha-nature, all else is considered a support for this outcome.

In times past, due to this approach, it was not uncommon for young monks with minimal reading skills to participate in a three year retreat and be introduced to the completion stage practices of the Six Vajra Yogas. At such an early age, they had not yet built the same degree of conceptual constructs as an adult and therefore a skilful master could introduce them to the nature of their mind with greater ease. Even without an understanding of what was taking place, a student could still develop a connection with their Buddha-nature which could then be nurtured and expanded upon throughout the course of their life.

As a result of degenerating times, the capacity of the students to be guided by masters began to deteriorate and this original purpose became less emphasised. While the tradition still continues to this day, it now serves as a way of blessing the mind of participants to create a strong connection with the *Sublime Realm of Shambhala* and the practice of *Kalachakra*. Once familiarity with the different practices is established, students either continue to practice in strict retreat or expand their understanding through an in-depth study of the Sutras and Tantras. Either way, everyone starts with a foundation of experience.

Such an experiential approach recognises that this human life is too precious to waste in the mere accumulation of conceptual understanding. As all concepts are provisional in nature, eventually they must be abandoned. Striving to make every second count by bringing the Dharma into our experience provides the skilful means of realising the definitive truth of our reality.

While this Jonang system of realisation works well in Tibet where monastic training often starts at an early age, the conditions are substantially different for Western students who generally encounter the Dharma as adults. Having already accumulated numerous concepts and beliefs regarding how the world exists, most adult practitioners begin practice with a mind oriented toward worldly pursuits. A different approach to engaging with the Kalachakra Path is therefore necessary. While the emphasis is still placed on practice, a number of initial remedial steps need to be taken.

In the early stages, the first major obstacle most Western students encounter is the *cultural difference* between the view of someone accustomed to Buddhism from an early age compared to growing up in a non-Buddhist environment. For instance, in most industrialised Western cultures there is a significant lack of understanding regarding the functioning of the mind, as their society focuses on physical phenomena. This is the opposite view to that held in Buddhism, where the mind is seen as primary. To remove the various biases and wrong views we have constructed, we need to analyse our present view of reality and establish a philosophy that is conducive to spiritual practice.

A *lack of faith* in a spiritual path is another obstacle that arises for many Western students. Growing up in a predominantly non-Buddhist environment and seeking a culturally different form of spirituality often indicates a scepticism or loss of faith in the wisdom traditions available to them. Although they may know what path they don't want to follow, they are still unsure of which path to take and so can be indecisive about committing to practicing anything. Consequently, there is considerable experimentation with different systems, resulting in a bouncing from tradition to tradition without stability or consistency. The only remedy for this is time and experience. The more that is learnt about one particular system, the more sense it makes and eventually confidence is developed so that we stop "seeking" and start "doing".

This is the ideal moment to begin practicing the *Kalachakra Path*. Having studied the teachings for a time, a general understanding of how the path works is formed and many of our afflicted doubts have been exhausted. We recognise that to experience the results described by the teachings requires greater seriousness and commitment. We do not have to cut ourselves off from what we have previously learned; it simply means choosing a path that can function as the heart of our practice. We take a single path as primary, a home base that brings stability and depth to our activities, and consider everything else to be a secondary support. With this attitude, we are ready to explore the specific features which make the practice of Kalachakra so unique.

THE VAJRAYANA APPROACH TO PRACTICE

Up to this point, our study of practice has been from the perspective of general Mahayana Buddhism, relying specifically on the teachings of the *Sutras of the Third Turning* and the treatises of the *Bodhisattva Maitreya* and *Arya Asanga*. This material has provided us with a theoretical foundation consistent with the teachings found in the *Kalachakra Tantra*. As we now progress to the actual system of practice, we transition from Mahayana to Vajrayana and therefore need to also shift the nature of our approach. This shift can be summarised in three points: (1) belief in our innate purity; (2) pure perception of the nature of reality and (3) working with the subtle body. We will now examine each point in greater detail.

Belief in Our Innate Purity

The ground of all Vajrayana practice is the innate purity of Buddha-nature. As it is completely free from all adventitious defilements, we are able to practice a path to reveal it. If our afflictions were an innate part of our nature, there would be nothing we could do about them and so practicing a path would be pointless.

Recognising this, the basic premise of Vajrayana practice is that we already have everything we need to manifest enlightenment. Our nature is primordially pure and this purity can be revealed through a process of purification. It is a subtractive approach in which the outer layers are peeled away until nothing remains but our essential nature.

From the perspective of Kalachakra, this purity is not a mere absence, but a sublime union of immutable bliss and empty-form—a field of infinite possibilities in which all enlightened qualities are simultaneously present. This reality is the definitive truth and is the experience we are trying to achieve. Everything else is a provisional truth, leading to that experience of reality as it is.

Pure Perception of the Nature of Reality

The Vajrayana approach to the path is built on the recognition that the result has the same nature as the ground. Whether we experience that ground as samsara or nirvana is based on the nature of our view. While the suchness never changes, our dualistic experience of it does. Tantric practice seeks to establish a view from the perspective of ultimate truth—a view that is completely free from all conceptual fabrications which obscure the nature of reality.

For this reason, the methodology is to recognise the purity of our ordinary experience by developing *pure perception*. Rather than grasping onto phenomena from the perspective of ignorance, we apply wisdom to the appearances that arise, revealing them to be pure manifestations of our Buddha-nature. When we have effectively integrated all appearances into this wisdom, our mind will be completely purified and able to abide in suchness.

Working with the Subtle Body

Philosophically speaking, the Vajrayana View is consistent with the Zhentong View of the Third Turning. What truly distinguishes this vehicle is its profound understanding of the relationship between the body and mind. Only in the teachings of Highest Yoga Tantras such as Kalachakra do we find detailed descriptions of the subtle energetic system that acts as a bridge between the physical and nonphysical.

Through the manipulation of this system, Vajrayana practitioners can cut the conceptual movement of their mind and manifest a non-conceptual experience of suchness. This experience can then be refined and expanded through a host of specialised techniques that rapidly dissolve habituation to dualistic grasping. In this way, what would normally take a bodhisattva billions of lifetimes to achieve can be accomplished within a single human lifetime.

Based on this understanding, many Vajrayana practices involve the use of elaborate visualisations. While the symbolic meaning of these meditations is an important method for cultivating greater wisdom regarding our experience, they also serve the purpose of purifying the channels and winds of our subtle body. When we dedicate ourselves to these practices, we shape the way our subtle body functions, transforming it into a suitable foundation for achieving enlightenment.

THE STRUCTURE OF THE KALACHAKRA PATH

Before entering the Kalachakra Path, it can be helpful to study the relationship between the different practices to understand how they fit together. The following overview highlights the key points of the path, providing a basic roadmap to follow for your own practice. Specific details for how to practice are covered in the remainder of this book and in Book Three of this series.

Many centuries ago, Jonang meditators would receive these practices in an experiential manner. Their teacher would bestow the teachings of a single practice and the student would then dedicate themselves to it until they achieved the signs of accomplishment. Recognising when the student was ready, the teacher would then bestow the next practice and the process would be repeated. In this way, the entire sequence would unfold in a controlled manner leading to perfect realisation.

Over time, it became tradition to give all the teachings at once in the form of a single three year group retreat. The first time a practitioner engaged in such a retreat, emphasis was mainly on receiving the necessary transmissions and establishing clarity regarding the way to practice each stage. After completing the group retreat, practitioners could continue in a private retreat, progressing through the path at their own pace.

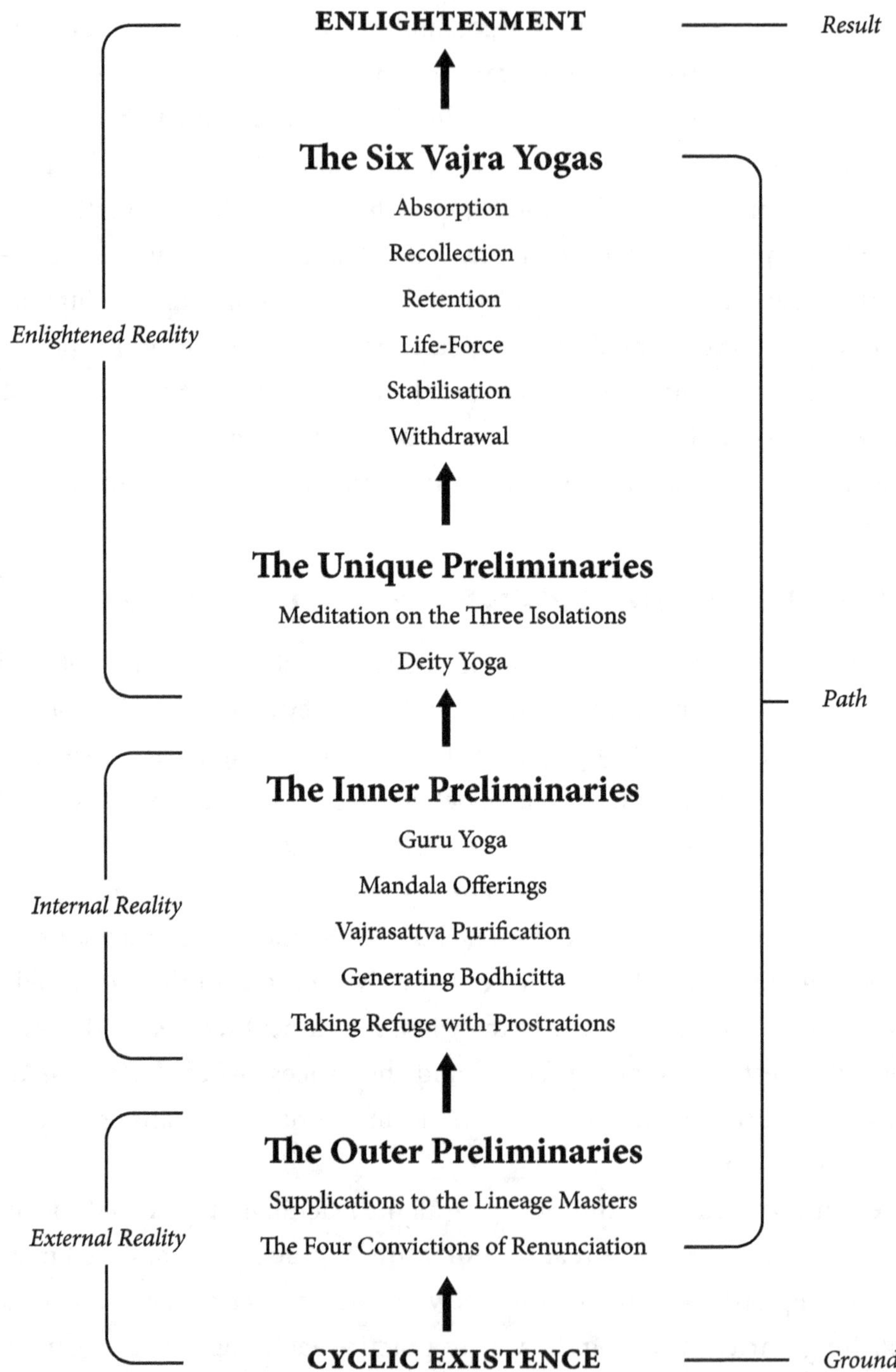

Figure 14-1: The Kalachakra Path to Enlightenment

Whether the retreat is based on accomplishments or on time, all the practices can be divided into two groups: (1) preliminary practices and (2) main practices. In a traditional three year retreat, approximately one year is spent on the preliminaries and two years on the main practices. This is only a general guideline as the time spent on each practice depends on the spiritual maturity of the retreat participants.

Preliminary Practices

The function of the preliminary practices is to purify the mind of gross and subtle grasping to help the dualistic consciousness become dormant. The aim is to bring the mind to a non-conceptual state that can be used to realise suchness. This is likened to trying to find a precious jewel hidden deep in the ground. After identifying where the jewel is located, a plan is formed to dig down to it. Since it is buried beneath many layers of rock and earth, great determination is required. Eventually with perseverance, we finally reach our destination. By clearing away the last layer of fine debris, the brilliance of the jewel is finally revealed.

In a similar way, there are three sets of Kalachakra preliminaries and each works with increasingly more subtle obscurations in order to create the conditions for realising our Buddha-nature. These preliminaries are: (1) the Outer Preliminaries; (2) the Inner Preliminaries and (3) the Unique Preliminaries.

Outer Preliminaries

The *Outer Preliminaries* are designed to dissolve our attachment to cyclic existence. If we fail to recognise its suffering nature, we will not make the effort to engage in spiritual practice. These preliminaries consist of two practices:

1. **Four Convictions of Renunciation:** This is the practice of contemplating the four topics of: (1) the karmic law of cause and effect; (2) the suffering nature of samsara; (3) the preciousness of a human rebirth and (4) the impermanent nature of this life. Their purpose is to turn us away from the *Eight Worldly Dharmas* and turn us towards the practice of *Sacred Dharma*.

2. **Supplications to the Lineage Masters:** This is the practice of developing awareness of the lineage masters through whom the Kalachakra teachings have been transmitted since the time of the Buddha. The main purpose is to fill the mind with devotion towards the lineage and inspire us to follow in their footsteps.

As a result of practicing the Outer Preliminaries, we are no longer interested in samsaric activities and our attention shifts to the achievement of genuine peace and harmony through the practice of the *Kalachakra Path*. This is like realising that a precious jewel is buried beneath the earth and knowing how to find it.

Inner Preliminaries

The practices of the *Inner Preliminaries* are designed to dissolve our gross conceptual mind and establish an experiential view that can be later refined through subsequent practices. This work focuses primarily on realising the emptiness of imputed natures which keep us bound to a dualistic perspective. There are five practices within this set:

1. **Taking Refuge:** The first obstacle to practicing a path is the belief that we can do it on our own. To overcome this *pride*, we engage in the practice of taking refuge in the Three Jewels while making physical prostrations. This ensures we have the necessary supports for practice, while the prostrations purify the subtle channel system, allowing the winds to flow more effectively. When the winds are free from obstruction, it is considerably easier to meditate and achieve states of meditative concentration.

2. **Generating Bodhicitta:** The next layer of obstacles is the afflicted minds which are rooted in *self-cherishing*. As long as the mind is dominated by self-cherishing thought, bias will be sustained, giving rise to attachment and aversion from which arise all derivative afflictions. To realise the empty-nature of our mistaken projections, we need to cut self-cherishing and maintain our focus on others. This allows our virtuous qualities to grow immeasurably, ensuring our practice of Kalachakra becomes a cause for full enlightenment.

3. **Vajrasattva Purification:** In this practice we use the wisdom-deity Vajrasattva as a support for dissolving our *gross self-grasping*. Through various visualisations and the recitation of mantra, we are reminded of the innate purity of our mind and that everything we identify with is merely an imputed reality with no inherent existence. When used as a meditation on emptiness, this practice leads to a conceptual realisation of the selflessness of persons.

4. **Mandala Offerings:** Just as the dependently arisen self is empty of all imputations, so too are all the phenomena of our external world. To overcome *grasping onto phenomena*, we practice offering the universal mandala to the enlightened beings. In this way we are reminded of the illusory nature of all things and that they are inseparable from our own mind. By offering these appearances we generate vast stores of merit that energise our practice and help us access the most profound layers of our experience.

5. **Guru Yoga:** The final obstacle to work with at this level is the mind which grasps onto the *subtle dualistic perspective of consciousness*. To dissolve this grasping we place our attention on achieving the non-dual awareness of Buddha-nature. When we stop perpetuating the dualism of a subject and object, these propensities lose their power and become purified. In this practice we learn to loosen our ordinary dualistic view and surrender ourselves to our true nature which is visualised in the form of our spiritual guide. By making supplications to the Guru, we strengthen our aspiration to realise our Buddha-nature and through meditating on our indivisibility with the Guru, we are reminded that this is already our innermost truth.

Thoroughly familiarising ourselves with these preliminary practices greatly reduces our grasping onto the gross appearances of the dualistic mind. This is like drilling down through many layers of sediment and rock to come within the vicinity of the precious jewel. All that now remains is to separate our awareness from the very subtle layers of grasping that prevent our Buddha-nature from manifesting clearly.

Unique Preliminaries

The above preliminary practices are common across all Vajrayana traditions and although they may be practiced slightly differently, the intended result of reducing grasping onto gross phenomena is generally the same. The following set of preliminaries are called the *Unique Preliminaries* as they are specific to the Kalachakra system of practice. Emphasis is placed on establishing the single-pointed concentration of Shamatha in a manner which facilitates the main practice of the Six Vajra Yogas.

The unique preliminaries consist of two practices which require tantric empowerment and instruction before they can be undertaken. This ensures you have a grounding in the tantric vows and sacred commitments necessary to practice these techniques authentically. The two practices are:

1. **Deity Yoga:** This practice is given after receiving the *Seven Empowerments of a Growing Child* which authorises the practice of the Kalachakra Generation Stage. It involves visualising oneself as an enlightened deity and the recitation of the Kalachakra mantra. This practice establishes a *divine pride* which identifies itself with the enlightened nature of Kalachakra. Through the use of mantra, it purifies the subtle channels and winds, shaping the subtle-energy system and enabling it to be used effectively in the main practices of the completion stage.

2. **Meditation on the Three Isolations:** Whereas deity yoga focuses on pacifying the subtle winds and establishing a subtle state of awareness, the actual state of single-pointed concentration is achieved through the practice of the Three Isolations. Instruction for this non-conceptual practice is only given after receiving the *Four Higher Empowerments* which authorise the practice of the Kalachakra Completion Stage. Its main purpose is to habituate the practitioner to the process of dissolving the gross dualistic mind and resting the awareness in the unconfigured space of the foundational consciousness.

As a result of practicing the unique preliminaries, we can bring our mind to a state of absorption that is very close to suchness. This is similar to standing in the doorway of a room; to enter, all that is needed is to step over the threshold.

Main Practices

When a mind has become fully ripened through the preliminary practices, it is ready to enter the main practices of the Kalachakra Path—the *Six Vajra Yogas*. The purpose of these profound methods is to establish an immutable state of absorption on suchness, which is then used to eradicate both the afflictive and cognitive obscurations. Through the incredible power of this absorption, it is possible to progress to the state of a fully-matured Bodhisattva within a single day; a feat which would normally take billions of years to accomplish using a grosser mind.

In order to realise suchness, it is necessary to transcend our conceptual mind and abide in non-dual awareness, therefore we cannot rely on conceptual meditations that perpetuate subtle forms of dualistic grasping. Although it is possible to release this grasping by resting the mind in its natural state, the process of refining and becoming habituated to non-dual awareness can take considerable time, depending on the spiritual maturity of the practitioner. While many methods are labelled as being "without effort", to maintain the un-distracted realisation of awareness in the face of dualistic perception actually requires significant exertion. To facilitate this process, the Kalachakra system relies on the interdependent relationship between mind and the subtle body.

The approach taken by the Six Vajra Yogas is to dissolve the conceptual mind by bringing the winds into the central channel so that aspects of suchness manifest naturally. On the basis of this realisation, awareness of suchness is then mixed with different types of appearances to dissolve the corresponding forms of subtle grasping. There are four levels of appearances to be purified:

1. **The Waking State:** These are the appearances which rely on the five sensory consciousnesses, such as form, sound, smell, taste and tactile sensation. They are purified by bringing the winds into the central channel.

2. **The Dream State:** These are the objective appearances which rely on the gross mental consciousness, such as thoughts or mental imagery. They are purified when the winds abide in the central channel without movement.

3. **The Deep-Sleep State:** These are the subjective appearances which rely on the subtle foundational consciousness. They are purified by dissolving the winds in the central channel.

4. **The State of Blissful Absorption:** These are the appearances of bliss that rely on a non-dual awareness. They are purified through gathering and melting the subtle essences in the body.

Through these successive stages of practice, increasingly more subtle levels of grasping are purified until eventually all experiences arise as suchness. When this occurs, there is no longer a dualistic support for perpetuating our karmic propensities. Like a wildfire blazing through a forest, all karmic conditioning of the body and mind are completely consumed and our mind becomes liberated from cyclic existence.

Having perfectly refined our realisation of suchness, we attain the *Twelfth Bodhisattva Stage*—the state of a Dharma King in the Sublime Realm of Shambhala. As one abides on the vajra throne of Kalapa, infinite forms are manifested to bring benefit to sentient beings in accordance with the *Four Methods of Gathering a Following*. In this way the accumulations of method and wisdom are quickly completed and the state of a fully enlightened Buddha is ultimately achieved.

ESTABLISHING A FORMAL PRACTICE

With a general overview of the way the Kalachakra Path unfolds, we can now begin the practice. The method we will use is the same as practiced by Jonang masters since the time of Kunkyen Dolpopa and Jetsun Taranatha. As such, we can be confident it has the capacity to transmit a profound blessing on our mind and create the conditions for realisations to manifest.

Known as a *Daily Recitation Practice*, it consists of a single text containing all the preliminary practices in a form that facilitates their daily recitation. The text traditionally used in most Jonang three year retreats is *The Divine Ladder: Preliminary and Main Practices of the Profound Kalachakra Vajrayoga* by Jetsun Taranatha. Taking approximately half an hour to recite from beginning to end, it is an ideal preliminary for use before engaging in the completion stage practices of the Six Vajra Yogas.

To understand how a recitation text works, we need only remember that meditation is about familiarising ourselves with virtuous states of mind. Familiarisation comes from repetition—every time we recite a practice, contemplate its meaning, generate a visualisation or repeat a mantra, we habituate ourselves to certain ideas and the states of mind they help to manifest.

With this in mind a recitation text functions on multiple levels. The most basic form of practice is to simply recite the words out loud to become acquainted with the structure of the text. Understanding the meaning is not necessary at this point as this be can be developed later. Ideally, as time progresses, memorising the words can be helpful to access the text at any time without the need for a physical object. This is obviously good for practicing in environments without light, but more importantly, it has the advantage of allowing your practice to flow. Rather than the constant need to look at the text and turn pages, the mind can instead maintain its inward focus on the meditations.

Internalising the text creates space to build meaning through reflection on the words and this is where we integrate the knowledge acquired from our teachers and from our study. For instance, to expand our understanding of the *Divine Ladder*, reading my book *Hidden Treasure of the Profound Path* provides detailed commentary explaining each line of the root text. The aim at this stage is to not only know what the words mean, but to also establish a clear understanding of each practice and how they relate to the context of the path.

At the next level of practice, the meaning of the text becomes the basis for realisation. We can think of the practices as instruments in an orchestra. Individually they produce their own specific sound but when combined, they form a powerful and dynamic arrangement of harmonious melodies. Likewise, each individual practice produces a specific experience in the mind that can be used as the basis for the experience of the next. Progress through the text effectively builds a multi-layered experience designed to introduce us to the very nature of reality.

Our goal is to become so familiar with the experience of each practice, simply reading the words is enough to trigger the experience. This sort of habituation takes time to develop and therefore requires great patience and determination, which is why it is called a *daily* recitation. Unfortunately it is not enough to practice every now and again when we feel like it. Instead, we need to strive to overcome our laziness and make the experience of the practice an integral part of our lives.

MAKING TIME TO PRACTICE

Over the centuries, Tibetan Buddhism has developed a number of traditions of skilful practice in order to achieve enlightenment. One such tradition consists of performing each of the inner preliminaries 100,000 times for a total of 500,000 repetitions. This was originally introduced as a way of providing practitioners with guidelines for intensive practice, before proceeding to more advanced ones. Within the context of a three year retreat, completing the accumulations was seen as a sign of understanding the practice and readiness to receive and progress to the next teachings. It did not however mean that realisations had automatically been attained.

In recent times, people have commonly taken two extreme views to this practice. There are those who fixate heavily on the numbers and try to accumulate as much as they can in the shortest time possible. For them, the preliminaries are like a race to be rushed through, and consequently they fail to connect with and really feel the practice. On the other side are those who outrightly reject the accumulations. While their preliminaries still allow them to go deeper, without the short-term goals to guide them, their practice tends to flounder without a sense of urgency or strength.

To practice effectively, a balanced approach is needed, as a steady progression along the path gives us sufficient time to generate realisations. I therefore recommend dedicating a particular amount of time to each stage of your practice. For instance, for the practice of taking refuge while making prostrations, rather than focusing on the number of prostrations you complete, identify the number of hours each day you can dedicate towards the practice and for how long you intend to maintain that discipline. In this way you set a specific goal without getting stressed about meeting daily quotas.

This approach is flexible and allows adjustment to the changing conditions of your life. Continuing with the refuge and prostration example, approximately 480 hours is generally recommended. If you are currently living an engaged lifestyle, you may be able to dedicate a few hours each day to the practice, in which case it would be completed in approximately eight months. If however, conditions come together to do a full-time retreat, you could potentially practice eight or twelve hours a day and complete the recommended time much quicker.

The following table provides some suggestions and estimates for how much time to dedicate to each practice in order to develop a good grounding for each before moving to subsequent practices. As every individual has unique karmic conditions, some practices may take more or less time, therefore it is always recommended to work closely with your spiritual guide to adjust your practice as needed.

Practices	Hours	1hr / day	2hr / day	8hr / day
Outer Preliminaries	960	32 months	16 months	4 months
Four Convictions of Renunciation	*840*	*28 months*	*14 months*	*3.5 months*
Supplications to the Lineage Masters	*120*	*4 months*	*2 months*	*2 weeks*
Inner Preliminaries	1920	64 months	32 months	8 months
Taking Refuge with Prostrations	*480*	*16 months*	*8 months*	*2 months*
Generating Bodhicitta	*480*	*16 months*	*8 months*	*2 months*
Vajrasattva Purification	*480*	*16 months*	*8 months*	*2 months*
Mandala Offerings	*240*	*8 months*	*4 months*	*1 month*
Guru Yoga	*240*	*8 months*	*4 months*	*1 month*
Unique Preliminaries	1200	40 months	20 months	5 months
Deity Yoga	*480*	*16 months*	*8 months*	*2 months*
Meditation on the Three Isolations	*720*	*24 months*	*12 months*	*3 months*
Six Vajra Yogas	5760	192 months	96 months	24 months
Withdrawal	*960*	*32 months*	*16 months*	*4 months*
Stabilisation	*960*	*32 months*	*16 months*	*4 months*
Life-Forcev	*960*	*32 months*	*16 months*	*4 months*
Retention	*960*	*32 months*	*16 months*	*4 months*
Recollection	*960*	*32 months*	*16 months*	*4 months*
Absorption	*960*	*32 months*	*16 months*	*4 months*
TOTALS	**9840**	**27.5 years**	**13.5 years**	**3.5 years**

Table 14-1: Suggested times for practice

You may think that spending thirteen years on study, reflection and meditation seems like a lot, but just consider the total number of hours that an average person has available to them in their life. For someone who lives to be eighty years old, their life consists of 691,200 hours. That means that to establish the path in our mindstream, we only need to dedicate 2% of our total lifespan. If you were to use every single moment of your day and night to practice this path, you could complete the 9840 hours in a little more than one year's time. Even if you only dedicate two hours a day, that is still only 8% of each day. When we consider the infinite benefit that we would receive from such a small investment of our time, there is really no excuse not to make the effort.

GENERAL ADVICE FOR A SUCCESSFUL PRACTICE

To help make the most of your recitation practice, I would like to offer the following points of advice. They are not hard and fast rules, but friendly suggestions to guide you past some common pitfalls.

Build Your Practice Gradually

When taken as a whole, the Kalachakra Path with its many practices can appear daunting and overwhelming to the beginner. Feelings of uncertainty are completely normal and need not be a cause for panic. It merely indicates a lack of familiarity with the practices, which is to be expected in the beginning.

Fortunately, this problem is easy to remedy by simplifying your recitation into stages and slowly building your practice over time. For instance, when starting out, focus on the the *Four Convictions of Renunciation*. Recite the verse, reflecting on its meaning and spend the remainder of the session practicing placement meditation, working with your breath or whatever object of meditation you feel is most suitable.

Once familiarity with this practice is established, move to the next step by reciting *Supplications to the Lineage Masters*. Spend the time to get to know their names and read their stories. You can find short biographies of each master in *Hidden Treasure* or more extensive histories in my book *Demystifying Shambhala*.

You could begin your session by first reciting the Four Convictions, and settling your mind through mindfulness of breathing. As you then recite the lineage prayers, you could pause at the names of the masters you would like to know more about and then read their history. This builds a connection between the verses and the story, helping you draw inspiration from the practice. When you are finished studying, continue with the recitation.

Letting your practice evolve slowly over time incorporates the complexity of the path in a gradual manner, step by step. As your focus shifts to a new practice, use the previous steps as its preliminaries and eventually you will become quite comfortable reciting the entire text from beginning to end.

Work with What You Have

Reading about the great yogis who have practiced the Kalachakra Path before us can sometimes create the belief that living in a cave on a remote mountain top is the only real way to practice. Based on this idea, we generate a particular image of what the "perfect" conditions are, and often wait for the day for them to arise so we too can properly start a practice.

This type of thinking only diverts our attention away from the conditions present in our lives and onto a potential future that doesn't yet exist. Rather than working with what is actually arising in our experience, we are too busy complaining about what is missing. This form of procrastination prevents us from ever really applying ourselves to our practice.

A much more beneficial attitude is to focus on our present conditions and identify the opportunities we can use to practice. Recognising that each day presents its own challenges, we can be content with things as they are. This develops a resilience toward whatever arises and we become skilled in finding creative ways to make the most of any given situation.

This of course does not mean we cannot seek conducive conditions. Having meaningful aspirations is an important part of practice but we don't have to experience aversion toward our current reality simply because it doesn't match our hopes. There is no contradiction between accepting the present for what it is, while still working to create the causes for our aspirations to manifest.

Don't be Afraid to Mix It Up

Anything we repeat on a daily basis risks becoming stale or boring. To avoid this danger in our practice, we can make use of alternative texts for the individual practices, such as when reciting the Divine Ladder, there are three Guru Yoga practices: (1) *Rain of Blessings* by Dolpopa Sherab Gyaltsen; (2) *The*

Anchor for Collecting Siddhis by Taranatha or (3) *The Foundation Guru Yoga.* You can feel free to use whichever text suits you at a particular time.

You can even choose to recite an entirely different text such as *Enlightening the Heart: A Secret and Profound Life Practice of Kalachakra Tantra.* I wrote this recitation text to facilitate learning the various meditations: it contains a number of expanded visualisations that are useful for enriching your understanding of the Divine Ladder. While I generally recommend focusing on the Divine Ladder due to its enormous blessings, there may be some who find Enlightening the Heart more suited to their karmic propensities.

As our practice should inspire the mind, incorporating different texts and methods can help us remain engaged and motivated. Practice shouldn't be viewed as a chore you resent, but as something you look forward to, like a special gift to yourself. After all, through your practice of the Kalachakra Path, you have the extraordinary opportunity to explore the nature of your mind and to connect with genuine happiness—a precious jewel indeed!

Avoid Thinking in Black and White

One tendency I see in many Western students is to think in very strict terms of the "right way" and the "wrong way". They approach their practice with a rigid mindset where everything must be exactly correct and they feel a great anxiety about making mistakes. As a result of grasping so tightly to the form of their practice, they often create many unnecessary obstacles for themselves.

The mind is not a black and white phenomena and its nature does not fit neatly into a box. When we lack flexibility in our practice, we fight against the nature of our mind, forcing it to be something it is not. This creates a barrier preventing us from going deeper, causing us to become stuck on the surface where we never actually taste the essence of our practice.

To overcome this obstacle, we should concentrate our effort on understanding the nature of each practice. We of course need to learn the instructions and practice in accordance with them, but we don't have to grab onto them as being set in stone. Investigate why the practice is structured the way it is, what its purpose is, and how that purpose is achieved. Reflect on its context and how it relates to the other practices.

With the development of such clarity comes the possibility of knowing how to adapt to different situations. Instead of forcing life to fit into the practice, use the practice to work with life. This is when the transformative capacity of the Dharma is revealed and our mind opens to new potentials. With greater flexibility, our attitude is more relaxed and our mind can rest in equanimity. Practice then becomes more enjoyable and easier to sustain.

Furthermore, when focusing on the meaning, the specific form our practice takes matters less, as making the connection is what is really important. This is illustrated in the story of a woman who recited a mantra that allowed her to transform rocks into food. Becoming proficient in the practice, she was able to save her entire village from starvation during a famine. One day her monk son heard her reciting the mantra and noticed she mispronounced one of the words. He told her to use the "correct" pronunciation but when she followed his advice, the new mantra didn't work. She subsequently abandoned it and went back to reciting it the way she had always done.

If you find yourself worrying about details, such as how mantras are pronounced in Sanskrit as opposed to Tibetan, then just remember the lady of the story. Choose a form you feel connected to, that communicates the meaning in a way you can understand. Likewise, when reciting your practice text, great blessings come from reciting in Tibetan, but if you don't understand the meaning of what you are saying, you are just making sounds. Therefore familiarise yourself with the practices using a language you understand, so you know what you are saying, then once you make the connection, you can recite in Tibetan if this is of interest or inspiration to you.

The Preliminaries are the Main Practice

In modern goal-oriented societies, there is a tendency for people to think the preliminary practices are secondary to the main practices. We have this notion that the higher practices are the most important and everything else can be skimmed across in order to jump straight to ultimate realisations. On the basis of this way of thinking, the preliminaries become a chore we want to get through as quickly as possible. We don't want to do them, but we know our teacher won't give us the higher practices until we do. It is just like a child who suffers through eating their vegetables because their mother has promised them ice cream.

The problem with this mentality is that it fails to recognise the crucial role the preliminaries play in creating the conditions for the higher realisations to manifest. To understand this relationship, we can think of a jigsaw puzzle. The only way to experience the final image is to put all the pieces together. If one piece is missing, the image is incomplete. Likewise, the entire Kalachakra Path is designed to produce a single, highly concentrated state of mind. That mind is the sum total of a whole series of secondary minds, so that if any are missing, the desired result cannot be produced.

The names "preliminary" and "main" are simply labels used to differentiate the practices. If we really think about it, each and every practice is a preliminary to the final moment before achieving enlightenment. Your main practice is therefore whatever practice you are currently focused on, which depends entirely on where you are on your spiritual journey. For some people the main practice is renunciation, for others it's purification. Whatever it is, the practices which precede it are fundamental conditions for achieving success.

Embrace the Process

In a world filled with weekend training seminars, three hour workshops and self-help apps, it is easy to develop an expectation that our practice will produce immediate results. We seem to be in a constant search for pearls of wisdom that will bring instant gratification to our lives. If a practice takes effort, we tend to look for ways to make it easier and more agreeable to our sensibilities. Rather than letting the Dharma change us, we try to change the Dharma and as a result, we end up diluting the teachings, preventing them from producing their intended outcome.

At the root of this problem is the belief that our practice is separate from our life. When life is good, we see no need to practice, but when it is bad, we scramble to find something to fix it. This behaviour shows a lack of wisdom that comes from focusing too narrowly on one's immediate experience.

To counteract this tendency, it can be helpful to view spiritual practice as a *lifelong project*; a process of development that starts from the moment you step onto the path, and continues until the moment you die, and beyond. By thinking in this way you integrate all of life's ups and downs into the context of your practice and although you see each day as an opportunity to progress, you recognise there are days which are more challenging than others. You may have every intention of practicing but things come up and you find yourself distracted. Instead of becoming disheartened and giving up, simply accept what is occurring, re-establish your intention and try again the following day.

Embracing the process means we don't let setbacks faze us. By taking a long-term perspective we don't need to worry if we stumble every now and again. The key is to always get back on our feet, dust ourselves off and continue moving forward. This is the determination we need in order to achieve our aims. Never think that just because you make mistakes, you are permanently stuck and cannot practice any more. Every moment is an opportunity for a fresh start.

REVIEW OF KEY POINTS

- For Western students, it is recommended to start the Kalachakra Path after having established a foundation in the Buddhist view and developed faith in the Kalachakra system.

- The Vajrayana approaches practice in a different way from other vehicles. This approach is characterised by three points: (1) belief in our innate purity; (2) pure perception of the nature of reality and (3) working with the subtle body.

- The Kalachakra Path is broken into nine preliminary practices and six main practices for a total of fifteen practices in all.

- The preliminaries are broken into three categories: (1) Outer Preliminaries; (2) Inner Preliminaries and (3) Unique Preliminaries. While the outer and inner preliminaries are common to other forms of Tibetan Buddhism, the unique preliminaries are specific to the Kalachakra system.

- The outer preliminaries are focused on removing our attachment to samsara. There are two practices: (1) The Four Convictions of Renunciation and (2) Supplications to the Lineage Masters.

- The inner preliminaries are designed to cut our grasping to gross forms of consciousness. There are five practices: (1) Taking Refuge; (2) Generating

Bodhicitta; (3) Vajrasattva Purification; (4) Mandala Offerings and (5) Guru Yoga.

- The unique preliminaries are used to purify the subtle body and achieve the state of single-pointed concentration. There are two practices in this set: (1) Deity Yoga and (2) Meditation on the Three Isolations.

- The main practices consist of the Six Vajra Yogas which are designed to establish an immutable state of absorption on suchness that can then be used to eradicate both the afflictive and cognitive obscurations.

- The main method to familiarise yourself with the Kalachakra Path is through a daily recitation practice. This involves reciting and meditating on a text such as the Divine Ladder by Jetsun Taranatha.

- It is important to create a practice that is flexible and capable of adapting to the conditions of your life. By establishing time goals for each practice, we ensure we are able to develop familiarity with the entire path during the course of this life.

- Take the time to build your practice slowly in order to avoid being overwhelmed by complexity.

- Instead of waiting for conditions to be perfect in the future, try to focus your attention on the opportunities presenting themselves right now in the present.

- If you find yourself getting bored with your practice, refresh your interest by using alternative practices from different texts.

- Avoid getting too caught up in the form of your practice: instead focus on understanding the essential meaning. This will give you clarity and help you adapt to changing conditions in your life.

- The preliminary practices are fundamental components of the path. Without them, your practice will not be a cause for enlightenment. Therefore, don't think that they are secondary to the Six Vajra Yogas.

- In order to overcome the setbacks and difficulties that arise while practicing, it is important to have a long-term perspective that fully incorporates your practice as a lifelong project.

The Preliminary Practices of Refuge and Bodhicitta

The Buddha taught three ways to make a spiritual practice meaningful. The first is to establish a meaningful motivation that orients the practice toward a beneficial result. As our motivation determines whether an action is virtuous, this step provides the context for everything we do. Without a strong motivation, the results of our practice will be uncertain.

The second is to engage in meaningful actions which accumulate merit and wisdom in our mind. The actions we choose will largely depend on the qualities that we need to cultivate. The Kalachakra Path provides us with the opportunity to do this by using a number of different practices which gradually refine the mind to eventually achieve the perfect realisation of Buddha-nature.

The third way to make spiritual practice meaningful, is to take the merit generated by the main practice and dedicate it toward a meaningful result. This has the effect of connecting the act with a virtuous result, thereby separating it from regular samsaric activity. This division prevents our samsaric actions from corrupting our merit made with virtue and ensures it will give rise to genuine happiness in the future.

Within the context of these three aspects, the first phase of the Kalachakra Path is dedicated to establishing a meaningful motivation which is done through the practice of the inner preliminaries of *Taking Refuge* and *Generating Bodhicitta*. In this chapter we will explore these practices in greater detail, specifically the steps to follow in order to perform them effectively.

USING VISUALISATION EFFECTIVELY

Before we delve into the practices, I would like to say a few words regarding the use of visualisation in meditation, which is used throughout the Vajrayana as a way of training the mind while simultaneously purifying the subtle body. While the word "visualisation" tends to have an overly visual connotation, the actual meaning is closer to the idea of *mind generation.*

When we engage in visualisation practice, we are actively trying to generate a particular experience in the mind. That experience may have visual aspects but it is not purely visual in nature. In fact, the most important aspect of a visualisation is the awareness of the meaning being expressed through visual forms. When we experience that meaning, we can be said to have generated the mind. Without the meaning, our practice lacks context and we are doing little more than creative day dreaming.

The implication of this is that the specific details described in the practices are only guidelines for focusing your attention and reminding you of the main features. It is then up to you to bring those descriptions to life in your own mind so they can trigger the necessary understanding of the meaning. This means that there is no single way that is correct; there is only what works for the mind that is meditating.

Another key point to remember is that authentic visualisation is not imaginary. It is not something that does not exist which you then create from nothing. All appearances have the nature of emptiness, whether they are the gross appearances of our physical senses or the subtle appearances of mental consciousness. As such, they all have the same capacity to support an awareness of reality. The only difference between sensory consciousness and mental consciousness is that we have minimal control over our senses, whereas the mind is much more malleable and able to generate appearances without constraint. When we work with generating specific states of mind, we shift our attention from sensory appearances as the only "reality" and begin to recognise a much deeper and profound layer of experience.

Throughout the practice of the Kalachakra Path we encounter the same basic pattern. First we establish a visualisation, then perform an action in relation to it and finally we dissolve the visualisation. This process is like a wave rising out of the ocean, where it swells up to take a particular shape and then returns back to where it came from. At no point is the wave anything other than water. Likewise, all our visualisations arise from the nature of the mind.

They abide for a time and then dissolve back into that nature. By repeating this pattern over and over, we familiarise ourselves with the way suchness manifests. This prevents us from grasping onto our visualisations as being "real" and instead recognises their provisional nature.

When you first encounter the instructions for a visualisation, the number of details can seem daunting, but don't let this scare you. In the beginning, focus on establishing a feeling for the scene as if you were closing your eyes in a room while maintaining a feel for the space. Even though you can't see the details, you have a sense of where everything is. Once you have this feeling, you can enhance it by slowly adding details, until eventually you become familiar with the visualisation, in the same way you feel at home in a particular space such as your bedroom or workspace.

WARMING-UP WITH THE OUTER PRELIMINARIES

The formal practices of the Kalachakra Path are predominantly concerned with cultivating awareness about the nature of our experience. This is an internal process that requires a temporary disengagement from our ordinary lives. As such, before we are ready to begin cultivating our motivation of refuge and Bodhicitta, we need to transition from an external focus to an internal one. We do this by spending some time reflecting on the outer preliminaries of the *Four Convictions of Renunciation* and by making *Supplications to the Lineage Masters*.

Settling the Body, Speech and Mind

As with any meditation, it is important to settle our body, speech and mind into their natural states so they can provide a conducive support for practice. If our mind is distracted, the subsequent meditations will be ineffective and we will not achieve the results we hope for. For this reason, spend a few moments with any or all of the following methods to help establish a neutral foundation.

Expelling the Stale Air

During the day our winds are conditioned by the many afflicted activities we participate in, so that when we sit down to meditate, there is a buildup of energy related to the three poisons of attachment, aversion and ignorance. These accumulations can be cleared away by a practice known as *Expelling the Stale Air*. The basic instruction is as follows:

> *Begin by closing the left nostril using the Pacifying Mudra and exhale three times through the right nostril, then change to the other nostril. Finish by exhaling three times through both nostrils. Visualise all afflictions and negativity leaving your body in the form of black smoke.*

There are three sets of three breaths, making nine rounds in total. We start with exhaling three times from the right nostril, imagining that we are expelling all the negativity related to attachment. We exhale in three rounds to expel gross, subtle and very subtle obscurations.

The *Pacifying Mudra* mentioned in the verse is created by curling your ring and middle fingers down towards the palm and holding them there with your thumb while the index and little fingers remain straight. If you can't make this gesture don't worry, simply block the nostril with your index finger.

The process is repeated with the left nostril, this time expelling the negativity related to aversion. Again, the three rounds expel gross, subtle and very subtle propensities. This has the effect of clearing the two main side channels and balancing the left and right energies. The final phase is to expel the winds through both nostrils, clearing the negativity related to ignorance. Once you have completed all nine rounds, rest your awareness in the experience for a few moments.

Blessing the Speech

Exhaling the stale breath facilitates a neutral frame of mind. As we are trying to cultivate as much virtue as possible, there are a number of things we can do to enhance our effectiveness, such as blessing our speech. During our recitation practice we recite a variety of verses and mantras. By blessing the speech we recognise that each word is an expression of Dharma and therefore each word we recite brings us closer to enlightenment. The actual practice is as follows:

> *Visualising a red RAM (ཨཾ) syllable on your tongue, imagine that as you recite the mantras, the RAM glows like a burning ember and all the negativities of your ordinary speech are completely burned away.*

OM A AA I II U UU RI RII LI LII E EE OH OOH AM AH SO HA

KA KHA GA GHA NGA | TSA TSHA DZA DZHA NYA | TA THA DA DHA NA | TA THA DA DHA NA | PA PHA BA BHA MA | YA RA LA WA SHA | SHA SA HA KSHA | SO HA

Repeat these mantras as many times as you like.

The first set of syllables represents the vowels of the Sanskrit language and the second set represents the consonants. These sounds are considered sacred as they were used by the Buddha to communicate the teachings. They also have the significance of being the basic building blocks for words which are used to communicate meaning.

Traditionally this technique is used at the start of the day, but it can be used at any time. It is particularly beneficial if you have been engaging extensively in worldly discussion prior to meditation.

Blessing the Mind

A final helpful technique is to remind ourselves of the mind's purity by reciting the short vajrasattva mantra. This ensures we start our meditation with a pure mind that is aware of its ultimate nature. The practice is very simple:

Take a moment to remind yourself that all appearances are in the nature of emptiness. They do not exist inherently in the way you impute them to be. With this awareness, allow all ordinary appearances to dissolve back into the mind and then recite the short Vajrasattva mantra.

OM VAJRASATTVA HUM

After reciting the mantra for a while, rest the mind for a few moments in a non-conceptual experience of the mind's own purity.

These three practices provide us with a blank canvas to work with during our meditation. Having temporarily dissolved the afflicted states of mind, we are now ready to generate the specific qualities of the Kalachakra Path.

Establishing a Connection with the Lineage

Different practice texts approach the order of meditations in slightly different ways. In the case of the outer preliminaries, traditionally we meditate first on the four convictions, followed by supplications to the lineage masters. It is however acceptable to reverse this order, giving the practice a slightly different flavour. To help promote flexibility of mind, here I will present the lineage first and the four convictions second as it is presented in *Enlightening the Heart*. To follow the traditional approach you can refer to my book *Hidden Treasure*.

The reason we meditate on the lineage is to remind ourselves that our ultimate aim is to realise our innate Buddha-nature, also known as the *Absolute Guru*. Through making supplications to the Guru in the form of Vajradhara or as the lineage masters, we form a bond between our present deluded self and our own enlightened nature. The following verses provide an example of how this connection is made.

Lama please hear me, I offer you my complete self.
I offer you my unwavering devotion and trust.
Lama, I and mine are all yours.

We invoke the Lama by establishing an attitude of devotion. This is the mind that recognises that only through realising the ultimate nature of reality are we able to achieve enlightenment.

From the centre of devotion at the lotus of my heart you dwell, glorious and supremely compassionate lama, embodiment of all the liberators. I pray with great devotion, may you rise through my clear and pure avadhuti (central channel) and sit above the crown of my head surrounded by a field of rainbow light. Your form with the divine marks emanating joyful spirit and radiance; your speech cutting through any cloud of doubt; your omniscient mind of divine wisdom and compassion; I supplicate you. May you bless me, I, who have faith and devotion.

We then visualise the lama rising up from our heart to take a seat above the crown of our head, establishing the feeling of their presence. When we ask for blessings, we are asking to receive inspiration to practice in accordance with the authentic teachings of the lineage.

Cast into samsara from overpowering karma without choice, habitual patterns possess me, creating unfortunate karma. I am born with the five poisons. May I transcend this endless deception and unveil my primordial awareness this instant.

Recognising that we have been experiencing suffering since beginningless time, we turn to the lama as our ultimate source of refuge.

I pray to the root and lineage Lamas.
I pray to the lineage of wish-fulfilling jewels.
Please bless me so the lineage transmission will enter within me.
May all these blessings enter my heart!
Please bless me so the darkness in my heart is cleared away!

Over the centuries, the wisdom of the lama has manifested in the minds of the lineage masters and through their dedication to the path, we now have access to these precious teachings. By reciting these verses, we strengthen our desire to practice the unique Dharma of the Vajrayoga lineage, recognising it as the method through which we can achieve lasting freedom.

May my consciousness dwell in the precious Dharma. May my Dharma practice remain secure and on the right path. May all obscurations on my Dharma path be pacified. May all my delusions transform into primordial wisdom.

These last requests strengthen our determination to practice the path and to achieve its results. By cultivating faith in the unbroken lineage of masters and the path they taught, we develop the confidence to face our obscurations and transform our experience. Once the feeling of trust and conviction arises, we should rest the mind naturally in this state for as long as we can.

Contemplating the Four Convictions of Renunciation

No matter how strongly we desire to follow in the footsteps of the lineage masters, as long as we remain attached to worldly pursuits, progress is difficult to make. For this reason the next step is to develop a mind of renunciation that turns away from cyclic existence and towards the practice of Dharma.

This is done through the cultivation of the *Four Convictions of Renunciation*, which are (1) the karmic law of cause and effect; (2) the suffering nature of samsara; (3) precious human rebirth and (4) the impermanence of this human life. These four topics are covered extensively in Book One of this series. Before continuing to the practice of taking refuge, spend some time familiarising your mind thoroughly with these meditations.

Over time as you work with these topics in detail, only a short glance meditation is required to remind you of your previous realisations. The following verses illustrate how to do this.

Karmic Law of Cause and Effect

Just as nature is conditioned and forms of the four elements arise and deteriorate, so it is that karmic causes and conditions dominate everything. I cause my own happiness and unhappiness. May I choose the right action.

In this meditation, the aim is to remind yourself of the role you play in conditioning your own experience. Far from living in a reality where everything is predetermined, you have a choice; you can choose to create causes for suffering or you can choose to create causes for happiness. In this way, you are in control of how your experience will manifest in the future and therefore it is your responsibility to make wise decisions.

Disadvantages of Cyclic Existence

Just as bees work tirelessly for honey, a candle flame attracts the moth, poison appears as an antidote and fish hurry towards the bait, the hook of samsaric pleasure throws us into oceans of suffering. May I have true renunciation of samsara.

When we examine the nature of our present experience, we see that it is unsatisfactory. Regardless of the form we take within the cycle of existence, we will always encounter suffering whether it be gross or subtle and as we fail to recognise this nature, we mistake the causes for suffering for the causes of happiness. Realising that samsara has nothing to offer us, we focus our mind on the achievement of liberation.

Preciousness of a Human Rebirth

A precious human birth is extremely hard to find. If taken to heart, eternal happiness will triumph. If wasted, a rare opportunity is destroyed. May I take action and embrace the essence of this treasure.

To free ourselves from suffering we need the right conditions, as without them, there is no opportunity to practice the Dharma and no opportunity to achieve realisations of the path. As these conditions are extremely rare, when we recognise we have them all, we should do whatever we can to take advantage of our situation.

Uncertainty of the Time of Death

Life is precarious, like a candle flame in the wind. The time of death is unpredictable and the causes of death are many. Conditions for survival cannot be guaranteed. For these reasons, may I never be lazy or procrastinate in my Dharma practice.

Ignorance is believing that something which is impermanent in nature will somehow last. As our precious human life is the result of specific causes and conditions coming together, it is inevitable that it will end. Sooner or later we will die. If we waste this life, doing nothing to create the causes for happiness, we will surely experience greater suffering in the future. For this reason, we need to abandon laziness and apply ourselves wholeheartedly to practicing the path.

TAKING REFUGE WHILE MAKING PROSTRATIONS

The outer preliminaries create a sense of determination to practice the Dharma. We then come to the inner preliminaries where we establish the foundational realisations allowing us to experience our most sacred truth. The first practice to cultivate is that of *Taking Refuge while Making Prostrations*.

There are many reasons to take refuge, such as our innate fear of suffering. We all want to experience happiness and we do not want to suffer. By meditating on the four convictions, we realise we need to change our habits in order to break free from samsara. But where do we start and how do we do it? When a person is drowning, how can they pull themselves from the water? When we reflect on these questions, we realise we cannot do it alone. Therefore we need to search for sources of refuge which have the capacity to help us change our direction.

Taking refuge also comes from developing faith in the teachings. By studying the topics presented in the first two parts of this book, we come to the realisation that the Dharma has the capacity necessary to guide us to liberation. The more we work to apply its principles to our lives, the more wisdom is implanted in our minds. This process increases our confidence, leading us to rely on the Three Jewels.

In the Mahayana, there is a very specific reason to make taking refuge our foundation. Just like us, all sentient beings are suffering due to the conditioning of their mind. To be of maximum benefit in helping them to break free from this cycle, we need to achieve the state of complete enlightenment, as personal liberation is simply not enough to do this. We therefore take refuge because we know that those who have attained the perfect state of enlightenment provide the best possibility for guiding others to that perfection. We turn to the Three Jewels as they represent everything we wish to become.

Through the practice of taking refuge we overcome two major obstacles that prevent our capacity to know reality as it is:

1. **Afflicted Doubt:** When beginning an unfamiliar journey, our mind is often filled with doubt. We question everything we do, causing us to frequently shift direction. The remedy to doubt is to develop clarity regarding the sources of refuge. As we come to understand how the field of refuge supports us on the path, our doubts are reduced in strength. Eventually, we come to the point where our faith in the Three Jewels outweighs our confusion, bringing stability to our practice.

2. **Pride:** The other major obstacle is a mind of pride and arrogance. These afflicted states create barriers to asking for help, without which we cannot internalise the guidance needed to achieve our goals. Pride is also responsible for reinforcing our sense of self-cherishing, which prevents the development of an authentic realisation of Bodhicitta. To remedy this obstacle, we rely on the practice of making prostrations to reinforce our humility and receptivity.

As a result of practicing refuge with prostrations, we give ourselves a solid foundation to build a meaningful motivation.

The Actual Practice

The practice of taking refuge is an integral part of any Buddhist practice. In its simplest form it involves bringing to mind the qualities of the Three Jewels while reciting a *refuge formula*. These verses are often combined with the generation of Bodhicitta as in the following verse:

I go for refuge until I am enlightened
To the Buddha, the Dharma and the Supreme Assembly.
By the virtuous merit created by meditating on the Dharma,
May I attain the state of Buddhahood for the benefit of all beings.

While this type of formula works well to trigger the states of mind we are already familiar with, it lacks the detail necessary to cultivate those minds in isolation. For this reason, when taking refuge is the main focus of your practice, it is customary to use a more elaborate process of visualisation. This helps to strengthen your awareness of the different objects of refuge as well as ensuring that you generate an authentic feeling of refuge. It is this feeling you need to familiarise your mind with.

The basic structure of the Refuge Practice consists of five steps: (1) generate a visualisation of the refuge field; (2) make prostrations to that field while (3) reciting prayers of homage; then (4) dissolve the refuge field and (5) dedicate the merit.

Figure 15-1: The Jonang Field of Refuge

Visualising the Field of Refuge

Just as a farmer relies on a fertile field to grow his crops, so too do we rely on a sublime field to develop our mind. The term *refuge field* is used to refer to the collection of enlightened beings that are the main support for our spiritual practice. Your practice of refuge begins by visualising this field in the space in front of you:

Having already dissolved all regular appearances, visualise yourself seated in a vast open plain with a soft ground, perfectly smooth like a mirror and of the deep blue colour of lapis lazuli. This ground is filled with golden vajras and ornamental script radiating out from where you are sitting. In the space before you there is a great palace encrusted with jewels and glowing with light. In the centre of the palace is a massive courtyard from which grows a wish-fulfilling tree. Its branches stretch outwards creating a vast canopy over the palace. The branches are filled with a rich array of leaves, flowers and fruit, each radiating light in all directions, filling the sky with a magical display of colour. Each branch and twig is encrusted with jewels that sparkle like stars. Bells hang down, filling the air with their melodic chimes.

Resting within these branches is a great lion throne with a lotus holding four discs of white moon, red sun, black rahu and yellow kalagni. Atop these cushions, your root lama appears in the aspect of (1) Vajradhara—the embodiment of tantric enlightenment. His body is deep blue in colour holding a vajra and bell crossed at his heart. He is adorned with many kinds of vajra ornaments.

Surrounding Guru Vajradhara are all the lineage lamas for the Jonang-Shambhala Lineage. Directly above his head are manifestations of the four Buddha bodies: (2) Primordial Buddha; (3) Vajradhara; (4) Kalachakra and (5) Shakyamuni Buddha. Surrounding them are the Thirty-Five Dharma Kings of Shambhala, including (6) the Seven Dharma Kings; (7) the Twenty-Five Kalkis and (8) the Three Kings of the Golden Age.

Above and to his right and left are the lineage masters from India and Tibet. They include (9) the great mahasiddhas of Nalanda; (10) the Vajrayoga masters of the Dro Lineage; (11) the omniscient masters from the Jomonang Valley, and (12) the eastern masters of glorious Dzamthang.

Beneath Vajradhara stands the (13) Yidam deity Kalachakra in full aspect form embracing his consort Vishvamata. The two are surrounded by the deities of the four classes of tantra including (14) the deities of Highest Yoga Tantra such as Hevajra, Chakrasamvara, Guhyasamaja and Vajrabhairava; (15) the deities of Yoga Tantra such as the five Buddha families of Vairochana and so forth; as well as the deities of (16) Performance Tantra and (17) Action Tantra. Together, they form a great assembly of Sambhogakaya forms.

Underneath the yidams are four major branches that stretch out in the four directions. In the centre of the front branch appears (18) Buddha Shakyamuni, seated atop an open lotus. He is surrounded by the other Sublime Nirmanakaya forms who make up (19) the One Thousand and Two Buddhas of this Fortunate Aeon.

On the branch stretching behind your Vajra Master there is a vast array of scriptures such as (20) the Teachings on Monastic Discipline, (21) the Sutras from the Three Turnings and (22) the Teachings on Higher Knowledge. There is also a complete collection of the Tantric teachings including (23) the Kalachakra Tantra and (24) the three Bodhisattva Commentaries written by the Great Kings of Shambhala. The words of these immaculate teachings resound into the ten directions like a great drum for all to hear.

On the branch that stretches to the right of your Vajra Master, there is an assembly of the Mahayana Sangha seated on lotus cushions. This includes (25) the Eight Great Bodhisattvas such as Avalokiteshvara, Manjushri and Vajrapani; as well as (26) the Two Supreme Ones and (27) the Six Ornaments. The branch that stretches to the left of your Vajra Master, holds an assembly of the Hinayana Sangha including (28) the Sixteen Shravaka Arhats and (29) the Ten Principal Disciples such as Shariputra, Subhuti and Maudgalyayana.

In the space above the tree are countless (30) dakas and dakinis, each working to fulfil the needs of sentient beings, while on the ground there is an army of (31) enlightened Dharma Protectors such as Vajravega and Mahakala; as well as (32) worldly protectors such as the Four Great Kings who guard the four directions.

This visualisation represents all the objects of refuge contained within the Three Jewels and in total there are thirty two points to remember. To help build the visualisation in stages, start with a general sense of the six main groups: (1) Vajradhara and the Lineage Lamas; (2) Kalachakra and the Yidam Deities; (3) Shakyamuni Buddha and the Buddhas of this Fortunate Aeon; (4) the Dharma Collections of Sutra and Tantra; (5) the Arya Sangha of the Mahayana and Hinayana, and (6) the Dakinis and Dharma Protectors. Once you have these groups, you can add in details by recalling the individual points related to each.

1. Primordial Buddha (Svabhavikakaya)	A. Thirty-Five Shambhala Kings
2. Vajradhara (Jñana-Dharmakaya)	B. Vajra Yoga Lineage Masters
3. Innate Kalachakra (Sambhogakaya)	C. Yidam Deities of the Four Classes of Tantra
4. Shakyamuni Buddha (Nirmanakaya)	D. Buddhas of the Fortunate Aeon
5. Kunkhyen Dolpopa	E. Dharma Texts of Sutra and Tantra
6. Jetsun Taranatha	F. Bodhisattva Arya Sangha
7. Kalachakra Yab-Yum	G. Shravaka and Pratyeka Arya Sangha
8. Shakyamuni Buddha	H. Dakinis and Dharma Protectors
9. Vajravega	

Figure 15-2: Legend for the Jonang Refuge Field

To complete the visualisation, spend a moment to imagine yourself surrounded by an ocean of sentient beings. To your left is seated your mother and to your right is seated your father. In the space in front of you, with an attitude of humility and respect, visualise those who have harmed you in some way or with whom you have difficulty. Then imagine everyone else stretching out as far as the eye can see.

Making Prostrations

Holding your awareness of this environment, cultivate a mind of deep devotion which recognises that you and all sentient beings have been circling in samsara since beginningless time. Without help, there is no way to break free from this never ending cycle of pain and torment. Only those who have already freed themselves can guide you out of this situation. For this reason you turn to the Three Jewels as your only source of refuge.

In order for the Three Jewels to benefit us, we need to abandon the pride that thinks we can do everything on our own. We can do this through the practice of making prostrations. The simplest form of prostration is to join your two palms together and bow your head in reverence. In the Buddhist tradition it is customary to curl your thumbs between the palms, creating a space that represents your essential nature. We bow our heads to humble ourselves before the field of refuge.

We can enhance this basic gesture by touching our head to the ground. This is the lowest we can go, symbolising our submission to the Three Jewels. Even better is to physically stretch yourself out on the floor in a *full prostration*. This act represents a complete surrendering of your ego and opens you to receiving the blessings the Three Jewels have to offer.

The actual technique to perform a full prostration is as follows:

1. While standing, cup your hands together with the fingers tucked between the palms as you would when praying.

2. Bring the hands up to the crown of the head.

3. Then bring them downward in stages, touching the forehead, the throat and the heart.

4. Now bring your hands to the ground, bracing yourself as you kneel.

5. After the knees have touched the ground, extend your entire body forward with your face down to the ground.

6. Bring your palms together with your arms stretched in front, as though you were reaching out to touch the feet of the Buddha. Then bring your hands up and over your head.

7. Reverse the motion back to a kneeling position and stand up.

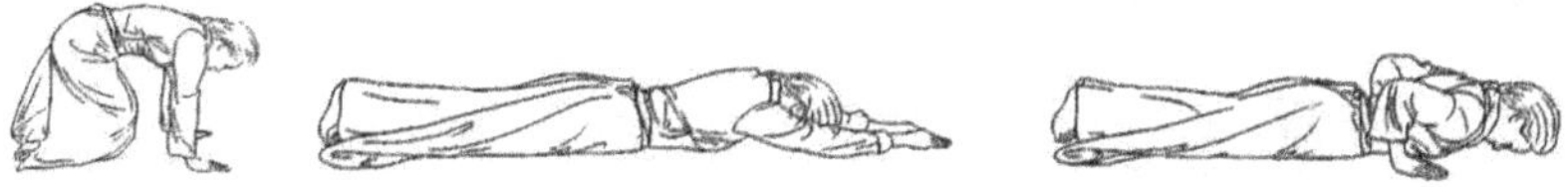

To amplify the karmic effect of this practice, as you make prostrations physically, imagine all the sentient beings you have visualised, also making prostrations with you. Imagining you are leading everyone to practice virtue and helping them create the causes for enlightenment is enormously beneficial for the mind.

Paying Homage to the Objects of Refuge

As you perform each prostration, you recite prayers to focus your mind on different objects of refuge. When you touch your crown, bring to mind the qualities of the object of refuge. As you touch your forehead, throat and heart, imagine you are offering your body, speech and mind to that object. As you extend your body on the floor, imagine you are completely surrendering all control of your life and as you rise, strengthen your determination to rely on the object with all of your heart.

During a session of prostrations, you should repeat a long or short refuge prayer that covers all the main objects of refuge. For instance in the Divine Ladder we use the prayer:

> *I take refuge in the Dharma Lords, the glorious Lamas.*
> *I take refuge in the enlightened mandala of Yidams.*
> *I take refuge in the Bhagavans, the perfect Buddhas.*
> *I take refuge in the immaculate Holy Dharma.*
> *I take refuge in the noble Arya Sangha.*
> *I take refuge in the Dakinis and all-seeing Dharma Protectors.*

In this verse, we focus on the six main groups of refuge objects. For each line, we perform one prostration. We can repeat the line once at the start, or we can repeat it continuously throughout the prostration. After reciting the entire verse once, we will have performed six prostrations.

A more elaborate method would be to recite prayers for each level of the Three Jewels: (1) Outer, (2) Inner and (3) Secret. This practice uses nine objects and is considered the most complete.

Outer Three Jewels

When prostrating to the outer Three Jewels, we concentrate on the four lower branches of the refuge field. This represents the Nirmanakaya level of practice where we take refuge in the Buddha as our teacher, the Dharma as the teaching and the Sangha as our community. This is the type of refuge generally followed by practitioners of the Hinayana and Mahayana. We begin by reciting the following prayer while bringing to mind the qualities of the Buddha:

> *Guide of the path, destroyer of deception, conqueror, the awakened one; in you I take refuge. May I overcome my uncontrollable cycle of birth, sickness, old age and death.*

We then focus on the qualities of the Dharma:

> *Genuine liberator of the nature of the two truths of pure Dharma, in you I take refuge. May my mind dwell pacified and awakened in the cool ocean of the Dharma.*

And finish with the qualities of the Arya Sangha:

Inspirational liberator who realised the truth, Arya Sangha and admirers of the precious Dharma, you are my companions; in you I take refuge. May I develop devotion, diligence, mindfulness, inspiration, a loving nature, concentration and wisdom.

Inner Three Jewels

For the inner Three Jewels, we concentrate on the objects of refuge in accordance with Tantra. They are represented by the central branches of the tree and the beings who surround it. While the three roots are usually presented as (1) Guru, (2) Yidam and (3) Dakini, we practice them as four objects of refuge, beginning with the Lama who is the manifestation of our pristine nature:

Glorious and all pervasive Lama, in you I take refuge.
May I realise the secret Vajrayana Dharma.

We then prostrate to Kalachakra who represents the Yidam we rely on as our path:

Kalachakra, embodiment of all the yidam deities, in you I take refuge.
May I achieve the two essences of the profound Vajrayana.

Next we consider the peaceful forces which inspire our practice:

Dakinis from the Khechari realm, skywalkers of the tantric family and all Khandromas; in you I take refuge. May I be blessed with a sacred companion to penetrate the incomparable secret realisation.

And the wrathful forces which protect us from our own delusions:

Authentic Dharma Protectors, in you I take refuge.
May all my external and internal obstacles be eradicated.

Remember that each of these objects is an aspect of our own Buddha-nature. They are not considered to be separate from our own mind.

Secret Three Jewels

Finally we have the secret Three Jewels which represent the objects of refuge in accordance with the completion stage practices of Highest Yoga Tantra. These objects are not represented in the refuge field visualised in front of you, but are found within your body. It is through reliance on our subtle energetic system of (1) channels, (2) winds and (3) essences that we can attain enlightenment within a single lifetime.

When making prostrations to the channels, we remember that by bringing the winds into the central channel, we overcome the proliferation of thoughts:

I take refuge in the 72,000 channels of my subtle body.
May I transcend and realise they are a Nirmanakaya emanation of the Buddha.

Then, when prostrating to the winds we remember that by stopping their movement, we cut the habitual propensity of grasping onto appearances.

I take refuge in the 72,000 inner winds of my subtle body.
May I transcend and realise they are a Sambhogakaya emanation of the Buddha.

Finally, while prostrating to the essences, we remember that by gathering the essences into a single point, we abandon our dualistic view and achieve a non-dual awareness of suchness.

I take refuge in the 72,000 white and red essences of my subtle body.
May I transcend and realise they are a Dharmakaya emanation of the Buddha.

This refuge teaches us to take full advantage of our precious human rebirth as it provides us with the basis for truly remarkable practices.

Dissolving the Field of Refuge

The visualisation of the refuge field described above, along with the understanding of its details, is known as the *causal refuge*. This is a provisional refuge we use as a support for practicing the path and achieving realisations. Of far greater importance however, is the definitive meaning of the *resultant refuge*. This is the perfect understanding that the sacred truth we seek to unveil through our practice is ultimately the same as that of all the Lamas, Yidams, Buddhas, Bodhi-sattvas, Arhats, Dakinis and Dharma Protectors. For every object of refuge, there is an ultimate version that represents the absolute truth of that object, for instance the ultimate Lama, ultimate Buddha and so forth. No matter what form they take, they are all one in suchness, collectively known as Buddha-nature.

Based on this understanding, the final step of this practice is to dissolve the field of refuge by visualising the objects melting into light and dissolving into your mindstream, as well as the mindstreams of the limitless sentient beings that surround you. The following elaborate dissolution has two stages. Firstly each object of refuge bathes the assembly of sentient beings (yourself included) with radiant yellow light that bestows a corresponding blessing on your minds, then the objects of refuge melt into light and dissolve into each other until they are unified in Lama Vajradhara, signifying their shared nature. Lama Vajradhara then comes to your crown and dissolves into you. This process is carried out in seven steps:

1. When a session is completed, light radiates from our root teacher and shines upon us. All our previous misconduct such as insufficient devotion and respect for our teacher, lack of respect for the Dharma and all other karmic debts are purified instantly by the radiating light. The blessings of our teacher and the lineage are thus received.

2. Light radiates from the Yidam deities, purifying all our prior misconceptions and wrong views including all impure perception, extreme views and abandonment of the Dharma. The blessings of the Yidam deities are thus received.

3. Light radiates from the Buddhas and all prior misdeeds such as lack of respect for the Buddha, images of the Buddhas and the Buddha's teachings are purified by the radiating light, and the blessings of all the Buddhas are received.

4. Light radiates from the Dharma texts which represent the teachings and realisations, and all previous misdeeds such as ethical misconduct and lack of respect for Dharma teachings and texts are purified by the radiating light. The blessings of the Dharma are thus received.

5. Light radiates from the Sangha and all previous negative actions such as criticism of the Dharma and of Sangha brothers and sisters, as well as lack of respect for the Sangha robes, are purified by the radiating light. The blessings of the Sangha are thus received.

6. Light radiates from the Dakinis and Dharma Protectors and all obstacles to Dharma practice such as mental afflictions, illness and faults of the

ego, as well as insufficient offerings to those beings, are purified instantly by the radiating light like a feather being burnt by fire. The blessings of the Dakinis and Dharma Protectors are thus received, and like a shadow, they remain with you always.

7. Finally, light radiates from the entire field of assembly to all beings and dispels their obstacles to enlightenment. Light radiates from Vajradhara to the Dakinis and Dharma Protectors who dissolve into the Sangha. The Sangha dissolves into the Dharma texts, the Dharma texts dissolve into the Buddhas, the Buddhas dissolve into the Yidams, the Yidams dissolve into the lineage masters and the lineage masters dissolve into the root teacher in the form of Vajradhara. The vast palace and wish-fulfilling tree also dissolve into Guru Vajradhara and Guru Vajradhara reduces to the size of the width of a finger, dissolving into your crown chakra and then into your heart chakra where he remains and blesses you.

If you are practicing refuge as a preliminary to Bodhicitta, you should stop before the last step of actually dissolving the refuge field and focus on receiving the blessings, remaining and resting in a non-conceptual state. If taking refuge is your main practice, you should fully dissolve the field at this point and rest your awareness in the feeling of being completely merged with the nature of the resultant refuge.

Dedicating the Merit

After completing the dissolution and resting in meditation for as long as you like, the virtue of this practice should be dedicated to the enlightenment of all beings. In particular, you should pray:

Through the power of this virtue,
May I complete the accumulation of merit and wisdom
And so attain the two kayas of enlightenment for the sake of all beings.

Advice for Accumulating Prostrations

Of all the preliminary practices, taking refuge with prostrations is one of the most physically demanding. To help you overcome some of the obstacles that may arise during this process, I would like to offer a few words of advice.

Working with Pain

Pain is an inevitable part of any process which engages in prolonged physical training. Prostrations are no different and it may be helpful to know that the fatigue and pain arising from a long session are signs that the practice is working. To understand why this is the case, we need to refer to our subtle body.

Due to the deluded way our mind relates to reality, over the course of a lifetime our subtle bodies become a tangled mess of incredibly inefficient broken or bent channels which prevent our winds from flowing freely. They can be likened to a river full of rocks and snags. For the water to travel down hill, it must slam against these obstructions, snaking its way through which creates substantial turbulence. Likewise, as the subtle energy tries to flow through our muddled channel system, uncontrolled movements are created in the mind, manifesting as afflictions.

Through the practice of prostrations, we can heal many of our channels and generate a subtle structure that is considerably more conducive to meditation. This requires our channels to be untangled. This process of purification can manifest as physical sensations such as stiffness of joints, temporary sickness or other unpleasant feelings. If we are unaware that this can occur, we may end this practice in favour of only focusing on the mental aspects, bypassing the physical benefits prostrations can bring.

We should try to remember that pain is not a permanent phenomenon and will pass. As the body is purified, the winds start to flow more effectively through the channels making you feel more flexible. Therefore have courage and don't give up.

Also don't forget that it is not a race so you don't have to go fast. It doesn't matter if it takes a long time to get up and down from your knees. By making the effort, you are enhancing the quality of your determination which is an important support for the rest of your practice.

Furthermore, don't be afraid to push yourself. If your mind is telling you to give up, resist the urge to immediately stop and try to do just a few more prostrations. Our aversion to unpleasant feelings often acts as an obstacle, preventing us from practicing virtue. When we accept the pain as part of the process, we develop the quality of patience.

Break up your sessions

Although we shouldn't give up at the first sign of trouble, we also should not push ourselves so hard that we are unable to walk. The body needs time to heal and rejuvenate its energy stores, therefore it is important to take breaks between sessions of prostrations.

A good way to do this is to break a single session into sections of equal length. You could start with a sitting meditation, contemplating the qualities of your object of refuge followed by making prostrations for the remainder. At the end of the section, sit down and imagine receiving the blessings from the object of refuge in the form of radiant light. Rest quietly in this generated feeling. Then continue to the next object of refuge and repeat the process of meditation and prostration, until the end of the session. Alternating between sitting meditation and prostrations allows your body to rest and reduces the intensity of strain on your joints. It has the added benefit of giving you the opportunity to really connect with each object and refresh your attitude of refuge throughout the session.

Rejoice in the Prostrations You Do

Placing too much emphasis on the number of prostrations you complete can be an obstacle to achieving realisations in this practice. We need to be careful to avoid cultivating a mind which tries to accumulate quantity over quality and instead remind ourselves throughout the practice that the goal is to cultivate faith in the objects of refuge.

There is however still benefit in counting the prostrations you make. Here the counting is not in order to reach a goal, but a way of recognising the effort you are making. When engaging in an activity that takes time to complete, having meaningful milestones can provide encouragement and inspire the mind to keep going.

For this reason, it is recommended you count each prostration and add them to a running tally. When you reach a milestone like 10,000 prostrations, take a moment to rejoice in your achievement and delight in the fact that you are doing something to bring incredible meaning to your life. Recognise that despite the obstacles you encountered along the way, you were able to overcome them—this is something that is certainly worth rejoicing.

GENERATING BODHICITTA

Reducing our pride through prostrations, we become aware that we are not the centre of the world and in fact there are countless other sentient beings that, just like us, wish to be free from suffering. The preliminary practice of *Generating Bodhicitta* is designed to expand upon this basic realisation and use it to establish a powerful motivation with the capacity to carry us through to enlightenment. The two main obstacles that prevent us from developing Bodhicitta are:

1. **Self-Cherishing:** The self-cherishing mind is the root of all bias and is the main cause for afflictions such as attachment and aversion. As long as it exists in our mind, our view of reality will be narrow and limited. Cultivating our connection with sentient beings by practicing the four immeasurables of love, compassion, joy and equanimity is a remedy for this state of mind. Only when our hearts are focused on the wellbeing of others can we generate the thought of achieving enlightenment for their benefit.

2. **Lack of Wisdom:** The second barrier to Bodhicitta is a lack of wisdom regarding the path. If we don't understand how enlightenment is achieved, we can not take the necessary steps to achieve it. We therefore need to study the path as extensively as we can to develop clarity regarding what we are attempting to do.

Successful practice of Bodhicitta leads to a mind that is vast and all encompassing—a motivation that is truly immeasurable, incorporating all sentient beings and all methods of practice. This is the attitude that will enable us to explore the deeper layers of our experience and to discover the sacred truth of our reality.

The Actual Practice

There are many ways to cultivate the extraordinary mind of Bodhicitta. We can practice concisely or in an extensive manner based on our personal preference and time available to us. Whichever way we choose, the foundational qualities of love and compassion form a basis for establishing an altruistic motivation.

If you have already spent considerable time studying and meditating on the Bodhisattva path, you can simply generate the aspiration of Bodhicitta and use meditation on love and compassion as a way of invigorating that aspiration, making it stronger and more expansive. This is probably the most basic form of practice.

For a more elaborate approach you may like to use the following sequence of meditations which are structured to ensure the development of the key components for authentic Bodhicitta. There are six steps to this approach: (1) generate a connection with sentient beings; (2) cultivate the four immeasurables; (3) cultivate the altruistic intention; (4) generate an engaged form of relative Bodhicitta; (5) meditate on ultimate Bodhicitta and then (6) dedicate the merit.

Generate a Connection with Sentient Beings

During our practice of taking refuge, the enlightened beings of the refuge field were our main focus. For this practice, our main support shifts to the countless sentient beings we visualise surrounding us. To establish a strong connection to these beings, spend some time reflecting on the loving relationships you have experienced with them over endless lifetimes. You may like to recite the following acknowledgement:

All sentient beings throughout time and space have been my beloved parents, children, partners and friends. They have adored and taken care of me and I am indebted to them. They yearn for happiness but do not know how to create the causes of happiness, instead creating the causes of suffering and dissatisfaction. They avoid suffering, not knowing how to abandon the causes of suffering; instead their efforts contradict their heartfelt desires. May I have great empathy toward all sentient beings.

As we consider the nature of our relationship with others, we bring to mind the countless lives we have had and recognise that within each one, we have been constantly cared for and supported by sentient beings who have been our parents, children, partners and friends. They have made numerous sacrifices to feed and shelter us and every moment of our happiness is due to their kindness. Without them, we would have nothing.

Contemplate the kindness our dear mother sentient beings have shown us and when feelings of gratitude and affection arise, connect with them and rest in the awareness. Then consider the conditions of your dear mothers and how they suffer right at this moment. Due to their ignorance of the true causes for happiness and suffering, they live in confusion. Despite their longing for genuine happiness, they constantly create the causes for themselves and those around them to suffer. Reflect deeply on this suffering until a sense of sorrow arises in your heart and empathise as much as you can with their pain, as a mother would hearing her only child cry out.

Cultivate the Four Immeasurables

Recognising that our dear mothers are suffering, the desire to help them naturally arises but if we do nothing, the sorrow we feel can overwhelm us and we may slip into depression. We therefore need to channel this energy into something beneficial for them, as well as ourselves. One of the most skilful responses to suffering is to cultivate the four immeasurable qualities of love, compassion, joy and equanimity.

To give this meditation a focus, bring to mind an individual or group of sentient beings you know or you have heard about. Visualise them in the space before you and reflect on the particular suffering they experience. Then recite the following two lines:

May all my dear sentient beings have happiness and its causes.
May all my dear sentient beings be free of suffering and its causes.

With each out-breath, imagine giving these beings all your virtue and joy in the form of radiant white light emanating from your heart, cultivating a sense of delight in your ability to help them. Whatever you have, give it freely so they can experience happiness now, while also creating the causes for their happiness in the future.

With each in-breath, happily draw in all their pain, sorrow and negative karma in the form of black smoke. Nurture the joy you feel from bringing them relief from their suffering. Imagine the smoke filling your heart and being burned up by the radiant light of your love.

Alternate the act of sending out light and drawing in smoke, focusing your attention on the sentient beings and developing the desire to do whatever it takes to help them. Imagine that there is no limit to the love you can offer and no limit to the suffering you can take. Continue by reciting the following:

May all my dear sentient beings never be separated from the bliss that is free from suffering.

Next imagine the visualised beings before you are now completely free from manifest suffering as well as the causes for suffering. Their hearts are filled with joy and their minds are no longer under the sway of their ignorance. They are content and at peace with themselves and their world. Witnessing their state of genuine happiness, and knowing they are finally able to experience their heart's deepest desire, take joy in the fact you were able to help them.

Complete the meditation by allowing the visualised beings to dissolve back into the space of the mind. Then recite:

May all my dear sentient beings be in equanimity, free of bias, attachment and aversion.

Reflect that the suffering and happiness sentient beings experience is due to their grasping onto reality as existing in a way that it does not. Recognise that although sentient beings experience pain and sorrow, this is not the true nature of their experience. All appearances of happiness and suffering are never anything other than emptiness. Rest your mind briefly in a state of equanimity that is aware of this ground of purity.

If you like, you can repeat this process by bringing to mind another sentient being and meditating on taking and giving. In this way, you can work with many others, using the suffering of each as a support to cultivate the four immeasurables. You could begin with people in your life, such as friends, enemies and strangers. Once your love and compassion is sufficiently strong, you can extend your awareness to the suffering of beings in each of the six realms, to eventually work with the whole of cyclic existence.

Cultivate the Altruistic Intention

While visualisations can have a powerful effect on our mind, they are still only visualisations. Unfortunately, imagining someone to be free from suffering doesn't make it so. However, even though this is true, it doesn't mean our visualisations are pointless. They are still skilful means for helping us cut through our self-cherishing mind and for the development of virtuous qualities. We simply need to recognise that if we truly wish to bring benefit to sentient beings, we need to do more than imagine a perfect world and that to manifest that reality, significant effort is required. For this reason, we cultivate the altruistic intention that takes personal responsibility for the welfare of sentient beings. We can do this by contemplating the following verse:

May all beings including myself, beloved ones, acquaintances, those that are harmful to me and those I don't know, reach the ultimate state of Buddhahood. I take the responsibility to liberate all, for it is the only way I will completely awaken and benefit all beings. I undertake limitless, incomparable, pure, awakened altruism such as the six perfections and four means of generosity. For the sake of all this I will meditate on the most profound, skilful pith instructions of the expedient and excellent Vajrayoga path.

In this moment, we recognise the limitations of our present capacity and acknowledge that we can barely help ourselves, let alone the countless sentient beings throughout the ten directions and three times. In order to truly bring them benefit, we need to free ourselves from the endless cycles of death and rebirth and this can only happen by practicing a spiritual path with the capacity to liberate us from our suffering. Only by walking such a path ourselves can we then show others the way. With these points in mind, we cultivate a strong aspiration to meditate on the profound Vajrayoga path of Kalachakra.

Generate Relative Bodhicitta

Establishing the aspiration to achieve enlightenment puts us on the path; to see it through to the end, fearless determination is necessary. We therefore recite the following verse:

For the sake of all beings I will reach the state of complete Buddhahood;
I shall therefore meditate on the profound Vajrayoga path.

The first line renews our aspiration to achieve enlightenment for the benefit of all sentient beings. This is our purpose. Our method to achieve this aim is meditation on the Vajrayoga path. Within these two lines we essentially have the expression of both *aspirational and engaged Bodhicitta*. When we repeat these words, we should bring to mind the commitments we have made to practice the *Six Perfections* and the *Four Methods of Gathering a Following*. In doing so, we use this opportunity to refresh our vows and generate a pure form of *relative Bodhicitta*.

Meditate on Ultimate Bodhicitta

As a final step to our meditation, we then recite:

> *The whole assembly in the enlightened field is delighted, they say well done, and dissolve into me.*

Reflect on the imputed nature of the field of refuge and all of the sentient beings. Recognise that the three spheres of the imputed agent, action and object are empty of inherent existence and allow the visualisation to dissolve back into the emptiness from which it arose. You can either use the elaborate dissolution process described in the Refuge practice or you can simply release the visualisation instantaneously. Either way, once it is dissolved, rest the mind in a non-conceptual state for as long as you can.

Dedicate Your Merit

As with any practice, we dedicate the merit with a few verses:

> *May the precious Bodhicitta arise which has not yet arisen, and may that which has already arisen not degenerate; may it increase.*

> *Through the power of this virtue,*
> *May I complete the accumulation of merit and wisdom*
> *And so attain the two kayas of enlightenment for the sake of all beings.*

This ensures our merit is directed towards enlightenment and is safeguarded against any potential deterioration.

Advice for Working with Bodhicitta

The practice of generating Bodhicitta is the very root of the Kalachakra Path. Without it, there is no chance of achieving enlightenment. Therefore it is vital to spend as much time as necessary to properly connect with these meditations. They should become so familiar they imbue every aspect of your activities. To help you achieve this level of realisation, keep the following pieces of advice in mind.

Bodhicitta is About Making Connections

Unlike prostrations, mantra recitation or mandala offerings, the practice of Bodhicitta is not based on how many times you recite a prayer or formula. The power of these meditations comes from the degree of connection you make with sentient beings. The stronger the connection, the more impact and meaning other meditations will have.

To enhance this connection, deeply examine your life experience and search for examples to use in your meditations. Think back through the different phases of your life and identify all the beings you have encountered including people you already feel a strong connection to or those you only met in passing. Whoever they are, whether human or otherwise, bring them into your visualisation and develop the four immeasurables towards them. Try to develop a sense for the vastness of the number of beings you are connected to.

By working first with people you have actually met, you avoid making your meditation too vague or generic. It provides you with something tangible to relate to, giving your meditations strength. Once the feeling of love and compassion has been stabilised, you can extend it by considering beings you only know indirectly through your knowledge of the world or through the teachings. This could involve considering people at different points in history or in different parts of the planet. You can also draw from the descriptions of beings living in the infinite worlds of the six realms of samsara. Try to be as thorough as you can, creating a sense that no one has been left out.

Focus Inside Before Outside

To effectively bring benefit to others, we need to increase our capacity by refraining from harm and cultivating virtuous qualities—such activities must be our first priority. This doesn't mean we cannot live an engaged life helping others, only that we should be smart in the way we go about it.

The key is to avoid the two extremes of distraction and indifference. Spending too much time working to relieve immediate suffering can become distracting and make it difficult to develop the wisdom required to offer long-term relief. Similarly, indifference to the suffering of others, means lacking the necessary connections to help them at a later time.

The middle way is to focus on what will bring the most benefit in any given moment. When an opportunity arises to help, consider the effect your actions could have and consider the amount of energy required to achieve that effect. If an action will bring benefit straight away and requires little effort it could be well worth doing. Not only would you be providing immediate help, you would establish a strong karmic connection allowing you to help them again in the future.

If however, helping requires the expenditure of significant energy, whether the results will offer temporary or lasting benefit should be considered. For a temporary result, your effort could be wasted on an action that doesn't fix the source of the problem. Investing your time and energy in this way may prevent you from helping other people with different problems. The wise choice could therefore be to focus on developing your capacity so you can offer a longer lasting solution.

Bring Bodhicitta into Daily Life

Entry to the Path of a Bodhisattva is to spontaneously generate Bodhicitta during every moment of our life so that it becomes so familiar, it is our default way of being. We can achieve this by maintaining mindfulness of Bodhicitta throughout the activities of our daily life.

One strategy is to identify regular routines you have and use them as triggers for remembering Bodhicitta. Consider the nature of the activity and try to find a way to relate it back to achieving enlightenment or benefiting others. For instance, every time you take a shower, you could think about helping sentient beings to wash away their obscurations by teaching them the Dharma. When walking up stairs, you are purifying your mind and ascending up through the Bodhisattva stages; as you come down, you are descending into the lower realms to bring benefit to those sentient beings. There is no limit to the number of triggers you can identify; you just need to be creative.

This process helps you to keep Bodhicitta present in your awareness at all times. The more you do this, the more habituated the mind becomes to seeing the world in this way. This creates a continuity of realisation that can flow into your formal meditations. Even spending a brief moment reminding yourself of Bodhicitta enables your activities to become a cause for achieving enlightenment.

REVIEW OF KEY POINTS

- There are three ways to make a spiritual practice meaningful: (1) meaningful motivation, (2) meaningful action and (3) meaningful dedication.

- Visualisation is the act of generating a state of mind through the use of mental imagery. Vajrayana uses visualisation as a skilful means to familiarise the mind with particular experiences while also purifying the configuration of our subtle body.

- To transition the mind from the external world to the internal world, we rely on the Outer Preliminaries. This involves three steps: (1) settling the body, speech and mind as a way to establish a neutral basis for meditation; (2) establishing a connection to the path by making supplications to the lineage masters; and (3) developing renunciation of samsara by contemplating the four convictions of renunciation.

- There are three reasons for taking refuge: (1) fear of suffering; (2) faith in the teachings and (3) compassion for sentient beings.

- Taking refuge while making prostrations overcomes two obstacles: (1) afflicted doubt and (2) pride. We overcome doubt by familiarising ourselves with the field of refuge and we overcome pride through making prostrations.

- The basic structure of the Refuge Practice consists of five steps: (1) generate a visualisation of the refuge field; (2) make prostrations to that field while (3) reciting prayers of homage, then (4) dissolve the refuge field and (5) dedicate the merit.

- Different forms of physical pain are likely to manifest as part of the purification process produced by making prostrations. Recognise that the discomfort is a sign that the process is working, make the effort to keep going at your own pace and don't be afraid to push yourself when aversion arises.

- To help the body recover from fatigue, try alternating between sitting meditation and making prostrations. This gives the body time to heal while helping you to build your realisation of refuge.

- It is good to count the number of prostrations you do so you can rejoice after achieving intermediate milestones. This practice will help encourage you in the face of obstacles that arise.

- The practice of generating Bodhicitta is designed to expand our connections with sentient beings and develop a meaningful motivation that can carry us through to enlightenment.

- There are two main obstacles to cultivating Bodhicitta: (1) self-cherishing and (2) lack of wisdom. We overcome self-cherishing by cultivating the four immeasurables of love, compassion, joy and equanimity. We overcome lack of wisdom by studying the path and learning how enlightenment is possible.

- The process for training in Bodhicitta can be broken into six steps: (1) generate a connection with sentient beings; (2) cultivate the four immeasurables; (3) cultivate the altruistic intention; (4) generate an engaged form of relative Bodhicitta; (5) meditate on ultimate Bodhicitta, and then (6) dedicate the merit.

- The strength of Bodhicitta is based on making connections with a vast array of sentient beings. First identify beings in your history that you have encountered and use them as the basis for meditation. Then extend outwards to include all those you have never met or have only learned about through the teachings. Keep expanding until no one has been left out.

- Until you increase your mental capacity, you need to be smart about how you help others. Try to avoid the extremes of distraction and indifference. Consider the balance between benefit and effort before committing to an action.

- To generate Bodhicitta arising spontaneously, you need to integrate it into every part of your life. You can do this by identifying mindfulness triggers that remind you of Bodhicitta.

CHAPTER SIXTEEN

Purifying Negativities through the Practice of Vajrasattva

Through the practices of *Taking Refuge* and *Generating Bodhicitta* we establish a meaningful motivation. The next phase is to engage in the most meaningful activity possible, that of establishing an experiential view of the ultimate nature of reality—a direct realisation of Buddha-nature. The remaining preliminary practices are intermediate steps to bring us to that realisation. Through the *Six Vajra Yogas*, we establish a taste of suchness and then extend that realisation to all of our experiences so that we can completely transcend our dualistic mind.

To understand how we bring about this transformation, we need to know what prevents us from abiding in suchness. From a general perspective, it all comes down to *grasping*. We grasp onto reality as existing in a way that it does not and this obscures the mind from realising its own nature. Specifically, there are three forms of grasping we need to overcome:

1. **Grasping onto a Self:** This is a mind which grasps onto the appearance of the five aggregates as being a self. It is this mind which forms the basis for the accumulation of karma and the experience of cyclic existence.

2. **Grasping onto Things:** This is a mind which grasps onto the appearance of distinct phenomena as being self-existent. It is this mind that solidifies reality into being "this" or "that".

3. **Grasping onto Dualistic Appearances:** This is a mind which grasps onto the nature of imputed reality as being real. It is this mind which locks awareness into a dualistic consciousness.

In Kalachakra, the root form of ignorance is the third type of grasping. By cutting our grasping of dualistic appearances we can abide in a non-dualistic awareness of suchness. Unfortunately, while the other two forms of grasping are active, this state is very difficult to achieve, therefore we need to reduce their strength before we can work with the root. We do this through the preliminary practices of *Vajrasattva Purification*, and *The Offering of the Universal Mandala*. The practices presented in Book Three of this series address how to remove the root of dualistic grasping.

With regards to self-grasping, the problem is a matter of identity. When appearances arise we tend to grasp onto some of them as being "me" or "mine" and when we do this, we incorporate those appearances into our identity. This acts like a glue that binds our conceptual interpretations together, providing a basis for the mind to be conditioned. This conditioning is what we know as karma. When karmic propensities are created on the basis of afflicted states of mind, we perceive reality in a distorted way. The greater the distortion, the harder it becomes too see things as they actually are. By reducing the strength of our self-grasping, we purify our mind of the karmic propensities which are based on ignorance.

TWO APPROACHES TO PURIFICATION

Any method used to remove obscurations can be considered a form of *purification*, although in the context of specifically purifying negative karma, there are a number of particularly effective techniques. The Kalachakra Path relies on the combination of two approaches which we will now examine in detail. They are: (1) the general approach taken in the Great Vehicle and (2) the uncommon approach taken in the Vajra Vehicle.

The Mahayana approach

Due to its emphasis on working with cause and effect to shape how experiences manifest, the Mahayana is known as a *causal vehicle*. With regard to the practice of purification, the Mahayana approach is based on recognising the conditions required for karma to ripen and the application of antidotes to prevent those conditions from arising.

The primary method used for purification is the application of *The Four Powers*: (1) the power of regret; (2) the power of reliance; (3) the power of the remedy and (4) the power of resolve. Each of these conditions effectively exhausts our negative karma, preventing it from manifesting.

For our purification to be effective, it is fundamental that all four powers are included, as missing even one step will mean it is incomplete. Just like trying to wash something dirty without soap and water, the job isn't done right. Similarly, all four powers are necessary to wash away negative karma.

When we introduce these powers, keep in mind that their order is not fixed. As a secondary factor, their arrangement is usually determined by the author of the text or the nature of the practice. So no matter how a practice unfolds, just be sure that all four powers are included at some point.

Power of Regret

The first power we will refer to is the *Power of Regret*, sometimes called the Power of Repentance. The purpose of this power is to genuinely acknowledge all of our negative actions without concealing anything. Recognising our past actions as being unwise, we expose our pride and reveal everything in front of the Buddhas and Bodhisattvas.

For those living in cultures where excessive guilt and self-criticism are common, it is important to clearly identify the nature of regret. When we realise we have engaged in negative behaviour, regret is the mind which sees that such actions contribute to an undesired result. There is no blame involved and there is no implication of a "bad person" who needs to be punished. True regret spurs us into finding a solution to our problems, rather than trapping us within feelings of guilt. Instead of crying over spilt milk, regret helps us see that we have spilled the milk and need to take steps to then clean it up.

Authentic regret should be based on a foundation of unconditional love for ourselves. It is important to give ourselves permission to accept every part of who we are and openly confess our negative tendencies. It can be helpful to remember that making mistakes and committing unwholesome actions is part of being human. Since we are born in samsara without choice, we are naturally afflicted by negative karma. As we traverse the Buddhist path it is inevitable that we will continue to make mistakes; just remember that breaking commitments and purifying them is how we learn to progress along the path.

Regret is generated by reviewing one's actions and reflecting on their nature.

Realising how much our mind is dominated by negative propensities creates a feeling of grave apprehension, as though we have just swallowed poison. With a strong sense of urgency, we want to find a remedy for this poison.

Power of Reliance

The next power is the *Power of Reliance,* also known as the Power of the Support. The essence of this power is to recognise that we need help to overcome our mistakes. This is similar to a person who has fallen down and relies on the ground as a support to lift themselves up again. Likewise, when we commit negative actions due to the strength of our afflictions, we turn to the Buddhas and Bodhisattvas as a source of refuge. With their support, we gain access to the wisdom needed to overcome our habitual tendencies. We can generate this power through the practices of taking refuge and generating Bodhicitta.

Relying on a valid source of refuge creates a sense of relief, similar to a doctor appearing before you with medicine after you swallowed a deadly poison. Knowing the doctor will cure you eases your mind, allowing you to focus on getting better. This is the power of reliance.

Power of the Remedy

The *Power of the Remedy* or Action is the cultivation of virtuous actions as an antidote to the harmful actions we have confessed. With a strong intention, we dedicate any virtuous deeds accumulated since beginningless time to serve as an antidote which will purify our negative karma. Such cultivation of merit may include making offerings, reciting prayers or mantras, reading Buddhists texts or engaging in acts of kindness and compassion. Whatever antidote or purification method we choose to apply, it must be carried out with intention and a sense of urgency. Within the Mahayana, there are a number of practices traditionally used to purify negative karma:

1. **Meditating on Emptiness:** All karma is based on a dualistic grasping onto the nature of reality. By meditating on emptiness, we cut through the ignorance that supports afflicted states of mind thereby cutting the creation of negative karma.

2. **Prostrating in Front of Holy Objects:** Making prostrations in the presence of real or visualised holy objects is a very effective way to cultivate vast oceans of merit while simultaneously reducing our self-cherishing which acts as a cause for many afflicted states of mind.

3. **Creating Buddha Images:** To purify negativities of the body, it is very beneficial to create manifestations of the Buddha's form such as statues or paintings. Not only does this create the causes for you to manifest those forms, it also generates positive propensities in the mind of those who see the images created. If you cannot produce the images yourself, sponsoring someone who can is a good alternative.

4. **Creating Holy Texts:** To purify the negativities of speech, you can personally create or help others to create texts which communicate the Dharma. This includes making transcripts of Dharma talks, assisting people to access the teachings or making translations.

5. **Creating Stupas:** To purify negativities of the mind, you can build or cause others to build stupas which are the physical manifestation of the enlightened mind. Such stupas can bring immeasurable benefit to those who encounter them by creating imprints to actualise their Buddha-nature.

6. **Praising the Buddhas:** By bringing to mind the qualities of enlightened beings and cultivating devotion towards them, you create the propensities for your own enlightenment. This action directly counteracts attachment to cyclic existence and orients your mind towards liberation. Within the Tibetan traditions, it is common to recite *Praises to the Thirty-Five Buddhas* or *Praises to the Twenty-One Taras* for this purpose.

7. **Offerings of Body, Speech and Mind:** To purify attachment you can focus on making extensive offerings of body, speech and mind. These can include physical offerings or those visualised within the mind. As we will see in the coming chapter, *Offering of the Universal Mandala* is a particularly effective method for purifying attachment, as well as accumulating vast quantities of merit.

8. **Dedicating Merit:** No matter what the virtuous activity, if the merit is dedicated towards overcoming a particular negative propensity, that activity functions as a method for purification.

Power of Resolve

The fourth and final power is the *Power of Resolve*. After confessing our negative actions and cultivating virtue to purify them, we make the conscious resolution to never commit them again. There are two important elements which determine whether our purification practice will be successful:

1. **A Firm Determination:** Once you have identified a mistaken form of behaviour, you should develop a strong conviction to never repeat that action again, even if your life is at stake. Even though you may think there is a possibility you will repeat the action, it is still worth making a promise not to. It is said that a strong and sincere resolve can be powerful enough to purify many lifetimes' of negative karma. This is not dependent on the amount of time spent considering your determination, but rather the genuineness and strength of your commitment. We can be specific with our resolution and promise to avoid a particular negative behaviour for a specific period of time or at least promise to exert substantial effort to avoid repeating it.

2. **Faith in Purity:** After performing the remedy and generating your resolve, you should feel confidence in having purified all your negative karma. This does not mean never having to purify again, but recognising that from the very start, your mind has always been pure. This can be done by reflecting that the agent who performed the negative actions, the negative actions themselves and the karmic propensities created, are all mere imputations and therefore are empty of inherent existence.

Incorporating these aspects into your practice ensures your purification will have a very powerful effect on your mind.

The Vajrayana Approach

Through the four powers, any spiritual practice can be skilfully transformed into an act of purification—including the methods presented in Buddhist Tantras. The main difference between the general approach of the Mahayana and the uncommon approach of the Vajrayana, is the perspective each uses. In the Mahayana, purification comes from recognising the presence of negative karma, which we then try to remove. In the Vajrayana, when we realise the ground of our afflicted experience is already suchness, karma no longer has the power to condition our experience. Because it relies on the understanding of the inseparability of ground and result, the Vajrayana is often referred to as the *resultant vehicle*.

The primary method of purification in the Vajrayana is to recite the hundred syllable mantra of Vajrasattva. This is usually combined with an elaborate visualisation practice with the deity Vajrasattva as the main focus. On a relative level, Vajrasattva was once a Bodhisattva who dedicated his enlightenment to purifying the negative karma of all beings. He pledged to purify and heal all those who thought of him and genuinely confessed their negative actions. By the power of this pledge and his connection to the sentient beings of this universe, we are able to receive his blessings when we offer our prayers, aspirations and practice.

On the ultimate level, Vajrasattva is another name for the innate purity of our own Buddha-nature. He is the absolute guru who spontaneously manifests in the form of a wisdom deity to provide us with a method for purifying our defilements. Through meditating on his nature, we can realise that we are inseparable from him. In this way, Vajrasattva is simultaneously the ground, path and result.

THE ACTUAL METHOD OF PRACTICE

The practice of *Vajrasattva Purification* is a complete form of purification that incorporates the four powers while also taking advantage of the skilful techniques of visualisation and mantra recitation. This practice can be divided into five steps: (1) establishing the visualisation of Vajrasattva as the main support for purification; (2) reviewing one's past misdeeds and acknowledging them as mistakes; (3) strengthening your resolve to avoid these actions in the future; (4) applying the remedy of recognising one's innate purity by visualising the flow of nectar and reciting mantras; and (5) concluding the practice by dissolving the visualisation and resting in one's pure nature.

This process may initially appear complicated, but remember it is only a matter of developing familiarity with each step, beginning with an understanding of the basic structure, which can be expanded upon by adding details. Try to remain mindful of the essence of the practice, so that regardless of how elaborate or concise it is, the desired results will be produced. If your resolve and intention are pure, the effectiveness of your purification practice will undoubtedly improve.

Visualisation of Vajrasattva

In this practice, we visualise ourselves as an ordinary human being whose mind is full of afflictive and cognitive obscurations. This impure state is our usual way of experiencing the world. It is important to have the impression of the vast quantity of negative karma we have produced since beginningless time, as this provides the basis for comparison with our innate purity which is visualised in the form of Vajrasattva.

Before engaging in this practice, spend time establishing a meaningful motivation through the practices of refuge and Bodhicitta. If purification is your main practice, the related prostrations and visualisations of those preliminaries can be left out and you can simply remind yourself of their meaning.

Begin the actual practice by reciting the mantra:

OM SVABHAVA SHUDDHA SARVA DHARMA SVABHAVA SHUDDHO HUNG

All existence including oneself enters into the true state of emptiness.

The purpose of this mantra is to purify all appearances into the pure natural state of emptiness—the ultimate truth which is empty of deceptive phenomena. Visualise your body and all appearances as an empty reflection, like the reflection of the moon on a lake. After reciting the mantra, rest a few moments in a non-conceptual state, then continue:

The true nature of conventional existence is self-less and non-conceptual; I remain in this state of emptiness. From this state of emptiness, I will meditate on purification and accumulation for obtaining Rupakaya.

Seeing myself as ordinary, above my crown the syllable PAM (པཾ) appears which is transformed into an eight-petalled white lotus flower. The syllable AH (ཨཱཿ) appears on top of the lotus flower and is transformed into a full moon disc.

On top of the moon disc appears the syllable HUNG (ཧཱུྃ) which then transforms into a white five-pronged vajra with a HUNG (ཧཱུྃ) syllable at its hub.

Slowly the natural state of emptiness becomes alive, like the reflection of a mirror. From this appears the syllable PAM, positioned an arrow's length above your crown, transforming into a white lotus flower symbolising the birth of your pure nature. The syllable AH represents the speech of all the Buddhas while the full moon disc symbolises compassion. The syllable HUNG represents the mind of all the Buddhas, and the vajra represents indestructible, unyielding spiritual power and wisdom. The vajra is made of translucent light, with five prongs at each end, representing the five Buddha-families or the five wisdoms of a Buddha.

To unveil the Dharmakaya or natural Buddha within us we need to accumulate merit and purify all defilements on a relative level. The lotus, vajra and seed syllables are then representations of the generation of merit and the process of purification during the different stages of existence—birth, life, death, transition and rebirth.

This HUNG (ཧཱུྃ) syllable radiates luminous light to all universes and makes limitless offerings to all Arya beings.

The light then radiates throughout samsara to all beings and purifies their obscurations and defilements; then the light returns and dissolves into the HUNG (ཧཱུྃ) syllable.

Vajrasattva Yab-Yum

The HUNG syllable is the essence of the mind of the Buddhas. When the HUNG radiates luminous light making offerings to all Arya beings, you are invoking the blessings of the Buddhas and visualising the light of those blessings dissolving back into you. This is a tantric way of making the practice powerful. Purifying the defilements of all beings with this same light is a unique method for accumulating merit. The purpose of making limitless offerings to enlightened beings and purifying the defilements of sentient beings is to attain the Rupakaya form body, which is the result of the accumulation of merit.

With this supreme offering and purification, the HUNG (ཧཱུྃ) syllable transforms into the divine form of Vajrasattva in union, transcending gender.

Vajrasattva, has a white body, one face and two arms, holding a vajra in his right hand and a bell in his left. He embraces the consort Vajratopa in Yab-Yum.

The form of Vajrasattva and Vajratopa is the Rupakaya aspect of enlightenment, representing the accumulation of merit needed in order to spontaneously benefit others. Although the practice still works visualising Vajrasattva alone, it is more effective to visualise him in an enlightened embrace with his consort Vajratopa. This is known as Vajrasattva Yab-Yum and signifies the union of method and wisdom in the ultimate state.

Vajrasattva has a radiant white body that is youthful, translucent, perfectly proportioned and attractive, which are features that symbolise the purification of all defilements. In Vajrayana, attributes like the vajra and bell are particular conditions to link you with the qualities of enlightenment, working on the principle of interdependence. The vajra embodies the quality of indestructibility, like that of a diamond, and represents the Buddha's mind. It is also the symbol of spontaneous great bliss and masculine spiritual qualities such as compassion. The bell, bearing the image of a Buddha's face and the inscription of a mantra, represents the enlightened body and speech, as well as the empty-form and feminine spiritual qualities such as wisdom.

Vajratopa is white in colour, holding a curved knife in her right hand and a skull cup in her left. They are both adorned with bone and jewel ornaments with legs crossed in the vajra-lotus posture. Great bliss manifests from their enlightened embrace.

The curved knife signifies method or the ability to cut through the dualistic mind, while the skull cup represents wisdom or the "consumption" of impure dualistic thought. Both Vajrasattva and Vajratopa are adorned with eight ornaments, representing the eight pure forms of consciousnesses. These include: (1) a crown; (2) earrings; (3) short necklace; (4) mid-length necklace; (5) long necklace; (6) shoulder ornaments; (7) bracelets and (8) anklets. Vajratopa's ornaments are made of bone, and Vajrasattva's are made from jewelled vajras.

The crossing of their legs in the vajra-lotus posture symbolises the indivisibility of samsara and nirvana and they appear with white translucent bodies, luminous like the moon and radiant like a snow peak lit by a hundred thousand suns. This visualisation provides the power of reliance.

Our visualisation should not be a flat image as with a picture or fresco, nor is it inert and inanimate like a clay or gold statue. Every detail is vividly present, appearing clearly and distinctly, even the pupils and whites of the eyes, and yet its appearance is empty. Without solid substances such as flesh, blood and internal organs it is instead like a rainbow appearing in space, or an immaculate crystal vase like the reflection of the moon in water. It is also imbued with wisdom in that Buddha Vajrasattva is identical in nature with your own compassionate root teacher, and his mind reaches out to you and all beings with boundless love.

At their forehead is OM (ༀ).
At their throat is AH (ཨཱཿ).
At their heart is HUNG (ཧཱུྃ).
At their navel is HO (ཧོཿ).

From the HUNG (ཧཱུྃ) at their heart, light radiates outward to the ten directions. The purification power of all the Buddhas and Bodhisattvas radiates back in the form of white nectar. The nectar dissolves and becomes inseparable from Vajrasattva Yab-Yum.

DZA (ཛཿ) HUNG (ཧཱུྃ) VAM (ཝཾ) HO (ཧོཿ)

The OM, AH and HUNG syllables at the forehead, throat and heart represent

458

the indestructible body, speech and mind of Vajrasattva. The HO at the navel signifies indestructible primordial wisdom. The light radiating to all the Buddhas and Bodhisattvas collects their blessings and empowers the heart of Vajrasattva with their purification power. This takes the form of thousands of luminous, translucent, milky-white drops of nectar, which are sometimes referred to as Bodhicitta.

As you recite the syllable DZA, the nectar converges to a single point and gathers above the crown of Vajrasattva; with HUNG it dissolves into him; and with VAM it fills Vajrasattva Yab-Yum's entire body. Finally, as HO is recited the nectar becomes inseparable from Vajrasattva Yab-Yum, causing them to radiate with pure white light. The nectar then overflows from every pore of their bodies, especially their secret place, and cascades down like a waterfall or a gentle shower of rain.

Confessing All Past Misdeeds

With the visualisation established, we now recall our negative actions from the past and confess them in the presence of our guru manifesting as Vajrasattva Yab-Yum. To help us develop mindfulness of these misdeeds, we recite the following verses:

Destroyer of Deception, Vajrasattva, please purify and cleanse all the negativity, obscurations and downfalls accumulated since beginningless time.

From beginningless time until now, with afflictions of attachment, hate and ignorance through the three doors, I have accumulated the ten non-virtues, five heinous crimes, five close crimes, four heavy non-virtues and eight wrong actions.

All downfalls of the Pratimoksha precepts, Bodhicitta pledges, tantric commitments and any misconduct towards my parents, teachers and precept bestowers, I confess them now.

In particular, any impure and judgemental perception, disrespect, lack of love or loyalty towards my Lama and Dharma family; Wrong actions towards the

Three Jewels, abandoning the Dharma, judging the Sangha incorrectly and harming any sentient being; I confess now.

During this time you should develop a deep feeling of regret for the mistaken activities you have engaged in. Thinking about specific negative actions can heighten the power of your feeling; therefore, you may like to review the following sets of actions:

1. **The Ten Non-virtues of Body, Speech and Mind:** (1) killing; (2) stealing; (3) sexual misconduct; (4) lying; (5) harsh words; (6) divisive speech; (7) idle speech; (8) covetousness; (9) ill will and (10) wrong views.

2. **The Five Heinous Crimes:** (1) killing one's father; (2) killing one's mother; (3) killing an Arhat; (4) drawing blood from a Buddha and (5) creating a schism in the Sangha.

3. **The Five Close Crimes:** (1) to degrade through sexual misconduct one's mother who is also an arhat; (2) to kill a "securely abiding" Bodhisattva; (3) to kill an Arya on the path of learning; (4) to misappropriate funds from the Sangha and (5) to destroy a stupa.

4. **The Four Heavy Non-Virtues:** (1) accepting homage from a more advanced practitioner; (2) taking advantage of a genuine practitioner's wealth; (3) preventing devotees from accumulating merit and (4) cheating one's spiritual master.

5. **The Eight Wrong Actions:** (1) criticising good; (2) praising evil; (3) interrupting the accumulation of merit of a virtuous person; (4) disturbing the minds of those who have devotion; (5) giving up one's spiritual teacher; (6) giving up commitments to one's deity; (7) giving up one's Dharma brothers and sisters; and (8) desecrating a mandala or disobeying the rules while on retreat.

Finally, we should acknowledge all transgressions in relation to the vows or commitments we have taken. This includes: (1) the external *Vows of Personal Liberation*; (2) the inner training of the *Bodhisattva Vows* and (3) the secret commitments of the *Tantric Vows*. If you have the time, it is a good idea to review each vow and make sure it has not been damaged. At the very least, bring to mind the essential nature of each set of vows and recognise when you have not acted in accordance with them.

In general, bring to mind all the promises you have not kept, all the lies you have told and everything you have done that is shameful or dishonourable. Nurture the sentiment that you are confessing them all in the presence of Buddha Vajrasattva and try to generate feelings of shame, fear and remorse so intense that your whole body breaks out in goose bumps. Such a reaction is a demonstration of the power of regret, assisting the mind to turn away from negative habits.

Promising to Avoid Misdeeds in the Future

With a clear awareness of the negative actions we have committed in the past, we now turn to establishing a determination to avoid these actions in the future. The attitude we are trying to cultivate is one which recognises that we have committed the same mistakes over and over again since beginningless time. Without the effort to now abandon these behaviours, we will continue to accumulate more causes for suffering. This understanding is captured in the verse:

All accumulated non-virtues committed by myself, including encouraging others to commit the same, and all other misconduct; All obscurations preventing Nirvana and omniscient Buddhahood, all non-virtuous causes for rebirth in samsara including the lower realms; Without pride, confessing all, from the depths of my heart, I will never commit these deeds ever again.

For our promise to have strength, we need to recognise why these actions are causes for suffering. By cultivating a discriminating wisdom that sees how we perpetuate our own and other's suffering, we develop an intense weariness towards those behaviours. Only then will we sincerely let go of these causes and abide in virtue.

Visualising the Descent of Nectar with Mantra Recitation

Having cultivated the correct attitude for purification, we now move to purifying our mind of the negative karmic propensities we have created. The method we use to do this is the visualisation of a shower of nectar cleansing our body and mind as we recite the one-hundred syllable mantra of Vajrasattva. We establish our visualisation first and then focus on the recitation of the mantra.

Combining genuine remorse with this precious prayer, white nectar flows powerfully from the Vajrasattva union. It pours through my external and internal body and washes away all negativity, illness, evil and obscuration of karmic negativities. These defilements appear as insects, spiders, worms and flies. See them being washed away like soot or charcoal from a chimney and dissolving into the earth. They then transform into desirable objects that satisfy the needs of those I am indebted to. My body is now as clear as crystal, filled with the divine pure nectar.

You can begin by imagining a moon disc at Vajrasattva's heart. On top of this disc is the syllable HUNG, surrounded by the hundred-syllable mantra which rotates in a counterclockwise direction. As we recite the long mantra, the HUNG produces beads of white luminous nectar, which drip down from the mantra syllable like ice being melted by fire. The drops emerge from the place of union between Vajrasattva and Vajratopa producing a steady stream of nectar.

This blissful healing nectar flows into your central channel through the crown of your head, soaking your entire body from top to bottom and purifying countless aeons of negative karma. Defilements emerge from the pores of your skin and the lower openings of your body, in the form of unpleasant substances or creatures such as black soot, smoke, worms, maggots, blood or pus. All these manifestations then dissolve into the ground beneath you. After continuing in this way for a while, imagine your body becomes crystal clear and filled with glowing nectar.

In this practice, the nectar represents our awareness of the pure nature of all phenomena. This awareness is the very heart of Vajrasattva Yab-Yum and is the actual remedy for purifying our mind. If we continue to reinforce our dualistic perception of reality, we will remain dominated by our karma, but by maintaining awareness of our true nature, we can overcome our dualistic mind. Vajrasattva represents this pure nature of suchness and our own nature is no different.

Through this visualisation, we come to see our negativities as dirt that is caked onto our skin. It is true that we have committed non-virtuous deeds, but they are not an inseparable part of who we are. They are adventitious stains, mere imputations created by our mind and are as illusory as a reflection in a mirror.

With the visualisation established in your mind, begin reciting the hundred syllable mantra of Vajrasattva. This version is known as the mantra of *Heruka Vajrasattva*, and is particularly powerful for purifying the mind:

OM SHRI VAJRA HERUKA SAMAYA MANUPALAYA | VAJRA HERUKA TENOPA | TISHTHA DRIDHO ME BHAVA | SUTOKAYO ME BHAVA | ANURAKTO ME BHAVA | SUPOKAYO ME BHAVA | SARVA SIDDHI ME PRA YAT CHA | SARVA KARMA SU TSAME | TSITAM SHREYANG KURU HUM | HA HA HA HA HO | BHAGAVAN VAJRA HERUKA MAME MUNTSA | HERUKA BHAVA MAHA SAMAYA SATO AH HUNG PHET

While it is best to recite this long mantra as much as you can, there is also a shorter version that can be used:

OM VAJRASATTVA HUNG

When Vajrasattva Purification is your main practice, you should concentrate exclusively on the long mantra. Although it takes more effort to memorise, with determination you will find it eventually rolls off the tongue with ease. Using this practice as a daily purification, you could recite the long mantra three or more times, followed by at least one mala of the shorter mantra.

Mindfulness of the Mantra's Meaning

Reciting mantra works on multiple levels. On the level of speech, each syllable causes the breath to be modulated in a particular way. This rhythm acts to purify the winds in the subtle body, making them more serviceable for meditation. Our goal is to develop an unbroken stream of sound that becomes an object for focusing the mind. To do this, we use not only the out-breath to produce sounds, but also the in-breath, a skill which will require practice to learn. In time, you will find that both the breath and the mind become increasingly more subtle.

On the level of the mind, we work with mantra by trying to maintain our awareness of the mantra's meaning. In the case of the long mantra, the literal translation of each line is as follows:

Words	Meaning
OM	Homage!
SHRI VAJRA HERUKA SAMAYA	According to glorious wrathful Vajrasattva's sacred pledge
MANUPALAYA VAJRA HERUKA TENOPA	O Vajrasattva, protect the Samaya
TISHTHA DRIDHO ME BHAVA	Remain firm in me
SUTOKAYO ME BHAVA	Grant me complete happiness
ANURAKTO ME BHAVA	Be loving towards me
SUPOKAYO ME BHAVA	Grow within me (increasing my virtue)
SARVA SIDDHI ME PRAYATSA	Bless me with all the siddhis
SARVA KARMA SU TSA ME	Show me all the karmas
TSITTAM SHREYANG KURU	Make my mind good, virtuous and auspicious
HUNG	Vajrasattva's essence (or seed syllable)
HA HA HA HA	The four immeasurables, four empowerments, four joys and four kayas
HO	Exclamation of joy
BHAGAVAN	O blessed one, embodiment of all the Buddhas
VAJRA HERUKA MA ME MUNTSA	Never abandon me
HERUKA BHAVA	Show me the vajra nature of the five wisdoms
MAHA SAMAYA SATTVA	O great wisdom being
AH HUNG PHET	Make me one with you!

Table 16-1: Meaning of the long Vajrasattva mantra

Based on this translation, the approximate meaning of the mantra is:

You—Glorious Heruka Vajrasattva—have awakened the holy mind of Bodhicitta according to your sacred pledge. Your holy mind gives birth spontaneously to holy actions releasing beings from the sufferings of samsara. Whatever happens in my life —happiness or suffering, fortune or misfortune—may your holy mind never give up on me but continue to guide me. Please stabilise all my happiness, including the happiness of the higher realms. Help me achieve sublime and common realisations, and please make the glory of the five wisdoms abide in my heart.

As you recite the mantra, try to connect this meaning to the words you are saying. In this way, each recitation becomes a prayer for achieving enlightenment.

Additional Visualisations for Purification

Reciting the long mantra with the above visualisation is the basic form of this practice. There are several other visualisations we can apply while reciting the mantra that are based on the pith instructions of great masters. An awareness of different forms of practice can be helpful for selecting a method most effective for you.

You can choose to alternate between methods or remain with a single one as you recite the mantra. When concentrating specifically on this practice, for example during a Vajrasattva retreat, it is useful to try all options to maximise the benefit of the practice. If, however, it is not your main practice, it is better to focus on only one of these options.

Whichever visualisation you choose, you should always recite the Vajrasattva mantra in a continual stream, as you recall the importance of genuine and heartfelt regret for the negative actions you have committed. Try to feel joyful that you have the opportunity to clear the obscurations in your mind and that through your actions, you are creating the causes for your own happiness, as well as the happiness of all beings.

Elaborate Shower of Nectar

This option entails a more elaborate form of the basic visualisation described above. Begin by visualising a moon disc at Vajrasattva's heart, with the syllable HUNG on top. Surrounding the HUNG syllable is the hundred-syllable mantra, rotating like a wheel in a counterclockwise direction. With this image in mind, as you recite the Vajrasattva mantra, visualise white light radiating outwards from the HUNG syllable onto the mantra. The HUNG syllable and the mantra both fill with light and nectar, which gradually permeate the bodies of Vajrasattva and Vajratopa. The nectar radiates from the pores of their skin to all the Buddha realms, and at the end of each ray, countless offerings to the Buddhas and Bodhisattvas appear, formed from the great bliss in the mind of Vajrasattva Yab-Yum.

The nectar returns empowered by the blessings of the body, speech and mind of all the Buddhas and Bodhisattvas. The blessings of their body appear in the form of countless Vajrasattva deities, the blessings of their speech appear as the all-pervasive sound of mantra, and the blessings of their mind appear as the enlightened mind of Vajrasattva, inseparable from your own pure awareness. Alternatively you can visualise the speech blessings in the form of mantra syllables and the mind blessings in the form of precious implements such as the vajra and bell. All of this dissolves into Vajrasattva and Vajratopa, causing the nectar to flow from the union of their sexual organs and into your central channel at the crown of your head.

This nectar flows throughout your entire body from top to bottom, purifying countless aeons of negative karma. These defilements appear as black soot, smoke, worms, maggots, blood and pus, pouring out of your feet and anus and being absorbed into the earth. Deep within the earth you visualise the deity Yama, the Lord of Death. He consumes all your defilements, converting them into qualities such as long life, and all karmic debts are repaid, resulting in smooth spiritual progress and the removal of obstacles. Your body then becomes crystal clear and you are filled with radiant white nectar.

After completing this visualisation, start again from the beginning. By repeating the visualisation over and over again, you incorporate vast offerings into your practice of purification, significantly increasing the virtue.

Purification of Illness and Negative Influences

Another option involves specifically focusing on the purification of illnesses, evil influences and maras. Maras include negative influences on a variety of levels: external beings who are obviously evil as well as internal obstacles such as afflictions, cognitive obscurations and other obstacles to spiritual realisation. Repeat the same visualisation described above, but this time visualise that the nectar flow is purifying illnesses caused by imbalances in your gross and subtle body. They pour out from the pores of your skin in the form of pus, dark blood, maggots, snakes and scorpions, before being absorbed into the earth. Recite the Vajrasattva mantra as you visualise yourself being purified.

Purification of All Sentient Beings

The next option is to extend the Vajrasattva practice to include all sentient beings. This is particularly relevant for Mahayana and Vajrayana practitioners whose motivation to practice embraces all others, not just oneself. For this reason, when you visualise light radiating from Vajrasattva in all directions, imagine an infinite number of Vajrasattva Yab-Yums taking up position above the head of each sentient being visualised around you. Just as the nectar flows into you, so too does it flow through the crown of all beings, soaking through their entire bodies and purifying countless aeons of negative karma. Their bodies then become crystal clear and full of blissful white nectar. You should have the conviction that all their defilements are purified.

Purification of the Energy Centres

Another method involves visualising the nectar flowing into your body, purifying each of the four main energy centres (chakras) in your subtle body. Starting at the forehead chakra located in the middle of the brain, visualise the nectar flowing into a network of branch channels extending from this central point. From the centre, there are eight branches corresponding to the eight directions and each splits into two, making sixteen in all. Imagine all these channels are healed and the obscurations related to the body are purified.

The nectar then continues down the central channel to the throat chakra, located just above the base of the neck. From the central channel, there are eight branch channels which split into two making sixteen. Each of those channels divides again to form thirty-two. As the nectar heals these channels, all obscurations related to speech are purified.

The next chakra is located at the heart and consists of eight channels branching out in the eight directions. As the nectar heals these channels, the obscurations related to afflicted forms of thought are purified.

The last chakra is located at the navel, four finger-widths below the belly-button. The navel chakra starts with four channels, that split into eight. The four channels of the cardinal directions then split into three branches with each dividing again into five, making sixty-four channels in total. As the channels are healed by the nectar, the obscurations of dualistic grasping are cleared away.

Transforming the Universe into Vajrasattva

The final variation of this practice is often used at the conclusion of a session. Visualise light radiating outwards from the HUNG at Vajrasattva's heart towards all beings, purifying their negativities of body, speech and mind and transforming them into the enlightened body, speech and mind of Vajrasattva. Imagine all appearances taking the form of Vajrasattva Yab-Yum; all sounds becoming the speech of Vajrasattva, resonating with the sound of the hundred-syllable mantra; and all thoughts transformed into the primordial wisdom mind of Vajrasattva Yab-Yum, the union of great bliss and empty-form.

Conclusion of the Practice

When you have completed your session of visualisation and mantra recitation, imagine light radiating from all the Vajrasattva Yab-Yums at the crowns of the beings around you. They melt into light and dissolve into those beings who then take the form of Vajrasattva Yab-Yum, symbolising their innate purity. As if drawn by a powerful magnet, all those Vajrasattvas melt into light and merge with the Vajrasattva seated above your own crown. With a mind filled with devotion and trust, recite the following:

Great protector, due to ignorance and confusion I have broken my samaya and let them decline. Compassionate Lama Vajrasattva, please purify my negativities and protect me. In you I take refuge, supreme vajra holder, treasure of compassion and rescuer of all beings.

I confess all downfalls of my body, speech and mind, including all breaches of my root and branch vows. Please purify and cleanse all the stains, downfalls and negative obscurations amassed during beginningless time in samsara.

Vajrasattva is pleased, smiles at you and says: "Noble son or daughter, you are purified of all negativities". You then dissolve the visualisation with the following verse:

Vajrasattva Yab-yum, with great joy, transforms into a white moon and dissolves through the crown of my head. Vajrasattva's divine body, speech, mind and indestructible primordial wisdom are now inseparable from my own.

Rest the mind in a non-conceptual state for as long as you can, abiding in the recognition that it is completely pure and free from all defilements. Feeling great confidence that your mind has been purified, recite the following dedication:

Through this virtue may I quickly reach the enlightened state of Vajrasattva and lead all beings without exception to this ground of purity.

Through this virtue may all beings complete the accumulation of merit and primordial wisdom and so attain the two kayas of enlightenment.

ADVICE FOR PURIFICATION PRACTICE

The practice of purification is one of the cornerstones of the Buddhist path as it is the primary method for working with karmic propensities so we can effectively cultivate virtue. To help you get the most out of this practice, I'd like to offer the following advice:

Acknowledge Your Dark Side

Our mind is presently filled with two main types of karma: virtuous and non-virtuous. As a result of the influence of the non-virtuous karma, we experience unpleasant situations and engage in destructive behaviours. As a result of the virtuous karma, we experience pleasant situations and engage in beneficial behaviours for ourselves and others. Both of these aspects, the light and the dark, are a part of our experience. They are our reality.

In order for purification to work, we must acknowledge this reality so we can then transcend it. Ignoring our dark side by trying to bury our demons in our subconscious in the hope they will not affect us does not benefit anyone.

Sooner or later we need to face them, and it is better to do so on our own terms rather than be forced into confrontation arising from changing conditions.

Purification practice shines a light into our mind, bringing everything we have hidden to the surface where it can be dealt with directly. Its pragmatic nature means we don't shy away, nor do we wallow in guilt, we simply allow ourselves to acknowledge what is there and apply as much wisdom as we can. With everything out in the open, we can clearly see the errors we have made. This robs our demons of their power, preventing them from affecting our future.

This process of healing can sometimes be scary because it exposes our weaknesses, but this too is part of the process. With each obscuration we clear, our mind is strengthened which allows us to dig deeper and face more fundamental problems. The more we uncover, the less threatened we feel and the more peaceful and harmonious we become. So be brave and be diligent, leaving no stone unturned in your search for truth.

There is Nothing That Cannot Be Purified

When we evaluate our actions with sincerity, we may feel we have done things we think are unforgivable, for instance, betraying someone close to us or committing a violent crime such as killing. You see the action, you know it was wrong, but instead of purifying it and vowing never to repeat this action, you allow guilt to overwhelm you and like a wound that never heals, you punish yourself over and over again.

To avoid this type of thinking, it is important to remember that all non-virtuous actions are a result of mistaken projections that distort our view of reality. If we could see reality clearly, we would not make such mistakes. The nature of reality is pure, completely free from the imputed reality we project onto it, therefore no matter how horrible an action may be, it can always be purified.

Recognising our innate purity means we always have the opportunity to start afresh. Just because we have made mistakes in the past, doesn't mean we have to continue making them in the future. Right now we can choose to heal our wounds by taking steps to develop the wisdom that removes the ignorance that underlay these unwholesome actions.

Maintain Mindfulness of Purity Between Sessions

A big part of purification is having faith in our pure nature. Without faith we continue to cling to our afflicted states of mind as an integral part of our being. For this reason, to help strengthen our differentiation between pure and impure, it can be useful to spend the time between formal sessions cultivating an awareness of the imputed nature of our experience. As you interact with the world, ask yourself, "What am I projecting?" Consider what is appearing to your six senses and how you interpret these appearances. What names do you use to describe them and what beliefs are you projecting onto those experiences?

The wisdom you generate by asking such questions acts as a direct antidote to self-grasping. When we become more aware of how imputations are fabricated by the mind, it becomes very hard to identify with them as being an integral part of who we are. They begin to feel like clouds gathering in a clear blue sky; while the clouds come and go, the sky remains pristine and unconditioned. This way of reflecting can help make your purification practice much more powerful.

Purify Frequently

At the start of our spiritual journey, the main challenge is to reverse the flow of our karmic habituation. After spending beginningless lives cultivating non-virtue, our habits have built up incredible momentum. Practicing Dharma goes against this flow and we therefore encounter considerable resistance in the mind. Even with a strong desire to change our habits, we will still make mistakes; this is just a part of the process.

Accepting the reality of this situation, we should take every chance to counteract the flow of negative karma by engaging in regular purification practices. For as long as our mind keeps falling back into destructive habits, we need to be diligent. Making the effort to incorporate purification into each day can help us reduce this tendency. At the very least, it will ensure the negative karma we have accumulated does not expand.

This is especially important if we have developed the aspiration to uphold an ethical discipline that involves vows and commitments. Until the discipline has been fully integrated into our behaviour, we are likely to frequently damage our vows. Purification practice repairs the damage and strengthens our mindfulness of the vows. When we maintain their purity, we create the momentum needed to progress along the path. For all of these reasons, try to purify your mind as much as you can.

SIGNS OF PURIFICATION

During a retreat, practitioners traditionally perform 100,000 recitations of the hundred-syllable mantra. Whether these recitations act as a method for purification depends on how well the four powers are understood and how strongly they are applied. Therefore the success of this practice largely relies on having a pure motivation and a clear understanding of the nature of karma.

After a prolonged period of purification practice, you may experience certain types of dreams which indicate that the mind has been purified. For example, you may dream of blood and pus coming out of your body, vomiting, washing your body, swimming across a big river or flying in the sky. These are good signs that your practice is having a deep effect.

Other signs of purification can be experienced in your daily life, such as your mind being much clearer than before, your compassion and devotion growing or being weighed down by fewer mental afflictions such as anger and laziness. Of the two types of signs, those in dreams and those in daily life, the signs in daily life are considered much more important as they demonstrate that the Dharma is actually taming the mind.

REVIEW OF KEY POINTS

- There are three forms of grasping we need to overcome to achieve a direct realisation of suchness: (1) the grasping onto a self, (2) the grasping onto things and (3) the grasping onto dualistic appearances. According to the Kalachakra Tantra, the third is the root form of ignorance and the final obstacle to achieving complete enlightenment. Before we can cut the root, we need to weaken the other two forms of grasping.

- To overcome self-grasping, we need to dissolve the negative karmic propensities which function to distort our perception of reality. We do this through the practice of purification.

- The Mahayana approach to purification is through the use of The Four Powers: (1) the power of regret; (2) the power of reliance; (3) the power of the remedy and (4) the power of resolve.

- There are eight methods commonly used in the Mahayana for purifying negative karma: (1) meditating on emptiness; (2) prostrating in front of holy objects; (3) creating buddha images; (4) creating holy texts; (5) creating stupas; (6) praising the Buddhas; (7) offerings of body, speech and mind, and (8) dedicating merit.

- The Vajrayana approach incorporates the four powers with the visualisation of the deity Vajrasattva while reciting the hundred-syllable mantra. This practice emphasises the innate purity of our mind and the adventitious nature of our afflictions.

- The practice of Vajrasattva Purification can be divided into five steps: (1) establishing the visualisation of Vajrasattva as the main support for purification; (2) reviewing your past misdeeds and acknowledging them as mistakes; (3) strengthening your resolve to avoid these actions in the future; (4) applying the remedy of recognising your innate purity by visualising the flow of nectar and reciting mantras; and (5) concluding the practice by dissolving the visualisation and resting in your pure nature.

- Effective purification requires that we face the dark side of our habitual propensities. Our goal should be to shine a light in the darkness and expose our mistakes so we can move on. This takes courage and determination.

- No matter how severe the negative actions you have committed may be, there is always the potential to purify them. Simply remember that all afflictions, whether good or bad, are still adventitious in nature. They do not exist as an innate part of your nature.

- In-between sessions, focus your mind on recognising the imputed nature of your experience. By meditating on the emptiness of imputations, you drastically reduce your self-grasping which significantly increases the effectiveness of your purification.

- To counteract the flow of your habitual tendencies, it is best to engage in purification practices as much as possible. Try to make sure that you purify your mind at least once a day.

- There are two types of signs that arise after prolonged purification practice: (1) dream signs such as blood and pus coming out of your body, vomiting, washing your body, swimming across a big river or flying in the sky; and (2) signs in daily life such as greater clarity, increased compassion or devotion. Of the two, the second type is more important.

CHAPTER SEVENTEEN

Accumulating Merit by Offering a Universal Mandala

All dualistic experience can be understood as being either subjective or objective in nature. Through the practice of purification, as we work to purify our mind of the self-grasping that binds us to cyclic existence, we focus primarily on subjective aspects. When we change the way we relate to our notion of self, we also change the way that self relates to the world. The next step on our journey is then concerned with the objective appearances that manifest in our experience.

It is necessary to examine these appearances because of the interdependent nature between subject and object; a relationship which is known as a *dependent designation*. This means that when we impute one, there is an implicit imputation of the other. The instant an "object" appears, there must also be an appearance of a "self". It is an implied reference point that the mind naturally grasps onto and uses to establish a dualistic perspective. As our ultimate aim is to achieve a non-dualistic awareness of suchness, we need to abandon both our grasping onto a self, and our grasping onto the objective phenomenon that appears to our mind.

Everywhere we turn we see objects. With an infinite possibility of appearances to deal with, every experience creates the conditions for grasping to occur. We could try to analyse each of these objects individually in order to dissolve our grasping towards them, however due to their infinite number, this is not a particularly efficient method. For this reason, we must approach this problem from a different angle.

The key to overcoming grasping is through the accumulation of merit. Merit is the habituation to virtue and virtue is the experience of reality as it is. Therefore, the accumulation of merit is essentially habituating ourselves to focusing on the true nature of reality. One of the methods we use to accumulate merit is through the practice of generosity. As we have seen, generosity is normally used as an antidote to attachment and stinginess. While this can be a very useful way to reduce our self-cherishing attitude, when combined with the wisdom that understands the empty-nature of the objects being given, it also acts on a much more subtle level to reduce our grasping onto objective reality.

The method we will use to accumulate merit is the practice of *Offering a Universal Mandala*. This type of offering is made to enlightened beings for the specific purpose of releasing our grasping onto ordinary appearances, allowing us to direct our energy to knowing their true nature. Due to confusion regarding the term *mandala*, before discussing the specifics of this practice, we will first clarify a few points.

TYPES OF MANDALA

In Tibetan, the word for *mandala* is "khyil kor", which literally means centre and surroundings. The *centre* is the meaning or essence, while *that which surrounds* is the symbolic representation of that meaning. A mandala therefore is a symbolic representation through which we can achieve understanding of a deeper meaning.

Mandalas play an important role in the practice of Vajrayana, and yet most people only have a vague idea of what a mandala actually is. To assist in our understanding regarding this subject, we will take a look at the two main types of mandala: (1) enlightened mandalas and (2) universal mandalas.

Enlightened Mandala

The first type of mandala, known as the *enlightened mandala*, is what people usually think of when they hear the word mandala. It is a visual representation of the enlightened body, speech and mind of the Buddhas and is used to communicate the way our Buddha-nature manifests.

During Vajrayana ceremonies, an enlightened mandala is often created using coloured sand to form an elaborate design of an environment filled with deities. The environment represents the reality of suchness and the deities represent the pure awareness of that reality. As everything within these images is symbolic in nature, by familiarising our mind with the structure of the mandala, we generate a powerful mindfulness of the aspects

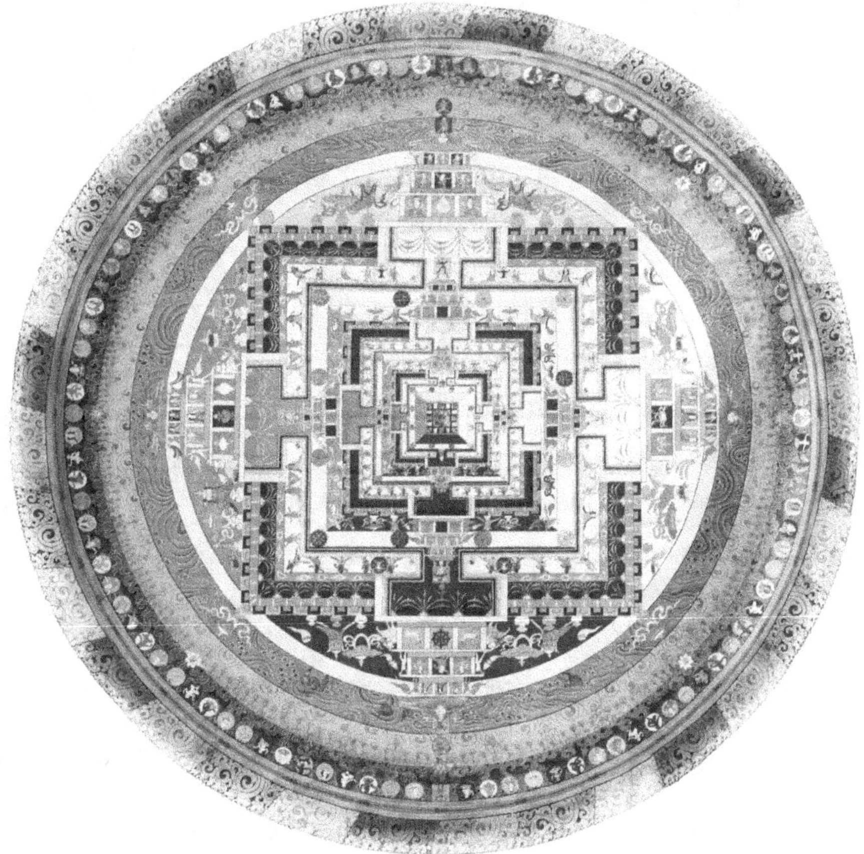

Figure 17-1: The Kalachakra Mandala

they represent. These aspects can then be used as a basis for meditating on the nature of reality.

Every system of Vajrayana practice uses different enlightened mandalas, but ultimately they are all representations of the same sublime truth of suchness. On a provisional level however, they manifest in different forms for the benefit of different types of practitioners. Some mandalas include only a handful of deities, whereas in complex systems such as the Kalachakra, mandalas can depict more than 636 deities. Regardless of the number of deities within a mandala, they are all considered manifestations of the central deity which is of one nature with our own Buddha-nature. This type of mandala will be explored in considerably more detail in Book Three of this series.

Universal Mandalas

The second type of mandala is called a *universal mandala* and represents the universe as it manifests to the mind of sentient beings. It is used as a basis for making offerings and accumulating merit. While an enlightened mandala emphasises the resultant state of Buddha-nature, a universal mandala is focused on the ground which is offered to purify the mind and to generate the manifestation of the enlightened mandala.

A universal mandala is usually presented as a physical object consisting of a circular base with three concentric rings. The rings are filled with semi-precious jewels or other offering substances and

Figure 17-2: A Mandala Offering

stacked on top of each other to create three layers, like a stepped tower. Resting on the uppermost level is a wish-fulfilling jewel or other auspicious symbol. This object is then used as a support for making symbolic offerings.

When making such an offering, the universal mandala represents the entirety of the ordinary universe that we presently experience. It includes all the sights, sounds, smells and so forth that manifest as a result of our individual and collective karma. Everything within this mandala is visualised in relation to how a single mind views the world and is not posited as a universe existing independently from that mind. As we are the only ones experiencing these appearances, we can say that we "own" them and therefore they are objects worthy of offering.

In order to accumulate merit, we present our offering of the universal mandala to all the enlightened beings represented in the field of refuge. While these beings don't need anything from us, due to their compassion and the recognition that making these offerings purifies our mindstream and cultivates virtuous qualities, they are happy to accept.

It may seem strange to offer ordinary worldly experiences to enlightened beings. We may also wonder how could it be beneficial to offer something impure to those who are completely pure. Is this not disrespectful? It is important to remember that from the perspective of enlightened beings, all phenomena appear with the innate purity of suchness; to their minds, there is no such thing as impure phenomena. It is only because of our ignorance that we see things in this way. By recognising the underlying nature of phenomena, our offerings are worthy and appropriate for the Buddhas and Bodhisattvas.

Due to the symbolic nature of the universal mandala, it is particularly suited to the accumulation of vast stores of merit. Through the power of our visualisation and the act of physically offering the mandala repeatedly, we can cultivate the qualities of non-attachment and generosity while also purifying our grasping onto phenomena as inherently existent. This method is so powerful that the Buddha once said:

Through offering to all the Buddhas in their pure realms
The entire billionfold universe,
Adorned with all kinds of desirable gifts,
The wisdom of Buddhahood is perfected.

Practicing this form of offering has many specific advantages. As it does not rely on the presence of any external resources, anyone, whether rich or poor, can offer the universe of their own experience. There is no limit to what we can offer, as anything we can imagine in our mind can be offered as part of the mandala. This means that regardless of our present karmic conditions, we always have the opportunity to accumulate the merit we need to progress along the path.

A second advantage is that because the offering is visualised in the mind, there is no limit to the size it can be. We can therefore make truly expansive offerings that would normally not be possible. The more expansive our offering, the bigger the impact it has on our mind and the greater the merit produced, allowing us to accumulate merit more efficiently than under normal circumstances.

Finally, offering the universal mandala is an extraordinarily powerful practice that carries with it enormous blessings. For centuries the great masters of our lineage have relied on this method to rapidly accumulate merit and ultimately achieve enlightenment. By following in their footsteps, we too can experience its many benefits.

Although offering the universal mandala is a fundamental part of the Kalachakra Path, it does not prevent us from also engaging in regular acts of generosity such as giving Dharma, protection or material resources. As it is not an either-or situation, if an opportunity arises to bring someone benefit, we can still do whatever we can. In this way, our main practice of mandala offering to enlightened beings is supplemented by a general practice of giving to sentient beings.

THE UNIVERSE ACCORDING TO KALACHAKRA

When we offer a universal mandala, we are offering our experience of the known universe. To those who have grown up in a materialistic society, the word "universe" tends to conjure up images of stars, planets and galaxies. This understanding is largely based on what we have learned through scientific exploration of physical phenomena.

In the context of the Kalachakra Path, the universe described is significantly different from what we are familiar with. This can lead some to question the relevance of the universal model presented in the ancient texts and may motivate them to alter the practice to match a more "scientific" view. While this is not necessarily wrong, it is limited and can reduce the benefit received from this practice.

To avoid this mistake, before we discuss the traditional description of the universe we will explore the nature of the conceptual models which we use to interpret our experience. By understanding the limitations of one model over another, we can see why it is important to use those which are more suited to our needs.

Working with Conceptual Models

A conceptual model is defined as a collection of ideas used to describe the relationship between different types of phenomena. We commonly use models to communicate the characteristics of phenomena which are normally hidden from our direct experience. For instance, even though most of us have never actually seen inside the human body, we can still refer to the brain, heart, or stomach because we have a conceptual model describing the major organs. This allows us to communicate our experience more effectively with others.

If we were to compare our models of anatomy to the models used by medical doctors, we would notice significant differences in detail and as such, doctors can recognise more subtle relationships between the corresponding phenomena. We would also notice that some doctors use specialised models to help them focus on particular groups of phenomena such as the digestive or nervous systems. Their models are designed to meet very specific purposes.

Another example to consider is the way we use maps. The most basic type of map identifies key landmarks used to navigate from point A to point B. If however we wanted to know the difference in altitude from one place to another, a map that featured elevation would be more appropriate for our needs. Likewise, if our purpose was to find the nearest train station, you wouldn't use an aerial navigation chart, you'd use a road map. What this shows is that as our purpose changes, the models we use also change.

Keeping these points in mind, we can consider the benefit of using one model of the universe over another. In regards to the universe as described by science, its purpose is to allow us to manipulate our physical environment in order to receive worldly benefit. The scientific model enables the accurate measurement of physical phenomena as they appear to us so that we can predict the ways in which they change over time. For this specific purpose, the scientific model has proven extremely useful, facilitating the achievement of many truly remarkable things over the last few centuries.

The Buddha however was not interested in measuring how things appear to us. His purpose for teaching cosmology was as a support for realising the nature of reality so we could ultimately transcend our suffering. Accordingly, the universe he described includes a number of features we will not find in scientific models.

The biggest difference is that the Buddha described the universe from the perspective of an individual being. As an experiential model, it can be used to understand the forces which influence how our experience arises. By gaining mastery over those influences, we can optimise our experience to achieve genuine happiness.

One of the implications of this system of cosmology is that there is no singular objectively existing universe that acts as a container for all sentient beings. What we have instead is a seemingly infinite number of subjective realities that correspond to the karmic propensities of individual sentient beings. When those realities are grouped based on the influence they exert over each other, we establish a *world-system*. This is merely a conceptual model that enables us to speak about the experiences shared across a group of sentient beings with collective karma. As there are countless sentient beings with an infinite combination of karmic connections, there are potentially countless world-systems.

Faced with the challenge of communicating the vast complexity of our potential experience, the Buddha drew from the models that were common during his time. By using terms familiar to his students, he made the teachings accessible to them and provided extremely skilful means for them to experience a much deeper level of meaning.

Since the time of the Buddha, the model he presented in the Kalachakra Tantra has proven to be an effective tool for refining subjective experience. For this reason, it has been passed down from generation to generation through the Kalachakra lineage masters and continues to be the model we practice with today. As the Kalachakra model was never intended to describe physical relationships between objects, it does not contradict the scientific model. Similarly, as the scientific model was never intended to express the subjective reality of sentient beings, it does not contradict the teachings of Kalachakra. Knowing this, we can begin to work with the Kalachakra model.

The Description of the Universe

The presentation of the universe according to Kalachakra is specifically designed to highlight the correlation between the external environment and the internal structure of a human being. When understood properly, these correlations allow a skilled practitioner to recognise how the environment influences individual experience and conversely, how individuals can influence the environment. This knowledge forms the basis for the Kalachakra sciences of astrology and medicine, both of which help to bring greater harmony into the experience of sentient beings. It also provides the foundation for the manipulation of the subtle energies in our bodies enabling the achievement of enlightenment.

Key to developing this awareness is understanding the relative sizes between the elements. As we will see, each element is presented using precise measurements, generally in terms of *yojanas*—a unit of measurement from ancient India. It is not necessary to take these numbers literally as their main purpose is to establish proportion. We can think of them like the scale on a map so that by changing the unit of measurement, we can scale the universe up or down while still maintaining the relationship.

The Kalachakra presents the universe in considerable detail, but we can summarise a single world-system as consisting of five groups of features: (1) the elemental foundations, (2) Mount Meru, (3) the great golden ground, (4) the celestial sphere and (5) the beings who inhabit the system. Together, they form everything in samsara and are the sum total of the factors which influence an individual's experience.

The height and width measurements of such a world-system are both 400,000 yojanas, forming a perfect square. This correlates to the height and width of a human being standing with their arms out stretched, a proportion famously depicted by the artist Leonardo Da Vinci in his drawing of the *Vitruvian Man*.

The Elemental Foundations

We begin by establishing the elemental foundations for our experience of a world-system. In Kalachakra cosmology, the universe is made up of six elemental components: (1) space; (2) wind; (3) fire; (4) water; (5) earth and (6) consciousness. Each of these represents a different aspect of our experience and together they form all the phenomena we encounter. Of the six, consciousness

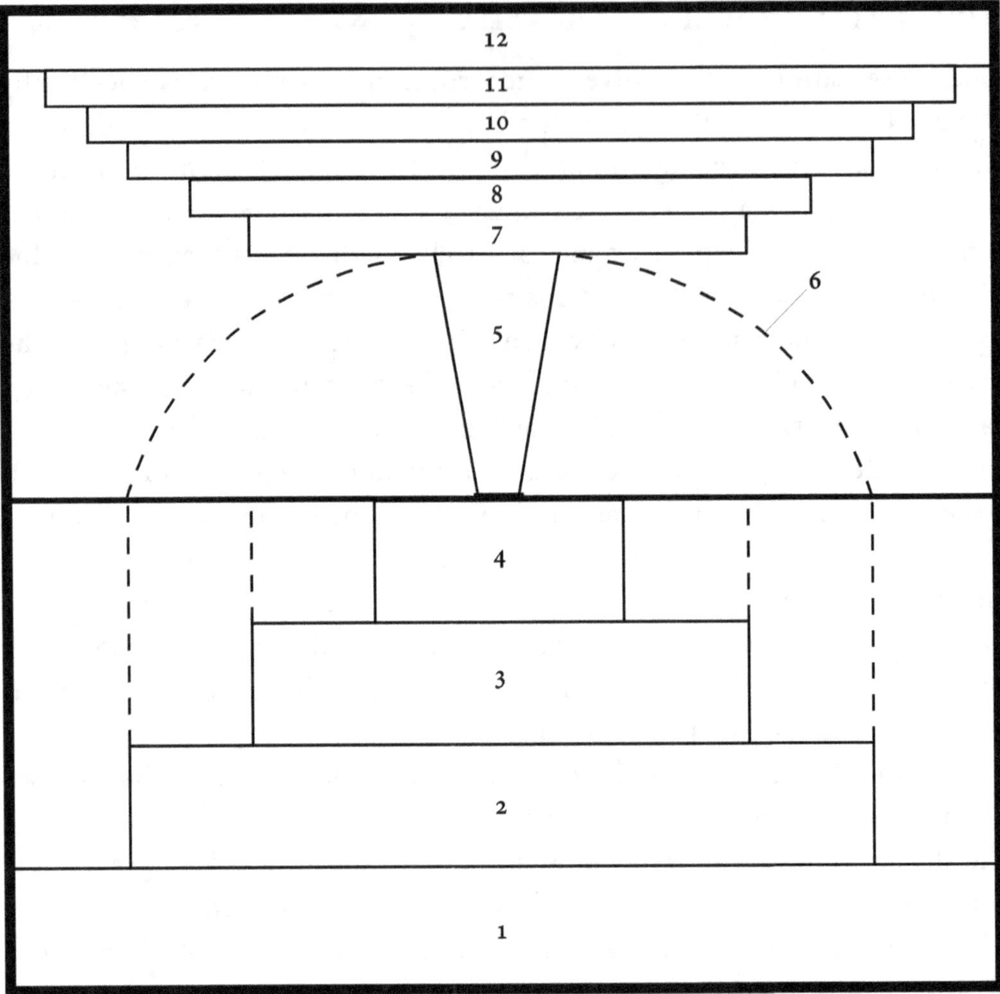

1. Wind Disc	7. Desire Realm Gods
2. Fire Disc	8. Form Realm Gods of the Earth Element
3. Water Disc	9. Form Realm Gods of the Water Element
4. Earth Disc	10. Form Realm Gods of the Fire Element
5. Mount Meru	11. Form Realm Gods of the Wind Element
6. The Celestial Sphere	12. Formless Realm Gods of the Space Element

Figure 17-3: The Kalachakra Model of the Universe

is the only element that is non-physical in nature with the remaining five being physical and pervaded by consciousness.

With reference to physical phenomena, we can group them based on the dominance of a particular element, such as particles dominated by wind. There is even the concept of a space particle which is merely a point where the other four elements are not manifest. In this way, we can determine a general relationship between the elements, organised from subtle to gross particles.

This relationship is depicted in a traditional mandala as being four circular discs that function as the foundation of a world-system. The first disc is dark-blue in colour and represents the wind element. It is 400,000 yojanas in diameter, forming the base of the world-system. The second disc is red, representing the fire element and is 300,000 yojanas in diameter. This is followed by white and yellow discs representing the water and the earth elements at 200,000 and 100,000 yojanas respectively. All discs are 50,000 yojanas in thickness for a total of 200,000 yojanas; half of the total size of the world-system. Their thickness roughly corresponds to the four hand spans that measure from the soles of the feet to the waist of a human.

From each of the first three elemental discs arises a corresponding material, bringing the element flush with the top of the earth disc. The wind material rises 150 yojanas, the fire material rises 100 yojanas and the water material rises 50 yojanas. You can imagine this being like four bowls nested one inside the other, all reaching the same level.

Mount Meru—The King of Mountains

As mentioned earlier, the consciousness element permeates every aspect of our world-system. Depending on where we are positioned within the system, consciousness will manifest in a different way. For instance, within the lower half of the system, the gross elements tend to dominate our experience. As we move upwards from the middle, the elements become increasingly subtle allowing consciousness to exert a greater degree of control over how it relates to reality.

The Buddha recognised that this refined degree of control could be used as a basis for a spiritual path to liberation. By establishing the *Union of Shamatha and Vipashyana*, a person could observe suchness directly and by the power of that realisation could then overcome all forms of ignorance. To help communicate this process, he visualised the path in the shape of the mythical Mount Meru. By "climbing" this mountain, you reach the pinnacle of your awareness to then attain the supreme siddhi of enlightenment.

In depictions of the world-system, Mount Meru is situated on top of the earth disc. It is circular in shape and rises upwards to a height of 100,000 yojanas. Meru's base is 16,000 yojanas in diameter while its top is 50,000 yojanas, giving it the shape of an inverted cone. The height of Meru from base to summit corresponds to the distance from the waist to the shoulders on a human body.

Above the summit of the mountain lies Meru's "neck, face and crown protrusion". These are labels given to the extremely subtle levels of wind and space that exist in this region. The neck rises 25,000 yojanas from the summit of Meru, the face is 50,000 yojanas and the crown protrusion is 25,000 yojanas. This corresponds to the proportions of a human neck, face and distance from the hairline to the crown. Together, the 100,000 yojanas of Mount Meru, plus the 100,000 yojanas of the space above Meru, give a total of 200,000 yojanas. When this is combined with the 200,000 yojanas for the elemental foundations, we arrive at 400,000 yojanas which corresponds to the span of a human body from the soles of the feet to the crown of the head.

The mountain itself is divided into five parts with corresponding colours: the central core of the mountain is green, the eastern side is dark-blue, the southern red, the northern white and the western yellow. The summit of the mountain consists of five peaks, each in relation to its five regions and colours. According to Taranatha, the green central peak is 25,000 yojanas in diameter and provides the main foundation for establishing the enlightened mandala of Kalachakra.

Although traditional descriptions of Meru speak of the mountain being made of precious substances such as emerald, blue beryl, ruby, crystal and topaz, we should not think of it as being the same as a regular mountain in our world. Mount Meru is a predominantly mental phenomena and therefore while it can be experienced, it is not through using gross forms of sensory consciousness.

Greater Jambudvipa—The Great Golden Ground

The world we currently experience is situated at the base of Mount Meru, on the surface of the earth disc. Beings who live here experience all five physical elements and their consciousness is generally dominated by sensory appearances. Within this bandwidth of experience, there are many specific environments people can be born into based on their karmic propensities.

According to the Kalachakra tradition, a ledge extends 1,000 yojanas from the base of Mount Meru, marking an impenetrable barrier preventing sentient beings from ascending Mount Meru by virtue of their physical bodies. The only way a being born below the barrier can transcend it is through meditation.

From the outer perimeter of this ledge and stretching for 16,000 yojanas, is a circular region measuring 50,000 yojanas in diameter. This region is divided into six concentric rings that form six inner continents, with each continent consisting of land and oceans surrounded by a mountain range.

Surrounding the sixth ring of mountains is a seventh broader circle called the *Great Golden Ground* (Greater Jambudvipa), which extends 25,000 yojanas outward to the edge of the earth disc. This area is divided into twelve equal regions, much like the face of a clock. For each region, there is a central continent surrounded by oceans.

The twelve continents of the Great Golden Ground are grouped into four sectors extending in the four directions: to the east is Purvavideha, to the south is Jambudvipa, to the north is Uttarakuru and to the west is Aparagodaniya. In each sector there are three continents, one central and two smaller to either side. The three continents of the eastern sector are in the shape of a semicircle with the straight edge facing Mount Meru. The three continents in the south are triangular, with their bases also in the direction of Meru. The three continents in the north are circular and the three in the west are squares.

From the edge of the earth disc, there is a great saltwater ocean that extends for 50,000 yojanas, corresponding with the boundary of the water disc. This ocean is enclosed by the *Great Indestructible Perimeter* which in turn is surrounded by the materials from the fire and wind mandalas respectively. Beyond the wind disc, there is only a vacuity, devoid of any attributes.

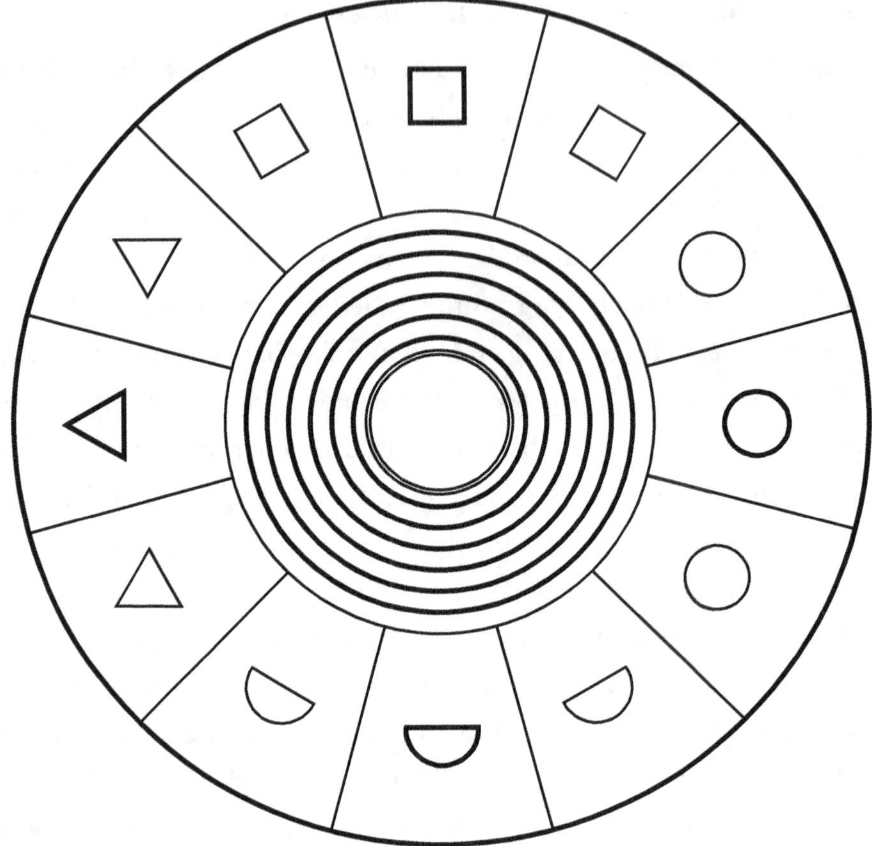

Figure 17-4: The Twelve Continents of Greater Jambudvipa

The Celestial Sphere

In the space above the Great Golden Ground, stretching like a dome from the upper rim of Mount Meru down to the mountainous ring of fire, there is a circular belt of wind called the *Celestial Sphere*. It is within this region that the appearances of the many celestial bodies of stars and planets arise. Although these bodies technically belong to other world-systems, their movements in relation to our own world-system, influence the types of experiences we have.

From the perspective of a being living in the southern continent of Jambudvipa in the Great Golden Ground, there are twelve houses of constellations that have significant impact on the quality of our experience: (1) Aries; (2) Taurus; (3) Gemini; (4) Cancer; (5) Leo; (6) Virgo; (7) Libra; (8) Scorpio; (9) Sagittarius;

(10) Capricorn; (11) Aquarius and (12) Pisces. These clusters of stars establish twelve regions in the celestial sphere, mirroring the twelve continents of the Great Golden Ground.

Within the astrological science of Kalachakra, ten planets are tracked as they move in orbits around the central axis of Mount Meru: (1) Sun; (2) Moon; (3) Mars; (4) Mercury; (5) Jupiter; (6) Venus; (7) Saturn; (8) Ketu; (9) Rahu and (10) Kalagni. The first eight of these planets move in counterclockwise orbits around Meru with the rest moving in a clockwise direction. Note that these celestial bodies are not necessarily understood to be planets in the scientific view, for example the Sun is a star, Ketu is a comet, while Rahu and Kalagni represent the solar and lunar eclipses respectively.

The Sun, Mars, Jupiter and Saturn are considered harmful, exerting influence over the winds moving in the right-side channels of our subtle energetic body, whereas the Moon, Mercury, Venus and Ketu are considered beneficial and exert influence over the winds moving in the left-side channels. We can think of the movement of the planets as having a magnetic pull that shifts the balance of energy in our bodies similar to the way the moon influences the ocean tides of the Earth. By understanding this causal relationship, we can identify optimal conditions for engaging in particular types of activities.

The Types of Beings Who Inhabit this Universe

So far we have described the aspects which form our specific world-system. This presentation represents how the universe exists in relation to a single sentient being. Our consciousness is always the centre of our own mandala and everything appears in relation to it. That being said, the overall shape of our world-system and how it manifests to us depends on the karmic connections we have created with other sentient beings.

As a result of our collective karma, we all experience a world-system with similar features. Although they are never one hundred percent identical, they are close enough to identify commonalities across our experiences. In this way, we can refer to beings "living in" different *Realms of Experience*. Within the Kalachakra teachings, there are thirty-one types of beings; eleven of the desire realm, sixteen of the form realm and four of the formless realm. Through the process of life and death, and the ripening of our karma, each of us constantly takes rebirth in these different regions of the world-system.

The *Desire Realm* encompasses approximately 308,000 yojanas from the bottom of the wind disc to the first third of the neck above Mount Meru. There are eleven types of beings that live in this sphere: (1) hell beings primarily live in the elemental discs of wind, fire, water and the lower half of the earth disc; (2) demi-gods and nagas occupy the upper half of the earth disc; (3) humans occupy the various continents that are located on the surface of the earth disc; they share these regions with (4) animals and (5) hungry ghosts; (6) the gods of the Heaven of the Four Great Kings are located in the region of Mount Meru stretching from the ground to the shoulder; (7) the gods of the Heaven of the Thirty-Three abide on top of Mount Meru; in the lower third of the neck are located the gods of (8) Non-Combat, (9) Tushita Heaven, (10) Enjoying Emanations and (11) Controlling Others' Emanations.

The *Form Realm* exists within the 67,000 yojanas of space from the top of the first third of the neck to the top of the face of Mount Meru. This space is divided into four, based on four elements: four realms related to the earth element are located in the remaining two thirds of the neck—(1) Heaven of Brahma, (2) Priests of Brahma, (3) Great Brahma and (4) Lesser Radiance; four realms related to the water element are located in the chin area—(5) Immeasurable Radiance, (6) Clear Radiance, (7) Lesser Virtue and (8) Immeasurable Virtue; four realms related to the fire element are located in the nose region—(9) Most Extensive Virtue, (10) Cloudless, (11) Increasing Merit and (12) Great Fruition; and four realms related to the wind element are located in the forehead region—(13) None Greater, (14) Without Torment, (15) Extreme Insight into Good and Bad and (16) Unexcelled.

The *Formless Realm* is located in the final 25,000 yojanas of space in the crown protrusion of Mount Meru. There are four types of gods living there: (1) the gods of Infinite Space, (2) the gods of Infinite Consciousness, (3) the gods of Nothing Whatsoever and (4) the gods of Neither Existence Nor Non-Existence.

HOW TO MAKE A MANDALA OFFERING

With a general understanding of the different parts that make up a world-system, we can now move on to offering that universe to the enlightened beings. This practice is divided into three steps: (1) preparing to make the offering by recalling the field of refuge; (2) building a universal mandala and offering it; (3) concluding the session by dedicating the merit.

Preparing to Make an Offering

As with any Mahayana practice, we begin the mandala offering by taking refuge and generating Bodhicitta. We should also include a brief Vajrasattva purification before our offering, as without the two conditions of purification and accumulation, there will be no spiritual development. Purifying alone is not enough to reach our goal, we also need the accumulation of merit to give us the strength to cultivate virtuous qualities.

Once you have completed the preliminaries, visualise your spiritual guide in the aspect of Guru Vajradhara. In the space in front of you sits a throne made of precious jewels, supported by eight snow lions. On top of this throne are four cushions, a white moon disc, a red sun disc, a dark-blue rahu disc and a yellow kalagni disc. Your Guru appears as dark-blue Vajradhara surrounded by a host of Lineage Masters, Yidams, Buddhas, Bodhisattvas, Arhats, Dakas, Dakinis and Dharma Protectors of the past, present and future. We look upon this great field as being inseparable from the Three Jewels, our ultimate source of refuge.

To ensure our practice of making offerings results in the accumulation of merit, you should pay particular attention to the state of your mind. The three most important elements you need to have are (1) a motivation based on compassion; (2) a focused mind that is not distracted, and (3) a constant awareness of the empty-nature of the person who makes the offering, the objects to whom we make the offering, the offering itself and even the act of making the offering.

When you have established the visualisation and adjusted your attitude, you can cultivate devotion by reciting:

You are the jewel-like lama,
The one whose kindness leads to the dawning of great bliss in a single instant.
I bow at your lotus feet, Lama Vajradhara.

I pay homage to the lama for whom my gratitude is beyond compare.
The light of your enlightened truth dispels my darkness.
You are the faultless wisdom eye, the sun-like lama of great immutable bliss.

As it can be difficult to recognise the master as the living embodiment of the Three Jewels, these verses help remind us that the master is more important than anything else. The "lotus feet" conveys the beauty of the Guru's body and refers to the throne upon which he sits. The vajra body represents the indestructible nature of the Guru's enlightened form, as he is a manifestation of all enlightened beings. Great bliss is our ultimate sacred truth which may take countless aeons to attain, but as we can instantly glimpse this state through the blessings of the vajra master, there is nothing more precious than he. Furthermore, the Guru is able to see through our hidden weaknesses with his "faultless wisdom eye", and like the sun, he is a source of radiant light that enables us to see all that is around us.

You are our mother and father.
You are the master of all beings, a true and noble friend.
You are the great protector who acts for the benefit of all sentient beings.
You are the great rescuer who steals away negative obscurations.
You are the one who abides in excellence,
You are the sole abode of all supreme qualities, completely free from all faults.
You are the protector of the lowly, the supreme conqueror of self-cherishing
and suffering; the source of all wealth, the wish fulfilling jewel, the supreme
victorious Dharma Lord, in you I take refuge.

The next verse conveys how the Guru is like a parent in a spiritual sense; as a father he guides and protects us on our spiritual journey and as a mother, he loves and nurtures us with our spiritual needs. He does not discriminate who he guides on the spiritual path, but accepts all beings, vowing to care for them until they reach enlightenment. As the supreme quality of omniscience is only attained through the Guru's Dharma teachings, we can say he is a manifestation of the Buddha in human form. He is also described as a "wish fulfilling jewel" as he manifests limitless enlightened qualities for the benefit of his devotees.

As you recite these verses, nurture your feeling of connection with your spiritual guide and with all enlightened beings. Remember their infinite kindness towards you and let your gratitude strengthen your devotion to them. With a great desire to honour and please them, you are ready to make your offering.

The Actual Offering of a Universal Mandala

The process of offering a universal mandala involves four steps: (1) gathering your materials; (2) preparing the ground; (3) visualising the objects to offer and then (4) making the offering.

Gathering Your Materials

Although it is possible to do this practice using nothing more than a hand gesture, making the effort to gather the materials to make a universal mandala and to then offer these physical substances is more effective for the mind. To do this you will need three things:

1. **Mandala Set:** A traditional mandala set consists of one base, three rings and a top ornament. They are usually made from gold, silver, or another type of metal such as brass or copper, but they can also be made of wood. While you should try to acquire as nice a set as you can afford, do not be worried if you don't have access to a complete set. The minimum you need is a flat circular surface such as a plate or rock.

2. **Perfume:** In order to bless the base, you will need perfumed liquid or powder. In ancient times, they often used cow dung as it was considered a traditional substance for purification. If you can't afford perfume, then simply use clean water as a substitute.

3. **Offering Substances:** An assortment of semi-precious gems is ideal to offer, however, if they are difficult to obtain, you can use grains such as barley or rice. When making many offerings, it is common to place all offering substances in a cloth draped over your lap. This way handfuls of offerings can be easily scooped up at different stages of the practice. Be sure to inspect the substances before making offerings to ensure no insects, dirt or stones are mixed in.

Preparing the Ground

Having gathered all your materials, you can begin the process of building the offering by taking hold of the mandala base and reciting:

OM VAJRA BHUMI AH HUNG

VAJRA BHUMI refers to the vajra ground which is represented by the circular disc and is the pure and powerful foundation of our present experience. OM AH HUNG is included to bring the blessings of the Buddha's body, speech and mind onto the base. While reciting this verse we clean the disc with the perfume, rubbing with the heel of our wrist in a circular motion. As we do so, we view the disc as our natural mind and the perfume as Bodhicitta, and our negativities are purified as the disc transforms into the natural mind of pure Bodhicitta. On top of this ground, visualise the four elemental foundations of wind, fire, water and earth. Continue by reciting:

OM VAJRA REKHE AH HUNG

VAJRA REKHE refers to the indestructible perimeter of wind and fire that surrounds the *Great Salt Water Ocean* and the *Great Golden Ground*. We symbolise this barrier by placing the largest ring on the mandala base. When we recite HUNG, we should say it slowly and imagine that all impure appearances dissolve into the emptiness of their own pure nature.

Visualising Objects to Offer

With the foundation established, we now begin placing heaps of offering substances into the mandala. Depending on the time you would like to spend, there are three versions you can use: long, medium or short. The main difference between them is the degree of detail.

When you are placing heaps of offerings onto your mandala, remember that in this practice, the cardinal directions are relative in nature. East is always considered to be the side of the mandala that is closest to you. This means south is to your left and north is to the right, with west on the far side of the mandala.

Long Mandala Offering

In the extensive mandala offering, there are fifty heaps of precious objects that are offered in sequence. As you place each heap, you should bring to mind the specific feature of the universe being offered and incorporate it into your visualisation. This is a good offering to make at the beginning of a session.

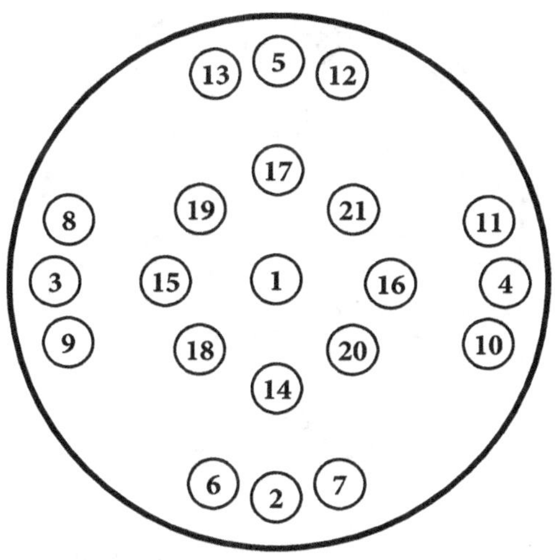

Figure 17-5: The first ring of offerings

Begin by placing a heap in the centre of the mandala base representing (1) *Mount Meru*. As you do this, reflect that through your practice of the Kalachakra Path, you can ascend Mount Meru and attain enlightenment within a single lifetime.

Continue by placing the *twelve continents* that represent the many beautiful sensory appearances of the human realms. There are four heaps in the cardinal directions: (2) to the east is Purvavideha; (3) to the south is Jambudvipa; (4) to the north is Uttarakuru; and (5) to the west is Aparagodaniya. Then place the remaining sub-continents to the left and right of the heaps you have already created: in the east is (6) Deha and (7) Videha; in the south is (8) Chamara and (9) Aparachamara; in the north is (10) Kuru and (11) Kaurava; and in the west is (12) Shatha and (13) Uttaramantrina.

Next is the offering of the *celestial sphere* of planets and constellations. In the space between Mount Meru and the continents, place four heaps: (14) to the east is black Rahu, (15) to the south is the red sun, (16) to the north is the white moon, and (17) to the west is yellow Kalagni. Here the sun and moon represent the right and left channels respectively, while Rahu and Kalagni represent the upper and lower central channel. Bring to mind the blissful appearances produced by the winds circulating in these channels, as well as the heavenly pleasures of the worldly god realms.

In the intermediate directions, place four heaps representing the *four incomparable treasures*: (18) to the south-east is the precious mountain, (19) to the south-west is the wish-granting tree, (20) to the north-east is the spontaneously harvested crops and (21) to the north-west is the wish-granting cow. These are four signs of the abundance and wealth of the human and god realms.

When you have completed these offerings, fill in the remainder of the ring with general offerings, imagining everything wondrous and beautiful within the human realms. In particular, offer anything you personally feel attachment to such as favourite foods, places, and people.

As you place the second ring on top, imagine the features that correspond to pure Bodhisattva realms such as the Sublime Realm of Shambhala.

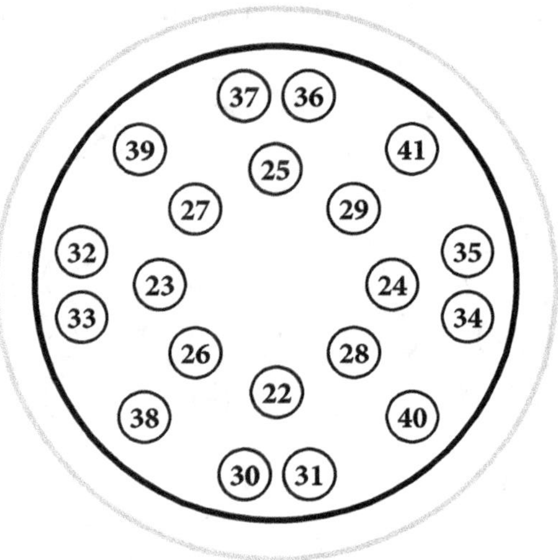

Figure 17-6: The second ring of offerings

We create an inner ring with the *seven precious emblems of royalty* and the *great treasure vase*: (22) to the east is the precious wheel, (23) to the south is the precious jewel, (24) to the north is the precious minister, (25) to the west is the precious queen, (26) to the south-east is the precious elephant, (27) to the south-west is the precious horse, (28) to the north-east is the precious general, and (29) to the north-west is the great treasure vase. As we place these heaps, we cultivate the aspiration to one day achieve the state of a Wheel-Turning King in Shambhala so as to bring limitless benefit to countless sentient beings.

Around this inner ring, extensive offerings to the enlightened beings are made by placing twelve heaps representing the twelve offering goddesses of Kalachakra: in the east place two heaps for the dark-blue goddesses of (30) perfumed water and (31) flowers; in the south place two heaps for the red goddesses of (32) incense and (33) light; to the north place two heaps for the white goddesses of (34) food and (35) fruit; to the west place two heaps for the yellow goddesses of (36) alluring beauty and (37) laughter; in the south-east place one heap for the green goddess of (38) music; in the south-west place one heap for the green goddess of (39) dancing; in the north-east place one heap for the blue goddess of (40) singing; and in the north-west place one heap for the blue goddess of (41) desire. As you fill in the rest of the ring, visualise the offering goddesses pervading all of space, filling every corner of the world-system with glorious offerings.

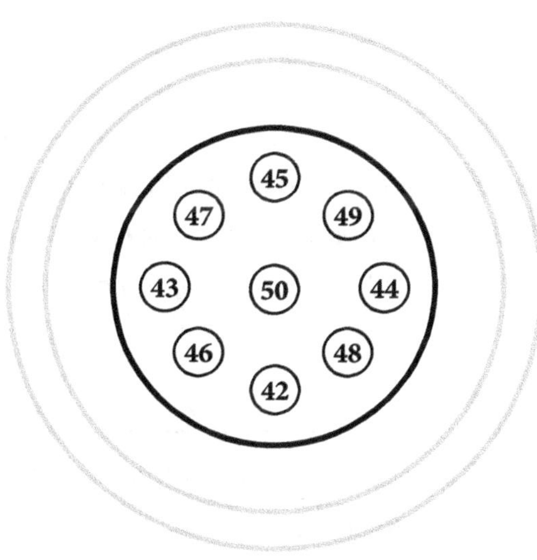

Figure 17-7: The third ring of offerings

To complete the mandala, place the third ring on top and offer the *eight auspicious symbols:* (42) to the east is the right-turning conch, (43) to the south is the precious umbrella, (44) to the north is the victory banner, (45) to the west is the golden fish, (46) to the south-east is the Dharma wheel, (47) to the south-west is the endless knot, (48) to the north-east is the lotus flower and (49) to the north-west is the vase of treasure. As you fill the remainder of the ring, imagine auspicious conditions arising so you and all sentient beings can achieve complete liberation from suffering.

Finally, place (50) the jewelled ornament on top and imagine the world-system you have visualised multiplying into the ten directions and that each of these mandalas multiplies into a further ten, and so on and so forth, until all of space is completely filled with universal mandalas. This type of visualisation is known as a cloud of *Samantabhadra offerings.* Remind yourself of the innate purity of these offerings, recognising that their nature is the sublime emptiness of suchness.

Medium-Length Mandala Offering

When mandala offering is your main practice, this briefer version of the offering is most commonly used. A typical prayer for a medium-length offering is as follows:

OM VAJRA BHUMI AH HUM

The foundation is the pure golden earth.

OM VAJRA REKHE AH HUM

The universe is encircled by a great iron fence and in the centre is Mount Meru—the king of mountains.

To the east is Purvavideha, to the south is Jambudvipa, to the north is Uttara-kuru and to the west is Aparagodaniya. The sun, moon, rahu and kalagni; all things pleasing and prosperous within the world of humans and gods, complete and lacking nothing.

All this wealth I offer with great devotion to my immaculate root and lineage lamas, and to the mandala of Yidams, Buddhas, Bodhisattvas, Pratyekas, Shravakas, Dakinis and all-seeing Dharma Protectors.

A heap of precious stones or grains is first placed in the centre of the base to represent (1) Mount Meru, and further heaps are placed around the centre beginning with the four continents. The first heap is placed in the easterly direction to represent the continent (2) Purvavideha, then in the south to represent (3) Jambudvipa, in the north to represent (4) Uttarakuru and in the west to represent (5) Aparagodaniya.

Next visualise placing objects in the sky as you continue to place them in the ring as before. In the east a heap represents (6) Rahu, in the south (7) the sun, to the north is (8) the moon, and to the west is (9) Kalagni. This forms the ground which is the basis of our practice.

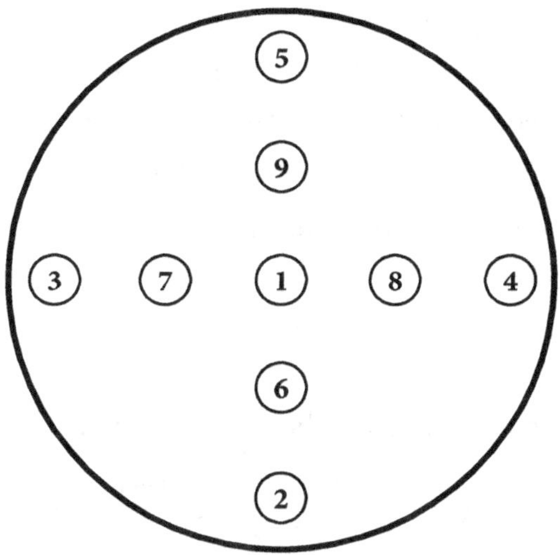

Figure 17-8: Medium-length mandala offering

After filling in the first ring with offerings, place the second ring to form another iron fence on top of the disc. As you place heaps of jewels or grains inside the ring, visualise them as representing the islands surrounding the four continents, the desire god realms such as the Heaven of Thirty-three, the form and formless realms, the eight auspicious symbols, the seven precious emblems of royalty, gold cloth, precious jewels, diamond palaces, beautiful gardens and the most precious and beautiful things the world has to offer, excluding nothing.

When the second ring is full, place the third ring on top and proceed to fill it in the same way as the second ring. When the third ring is full, place a victory banner on the top of the mound, sealing the mandala and making it shine forth in all directions.

Short Mandala Offering

The final version of the mandala offering is the shortest and most suitable for accumulating large quantities of offerings. The prayer most often used is:

The ground is anointed with perfume and strewn with flowers.
Its centre is adorned with Mount Meru, surrounded by the four continents,
the Sun and the Moon.
This I offer as a Buddha-field for all beings to enjoy.

In this practice, clean the disc in the same way as before and place seven heaps of offering substances to represent Mount Meru, the four continents, the sun and moon. Quickly offer this and repeat the process again and again, along with the short mandala offering prayer and subsequent mantra. Traditionally, a practitioner will complete 100,000 offerings in this way, however the actual number is not as important as the feeling and motivation of the practice.

When making many short offerings, you may like to refresh the details of your visualisation by inserting a long or medium-length mandala offering every now and then. For instance, you could do one extensive offering every time you complete one hundred small offerings.

Making the Offering

Having established the visualisation and constructed the mandala, you can now make your offering. Remind yourself of the presence of the refuge field and with a heart full of devotion, recite the following mantra:

GURU IDAM RATNA MANDALA KANG NIRYATAYAMI

This prayer essentially means "To the Guru, I offer this jewelled mandala." As you recite it, imagine everything you offer turning into brilliant light and dissolving back into the field of refuge. Develop the sense of holding nothing back and try to feel as though you are letting everything go.

If mandala offerings are your main practice, you should return the offering substances back into your lap, clearing everything from the mandala base. Return to preparing the ground and repeat the process of building the mandala and offering it. Continue in this way for the remainder of the session.

Concluding the Session

To conclude a session of practice, visualise the objects of refuge in front of you as before and request them to accept your offerings for the liberation of all beings, and to especially bless you with the realisation of the Kalachakra Six Vajra Yogas. Once again perform a short mandala offering and chant:

Out of compassion accept this mandala for the sake of all beings
And having accepted this offering, please bless me!

Recollecting the virtue of body, speech and mind gathered by myself and all beings during the three times, together with the collection of excellent

Samantabhadra offerings in this precious mandala; both real and visualised, I offer this all to my lama and the Three Jewels. Please accept this with your compassion and bless me!

When you finish this section, visualise the objects of refuge dissolving into you like water being poured into water, merging inseparably with them. Then dedicate the merit of this practice to the enlightenment of all beings.

ADVICE FOR MAKING OFFERINGS

There are few practices that are as effective in generating merit as that of offering the universal mandala, therefore it is highly recommended to make this practice a central part of your training. The following words of advice are just some ways to maximise the benefit you receive.

The Offering is In the Mind

The offering of a universal mandala takes place in the mind but unlike usual gifts, there is no physical exchange taking place, only a symbolic one. The real power of the training lies in the building up of appearances, which are then let go. This moment of release is the counterforce to grasping and is what allows our mind to abide in virtue.

For this reason, it is important to take the time to visualise the objects of offering and avoid simply throwing rice on a plate over and over again. Instead, try to bring meaning to each handful. As you scoop up offering substances, let a mental image form of something you find beautiful or pleasant and as you place the next heap on your mandala, imagine letting the image fade back into the mind.

Before you start a session, it may help to think of the different things you would like to offer and as you build the mandala, work your way through each, one at a time. This is especially useful during the short version where offerings are made quickly. For instance, in one round, you could offer different types of flowers and in another, offer different forms of light. Really explore the range of your experience so that through the process, you feel as though you have given everything away.

Offer Anything Beautiful

Making offerings does not have to be limited to formal practice. In fact, it is very beneficial to incorporate the act of offering into all aspects of your life. One of the easiest ways to do this is by offering your beautiful experiences to the Three Jewels. During the day, whenever you encounter something you find pleasing, whether it is the sight of a beautiful flower, the smell of a fragrant breeze or the taste of a flavourful meal, offer the experience to the Guru and the Three Jewels.

It doesn't have to be an elaborate process. When you experience something you like, mentally recite "GURU IDAM RATNA MANDALA KANG NIRYATAYAMI", then release the experience. Cultivate a sense of delight in making these offerings and at the end of the day, dedicate any merit you have generated.

Offer Your Attachments

While offering pleasant experiences is great for accumulating merit, offerings can also be used as a way of accumulating wisdom. Throughout the day, try to be mindful of your reactions to different experiences, recognising when attachment has arisen.

Identify the object of your attachment and consider the nature of what is appearing to you. How did this appearance arise? What qualities are you projecting onto it? Are those qualities an inherent part of the appearance? What is the ultimate nature of the appearance?

As you analyse the object, try to get an impression of its illusory-like nature. Imagine you are in a dream and that everything appearing to you is nothing other than your mind, then offer this experience to the Guru and the Three Jewels.

SIGNS OF SUCCESS

In the Jonang tradition, the mandala offering practice is normally performed in full-time retreat over a period of twenty-one days. This is however not the only time you should do this practice. Mandala offerings can be accumulated gradually during daily life, and a consistent practice will clear your mind and help you let go of attachment to fleeting thoughts.

With diligence, this practice will eventually lead to signs of your merit ripening. These include dreams or visions of being seated on a lion throne, seeing a halo above your head, wearing Dharma robes or seeing many people prostrate in your direction, although if your mind becomes clearer, has fewer afflictions and is always engaged in virtue, this is the best sign that your cultivation of merit has been successful.

REVIEW OF KEY POINTS

- The offering of a universal mandala is specifically designed to help accumulate merit while also cutting our habit of grasping onto objective reality.

- There are two types of mandalas used within the practice of Vajrayana: (1) enlightened mandalas which symbolically represent the universe as experienced by enlightened beings and (2) universal mandalas which represent the ordinary universe as experienced by sentient beings. Enlightened mandalas are used to help us become familiar with our Buddha-nature, while universal mandalas are used as offerings.

- There are three advantages to offering a universal mandala: (1) anyone can accumulate merit through offering a mandala, regardless of the resources they have; (2) there is no limit to the size of mental offerings, therefore you can generate vast stores of merit; and (3) the practice is incredibly blessed by countless practitioners who have used it to achieve enlightenment.

- A conceptual model is a collection of ideas used to describe the relationships between different types of phenomena in order to fulfil a purpose. Because they are only an imputed interpretation of reality, there is no conflict between switching models based on the context of your needs.

- The Buddha's model for the universe is based on the subjective experience of a single individual and emphasises the various factors which influence that experience. It was originally presented using familiar terminology to ancient Indian cosmology as a skilful means to communicate complex ideas.

- The Kalachakra universe can be summarised by five groups of features: (1) the elemental foundations; (2) Mount Meru; (3) the great golden ground; (4) the celestial sphere and (5) the beings who inhabit the system.

- The universe is comprised of six elements: (1) space; (2) wind; (3) fire; (4) water; (5) earth and (6) consciousness. The first five are the physical elements, whereas the last is non-physical and pervades the other five. The foundation of the universe consists of four elemental discs of wind, fire, water and earth.

- Mount Meru is situated at the centre of the earth disc and symbolises the state of concentration of an individual's mind. By ascending Mount Meru, you can achieve more subtle states of mind that can be used to dissolve ignorance and achieve liberation from suffering.

- The surface of the earth disc is divided into three parts: (1) an impenetrable ledge surrounding the base of Mount Meru, (2) an inner ring of six continents with surrounding mountain barriers, and (3) an outer ring divided into twelve continents and surrounded by a great salt ocean. All of this is contained within an indestructible perimeter of fire and wind.

- In the space above the Great Golden Ground is the celestial sphere consisting of the constellations and planets that appear to an individual on the ground. The movement of these entities affects the balance of the winds in the physical body and has an impact on the quality of experience.

- Due to collective karma, a wide variety of beings appear within our experience. The Kalachakra identifies thirty-one types: eleven of the desire realm, sixteen of the form realm and four of the formless realm. The desire realm includes all the elemental discs as well as the Great Golden Ground and Mount Meru, and the form and formless realms exist in the space above Meru.

- There are three steps to making a mandala offering: (1) preparing to make the offering by recalling the field of refuge; (2) building a universal mandala and offering it; (3) concluding the session by dedicating the merit.

- Throughout the practice you should maintain a mind with three qualities: (1) a motivation based on compassion; (2) a focused mind that is not distracted; and (3) a constant awareness of the empty-nature of the person making the offering, the objects to whom the offering is made, the offering itself and even the act of making the offering.

- There are four steps to making an offering: (1) gathering your materials; (2) preparing the ground; (3) visualising the objects to offer and then (4) making the offering.

- The offering of the mandala occurs in the mind, therefore make the effort to build your visualisation and ensure each handful of offering is imbued with meaning.

- During the time between sessions, you can develop the habit of offering any pleasant or beautiful experience you have.

- To make your offering an offering of suchness, consider briefly the illusory-like nature of the things you are attached to and offer the purified appearance to the enlightened beings.

- With a persistent practice of offering mandalas, your mind will have less attachment to thoughts and will have greater clarity.

Appendices

The Jonang-Shambhala Lineage of Sutra and Tantra

The following diagram presents the two main lineages of the *Jonang Tradition:* (1) the tantric lineage of the *Six Vajra Yogas of Kalachakra* and (2) the sutric lineage of *Zhentong Madhyamaka.*

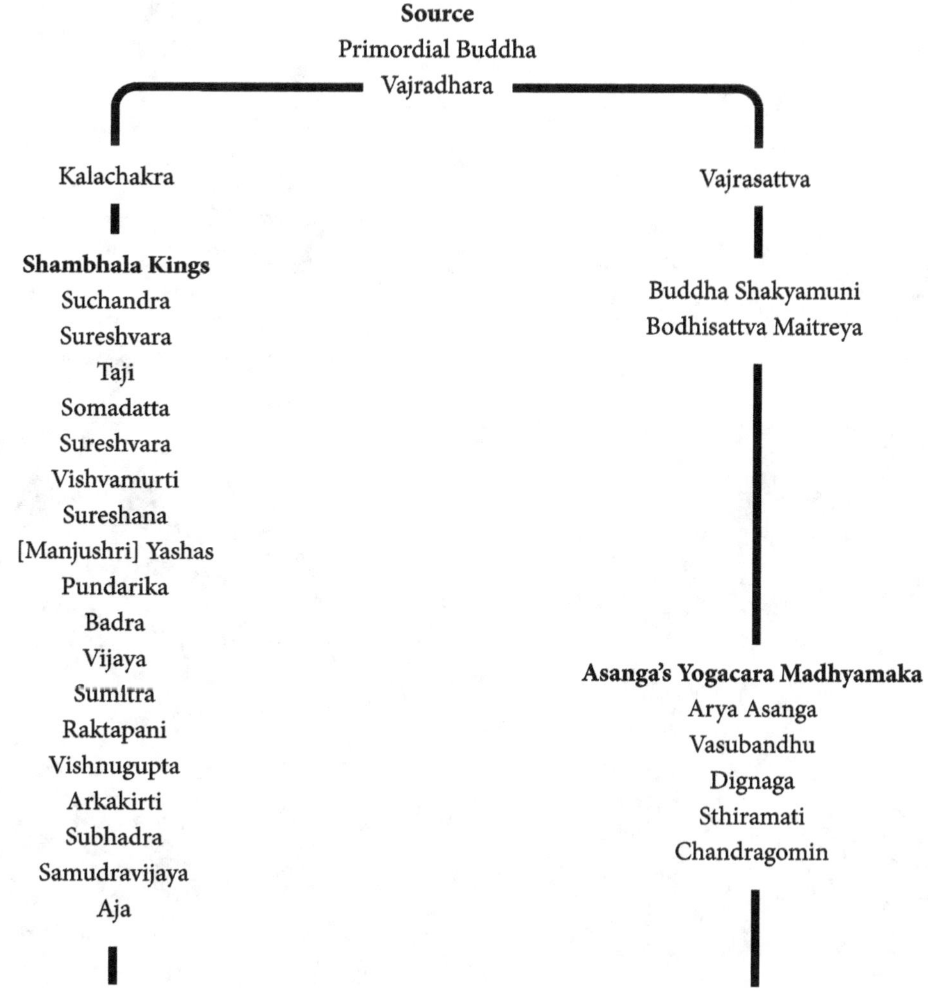

Nalanda Tradition of Kalachakra
Manjuvajra
Shri Badra
Bodhibadra
Somanatha

Dro Lineage of Six Vajra Yogas
Drotön Lotsawa
Lama Lhaje Gompa
Lama Drotön Namseg
Lama Drupchen Yumo
Tséchok Dharmeshvara
Khipa Namkha'i Öser
Machig Tulku Jobum
Lama Druptop Sechen
Chöje Jamyang Sarma
Kunkhyen Chöku Öser

Jonang Kalachakra Lineage
Kunpang Thukje Tsondru
Jangsem Gyalwa Yeshe
Khetsun Yonten Gyatso

Maitreya's Contemplative Tradition
Maitripa
Ratnakarashanti
Anandakirti
Sañjana

Lotsawa Gawa'i Dorje
Tsen Kawoche Drimé Sherab
Dharma Tsondru
Yeshe Jungné
Jangchup Kyap
Zhonnu Jangchup

Narthang Lineage
Monlam Tsultrim
Chomden Rigpé Raldri
Kyiton Jamyang Drakpa

Kunkhyen Dolpopa Sherab Gyaltsen
Chögyal Choklé Namgyal

Tsungmed Nyabön Kunga

Drupchen Kunga Lodrö
Jamyang Konchog Zangpo
Drenchok Namkha Tsenchen
Panchen Namkha Palzang
Lochen Ratnabhadra
Palden Kunga Drolchok

Kenchen Lungrik Gyatso

Jonang Zhentong Lineage
Chöjé Pal Gonpo
Lodrö Gyatso
Donyöd Pal
Panchen Shakya Chokden
Donyon Drubpa
Jamgön Drubpa Pawo
Kunga Gyaltsen
Drakden Drubpa

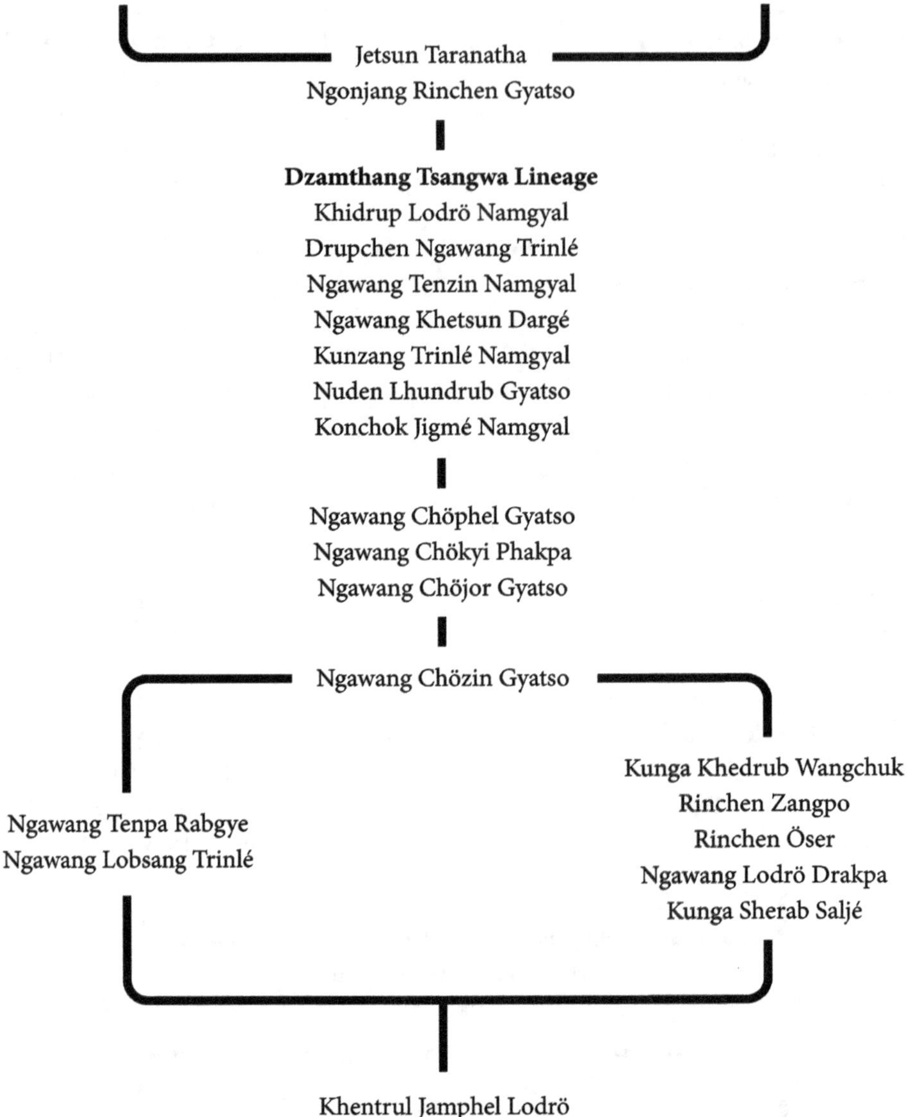

Jetsun Taranatha
Ngonjang Rinchen Gyatso

Dzamthang Tsangwa Lineage
Khidrup Lodrö Namgyal
Drupchen Ngawang Trinlé
Ngawang Tenzin Namgyal
Ngawang Khetsun Dargé
Kunzang Trinlé Namgyal
Nuden Lhundrub Gyatso
Konchok Jigmé Namgyal

Ngawang Chöphel Gyatso
Ngawang Chökyi Phakpa
Ngawang Chöjor Gyatso

Ngawang Chözin Gyatso

Kunga Khedrub Wangchuk
Rinchen Zangpo
Rinchen Öser
Ngawang Lodrö Drakpa
Kunga Sherab Saljé

Ngawang Tenpa Rabgye
Ngawang Lobsang Trinlé

Khentrul Jamphel Lodrö

The Refuge Commitments and Vows of Personal Liberation

PRECEPTS FOR TAKING REFUGE IN THE THREE JEWELS

There are three sets of precepts related to *Taking Refuge in the Three Jewels*: (1) the three things to be abandoned, (2) the three things to be adopted and (3) the three complementary precepts.

Three Things to be Abandoned

1. Abandon sentient beings as ultimate sources of refuge.
2. Abandon harming sentient beings.
3. Abandon the influence of worldly friends.

Three Things to be Adopted

1. Honour and respect the symbols of enlightened mind.
2. Honour and respect the symbols of enlightened speech.
3. Honour and respect the symbols of enlightened body.

Three Complementary Precepts

1. Respect, honour and venerate the Three Jewels.
2. Be mindful of the blessings of the Three Jewels.
3. Cultivate gratitude towards the Three Jewels.

VOWS OF PERSONAL LIBERATION

There are two sets of vows normally taken by lay practitioners: (1) the *Five Lay Precepts* or (2) the *Eight Twenty-Four Hour Precepts*. As the twenty-four hour precepts are temporary, they are not counted as fully qualified vows of personal liberation.

Five Lay Precepts

1. Abandon killing.
2. Abandon stealing.
3. Abandon sexual misconduct.
4. Abandon lying.
5. Abandon all intoxicants.

The Eight Twenty-Four Hour Precepts

1. Abandon killing.
2. Abandon stealing.
3. Abandon all sexual activity.
4. Abandon lying.
5. Abandon all intoxicants.
6. Abandon expensive or high-beds.
7. Abandon dancing and ornamentation.
8. Abandon eating after noon.

BRANCH COMMITMENTS

There are five sets of actions which should be abandoned after taking refuge: (1) the *Ten Non-Virtuous Actions*; (2) the *Five Heinous Crimes*; (3) the *Five Close Crimes*; (4) the *Four Heavy Non-Virtues* and the *Eight Wrong Actions*.

The Ten Non-Virtues *

1. Killing
2. Stealing
3. Sexual Misconduct
4. Lying
5. Harsh speech
6. Divisive speech
7. Idle speech
8. Covetousness
9. Ill will
10. Wrong views

** The first four non-virtues are the same as the four root lay precepts.*

The Five Heinous Crimes

1. Killing one's father
2. Killing one's mother
3. Killing an Arhat
4. Drawing blood from a Buddha
5. Creating a schism in the Sangha.

The Five Close Crimes

1. Degrade through sexual misconduct one's mother who is also an arhat
2. Kill a "securely abiding" Bodhisattva
3. Kill an Arya on the path of learning
4. Misappropriate funds from the Sangha
5. Destroy a stupa.

The Four Heavy Non-Virtues

1. Accepting homage from a more advanced practitioner
2. Taking advantage of a genuine practitioner's wealth
3. Preventing devotees from accumulating merit
4. Cheating one's spiritual master.

The Eight Wrong Actions

1. Criticising good
2. Praising unwholesomeness
3. Interrupting the accumulation of merit of a virtuous person
4. Disturbing the minds of those who have devotion
5. Giving up one's spiritual teacher
6. Giving up commitments to one's deity
7. Giving up one's Dharma brothers and sisters
8. Desecrating a mandala or disobeying the rules while on retreat.

The Vows and Commitments of a Bodhisattva

TRAINING IN ASPIRATIONAL BODHICITTA

Training in aspirational Bodhicitta is divided into two sets: (1) the *Precepts to Prevent Your Bodhicitta from Declining* in this life and (2) the *Precepts to Generate Bodhicitta in Future Lives.*

The Precepts to Prevent Your Bodhicitta from Declining

1. Contemplate the benefits of developing Bodhicitta
2. Generate the aspiration of Bodhicitta throughout the day
3. Accumulate merit and purify negativities
4. Never abandon any sentient being

The Precepts to Generate Bodhicitta in Future Lives

Abandoning the Four Black Practices that Weaken Bodhicitta

1. Confusing one's teachers
2. Making others feel regret about that which is not regrettable
3. Abusing or slandering those who have correctly entered the Mahayana
4. Using deceit and misrepresentation to manipulate others

Adopting the Four White Practices that Strengthen Bodhicitta

1. Avoid all forms of lying
2. Helping others practice Dharma
3. Showing honour and respect to Bodhisattvas
4. Maintain an altruistic intention towards sentient beings

TRAINING IN ENGAGED BODHICITTA

The training in engaged Bodhicitta is divided into two sets of vows: (1) the *Eighteen Root Vows* and (2) the *Forty-Six Branch Vows.*

The Eighteen Root Vows

The following actions should be abandoned completely:

Four Root Vows According to the Tradition of Asanga

1. Claiming to have false realisations
2. Not giving material aid or teachings
3. Not forgiving someone who has apologised
4. To abandon the Mahayana and present false teachings

Fourteen Root Vows According to the Tradition of Nagarjuna

5. To steal the property of the Three Jewels
6. To reject the teachings
7. To punish the immoral
8. To commit deeds of direct retribution
9. To profess wayward views
10. To destroy a dwelling, town, city, region or nation
11. To teach emptiness to the untrained
12. To cause another to give up Bodhicitta
13. To make someone abandon the foundational precepts
14. To assert that the Foundational Vehicle does not conquer afflictions
15. To praise oneself and belittle others
16. To exaggerate one's realisations
17. To cause a king to inflict a fine
18. To steal possessions from practitioners

The Forty-Six Branch Vows

These actions should be avoided as much as possible:

The Precepts Related to the Perfection of Generosity

1. Not performing the three kinds of devotion to the Three Jewels
2. Allowing desire to remain unchecked
3. Failing to respect one's spiritual elders
4. Refusing to reply to questions
5. Not accepting an invitation
6. Not accepting gold and other forms of wealth
7. Refusing to teach Dharma to those who seek it

The Precepts Related to the Perfection of Ethical Discipline

8. Abandoning those who are immoral
9. Not training oneself in a way that engenders faith in others
10. Engaging in few activities for the sake of sentient beings
11. Failing to act with sympathy
12. Persisting in wrong forms of livelihood
13. Engaging in mental excitation and excessive merriment
14. Regarding samsara with complacency
15. Failing to dispel a bad reputation
16. Failing to apply a distressing measure

The Precepts Related to the Perfection of Patience

17. Retaliating to harm
18. Ignoring those who have been angered
19. Refusing to accept an apology
20. Allowing anger to remain unchecked

The Precepts Related to the Perfection of Joyful Effort

21. Gathering a following out of desire for gain and honour
22. Failing to dispel laziness and the like
23. Engaging in idle speech with a sense of attachment

The Precepts Related to the Perfection of Meditative Concentration

24. Failing to pursue single-pointed concentration
25. Failing to eliminate the hindrances to meditative concentration
26. Regarding enjoyment of the states of meditative absorption as a good quality

The Precepts Related to the Perfection of Wisdom

27. Rejecting the teachings of the Foundational Vehicle
28. Failing to pursue the teachings of the Great Vehicle
29. Studying Non-Buddhist teachings more than Buddha's teachings
30. Delighting in the study of Non-Buddhist texts
31. Denigrating the teachings of the Great Vehicle
32. Praising oneself and disparaging others
33. Failing to pursue learning
34. Showing disrespect toward a Dharma teacher or the Dharma

The Precepts Related to the Benefitting Others

35. Failing to assist others
36. Failing to care for the sick
37. Failing to assist those who are suffering
38. Not indicating what is proper to others
39. Failing to return a benefit received from others
40. Failing to dispel the grief that others are experiencing
41. Failing to provide food and the like to those who seek it
42. Failing to assist one's followers
43. Failing to comply with the wishes of others
44. Failing to praise those who deserve to be praised
45. Failing to suppress those who engage in misconduct
46. Failing to use one's miraculous powers

Chöd

Cutting the Demons of Ignorance and Self-Cherishing

The essence of the Kalachakra Path is the nurturing of love and compassion as a means to achieving enlightenment. One of the main obstacles on this path is our self-cherishing attitude which fuels our feelings of bias and the many afflictions that are derived from this state of mind. To practice Kalachakra effectively, this obstacle needs to be removed as quickly as possible.

This task can be approached by using either indirect or direct methods. An indirect method works with the conditions of self-cherishing, preventing them from arising in the future, whereas a direct method works with the actual mind of self-cherishing to remove its capacity to harm us. In general, indirect methods tend to be gradual and peaceful in nature while direct methods are much more immediate and forceful.

In the main presentation of the Bodhisattva Path earlier in this book, we were introduced to various indirect methods to reduce the strength of our self-cherishing and help generate the supreme aspiration of Bodhicitta. In this appendix we will explore a more direct method that can be used to supplement our practice and progress along the path in an accelerated manner. Within the context of the Kalachakra Path, these practices should be considered part of our training in the inner preliminaries.

The method we will examine is called *Chöd* or Object Severance. Universally recognised as one of the best ways to eradicate the self-cherishing mind, this unique practice lineage can be found in all the major traditions in Tibet. The word *chöd* literally means "to cut". Cutting is not a smooth and gentle action, but decisive and abrupt. The moment a cut is made, a connection is severed—this is the nature of Chöd. If we need to rid ourselves of a tree, we don't concern ourselves with cutting the leaves and the branches, we go straight to the root. By cutting the root, all else will wither away.

Prajñaparamita—The Perfection of Wisdom

THE SOURCE OF THE CHÖD TEACHINGS

The teachings of Chöd have arisen from Prajñaparamita. This is another name for Buddha-nature manifesting in the aspect of the Great Mother—the wisdom which realises the empty-nature of all phenomena. Unlike a human, she is not born from a mother and father but from the pristine awareness that abides non-conceptually in selflessness and as such, she is inseparable from the Buddha Vajradhara, Kalachakra and our own root Guru. The teachings of Prajñaparamita manifest partially in the Second Turning of the Wheel of Dharma and completely in the Third Turning.

These teachings were eventually brought to Tibet in the eleventh century by the Great Indian Mahasiddha Padampa Sangye. Born into a Brahmin family in India, Dampa Sangye was ordained in Vikramashila at the age of fifteen and given the name Kamalashila. After studying under fifty-four renowned yogic practitioners, he received a profound education in both the Sutras and Tantras. For much of his life, Dampa travelled across India and Nepal, meditating at sacred sites such as Bodhgaya and Svayambhunath Stupa.

On numerous occasions Dampa Sangye journeyed to Tibet to give teachings and although he could understand and speak Tibetan, he chose to give symbolic teachings through non-verbal gestures, bestowal of items and short pith instructions. These teachings were committed to writing by his close disciples, acting as the main interpreters of his wisdom. The cycles of teachings that directly originated from him are known as the tradition of *Zhije*, meaning "pacification".

Padampa Sangye was particularly interested in supporting female practitioners who he felt faced additional obstacles to their spiritual practice due to the societal conventions of the time. Of his many students, his most famous female disciple was Machik Labdron who studied with him over the course of a year. During this period, she spent significant time practicing in accordance with the Prajñaparamita Sutras and received teachings directly from Padampa Sangye as well as his main disciple, Kyoton Sonam Lama.

Machik's story is truly inspirational. Very early in life she faced a series of deaths in her family. Her father passed away when she was thirteen, her mother followed three years later when she was sixteen and when she turned twenty, her older sister also died. In the space of only seven years, she lost almost everyone close to her. These tragedies strengthened her focus and energy on the practice of Dharma, particularly the study of the Prajñaparamita Sutras with which she felt a great affinity. Under the guidance of Drapa Ngonshé, she became known for her great ability to recall texts and would often be asked to recite the Long Prajñaparamita Sutra on behalf of her master's students. As a result of this practice, the wisdom of emptiness arose, liberating her mind and from that moment on, wherever she went, she never developed attachment towards people or places.

One day she met a wandering yogi named Topa Bhadra and became his consort. She gave birth to three sons and two daughters: Nyingpo Drubpa, Drubchung, Yangdrub, Kongcham and Lacham. When she turned thirty-seven, she chose to return to the life of a female renunciate, travelling far and wide throughout Tibet, Nepal and India. As no one believed she was a female mahasiddha, she was often tested. Each time she rose to their challenges, demonstrating the depths of her incredible realisations. Accordingly, she gathered many disciples, most notable of which were her sons.

The Chöd system of practice she taught was extremely innovative and arose through the power of her realisations. While it incorporated many of the principles of Padampa Sangye's Zhije, the actual practices were unique. Due to their astounding efficacy, the practices of Chöd spread throughout Tibet and were eventually incorporated into all the major traditions. Word of Machik's incredible teachings even spread to India and she was requested to transmit them there as well.

If you are interested in practicing this system, it is important to first familiarise yourself with the lineage masters to develop your connection with the teachings. This is a truly profound practice and without the blessings of the lineage, the intended benefits are unlikely to be gained. This appendix only provides a general introduction to the practices which can then be used as a basis for working with a qualified lineage master.

CUTTING THE ROOT OF SAMSARA

According to the teachings of Chöd, the root of cyclic existence is the concept of a truly existent self. On the basis of our grasping at this concept, we experience suffering and conflict. Everything comes back to the basic feeling of "I am". By removing this grasping, we cut the root of samsara.

To a sentient being, the self appears to exist, but to an enlightened being, it does not. Right now, what we think of as the self is actually an illusion which does not exist in the way it appears to us. But if this is the case, then who are we? Ultimately, we can say that we are Buddha-nature. This is our sacred truth, our pure self. However, this is not a self in the way that we normally think. As it is a self based on a non-dualistic mind, it completely transcends all notion of subject and object.

Fortunately, we can know this truth through experience. If we take our strong feelings of "me" or "mine" and investigate their nature, they completely fall apart. That which we think is so solid and real vanishes under analysis, proving to be baseless—without essence. Reality however does not fall apart under analysis. Even after clearing all concepts, the pristine awareness of the mind persists—it is not nothing. This mind is ineffable in nature because it is beyond our labels and while we can chose to call it a "pure self", this is merely a label we use to understand the nature of reality. It is not reality itself.

Chöd recognises our current confusion regarding what is and what is not the self. Usually we see this body and think this is the self. We may understand the concept of selflessness, but deep down we still feel we are the same as our body and this is why the thought of death terrifies us so much. We cannot imagine being separated from this precious body. It is for this reason Chöd focuses on cutting through our attachment to the body, enabling us to experience the nature of the mind.

Imagine you were renting a house which caught on fire. The first thing you would do is get out of the house, removing yourself from danger as quickly as possible. Once you were safe outside, you could watch the house burn and although it might be difficult to lose your home, you wouldn't be afraid as you would know the fire couldn't harm you.

Similarly, our body is like the house. When our body comes under threat, we are immediately gripped with fear. Deep down we think if our body is harmed then we too will be harmed. We conflate the two and mix them together, but no matter what happens to the body, the mind can never be harmed. It may certainly be unpleasant to lose our body, but the fundamental nature of our mind remains pure and undamaged. Recognising this, in the practice of Chöd, we separate our body and mind to then offer the body to others as a method for generating merit.

This provides only one example of how Chöd helps us remove self-grasping. The system works with multiple levels of grasping to eventually clear away everything that limits our mind. In order to fully understand how this works, we need to discuss the role maras play in our experience.

WORKING WITH MARAS

A "mara" is any force that obstructs our capacity to achieve liberation from samsara. It is a sanskrit term which is generally translated as "demon" or "devil". The root of all maras is the mind which grasps onto a self, projecting a reality based on what is perceived as being "I" or "mine". This is the main demon we must overcome.

While demons are commonly portrayed as physical entities; bloodthirsty beasts with menacing claws and fangs; in the context of Chöd, anything which provides the basis for ignorance or affliction to arise is considered a mara. As this is the case, even friends and family could potentially become maras if we grasp onto them with attachment.

The practice of Chöd cuts the strength of maras so they no longer have the capacity to influence our mind. By clearly identifying the different types of maras and learning how to face them with bravery and determination, we develop an unwavering fearlessness that propels us forward along the path. To this end, we can classify two sets of maras we need to be aware of: (1) the four common maras as understood in the sutras and (2) the four uncommon maras as presented in Chöd.

The Four Common Maras

We can speak of four types of mara that act as the principal obstacles for progressing along a spiritual path:

1. **The Mara of the Aggregates:** The aggregates include everything that is labelled as either body or mind. They are produced as a result of our karmic conditioning and provide the basis for the imputation of a "self". When the appearance of a self arises, we grasp onto it as being inherently real. As long as we continue to perpetuate this form of *self-grasping*, we will be doomed to experience an endless cycle of suffering and torment.

2. **The Mara of the Afflictions:** On the basis of self-grasping, the mind develops layers of distorted misperception that prevent us from recognising the true nature of reality. Ignorant of how things actually exist, we come to hold the self to be more important than everything we consider to be "other". In this way, a biased attitude of *self-cherishing* is born that fuels all the afflicted states of minds.

3. **The Mara of the Lord of Death:** The moment self-cherishing takes hold, we are faced with the challenge of protecting our aggregates from threats to its survival. The greatest threat is death, when the body and mind dissolve and the self we currently cherish is destroyed. This mara manifests as a constant sense of fear and anxiety about change and impermanence. On the basis of this fear, *aversion* arises towards anything that is perceived as a threat. When this aversion dominates the mind it leads us to engage in activities which bring harm to others and thereby creates the causes for the experience of suffering to arise.

4. **The Mara of the Sons of Gods:** The last mara is based on the mind that wishes to please the self which is cherished. Throughout the varying experiences in our lives, we find some more pleasant than others. Over time, we develop a deeply ingrained bias of *attachment* towards having more of those we desire and having less of those we don't. This mara manifests most prominently in our spiritual practice at times when we lose interest in Dharma and we return to old habits. Instead of striving to overcome our maras, we let our attachments get the better of us.

Of these four, the first is considered the root of samsara, the second derives from the first and the last two derive from the second. In this way, by cutting self-grasping, we effectively cut all self-cherishing, aversion and attachment. If we take an indirect approach, we meditate on subjects such as renunciation, impermanence, love and compassion. This weakens the influence of the last three maras, providing the conditions to then work with the first mara by meditating on the empty-nature of the aggregates.

The Four Uncommon Maras

The approach used in Chöd is to work directly with the nature of the mind in order to cut through to the root of our self-grasping. As such, the four maras are understood in a slightly different way. In Chöd we speak of (1) the tangible mara, (2) the intangible mara, (3) the mara of exaltation and (4) the mara of inflation. Each of these maras highlights a specific aspect of the mind that can be used to establish a realisation of the mind's empty-nature.

The Tangible Mara

The first mara focuses on the sensory appearances of form, sound, smell, taste and sensation which form the foundation for our experience of the external world. For this reason, we call them "tangible". In dependence on sensory experience, we develop attachment towards what we enjoy and aversion towards what we don't. This establishes the conditions for us to harm sentient beings and perpetuate our suffering.

Here, the tangible mara is our *grasping onto objective appearances* as being inherently existent. By clinging to them as existing in this way, all the afflictions are formed. Therefore, the antidote to this mara is to meditate without attachment or aversion on the empty-nature of appearances. We rest the mind naturally within each sense base and recognise that even though appearances arise, they are not established as validly existing in one way or another. Once this is recognised, the appearances take on an illusory or dream-like nature and cease to have power over the mind.

The Intangible Mara

While the tangible mara relates to the nature of objective appearances, the intangible mara is concerned with our subjective responses to those appearances. It consists of the conceptual constructs of "good" and "bad" that we project onto the world, determining whether we experience appearances with fear and dislike, or with joy and desire. As these emotional responses do not exist anywhere beyond the mind, they are called "intangible".

As appearances arise in the mind, we immediately project characteristics onto them. The characteristics we like, we call "qualities", whereas those we don't, we call "faults". If a person appears to have many faults, we call them a "demon", but if they appear to have many qualities, we call them an "angel". In this way, we grasp onto a reality that is completely fabricated based on our interpretation of what is appearing to us. All of these distinctions are completely without essence.

The intangible mara is the *grasping onto conceptual fabrications* as being an inherent part of appearances. To overcome this mara, we need to recognise that these concepts of good and bad are all merely projections. We can do this by resting the mind naturally without preference regardless of the sensations that arise. The content of thoughts and memories that come up is not important, as rather than focusing on them or reflecting on their meaning, we simply hold our awareness still within the vastness of the mind's empty-nature. This causes the mind to naturally settle and the proliferation of thoughts to diminish significantly. This is a practice of non-action, where the goal is to break our habit of reacting to everything we experience.

The Mara of Exaltation

Through working with the tangible and intangible maras, many meditative experiences can arise. These attainments might come in the form of worldly prestige, a large following of disciples, visions of deities, supernatural powers and so forth. If we develop attachment towards these attainments we experience considerable pride and arrogance. This is the mara of exaltation and if we don't remove it, we will become complacent and unable to progress along the path.

The essence of this mara is the mind that *grasps onto the desirable qualities of the self*. It is by nature similar to the intangible mara, however it has an inward focus on our sense of identity—the conceptual construct of who we think we are. To overcome this mara, we need to recognise that the qualities we perceive are not a true self. Just like all other appearances to the mind, whether tangible or intangible, they have absolutely no essence and are therefore illusory in nature. Like a dream, they manifest for a time and then dissolve away. By familiarising ourselves with this nature, we don't exaggerate our status and learn to remain humble in the face of whatever arises. This receptive attitude allows us to cut through to deeper levels of experience.

The Mara of Inflation

The last mara is considered the root of the other three. When the mind falsely grasps onto the appearance of a self as existing, a fixed reference point is created. From this reference point, conceptual fabrications arise describing how that self feels about the objects appearing to it. These fabrications obscure the mind and lead to engagement in afflicted behaviours. This process of accumulation of obscurations is known as "inflation".

In order to overcome inflation, we must learn to cut the dualistic *grasping onto subject and object*. We do this by resting our awareness in its own natural luminosity so we can realise the empty nature of all phenomena. When we habituate ourselves to this realisation, the mind no longer grasps onto objects as separate entities and so no longer generates conceptual fabrications. When the mind is free from the movement of concepts, it naturally rests in its own fully established nature—the sublime emptiness of suchness. In this way, by abandoning the four maras, we realise the ultimate nature of reality and completely eradicate all forms of self-grasping.

THE PRACTICE OF CHÖD

With an understanding of the uncommon meaning of the four maras, we can now begin to practice the profound methods of Chöd. This consists of two types of practice: (1) formal practice and (2) informal practice. The formal practice involves a unique visualisation practice designed to cut through the mind which grasps onto and cherishes the self, whereas the informal practice heightens our awareness of the self so we can work with it directly in formal practice.

While these practices are based on teachings from the Sutras, they belong to a profound lineage of pith instructions. For this reason you should first receive the transmission of the teachings from an authentic lineage holder before putting them into practice. Through the blessings of the lineage, you will avoid unnecessary obstacles and be ensured of beneficial effects on your mind.

Formal Practice

The formal practice of Chöd is essentially a practice in extreme generosity. Unlike regular offerings where you imagine giving away beautiful objects such as flowers, food or precious substances, the object of offering is our own body; the object we hold most tightly to and our most prized possession. By repeatedly visualising giving our body to others, we reduce our attachment to the very basis of our self-cherishing attitude. This dissolves the connection between body and mind, allowing us to focus on the nature of the mind, to ultimately cut the root of our ignorance.

The practice itself is divided into four steps: (1) preliminaries; (2) transference of consciousness; (3) offering the body and (4) dedication of merit.

Preliminaries

Before engaging in the main visualisation, spend some time establishing a meaningful motivation by reciting the following verses:

> *I take refuge in the Three Jewels to lead all mother sentient beings to Buddhahood,*
> *I take refuge to dispel my self-cherishing and offer my body to all beings,*
> *I take refuge to understand that all fearful beings were once my beloved ones,*
> *I take refuge to realise all beings are enlightened in actual truth.*

As you recite these words, imagine all the Lineage Masters, Yidams, Buddhas, Bodhisattvas, Dakas, Dakinis and Dharma Protectors gathered around you, witnessing your pledge. With their support, you should have great confidence in your ability to do whatever is necessary to benefit sentient beings.

I generate immeasurable love and compassion to develop the precious jewel of Bodhicitta, just like all the Buddhas and Bodhisattvas of the three times.

Bring to mind a vast sea of sentient beings around you and recall the suffering they are experiencing. Cultivate an intense longing to abandon the mara of self-grasping so you can actualise your greatest potential and achieve the state of a fully enlightened Buddha.

Then, imagine that the entire field of refuge melts into light and transforms into the radiant white form of Machik Labdron, with one face and three eyes. She plays a damaru drum in her right hand, holds a bell in her left and dances to the rhythmic beat of the music.

Recognising Machik as inseparable from your root Guru, cultivate a mind filled with faith and devotion towards the profound teachings of Chöd. Visualise Machik coming to the crown of your head and melting into light, becoming inseparable from your own Buddha-nature. Rest your awareness for a few moments in a natural state free from grasping.

Transference of Consciousness

In order to offer our body to others, we must first dissolve the connection between mind and body. If you are already familiar with meditating on the nature of the mind, you can do this by instantly recalling that nature, and resting your awareness single-pointedly without concepts for a few minutes, or you can use the following visualisation to facilitate the dissolution.

My consciousness as a pink drop at my navel chakra shoots upwards through my central channel:

PHET...PHET...PHET...PHET!

My mind dissolves into space and my body falls like a corpse.

Begin by imagining your consciousness appearing as a white and red drop of vibrating light, situated in the centre of your navel chakra. Reflect that this drop is you and identify with it. Forcefully recite the word PHET and imagine that you rise up through the central channel, from the navel to the heart chakra. On the second PHET, imagine moving from the heart to the throat. On the third PHET, you move from the throat to the crown chakra and on the final PHET, imagine you shoot out of the crown chakra and into the space above your body. Imagine looking down on your body as it falls lifeless to the ground.

OM SVABHAVA SHUDDHA SARVA DHARMA SVABHAVA SHUDDHO HUM

With this mantra, remind yourself that all phenomena are completely empty of their imputed natures and rest for a few moments in the dream-like quality of what is appearing to you.

All phenomena dissolve into emptiness and from this, appearing as the sublime Dakini Machik Labdron, is my glorious root Lama, surrounded by the five classes of Dakinis and the lineage masters. To you I pray, grant your blessings.

From within the sphere of emptiness, imagine your root Guru appearing as Machik Labdron along with a host of Dakinis and lineage masters. You request their blessings, permitting you to perform the profound offering practice of Chöd and thereby cutting the mind of self-cherishing from its root.

My consciousness appears as red Vajrayogini.

Imagine light radiating out from the merit field and bathing you in the blessings of this sacred lineage. From within this light, your consciousness instantly transforms into the enlightened form of Vajrayogini, with a red body, one face and two arms. You hold a curved knife in your right hand and a skullcup in your left.

Offering the Body

The next step is to prepare the body for offering. Imagine your body laid out naked on the ground in front of you. Spend some time looking at it, as you would a dead animal or a slab of meat.

Slicing the top off the body's skull, it is transformed into an offering bowl as large as a continent. Skin, flesh, blood, tendons, bones, lungs, liver, intestines, sense organs, everything is carved up and put into the offering bowls, transforming into enlightening nectar of liberation.

With your curved knife, imagine slicing off the top of the body's skull. Turning it upside down and placing it in front of you, it instantly transforms into a set of large offering bowls. Begin to slice up the body, piece by piece and in one bowl place all of the skin and in another, place the fleshy meat and fat. Continue in this way until the entire body has been broken down and divided up into the bowls. Imagine each bowl overflowing with offerings.

You can now offer the body in different ways to different types of beings. There are basically two styles of offerings you can perform: (1) White Feasts and (2) Red Feasts. A white feast reduces self-cherishing by making peaceful offerings out of love and compassion towards others. Red feasts directly confront our self-cherishing attitude by making wrathful offerings. While the first emphasises bringing benefit to others, the second focuses on bringing wisdom to bear on the experience of self-cherishing itself.

White Feasts

We first make offerings of nectar to the assembly of enlightened beings:

The nectar appears as flowers, light, music, incense, food, perfume, silk and ornaments. This is offered to the lineage masters, Yidam deities and all enlightened beings.

In the space in front of you, imagine the sky filled with Yidams, Buddhas, Bodhisattvas, Dakinis and all enlightened beings. Remembering their infinite kindness towards you and all sentient beings, imagine the substances in each offering bowl glowing and then dissolving into radiant white nectar. From your heart, countless offering deities emanate, taking the nectar and distributing it to the enlightened assembly. Imagine they are overwhelmed with joy and greatly pleased by your magnificent offering.

The nectar then appears as a treasury of wealth, beauty, youth, medicines, food, clothing, decorations, gardens, houses, friends and loved ones and whatever is needed, raining down upon all kind mother beings of the six realms, especially demons, ghosts, earth, water and air spirits, demigods, protectors and all my karmic debtors, who have been my nearest and dearest over countless lifetimes. For these beings the offerings become as vast as rivers, oceans and mountains.

Bringing to mind the countless sentient beings who have been your dearest mothers since beginningless time, nurture a heart full of gratitude and affection for everyone without exception. Think of the suffering that each of your dear mothers experience and cultivate the desire to repay their infinite kindness. Imagine you again emanate a host of offering goddesses who scoop up the nectar and carry it to the six realms. As they pour the nectar onto the inhabitants of each realm, it transforms into whatever your dear mothers need and their minds are completely satisfied and filled with peace and harmony.

There is no discrimination between all types of beings of the six realms as they have all equally been so kind to me as my parents, partners, children, teachers and precious ones. Each of these beings I cherish as a priceless treasure for accomplishing the path to enlightenment.

Finally, with a mind that cherishes each and every one of your dear mothers, imagine that as a result of offering your body as a wish-fulfilling gem to all sentient beings, they are established on the path to liberation. Through their practice of the precious Dharma, they clear their obscurations and achieve full enlightenment. Feeling incredible joy, dissolve the visualisation and rest in your awareness. When you are finished, continue with the next section.

Red Feast

For the red feast, bring to mind a vast assembly of horrifying demons and ravenous beasts. Imagine these beings are the manifestation of all those you have harmed as a result of your self-cherishing attitude. They snarl and growl, circling around you like a pack of hyenas waiting to feed. Try to generate the feeling that your life is in danger as this will arouse the mind of self-grasping, giving you a clear object to work with.

Then imagine this self-cherishing manifesting as your body spread out naked on the ground. Repeat the process of cutting it up, but this time pile up the parts into mountains of flesh and bone. The wrathful beings swarm around the offerings, devouring every last morsel. Think of how satisfied they become and that your karmic debt has been paid. Then contemplate the following:

There is no fear of any type of beings as no true beings exist as we perceive or as we imagine. There is no discrimination between beings of the three realms and enlightened beings, as everything already possesses the full qualities of enlightenment and so is equal in the ultimate truth.

OM GATE GATE PARAGATE PARASAMGATE BODHI SVAHA

As you repeat the mantra, allow all appearances to dissolve into emptiness. Recall whatever understanding of emptiness you have developed. When you tire of the mantra recitation, rest your mind in a non-conceptual state free from grasping for as long as you can.

Dedication of Merit

To end your session, you should dedicate the merit you have generated towards attaining Buddhahood. Finish by reciting the following verses:

The virtuous roots of having offered and given my body in charity, the virtuous roots of caring for gods and demons with my resolve for enlightenment, as well as any virtuous roots that I have amassed throughout the three times—all of this I dedicate to the welfare of hostile gods and demons and all sentient beings of the three realms.

Based on the power of dedicating in this way, may all negative karma, evil deeds and obscurations that are present in hostile gods and demons and all other sentient beings be purified. May they completely consummate the six perfections and reach the ultimate state.

May they be empowered by the intention of the unborn Mother and attain the citadel of Vajradhara, the lord of father-families of all victorious ones. Once they have attained such a state, may they bring about vast and great benefit for beings through various enlightened activities until cyclic existence is emptied.

May all those who practice Object Severance
Cut the string of self-grasping
By not seeing their own minds as devils.

May they be free of conceit
No matter what good qualities arise.
May they not create self-grasping
No matter what bad thoughts occur.

May this holy Dharma, the Severance of Evil Objects,
Pervade all times and directions
Like the sun rising in the sky.

Informal Practice

The informal practice of Chöd covers the two main activities performed by a Chöd practitioner between their formal meditation sessions: (1) the External Chöd of travelling to frightening places and (2) the Internal Chöd of cutting the proliferation of thoughts.

External Chöd

The first informal practice of external Chöd is focused on making the self-cherishing mind manifest clearly so it can be cut through using internal Chöd. This is done by physically travelling to scary places which induce fear. When the self feels threatened, our self-cherishing becomes strong. By maintaining mindfulness as it manifests, we can see the many layers of conceptual fabrication the mind generates to protect the self.

This is a direct and powerful method which requires wisdom to practice correctly. It is necessary to build our capacity to face frightening situations in a gradual fashion, as pushing too hard, too early, may cause our self-cherishing to overpower us, and prevent us from practicing at all. It is therefore recommended to start with peaceful environments such as your home or a public place where you feel safe, where you can sit and do the formal practice of offering your body.

Once you have developed familiarity with the practice, you can shift to a scarier environment, like a forest at night. It shouldn't be terrifying, but potentially creepy. As you settle in, take note of any uneasiness you feel and perform the formal practice.

Continue to practice in progressively more frightening locations. Unless you are a highly realised practitioner, it is not recommended to go into needlessly dangerous situations. Remember that you are trying to scare yourself, not get yourself killed, so be smart and know your limits. Ideal places are those where many deaths have occurred or have a history of being haunted, such as abandoned homes, prisons, cemeteries and battlefields. Consider places that have a strange and uneasy feeling.

The benefit of this practice is the drastic reduction of your self-cherishing and attachment towards your body, which will help you develop fearlessness, strength and conviction in your practice. Without self-cherishing, your heart of love and compassion can become vast and immeasurable and in the face of adversity you will have an unwavering patience. All of this enables you to practice with joy regardless of the external conditions.

Internal Chöd

The process of inflation is triggered by the proliferation of thoughts that arise due to self-cherishing. When the self is threatened, an inner dialogue starts up, saying things like, "What was that noise? I feel like I'm being watched. Is that something over there?". If you are successful in your practice of external Chöd, you will become familiar with the layers of conceptualisation that are triggered by fear.

Internal Chöd is concerned with cutting this proliferation with an intense form of mindfulness. Each time you detect the mind generating thoughts, forcefully recite the syllable PHAT. This has the effect of cutting your train of thought and creates a space immediately after the syllable in which to rest your awareness. As the thoughts stir again, recite PHAT and rest the awareness in a state free from concepts. With diligence, the proliferation of thoughts will gradually subside, and the mind becomes clearer, enabling you to experience the nature of the mind directly.

As making loud and sharp noises in public can lead to unwanted attention, you are not obliged to vocalise the syllable. It is just as effective to silently recite PHAT within the mind. The main thing is to make it forceful, like a strong blast of air that completely clears out the mind.

When used together, the formal practice of offering the body and the informal practices of visiting scary places and cutting the flow of thoughts are very effective for defeating the four maras. In a direct way, they can rapidly cut through many layers of obscurations and bring us closer to an experience of emptiness. Within the context of the Kalachakra Path, while this would not be considered our main practice, it can still be an extremely beneficial supplementary practice to help prepare our mind before engaging in the Kalachakra Generation and Completion Stages.

Outline of Book Two

PART TWO: ENTERING THE PATH OF A BODHISATTVA

PART THREE: PREPARING THE MIND FOR TANTRA

About the Author

Khentrul Rinpoché Jamphel Lodrö is the founder and spiritual director of Dzokden. Rinpoche is the author of many books including Unveiling Your Sacred Truth, The Great Middle Way: Clarifying the Jonang View of Other-Emptiness, A Happier Life, and The Hidden Treasure of the Profound Path.

Rinpoche spent the first 20 years of his life herding yak and chanting mantras on the plateaus of Tibet. Inspired by the bodhisattvas, he left his family to study in a variety of monasteries under the guidance of over twenty-five masters in all the Tibetan Buddhist traditions. Due to his non-sectarian approach, he earned himself the title of Rimé (unbiased) Master and was identified as the reincarnation of the famous Kalachakra Master Ngawang Chözin Gyatso. While at the core of his teachings is the recognition that there is great value in the diversity of all spiritual traditions found in this world; he focuses on the Jonang-Shambhala tradition. Kalachakra (wheel of time) teachings handed down from the Kalki Kings of Shambhala, contain profound methods to harmonize our external environment with the inner world of body and mind. This tantra is connected directly to the Karma of our earth to bring about the Golden age of Peace and Harmony (Dzokden). Khentrul Rinpoche has made it his life mission to spread these precious teachings in as many languages as possible globally so that we can truly transform our world, one person at a time from their inside out.

RINPOCHE'S VISION

Dzokden was founded with the express purpose of supporting Khentrul Rinpoche in realizing his vision to bring about the Golden Age of peace and harmony in this world. As our community continues to grow and develop, more and more people are getting involved with this extraordinary effort.

To provide a sense of the scope of Rinpoche's vision, we can speak of eight goals that reflect Rinpoche's short and long term priorities:

Immediate Goals

Ultimately speaking, lasting genuine happiness is only possible through profound personal transformation. Now more than ever, we need methods to develop our wisdom and actualise our greatest potential. It is for this reason that Rinpoche places such a heavy priority on the preservation of the Jonang Kalachakra Lineage. There are four ways in which Rinpoche proposes to do this:

1. **Create opportunities to connect with an authentic and complete Kalachakra lineage in close collaboration with dedicated meditators in remote Tibet.** Our goal is to create all of the supports for practicing Kalachakra in accordance with the authentic lineage masters who have upheld this tradition for thousands of years. We do this by commissioning statues and paintings, writing books and giving teachings around the world. We place particular emphasis on ensuring the authenticity of our materials, drawing on the profound experience of highly realised meditators who are dedicating their lives to these practices.

2. **Establish international retreat centres for the study and practice of Kalachakra.** In order to integrate the teachings into our mind, it is crucial to have the opportunity to engage in periods of intensive practice. Therefore, we are working to create the necessary infrastructure to support and nurture the members of our community to engage in both short and long-term retreats. This includes the purchase of land and the construction of everything needed to conduct group and solitary retreats. Our long-term aim is to develop a network of such centres around the world, forming a global community that supports a wide variety of practitioners.

3. **Translate and publish the unique and rare texts of Kalachakra masters.** The Kalachakra System has been the subject of countless texts over the course of Tibet's long history. So far, only a small fraction of these texts has been translated and made accessible in the West. While the theoretical texts are im-

portant, we aim to focus particularly on the pith instructions which will guide dedicated practitioners to a deeper experience of these profound teachings.

4. **Develop the tools and programs for a structured learning experience.** With pockets of students distributed throughout the world, we believe it is important to make the most of modern technologies to facilitate the process of learning for our students. Our aim is to develop a robust online educational platform that allows our international community to access quality study programs that are intuitive, structured and engaging.

Long-Term Goals

Whilst we each work towards achieving ultimate peace and harmony in our own mind, we must not lose sight of the fact that we exist within the context of a world filled with a great diversity of individuals. These individuals give rise to a wide variety of beliefs and practices that in turn shape how we relate and interact with each other. In this interdependent reality, it is vital to find viable strategies for promoting greater tolerance and respect. To this end, Rinpoche proposes four specific areas of activity:

1. **Promote the development of a Rimé Philosophy through dialogue with other traditions.** With the desire to be constructive members of a pluralistic society, we need to learn ways of reconciling our differences. We therefore aim to help people develop the positive qualities that promote an attitude of mutual respect, openness to new ideas and an inquisitive desire to overcome our ignorance.

2. **Develop highly realised role models by offering financial support to dedicated practitioners.** To ensure the authenticity of our spiritual traditions, it is imperative that there are people who actualise the highest of realisations. Therefore, we aim to create a financial scholarship program which facilitates genuine practitioners who wish to dedicate their lives to spiritual development, regardless of their system of practice. By helping people actualise the teachings, they become positive role models for those around them, inspiring and guiding the generations to come.

3. **Actualise the great potential of female practitioners by developing specialised training programs.** The Tibetan culture has a long history of cultivating highly realised masters through the intensive training of those who are recognised to have great potential. Unfortunately, all too often the search for potential has focused only on male candidates. Rinpoche believes that it is increasingly important to have strong, highly realised, female role models who can help bring greater balance into our world. For this reason we are working to develop a unique training program to provide women with the opportunity to actualise their spiritual potential. It is our aim to design a specialised curriculum as well as the financial infrastructure to fully support all aspects of their education.

4. **Promote greater flexibility of mind and a broader understanding of reality through modern educational programs.** In a world that is rapidly evolving, we need to rethink the types of skills we are teaching our children. The rigid structures of the past are often ill equipped to prepare students for the challenges they will face during their lives. Therefore, we aim to develop a variety of educational programs that can help children to become more flexible and more capable of adapting to their environment. An important part of these programs is the development of greater awareness of the role that our mind plays in our day-to-day experiences. We also aim to bring reforms into the monastic education system to help make them more relevant for this modern world.

HOW CAN YOU HELP?

The above will not be possible without your support and participation. A vision of this magnitude requires a great deal of merit and generosity from many benefactors over many years. If you would like to offer your support, please do not hesitate to contact us.

Dzokden

3436 Divisadero Street

San Francisco, California 94123

United States of America

www.dzokden.org